A HISTORY OF MUSIC IN AMERICAN LIFE

Volume I

THE FORMATIVE YEARS, 1620-1865

A HISTORY OF MUSIC IN AMERICAN LIFE
Volume I

THE FORMATIVE YEARS,
1620-1865

by
Ronald L. Davis

ROBERT KRIEGER PUBLISHING COMPANY
MALABAR, FLORIDA
1982

Original edition 1982

Printed and Published by
ROBERT E. KRIEGER PUBLISHING CO., INC.
Krieger Drive
Malabar, FL 32950

Copyright © 1982 by
ROBERT E. KRIEGER PUBLISHING CO., INC.

Printed in the United States of America

Library of Congress Cataloging in Publication Data

Davis, Ronald L.
  A history of music in American life.

  Includes bibliographies.
  CONTENTS: v. 1. The formative years, 1620-1865.—
v. 2. The gilded years, 1865-1920.—v. 3. The modern era,
1920-present.
  1. Music—United States—History and criticism.
I. Title.
ML200.D3   780'.973   79-25359
ISBN 0-89874-004-5 (v. 3)

In Memory
of

BLANCHE M. MARTS
my own incredible Auntie Mame,
who showed me the meaning of
beauty and adventure

and

WALTER PRESCOTT WEBB
who loved the arts
as he loved the West,
and who affected many lives,
including mine

Introduction

Although immigrants came to the New World singing, frontier America had little time for the serious arts. Music, perhaps the most sensuous of Western Civilization's aesthetic expressions, was particularly neglected by a country whose cultural ideals emphasized hard work, material and social success, and emotional restraint. The Protestant ethic, reinforced by the wilderness experience, led the Puritans and other religious zealots to consider music a waste of time unless specifically contributing to the task at hand. The power of music to affect human emotions caused the Calvinist denominations especially to view it with more suspicion than fondness and therefore to restrict its role even in worship. An infant nation admiring reserve and control was far more comfortable with intellectual pursuits than with an art form prone to excite the senses.

With adolescence came an early nostalgia for vanishing innocence and a tendency to mistake sentimentality for honest feelings. As gentility was sought in the urban centers of the East, theaters and concert life slowly appeared as appendages of an aspiring commercial class who needed public arenas in which to display their newly acquired wealth and refinement. Serious music became prized as a demonstrable link with established civilization, an exotic and edifying experience that could be appreciated only with effort. Since men were consumed with economic and political matters, art in the young nation fell increasingly under the domination of women. Gradually the notion grew that serious music was not masculine. While music was essential for a sophisticated image, it was at the same time threatening to manhood if pursued in more than a cursory way. "I do not think," conductor Walter Damrosch would write, "there has ever been a country whose musical development has been fostered so almost exclusively by women as America."

Fawned over by the leisured classes, art music in the United States remained separate from life itself—an adornment imported from Europe for social purposes rather than an extract from the American experience. Until World War I serious music in America was dominated by immigrants and foreigners—first British, later Italian and especially German. Successful concert artists doted on the spectacular. John Philip Sousa at the turn of the century observed that life in the United States was more hurried than almost

VII

anywhere else; being restless, American audiences demanded variety and more in the way of showmanship.

By the middle of the nineteenth century vernacular music had been largely turned over to the minorities. Black entertainers, when outside the restrictions of the genteel tradition, often devised spontaneous expressions that were original, uniquely American, and frequently voiced the repressed emotions of whites as well as blacks, creating an idiom that would eventually develop into a national music. Even white performers in blackface could be less inhibited, less self-conscious, and therefore more honest about the issues and feelings that bothered or inflamed them. Later, with the advent of vaudeville and the rise of the commercial music business, the Jew came to dominate popular music in America, a phenomenon that continued at least until the end of the big studio era in Hollywood.

Meanwhile serious musicians were consistently being told they could not hope to win acceptance unless they had studied and been acclaimed in Europe. Since there were few symphony orchestras and no provincial opera houses in the United States, singers and conductors either went abroad to gain experience or turned to mass media, out of necessity spanning the gulf between vernacular music and the cultivated tradition. Eugene Ormandy, long the mainstay of the Philadelphia Orchestra, was first given a chance to conduct at the Roxy Theater in New York, one of the original movie palaces. Soprano Rosa Ponselle came to grand opera from vaudeville, whereas baritone Robert Merrill had worked in movie houses, the "borscht circuit," and radio before winning his Metropolitan Opera contract. Even then Merrill sought the best of both worlds—grand opera *and* popular entertainment— and was once fired from the Metropolitan for canceling performances to make a film in Hollywood. Beverly Sills, who made a sensational debut at the Metropolitan in Rossini's *The Siege of Corinth* after performing the same role at La Scala, began her professional career as Bubbles Silverman singing "Rinso White" commercials on radio. And American-born Klara Barlow, who made a hasty entrance into the Met as Isolde early in 1974, had been a cigarette girl in New York's Latin Quarter for a time.

While maturity and world leadership have brought increased sophistication, Americans have remained basically a vernacular people. The minstrel show, burlesque, vaudeville, Hollywood films, radio, and television have been the entertainment forms revered by the multitude, for whom musical comedy is high art. Symphony orchestras, opera, and recitals for most Americans suggest the unapproachable, the exalted, the tedious. Dynamic personalities—a Callas or a Bernstein—can occasionally break through this general reticence, but seldom does the music itself have such power. If the New Orleans opera company offers a nude Thais, as it did in 1973, *that* will make the national news. But barring the extreme, art music in the United States remains in the background—ardently supported by a select few, noticed in passing by the great majority.

American popular music, on the other hand, is heard around the world. Berlin, Kern, Porter, Rodgers, and the other giants of Tin Pan Alley wrote standards that are still performed wherever there is a piano or a dance orchestra. *South Pacific, My Fair Lady, Hello, Dolly!* and *Fiddler on the Roof* have played with immense success in London, Tokyo, and Tel Aviv, as well as year after year in dinner theaters and stock productions across the United States. Discos in Madrid or Rome or Mexico City throb with contemporary American hits, while Willie Nelson and Waylon Jennings have made their way from Texas to the Orient via Nashville, making those decades when American music was dismissed almost without a hearing seem quaint and long ago.

Yet there are those around who remember well when music that was considered any good at all came from Europe, and native works still have difficulty finding their way into American concert halls and opera houses. Music's dramatic struggle to take root in the United States has been far more than a story of art at war with barbarism, more than the determination of the creative spirit to triumph in the face of diffidence and even ridicule. When viewed collectively, the nation's history has been written in music, as vividly as it has been chronicled in words. So have its values and aspirations, its tensions and fears, its joys and yearnings for self-expression, along with the never-ending search for both personal and collective identity. What the historian has phrased in words, the musician has captured with notes, preserving the spirit and dimension of American life with accuracy and insight.

Dallas, Texas   RONALD L. DAVIS
March 28, 1980

Acknowledgments

A fourteen-year writing project carries with it innumerable frustrations and counterbalancing rewards. High among the latter has been the opportunity to meet an assortment of helpful, talented people. My gratitude literally extends from coast to coast, and one of the frustrations has been a temptation to rewrite portions of the story long ago completed when subsequent conversations with performers and musicians have opened up nuances too tantalizing to ignore. But as that great legend of popular song Ruth Etting told me in a long distance telephone conversation a matter of days before her death in Colorado, "There comes a point at which time stops." Certainly there comes a point at which any writer must stop, even though he knows there is more to tell and often wants desperately to go on.

I must first thank David D. Van Tassel of Case Western Reserve University, who initially suggested a broader topic as the logical successor to my previous books on opera in Chicago and opera in the American West. Van Tassel later admitted he had in mind a brief paperback survey of American music with emphasis on interpretation. Obviously I misunderstood and went my own direction, preferring to write a longer version with the undergraduate cultural history student and the curious layman in mind. A grant from the Graduate Council of Humanities at Southern Methodist University enabled me to begin my research in 1966, and I soon found gracious assistance in SMU's Fondren Library, especially from Dorothy Bosch, Margaret Hamzy, and Esther Smith. Much of the material needed was furnished through Inter-Library Loan, and there were many trips to the University of Texas at Austin, where a competent staff turned tedious work into an adventure. Most of the photographs in these three volumes came from the Hoblitzelle Theatre Arts Collection in Austin, and a special thanks goes to W. H. Crain and the dedicated personnel in the Humanities Research Center on the University of Texas campus.

Robert W. Richmond of the Kansas State Historical Society read the entire manuscript and offered constructive criticism at a formative stage of the writing, while my colleagues Luis Martin and R. Hal Williams provided encouragement when I needed it most. Richard B. Allen at the William Ransom Hogan Jazz Archive of Tulane University made useful notations on the jazz chapters and earlier opened a mass of invaluable material for my use. Lee Breeden read the introductory volume from a musician's viewpoint, as did Ann Burk some time later. Eleanor Solon typed and retyped the whole manuscript, read galley proofs, and labored over index cards above and beyond the call of duty. My appreciation to her is boundless. Mary Plunkett and JoAnn Brown also read galley proofs, volunteering fresh eyes when they were especially welcome.

Two sections of the work, "Sentimental Songs in Antebellum America" and "Early Jazz," have appeared in the *Southwest Review*, and as always Margaret Hartley proved a dream editor. Valcour Lavizzo edited the final copy, rescuing me from any number of foolish errors.

I owe a special debt to Clifford L. Snyder, who has aided my writing ventures repeatedly over the years and was instrumental in the completion of this one. Also I have been fortunate in having the cooperation of Robert E. Krieger and his production staff.

Personal gratitude must be expressed to Joe B. Frantz, Anne Russ, Bruce H. Beard, Robert R. Wade, Frank and Jane Moffit, and William and Elaine Sweet, all of whom gave supportive strokes between chapters.

R.L.D.

Illustrations

Contents

The Colonial Experience

1607-1776

The New England Puritans

The Puritans, more than any other group in colonial America, contributed to that complex of values identified with the American character. Their sense of practicality, their devotion to hard work, their obsession with materialism, and their certainty of moral absolutes were all indelible stamps made by the Puritans on the American temperament. Convinced that through untiring effort and religious dedication they could perfect a utopian "city on the hill," the New England Puritans set for themselves the tasks of clearing the forests, planting fields, building cities, establishing industry, and otherwise touching civilization's wand to wilderness conditions which they tended to identify with depravity. Their mission, the Puritans were confident, was to bring enlightment and decency to a colonial frontier threatened by continued barbarism

With such a strenuous program envisioned, Puritan communities had little time for music, or any other diversion for that matter. Until the 1930s most historians viewed Puritans as severely loathing fine clothing, good food, wine, social pleasures, recreation, and music, and insisted that the Puritan elect feared that if such trifles were allowed to flourish, their followers would be distracted from the worship of God and prevented from doing His work. Secular music, traditionalists held, was considered by Puritan leaders to be a distinct menace to salvation, if not actually the work of the Devil; while some authorities even insisted that the Puritans doubted the validity of singing psalms in church, since the tunes used were not inspired by God but composed by sinful man. Other writers claimed that the Puritans would have abandoned psalm-singing altogether had not the Scriptures clearly indicated that the ancient Hebrews enjoyed the practice in their religious services.

But in 1934, with the publication of Percy A. Scholes' *The Puritans and Music in England and New England*, scholars began shifting their views on the Puritan attitude toward music. Scholes, himself an Englishman, demonstrates convincingly that the Puritans were *not* music haters, that outside the church they enjoyed music in wide and varied forms. True, Puritan leaders staunchly opposed the use of organs and trained choirs in the worship of God—since both smacked of Catholicism—but their attitude toward secular music was much more liberal. Anne Bradstreet's poetry, Scholes points out, contains any number of allusions to music, while Judge Samuel Sewall obviously was a serious devotee of the musical arts.

Judge Sewall certainly enjoyed singing psalms, for he led the congregational singing at Old South Church in Boston for twenty-four years. At formal dinners the Judge was accustomed to listening to instrumental music, and he delighted in public concerts when visiting England. A notation in his *Diary* for December 1, 1699, indicates that while on other business, he stopped by Mr. Hiller's shop "to enquire for my Wife's virginals." Hiller, it seems, either sold or repaired these instruments, and apparently, since Sewall was much a part of the religious establishment, their use for amusement was not condemned.

The notorious "blue law" of 1675 stating that "no one shall read Common-Prayer, keep Christmas or Saints' Days, make minced pies, dance, play cards, or play on any instrument of music except the drum, the trumpet, and the jew's harp," Scholes insists was a fabrication of the Reverend Samuel Peters, whose ability as a prevaricator evidently far outstripped his reliability as an historian. Reference to the alleged law first appeared in Peters' *General History of Connecticut* (1781), a work which Scholes and others find more fairytale-like than factual; but the book is in part responsible for our view of the Puritans as stern, scowling pleasure-haters. Peters exempted the drum, trumpet, and jew's harp from his imaginary ban, Scholes argues, to give his history some semblance of credulity, since all three instruments were commonly known to have been used throughout New England. Drums and trumpets were employed both for military and civil purposes, while the jew's harp was the favorite instrument among artisans and farmers and a common item of trade with the Indians.

The cutting down of the Maypole at Merry Mount, long held as a classic example of Puritan intolerance toward dancing and music, Scholes feels has been misinterpreted. William Bradford in his account of the incident does mention singing and dancing, but he condemns the offenders' "quaffing and drinking both wine and strong waters in great excess," which led to their "dancing and frisking" with Indian women of easy virtue and other "worse practices." The Puritan dislike of May Day celebrations, according to Scholes, did not stem from a basic hatred of music, but rather from the pagan origins of the feast, along with the fact that Maypole dancing often resulted in drunkenness and sexual excesses.

While the Scholes thesis is still highly regarded, the controversy over the Puritan attitude toward music has continued, reaching additional complexity in 1951, when an article by Cyclone Covey appeared in the *William and Mary Quarterly*. Covey flatly brands Scholes and his followers as Puritan apologists and indicates that the English revisionist badly overstated his evidence. Essentially advocating a return to the discredited position that the Puritans looked upon music with suspicion, Covey suggests that the Puritan environment, both in England and America, was lethal to the development of music as art. The Puritans produced no great musicians, the argument continues, for their world outlook and value system were basically incompatible with musical creativity. What concerts, operas, and oratories were produced in colonial New England, Covey maintains, were patronized not by Puritans, but by Anglicans and a sprinkling of Roman Catholics and Lutherans. Since balls were most frequently held in honor of the King's birthday or coronation, they were predominantly attended by Anglicans. All in all, Covey's conclusion is that Anglican New England was far more musical than its Puritan counterpart.

Yet the question appears to be not so much whether or not the Puritans hated music as how much time they were willing to devote to it. Elizabethan England, after all, had been a very musical age, one during which madrigals, ballads, and all sorts of popular song abounded. Even among the common people a strong oral tradition of singing developed, continuing into the colonial period. Puritans were no less a product of this heritage than Anglicans and apparently enjoyed singing on proper occasions—so long as the diversion was moral and did not distract its pursuer from more serious endeavors. English Puritans of no less stature than Oliver Cromwell, John Milton, and John Bunyan give evidence of unapologetic participation in musical recreation. Milton enjoyed playing the organ; Cromwell engaged a group of musicians for his daughter's wedding; and Bunyan kept a "chest of viols" for his private amusement.

Samuel Eliot Morison, the historian of Harvard, has brought to light two books indicating that secular ballads were sung by Harvard students shortly after Puritan leaders founded the college in 1636. But in 1661, when Josiah Flynt (a Harvard freshman at the time, studying for the ministry) wrote his uncle, Leonard Hoar (later Harvard's president), asking for a fiddle from London, the uncle refused. "Musick I had almost forgot," replied Hoar. "I suspect you seek it both to soon and to much. This be assured of that if you be not excellent at it, Its worth nothing at all. And if you be excellent it will take up so much of your mind and time that you will be worth little else." And yet while the uncle found it inadvisable to purchase a fiddle for a future minister, whom he felt should be concentrating on his studies, he did supply young Flynt's sisters with musical instruments. For the girls "tis more proper," Hoar commented, "and they also have more leisure to looke after it."

The point seems to be that even the early Puritans did not consider music a "snare of the devil," but instead found secular music a waste of time. So strongly was the Protestant Ethic ingrained into the Puritan mind that any form of idling was viewed with disfavor. In a frontier environment existence itself can be precarious; Puritan colonists were confirmed in their belief that even leisure must be constructively spent. Since music resulted in no material gain, it was considered a frivolity and therefore not worthy of serious consideration. Although the Puritans were not willing to outlaw nonreligious music, they did limit its place in their active lives and insist that musical activities be kept respectable. Bawdy or indecent songs and lacivious dancing *were* condemned in the most caustic terms. But so long as musical pleasures were restricted and held within the Puritan concept of decency, even church leaders seem to have accepted music-making without protest.

Yet the Puritans' theological orientation predicated their belief that the noblest form of musical expression was manifested in religious worship. Pragmatic to the core, the Puritan elect might consider dancing and ballad singing as frittering away one's time, but raising one's voice in the service of God was an eminently practical affair. Singing hymns was not permitted until the eighteenth century, for these were solely the creation of mortal man and had no Biblical sanction; the psalms of David, however, were another matter entirely, since they were scriptural. St. James had said, "If any be merry, let him sing psalms." And undoubtedly Puritan congregations had their joyful moments and took great pleasure in psalm-singing, considering it perfectly holy so long as the psalms were rendered in an accurate metrical translation, in unison, and without instrumentation. Part singing and organs, being identified with the Catholic Mass, were militantly avoided.

The singing of psalms, of course, was not exclusively a Puritan characteristic, since most of the Protestants in England and elsewhere during the sixteenth and seventeenth centuries (Lutherans being the notable exception) centered their church music on the singing of vernacular translations of the psalms by the whole congregation rather than by a choir. To aid the congregation in its singing, a number of psalters appeared; the first complete one in English, commonly known as Sternhold and Hopkins, was published in 1562. Begun by Thomas Sternhold before 1550 and later edited by a committee headed by John Hopkins, this psalm book was cast in popular ballad meters and included the notes, or at least the melody, of the tunes to be sung. Only one of these tunes is familiar today—that of "Old Hundredth," known to modern congregations as the "Doxology." Although later generations found its language stiff and ungainly, Sternhold and Hopkins became universally adopted throughout Elizabethan England, was admitted into the services of the Church of England, and went through many later editions. As Thomas Warton remarked, "Had they been more poetically translated, these psalms would not have been acceptable to the common people." In 1621 Thomas Ravenscroft's psalter was printed, containing almost a hundred melodies, some in four-part harmony; it was shortly recognized as the best English musical setting of the psalms available in the seventeenth century.

Nevertheless, the Separatist congregations that fled England for Holland rejected both Sternhold and Hopkins and Ravenscroft, preferring instead the *Book of Psalms* compiled by Henry Ainsworth, published in Amsterdam in 1612. Ainsworth was a recognized Biblical scholar with a knowledge of Hebrew, Latin, Greek, French, German and Dutch. He had studied at

Cambridge, became active in the Separatist movement, suffered hardships because of his views, and left England in 1593 for Holland. For a number of years he served as the teacher of the principal Separatist colony in Amsterdam, during which time he wrote a series of commentaries on the Scriptures. His *Book of Psalms* was a much closer translation of the Hebrew text than Sternhold and Hopkins, but was more complicated musically. The collection included thirty-nine psalms, melodies only, printed in the diamond-shaped notes customary of the period. About half of the entries were taken from the English psalm books, while the longer and more involved ones were drawn from French and Dutch sources.

When the Mayflower Pilgrims arrived in Plymouth in 1620, they brought with them copies of the Ainsworth psalter they had used in Holland. Edward Winslow recalled their sojourn in Leyden: "Wee refreshed ourselves after our teares with singing of Psalmes, making joyfull melody in our hearts, as well as with the voice, there being many of the Congregation very expert in Musick." After coming to America the Pilgrims continued singing psalms in a lively manner, often in the style of Renaissance madrigals. But as the years went by and as the colonists' ability at singing by note declined, the more difficult of the Ainsworth tunes became impossible. One Plymouth churchman later wrote, "many of the psalms in Mr. Ainsworth's translation had such difficult tunes, that none in the church could set [them]." Citizens of Salem and Ipswich, who also used the *Book of Psalms,* admitted they could not sing the longer tunes "so well as formerly" and gave up Ainsworth in 1667. But in Plymouth the Pilgrims continued its use until 1692, a year after the settlement was incorporated into the larger Massachusetts Bay colony. With the merger Plymouth adopted the *Bay Psalm Book* which the Boston Puritans had authorized a half century earlier.

Although the founders of Massachusetts Bay arrived in the New World a decade after the Pilgrims, their associates came in greater numbers, and the Puritan colony quickly became the stronger. Musically, however, the settlers of Massachusetts Bay appear from the beginning to have been less sophisticated than their Separatist neighbors. Initially the Massachusetts Puritans sang from copies of Sternhold and Hopkins imported from England, although they were dismayed by the looseness of the translation. Calvin had insisted that the only words appropriate for singing in worship came directly from the Scriptures. Sternhold and Hopkins had clearly taken liberties in translating the psalms into metrical verse, and the New England ministers were knowledgeable enough of Hebrew to realize that mistakes had been made. Ainsworth's rendering might be more palatable to the Puritans, but musically he was too complex. Besides his was the psalter used at Plymouth, and the competition between the two colonies and their conflicting religious views were too great for the Massachusetts Bay group to accept the compilation that was used by their rivals.

The obvious alternative was for the Bay colonists to devise their own translation, one that would be in keeping with their literal view of the

Scriptures and yet consistent with their musical ideals of directness and simplicity. In 1636, the same year that Harvard College was founded, a committee of thirty learned ministers was selected to produce a fresh metrical transcription of the psalms. The ministers sought "too keep close to the original text," making "a plain and familiar translation" in rhyme, but without "the sweetness of any paraphrase." The result was *The Whole Booke of Psalmes Faithfully Translated into English Metre*, more commonly known as the *Bay Psalm Book*, published in Cambridge in 1640 on a small press set up in the home of the Harvard president. The psalter is generally considered the first book printed in the Anglo-American colonies.

The early editions of the *Bay Psalm Book* contained no music—possibly because no one was available to engrave the plates—but included detailed suggestions as to how the tunes should be sung. That the ministers had not produced memorable poetry was evident from the beginning, but this was not their primary intent. "Conscience rather than Elegance, fidelity rather than poetry" was their purpose, and this they achieved, although the strain of adhering to the literal sense impeded their originality and cramped the flow of their verse. While the *Bay Psalm Book* contained some lines of distinction, the meter used was much less complex than Ainsworth's, probably one reason for the popularity of the Puritan translation. Whereas Ainsworth had employed no less than fifteen types of meter, the *Bay Psalm Book* involved only six, and these were uncomplicated.

The psalter was almost immediately adopted by congregations throughout the Massachusetts Bay Colony, its use eventually spreading all over New England and as far south as Philadelphia. A conservative minority among the Puritan communities did grow somewhat alarmed as they noticed that their companions were obviously enjoying the new book and not infrequently singing with considerable gusto. Most of the opposition was squelched, however, when the highly respected John Cotton wrote his *Singing of Psalmes, a Gospel Ordinance* in 1647, a tract in which he defended psalm-singing on scriptural grounds.

Three years later (1651), the *Bay Psalm Book* went into its third edition; for the revision many of the psalms were rewritten and the rhyme improved. Known as the *New England Psalm Book*, this version became the definitive one, used not only in America, but in England and Scotland as well and holding its own against competition until the middle of the eighteenth century. A ninth edition, printed in Boston in 1698, inserted thirteen tunes in two-part harmony at the back, the first known book with music published in the colonies. The tunes were those in frequent use at the time, taken from John Playford's *Introduction to the Skill of Musick*, reprinted in London eleven years before. The music—eight short tunes and five long ones—was engraved in wood in diamond-shaped notes, without bars except at the end of the line. This edition also provided instructions "for ordering the Voice," again taken from Playford. The range of the tune must first be observed, the leader was instructed; then "place your first Note" so that "the rest may be sung in the compass of your and the peoples voices, without Squeaking above, or Grumbling below." In still later editions the melody alone was printed, since the psalms were sung in unison.

But as the seventeenth century progressed, the New England Puritans appear to have had increasing difficulty in singing by note. Since no instruments were used as accompaniment in the churches, congregations had to rely on a deacon to "set" the tune. Although the Plymouth Pilgrims remained more adept at singing than neighboring colonists, toward the end of the century even they found difficulty in following Ainsworth's lengthier melodies. The Massachusetts Bay congregations, on the other hand, had recognized much earlier that Ainsworth was too difficult. As the years went by, the number of tunes that these colonists could sing dwindled, according to some accounts to four or five, although several psalms were sung to the same melody.

With fewer and fewer members of the congregations able to read music after 1650, coupled with a shortage of psalters, singing by ear became more common. Toward the latter part of the century, the general practice in New England churches was for a deacon to read a line of the psalm aloud, after which the congregation would sing it, and so on alternately through the whole verse. This "lining-out" process, as it was called, was also in use in rural England and Scotland, but as frontier conditions in America necessitated a simplification of technique, the British colonists fell back on the more commonplace traditions of the mother country, no less in music than in other cultural areas. From the standpoint of the arts, few distinctly American characteristics appeared during the seventeenth century, since most of the changes that took place involved modifications of practices established earlier in England. The "lining-out" method, although well suited to American needs, was definitely not a frontier innovation. The abrasive forces of the primitive environment, however, did enforce simplicity, for the hardships of the frontier obviously permitted little opportunity for musical education. With the passage of time settlers either forgot or, in the case of later generations particularly, never learned how to sing by note. Therefore, the folk method of singing that was common in England was adopted in America with only slight alterations.

To the traditionalist the "lining-out" process was awkward and highly inartistic, if not downright barbarous. The pause at the end of each line necessarily interrupted the flow of the music and often distorted the sense of the verse. George Hood cites an example of such distortion in his often unreliable *History of Music in New England* (1846). The verse was:

> *The Lord will come, and He will not*
> *Keep Silence, but speak out.*

According to Hood the lines were read by the deacon:

> *The Lord will come, and he will not.*

The congregation repeated this, upon which the deacon continued:

> *Keep silence, but speak out.*

As the "lining-out" procedure continued, the pace of the singing became slower. Some of the less skilled members of the group tended to sing more slowly than the rest, holding back the entire congregation. To compensate, the better singers began embellishing their singing, adding many grace notes, turns, and flourishes to fill in time, while the slower singers caught up. Pitch and time became rather arbitrary, as everyone began to sing pretty well as he pleased. "Old Hundredth" might sound, as many of the psalms did to contemporary critic Thomas Walter, "like Five Hundred different Tunes roared out at the same time," because "no two Men in the Congregation quaver alike." Synchronization, obviously, was destroyed. And since the "lining-out" system was an oral tradition with little concern for singing the tunes as printed, melodies differed tremendously from congregation to congregation; no two communities sang a tune exactly the same.

If the deacon had a good ear for music, an accurate sense of pitch, and a strong voice, he might keep his followers on key and reasonably on tempo. But by the 1690s even the deacons frequently had trouble singing the tunes as written. The melody would often be pitched too high or too low, forcing improvisation if the singing was to continue in the set key. The normal procedure was for a congregation to sing through the entire psalter in sequence without regard for the text of the sermon for the day. The few tunes in use were repeated, some of them once or twice every meeting.

Yet by the turn of the century the seaboard area of the English colonies had passed through the more rustic stage of frontier development. Cities, although scattered, were becoming far more important in influence than number, serving as centers from which trade and ideas radiated. As the degree of urban sophistication increased, as the wealth of successful businessmen became more abundant, as the impact of women grew, and as leisure time became a more visible aspect of city living, a concern for gentility and refinement became increasingly apparent among the established classes. The educated and the wealthy began seeking the trappings of culture and elegance with an almost frenzied dedication, as if attempting to assure themselves that their contact with primitive surroundings had not resulted in a reversion to barbarism. While the Puritan *ideal* might be to live humbly, without ostentation, their theology also taught that God's elect were favored with material rewards. To demonstrate their elect status, wealthy Puritans by the beginning of the eighteenth century became conspicuous in their devotion to fashion, taste, and sophistication. The portraits of Robert Feke and John Singleton Copley reflect that eighteenth-century Puritan merchants were something less than modest in their dress, while homes for those who could afford them grew to mansion proportions and were furnished in appropriate luxury.

As the search for propriety continued, the more educated New England clergymen became genuinely alarmed about the degenerated state of congregational singing. Critics bemoaned that the "lining-out" method had resulted in sounds that were absolutely painful to the ear. Thomas Walter, an educated young clergyman, deplored in 1721 that psalm tunes "are now miserably tortured, and twisted, and quavered, in some Churches, into an horrid Medly of confused and disorderly Noises." They were exposed "to the Mercy of every unskilful Threat to chop and alter, twist and change, according to their infinitely divers and no less odd Humours and Fancies." The young minister admitted, "I myself have twice in one note paused to take breath." Cotton Mather in 1718 found that the singing of some congregations could best be described as "an odd noise." Judge Samuel Sewall, that great lover of music, found the "lining-out" process so unsatisfactory that he eventually resigned his position as precentor of Old South Church. Anecdotes abound of the bedlam created by the folk method of singing. One New England deacon supposedly suffered from failing eyesight and found great difficulty in reading the psalms to be sung. Apologizing to his congregation, he observed, "My eyes, indeed, are very blind." Thinking this was the first line of the psalm, his followers sang it back to him, whereupon the deacon explained, "I cannot see at all." Again the congregation sang the line as if it were straight from Scripture. In amazement the deacon cried out, "I really believe you are bewitched," and back came the line loud and clear, "I really believe you are bewitched." At wit's end the elderly deacon added, "The mischief's in you all," and when the group sang that too, the poor man sat down in disgust and disbelief.

England had its critics of folk singing too. One British writer as early as 1676 said, "'Tis sad to hear what whining, tooting, yelling, or screeking there is in many country congregations." In America, like England, the rebuke focused in the cities, where the impulse toward gentility was greatest. Plymouth, for example, did not forsake singing by note for the "lining-out" system until around 1692, about the same time that the colony abandoned the Ainsworth psalter. Before the decade was over, however, more sophisticated Boston began abolishing the practice, at least in the larger churches. By the dawn of the eighteenth century folk traditions had become identified with backwardness and rural crudeness. A progressive city like Boston could not afford a boorish image, while Plymouth, smaller and not yet touched by the cult of respectability, was far less concerned about its cultural facade. As the urban influence came to dominate all of New England, the "lining-out" method disappeared from that area, but continued to be popular in the undeveloped frontier regions.

Nevertheless, the rural folk in New England did not give up their chosen method of singing without a struggle, and throughout the eighteenth century a battle raged between singing by note or "regular singing" (that is, singing by rule) and the "common method" or "lining-out" system. Singing by ear had become not only an expedient, but a meaningful musical experience for the common people, old and young alike. They frankly enjoyed the permissive folk style which allowed them to improvise and embellish as they saw fit, much as the jazz men of a later day exalted in the freedom and spontaneity of the early jazz style. The countless variations permitted by the "common method" served as a natural outlet for emotion and a satisfying means of personal expression. Singing by note, on the other hand, was found restrictive and artificial by the common folk of colonial New England. Consequently, these people clung tenaciously to their preferred way of singing, and as the Reverend Nathaniel Chauncey wrote at the time, were "very loath to part with it."

Even as late as August 21, 1771, John Adams wrote in his diary: "Went to meeting at the old Presbyterian Society; the Psalmody is an exact contrast to that of Hartford. It is in the *old way* as we call it—all the drawling, quavering discord in the world." Within another decade, however, the "lining-out" controversy was all but over in the towns. In 1779 the young singers at Worcester, Massachusetts, drowned out their old-fashioned deacon, who, realizing his day was over, seized his hat and withdrew from the church in tears.

Actually the "common method" never really died out. Although thoroughly pushed out of seaboard New England by the time of the Revolution, the tradition lingered on the various frontiers until eventually those areas, too, became concerned with creating an aura of sophistication and respectability. In time the "lining-out" method was confined to the isolated hinterlands, most notably the hill country of Kentucky and Tennessee, where it remained relatively undisturbed until the twentieth century. The rural folk in these regions, largely uneducated and remarkably out of touch with urbanized, industrialized America, developed little concern for genteel appearances or cultured mannerisms. As a result, they sang as they wanted—in the "common way"—and their way of life served as an isolated refuge for the dying folk technique. Later, revivalists of folk music would rely heavily upon the music of the hill country, finding it a genuine example of the American folk tradition.

It was assumed in the eighteenth century, and it has been assumed since, that the "common method" of singing is inferior. Most of the colonial reformers after all were clergymen educated at Harvard, who were sufficiently steeped in the conventional viewpoint to feel that singing by note was the only correct way, and in their newly achieved sophistication they were unwilling to tolerate a practice which to them represented the barbarism they had fought so hard to escape. By the same token virtually all of the contemporary accounts of early New England psalm singing were written by supporters of "regular singing," since the common people wrote practically nothing. All of this raises two questions: was the folk method of singing as abominable as its critics have said? Or was their prejudice against it so strong that they condemned its artlessness simply because it did not measure up to *their* conception of propriety? Musicologists are now inclined to feel that pushing the folk tradition into the back country, out of the pale of respectability, may well have denied American music a dynamic element. Certainly, the cult of gentility, by forcing American music into a rural prison, severely retarded its potential for growth along independent lines, and injected the fledgling nation's cultural efforts with an imitative and synthetic quality. Music, largely because of its close association with high society, suffered most of all.

But the reformers of the early eighteenth century were adamant that the folk method of singing was deplorable. Following a similar development in London by about a decade, the movement for "regular singing" in the colonies emanated from Boston, the recognized intellectual center. Sermons (printed and oral), published tracts, and essays all appeared denouncing the "lining-out" system in passionate terms, their arguments more doctrinal than musical. In 1720 the Reverend Thomas Symmes (a graduate of Harvard and the minister at Bradford, Massachusetts at the time) published his *The Reasonableness of Regular Singing*, and with that the first guns of New England's "singing war" were really sounded. The sharp-tongued Symmes argued in this and later commentaries that learning to read music was essential and advocated that singing schools be established for that purpose. Ministers should take the lead in creating these schools, which, Symmes suggested, would meet "Two or Three Evenings in the Week from five to six to eight o'clock." In addition to improving the congregation's musical abilities, Symmes felt the singing schools would have "a tendency to divert young people...from learning idle, foolish, yea, pernicious songs and ballads, and banish all such trash from their minds." He denied the contention of a number of his adversaries that singing by note would lead to the use of musical instruments in worship services. Not easily quieted, the opposition continued. A disgruntled writer in the *New England Chronicle* observed in 1723: "Truly I have a great jealousy that, if we once begin to sing by note, the next thing will be to pray by *rule*, and preach by rule; and then comes Popery."

Into the fray stepped the Reverend John Tufts of Newbury, another Harvard graduate, who at an undetermined date (probably 1721, although some evidence indicates as early as 1712) published *A Very Plain and Easy Introduction to the Singing of Psalm Tunes*, a pamphlet containing at least twenty-eight tunes and rules on how to sing them. Selling for six pence, or five shillings a dozen, and a size that could easily be bound with the *Bay Psalm Book*, Tufts' pamphlet was the earliest book of instruction in music compiled in the English colonies and was an immediate popular success. His tunes were printed in three-part harmony and were taken from Ravenscroft. His "easy" method of singing, derived largely from Playford, used letters (signifying *fa, sol, la, mi*) rather than notes on the staff, with rhythm indicated by punctuation marks. The letter by itself represented a quarter note, the letter followed by a period a half note, and the letter followed by a colon a whole note. Tufts himself traveled about Massachusetts, organizing singing schools and lecturing on his method; the system by result became widely used, his booklet passing through at least eleven editions in twenty-five years. Although champions of the "common way" occasionally insisted that the *fa, sol, la* method was nothing short of Popery in disguise, Tufts' pamphlet fortified the battlers for "regular singing" for their first strategic wedge into enemy lines.

A more detailed text was *The Grounds and Rules of Musick Explained: or An Introduction to the Art of Singing by Note: Fitted to the Meanest Capacities* by the twenty-five-year-old Reverend Thomas Walter of Roxbury, Massachusetts. Walter's work, unlike Tufts', used diamond-shaped notes instead of letters with bars dividing the measures. Forty-three tunes in three-part harmony were included, along with instructions on singing by note and some "Rules for Tuning the Voice." The book was printed in 1721 on James Franklin's press in Boston, at a time when James' fifteen-year-old brother Benjamin was working as an apprentice in the shop. Even more extensively used than Tufts, Walter's manual enjoyed a number of editions, the last of which appeared in 1764.

Before the singing controversy was over, no less a figure than Cotton Mather had joined the ranks of the pamphleteers advocating "regular singing." Called *The Accomplished Singer*, Mather's treatise recommended the establishment of singing schools as the most efficient way of teaching congregations to read music. The venerable clergyman also corresponded with the English theologian Isaac Watts, who had published his *Hymns* in 1711 and his *Psalms of David Imitated* eight years later in an attempt to broaden the repertoire of Protestant congregations in England. Although Watts' hymns were not strictly scriptural (often paraphrases of the psalms), Cotton Mather approved of their use in private devotional readings.

The reformers, while differing in musical method, agreed on the singing school as the principal vehicle for learning to sing correctly. Again Boston took the lead. By this time it was a city of twelve thousand, supporting eleven churches, and two grammar schools. Boston had the population, the economic solidarity, and the intellectual leadership necessary for the singing school movement to emerge. Sometime around 1720 a Society for Promoting Regular Singing was created in the city, its citizens responding so favorably to the initial instruction that by 1724 Cotton Mather felt that the battle for "regular singing" in Boston had been won. Roxbury, Cambridge, Dorchester, Bridgewater, Charlestown, Ipswich, Newbury, Bradford and other more progressive towns shortly followed Boston's example, although many of the smaller communities in the Massachusetts hinterland were, in Mather's words, too "sett upon their old Howling" to join the trend toward singing by note.

Singing schools were commonly set up in a town after a committee, formed either by the minister or active members of the congregation, had secured underwriters for the project. Then a teacher was selected, and a meeting place for the school was chosen. While the churches in some cases provided a room in which the singers could meet, the village tavern or schoolhouse often served the purpose. Sessions were held two or three evenings a week, usually for something like twenty-four evenings. Singers were asked to bring their own candles and a board to hold both the candle and a music book. Instruction consisted of teaching the basic elements of notation, followed by a series of voice-placement exercises. Gradually, as the class became more proficient, new tunes were learned. Aside from its musical functions, the singing school was also a social gathering, especially for the young people, although the older folk enjoyed gathering with neighbors and chatting on the way home. Undoubtedly the diversion offered by the schools went a long way toward explaining their immense popularity.

The masters of the singing schools were the first really professional musicians to appear in colonial New England; that is, they were the first to make their living exclusively from music. Most of them were itinerants, traveling from town to town, spending several weeks in each one. Since classes needed additional music as students progressed in their singing ability, teachers supplemented their incomes by selling tune books. Particularly if the teacher returned to a community year after year, new material was essential if he were to continue attracting a class. As the singing school movement spread, the demand for the publication of new books, with more complicated music, increased. At the same time the Puritan insistence on a literal rending of the scriptural psalms weakened.

Among the numerous English publications, Tate and Brady's *New Version of the Psalms* (originally published in 1696) and, more especially, Isaac Watts' *Hymns* and *Psalms of David Imitated* became popular with New England singing schools. The literary quality of these later works was far superior to that of the *Bay Psalm Book*, with the result that the beloved psalter of the previous century was gradually superseded by the more sophisticated translations. The urban dilettantes of eighteenth century America particularly found the poetry of the *Bay Psalm Book* archaic and uncouth. Watts' verse, on the other hand, was more in keeping with the style of Addison and Pope, which the educated elite of the colonies had come to admire. Benjamin Franklin published an edition of Watts' *Psalms* in Philadelphia in 1729, but the Englishman's great American popularity really did not begin until 1739-41, when the famous British evangelist George Whitefield toured the colonies, promoting Watts' *Hymns* and *Psalms* as he went. A number of congregations, such as Jonathan Edwards' at Northampton, compromised the issue by alternating Watts hymns with the traditional psalms. By the end of the century Watts dominated hymnody in most New England churches, at least in the larger towns, much as the *Bay Psalm Book* had dominated earlier.

Compilations originating in the New World, however, appeared as well and came in for extended usage. Francis Hopkinson's *Collection of Psalm Tunes*, prepared for Christ and St. Peter's Churches in Philadelphia came out in 1763, although none of the tunes were written by Hopkinson. A year later,

Josiah Flagg, a Boston publisher, concert manager, and the leader of the city militia band, published his *Collection of the Best Psalm Tunes*, the music for which was engraved by silversmith Paul Revere. Flagg's collection, containing 116 tunes and two anthems, was the largest collection yet published in the English colonies. Slowly new tunes began winning acceptance, a few even composed by American musicians. James Lyon of Philadelphia published his *Urania* in 1762, a collection of psalm tunes, at least six of which were Lyon's own. But colonial America's most successful church composer was William Billings, who became deeply involved in the singing school movement and wrote a substantial amount of music, in a fairly original style, for choral use.

By the beginning of the nineteenth century over 130 collections of hymns and psalms had been published in the various cities along the Atlantic coast. Anthems were more frequently included in these books as time went by, indicating that church choirs were beginning to make a notable appearance.

Choirs emerged gradually and informally and seem to have incurred surprisingly little opposition. Members of a local singing school, partly because of their repeated social contact, often chose to sit together in church. Eventually, the more advanced churches began reserving the first seats of the gallery for the better singers and allowed them to lead in the psalm singing. From this the church choir naturally developed. Although there is slight documentation for when the transition actually occurred, the larger urban churches seem to have had something approaching a choir around 1750. While the formation of choirs in the smaller communities later on became embroiled in controversy, the early evolution among the bigger churches apparently took place so smoothly that the conservative faction was seemingly caught off guard and offered minimal dissent. Once the choirs were recognized, they began demanding more complex music to sing. To fill their desire for more ornamental pieces, the anthem, used earlier in the singing schools, became accepted into ordinary worship services beginning in the 1760s. With the anthem, part-singing (tenors customarily assumed the melody) became more wide-spread, although the old practice of singing the psalms in unison had doubtlessly broken down earlier.

The willingness of Puritan congregations to accept choirs and anthems—both of which had been heatedly condemned as Catholic less than a century before—indicates that in their great push for sophistication, New Englanders had become more liberal in their theology. The religious zeal of the first generation Puritans became less conspicuous among later generations, while their revulsion with primitivism and their desire for urbanity steadily increased. When religious dogma and the search for gentility clashed, church doctrine came to yield more and more as the eighteenth century progressed. While religious convictions remained important to New England Puritans, their concern with materialism and the trappings of respectability became greater in the urban centers, where colonial society was gradually becoming secularized. The "city on the hill" became less a spiritual vision than an earthly one, as the desire for prosperity, enlightenment, and cultural refinement became dominant.

The introduction of musical instruments into the Puritan church service, however, did produce fairly serious opposition. Still, by the middle of the eighteenth century, conservatives had pretty well lost this battle too. The tuning fork and bass viol (or cello) had been commonly employed in the singing schools, particularly when these schools met somewhere other than the church, and it was natural for choirs, who had grown accustomed to these instruments, to want them as support for church music as well. The tuning fork was accepted first, a much surer aid for setting the correct pitch than the precenter had ever been. Later, with the rise of part-singing, the bass viol was introduced as an accompaniment for singing and eventually became known as "the Lord's fiddle." Still later, flutes, the hautboy (oboe), the clarinet, the bassoon, and finally the fiddle found admittance into Puritan worship. The fiddle particularly brought cries of protest, since the instrument had long been associated with dancing. For a time churches that used stringed instruments were derided as "catgut churches."

Even more soundly condemned was the use of organs in Puritan churches, since the Puritans had come to look upon the organ as the very symbol of Popery. Then too, the majority of the early colonists, coming as they did from rural districts and villages, had probably never heard an organ. The instrument was fairly rare even in England during the seventeenth century, found only in cathedrals, college chapels, and in the larger city churches. It was an easy matter for the Puritan colonists to abhor what they had never known.

The first organ in New England was brought over in 1711 by the wealthy Bostonian Thomas Brattle and installed in his home. Brattle was an esteemed churchman, had helped organize the Brattle Square Church in Boston, and was the brother of the minister at Cambridge. His Puritan peers accepted and even admired the organ, so long as it was used only for personal enjoyment and private entertainment. On May 29, 1711, the Reverend Joseph Green noted in his *Diary*, "I was at Mr. Thomas Brattle's; heard ye organs and saw strange things in a microscope." The good Reverend apparently found nothing wrong with listening to "ye organs," at least not in Mr. Brattle's house. But two years later, Brattle died, leaving the organ in his will to the Brattle Square Church, of which he was a leading member. Should the church refuse his gift, the will specified that the organ was to be given to King's Chapel, where the Episcopalians worshipped. A further provision stated that whichever church accepted the instrument should "procure a sober person that can play skillfully thereon with a loud noise."

Although the Brattle Square Church was a highly liberal one—its congregation having been the very first in Boston to abolish the "lining-out" method back in 1699—the church voted overwhelmingly against accepting the organ. "We do not think it proper to use the same in the public worship of God," a spokesman wrote. Consequently, Brattle's gift went to King's

Chapel, the Episcopal congregation promptly importing an organist from London, one Edward Enstone, to play it. King's Chapel, therefore became the first church in New England to possess an organ; not until 1770 did the First Congregational Church of Providence become the initial congregational church to permit the use of the instrument in worship services. The Brattle Square Church changed its mind about the matter in 1790 and had an organ built in London. But even as late as 1800, there were something less than twenty organs throughout New England, most of them in Anglican churches. Religious prejudice, of course, was not the only issue at stake. The transportation problem, the cost of the instrument, and the difficulty of finding trained organists all contributed to the scarcity of organs in colonial America.

High shipping costs in fact served as a general deterrent to the importation of musical instruments into the colonies. References to instruments of any kind are rare in New England throughout the seventeenth century, although the Puritans seem to have approved of their use outside the church and had no restrictions on their importation. Probably the earliest notation of a musical instrument in the New England colonies was recorded by Isaac de Rasieres, secretary of the Dutch colony at Manhattan, who visited Plymouth in 1627. De Rasieres observed that the Pilgrims "assemble by beat of drum, each with his firelock or musket, in front of the captain's door." According to the town records of Windsor, Connecticut, a platform was added to the top of the meetinghouse there in 1638, making it possible "to walk conveniently to sound a trumpet or a drum to give warning to meeting." More frequently mentioned in the early accounts is the jew's harp, particularly as an item of barter.

The will of Nathaniel Rogers in 1661 lists a "treble Viall" among the deceased's possessions, while Edmund Browne left a "base vyol" to his heirs upon his death in 1678. Harvard students are known to have played musical instruments. John Foster (a classmate of young Josiah Flynt, who wanted so much a fiddle from London) owned a "violl" and a "gittarue," and Michael Wigglesworth (later the author of America's first best-seller, the graphic *Day of Doom*, but in 1653 a tutor at Harvard) wrote in his diary of hearing a student "in the forenoon with ill company playing music." While not plentiful, enough references to musical instruments exist from seventeenth century New England to confirm that instruments existed and were used for a variety of secular purposes.

But with improved shipping and an increase in both prosperity and leisure, the number of instruments coming into colonial America for household use had grown appreciably by the opening of the eighteenth century. An advertisement in the *Boston News-Letter*, April 16-23, 1716, clearly indicates that there were virginals and spinnets in Boston to be tuned and that a fairly large selection of musical instruments were available for purchase at Enstone's dancing school. Even in the frontier regions musical instruments were known, although occasionally put to fairly bizarre uses. A

Reverend Hugh Adams, who preached in a small village out on the Indian frontier, had obviously read the ninth verse of the second chapter of Numbers: "And if you go to war in your land against the enemy that oppresseth you, then ye shall blow an alarm with the trumpets...and ye shall be saved from your enemies." Adams located two old horns and instructed his sons in how to blow them. Repeatedly the boys blew the horns out the front door of their rustic cabin, a ritual which Adams was convinced had saved his family from Indian attack.

Instruments, even in the seventeenth century, were used as accompaniment for secular singing, and outside the church part-singing was common and acceptable from the beginning. The Puritans seem to have enjoyed a wide diversity of musical recreations at home, encouraging the participation of young people and delighting in the discovery of a new tune. Again, since most of the New England settlers had emigrated from the rural sections of the mother country, the music they brought with them was largely of the folk tradition, rather than from the art music repertoire of Elizabethan England. Still, as one contemporary wrote, the early Puritans possessed a sizable store of "neat and spruce ayres." In the towns the various trades all had their special songs, ballads were almost universally popular (especially among the urban youth), sailors' chanties could be heard along the coast, mothers sang lullabies to their children, while trappers, hunters, lumbermen, and farmers could be heard singing snatches of refrains as they went about their work. Harvard students are known to have sung such sentimental ballads as "The Last Lamentation of the Languishing Squire" and "The Love-Sick Maid"—the latter beginning, "Begone, Thou fatal fiery fever." Most of the songs were transmitted orally to succeeding generations, although broadsides containing lyrics were printed fairly early in the larger towns.

As time passed, the real center for popular song in colonial America became the tavern. As a rule located near the meeting house, the tavern was a natural gathering place, and in the early days the town council and courts often assembled there. Gradually the taverns emerged as dens for the idle, marked by a proportionate growth of drunkenness and rowdiness. Singing increased as well, but the preferred lyrics were of the bawdier variety. And, since the Elizabethans had lent an appreciative ear to the earthy ballad, the more urbane colonials had a substantial stock of ribaldry to draw upon. The titles alone indicate something of the nature of these ballads—for example, "Kiss Me Quick, My Mother's Coming," "Bonny Lass under a Blanket," or "Sweetest When She's Naked." But what was fun and frivolity to Elizabethan England was anathema to Puritan America. Cotton Mather complained that by his day every other house in Boston was an alehouse. The Reverend Benjamin Wadsworth warned his congregation against taverns, lamenting that "those wedded to bad Company have often a greater relish for Playbooks, Romances, filthy Songs and Ballads than for the Holy Scriptures." And Increase Mather had admonished his people earlier, "Tarry not in Taverns or

Ordinary's or in Houses where Strong Drink is sold....It is a sad thing, that Professors and Church-members should many of them be guilty of Scandalizing the world in this respect."

Eventually reservations were also expressed about the sale of broadsides, for in 1713 Cotton Mather wrote, "I am informed that the Minds and Manners of many People about the Countrey are much corrupted, by foolish Songs and Ballads, which the Hawkers and Pedlars carry into all parts of the Countrey." The concern of the Puritan clergymen was not that secular singing existed, but that it had come to occupy such a time-consuming place in the lives of some of their parishioners. In the case of tavern singing, idleness was compounded by lewdness, an obvious affront to the Puritan sense of morality. Even in the relatively sophisticated eighteenth century, indolence and obscenity were two infractions Puritan leaders could not tolerate.

The attitude toward dancing was much the same. Lascivious dancing, such as that interrupted at Merry Mount, was definitely frowned upon, and some of the more conservative clergymen disapproved of men and women dancing together. Increase Mather in 1684 wrote, "Concerning the Controversy about Dancing, the Question is not, whether all Dancing be in it self sinful....But our question is concerning *Gynecandrical Dancing*, or that which is commonly called *Mixt* or *Promiscuous Dancing*, viz. of Men and Women...together." Regulations were passed in the interest of public order restricting dancing in taverns, and dancing with the Indians was prohibited. But within these limitations, the Puritans apparently accepted dancing with few qualms. When Jonathan Edwards' father, for instance, was ordained in 1694, a dance was held at his house, and historian Henry Bamford Parkes claims that "by 1700 everybody danced except a few of the clergy and graver laymen."

Dancing schools are known to have existed in Boston during the early eighteenth century and give evidence of doing a handsome business, despite conservative opposition. In 1714 Edward Enstone, the Anglican organist brought to King's Chapel in Boston, requested permission to open a school of music and dancing, but was refused by officials. Nevertheless, two years later, with or without sanction, he was advertising his services as a music and dancing teacher and was selling musical instruments as well. Newspapers reveal that in 1720 he was still in business. As the impulse toward social refinement became more pronounced among the Puritan *nouveau riche*, the patronage of dancing schools broadened.

Theatrical entertainment, however, was held in considerable disrepute by Puritan communities throughout most of the eighteenth century. The Boston prejudice against the theater culminated in the passage of a series of blue laws in 1750 which remained in effect until well after the Revolution. The ballad opera companies so enthusiastically received in New York, Charleston, and Philadelphia (in spite of Quaker objections in the latter) scarcely ventured into Boston. Even as late as 1792 a ballad opera performance in Boston was raided by civic authorities.

Concerts were looked upon with greater favor, and as the singing schools became more proficient and as musical instruments were imported in greater numbers, public concerts became fairly common. The first known concert in the English colonies, advertised in the *Boston News-Letter* of December 16-23, 1731 as a "Concert of Music on Sundry Instruments," was held in the great hall of Peter Pelham's house. Pelham himself was a Boston dancing master, an engraver, an instructor in reading and writing, a dealer in Virginia tobacco, and an Anglican. This concert in Boston preceded the first given in Charleston by only three and a half months; it is highly probable that earlier concerts were given in the colonies, but no record of them has survived. Considering that the first public concerts in London were not held until the latter part of the seventeenth century, the Americans were actually not so far behind.

After 1731 concerts seem to have been presented in Boston fairly often—at least one or more a year. Oscar Sonneck, the pioneer historian of early American concert life, concluded that a regular concert season was offered in the city by 1751. From 1732 until 1744 most Boston concerts were heard in the Concert Room in Wing's Lane. Then in 1744 Faneuil Hall became the accepted place, offering vocal and instrumental music both by local amateurs and itinerant musicians. After 1755 the Concert Hall in Queen Street was the city's music center, housing concerts and, later, dancing classes. The Music Hall in Brattle Street was also popular, particularly with the wealthier set; a notice of a concert occurring there on November 1, 1768, indicated that after the performance, "the Ladies and Gentlemen may have a Ball till eleven o'clock." In the years right before the Revolution, William Selby, an Anglican who became the organist at King's Chapel, managed most of the Boston concerts, especially the importation of European artists and the high society affairs. Tickets for these events were sold at the British Coffee House.

The various New England singing societies presented occasional concerts that were held in the churches since these groups concerned themselves almost exclusively with religious music. Their offering focused principally on anthems and oratories. The Boston Musical Society under Selby, for instance, once presented selections from the *Messiah*, a chorus from Handel's *Samson*, and several pieces played by Selby on the organ, including a Bach sinfonia. Only rarely did the singing societies participate in secular events, although a notable exception occurred in Boston in October, 1789, when one of the groups there welcomed Washington's arrival in the city with a special ode written to the march from Handel's *Judas Maccabacus*.

Most of New England's concert life does seem to have rested in Anglican hands, and the secular events particularly appear to have had strong Tory ties. As the eighteenth century progressed, Boston became not only a more sophisticated city, but also more closely linked to the mother country, economically, politically, and socially. Much of the social gaiety of the city came to center around the military set and an elite circle of royal officials. Wealthy Bostonians mixed freely with the English social set up to and, in many cases, during the Revolution, and it was this nucleus that was responsible for the bulk of the city's musical activities—activities patterned after the European example.

And yet, the fact that the Anglicans promoted most of the formal concerts in eighteenth century New England does not validate the age-old argument that the Puritans hated music. While the first-generation Puritans had never been as straight-laced and narrow as their critics have indicated, most of them had grown out of touch with the more genteel aspects of Europe's cultural life, dedicated as they were in the seventeenth century to clearing the forests, establishing a solid economic footing, and fashioning their ideal religious community. But by the 1750s Puritan ideology had come in for an appreciable reorientation, initially prompted by the Puritan interest in logic and science but intensified by their growing concern for commerce and the rewards of material success. As the Puritan outlook became more secular, their interest in fashion and respectability became increasingly marked. Since England in the colonial mind was considered the center of style, it was natural that the later English immigrants to America, many of whom were merchants and professional people of some standing, were looked upon by second and third generation Americans as connoisseurs of elegance and sophistication. That most of these later arrivals were also Anglicans is understandable and somewhat beside the point; their recent acquaintance with the mother country caused them to be viewed as a source of cultural wisdom.

When the impulse for propriety entrenched itself in the American colonies early in the eighteenth century, cultural leaders were drawn from two sources: the educated clergy from the colonial seaboard and the wealthier recent immigrants from England. Gradually, with the great wave of Puritan migration over, and as the New England colonies came under royal control, Anglican leadership in cultural affairs became increasingly evident. While the Puritan impact on economics and moral attitudes continued, New England's musical life, more and more a model of Great Britain's, became conspicuously dominated by Anglicans. Puritans maintained a lively interest in religious music and attended concerts, when they were made available, without moral compunction, but the role of leadership in formal secular music was filled mainly by Anglicans.

Above and beyond everything else the New England Puritans were motivated by a sense of practicality, staunchly insisting that pragmatic matters be placed first. To the Puritan mind adherence to their deep religious and moral convictions, coupled with their growing concern for economic success, must take precedence, and the Puritan energy was mainly directed toward these ends. Musical activities were clearly viewed as peripheral in importance. The early Puritan immigrants brought few musical instruments with them from the Old World simply because the frontier environment of the New World offered them an invigorating challenge—a grandiose opportunity to express their great admiration for work. In their devotion to the "Protestant Ethic," the seventeenth century Puritans could concern themselves only slightly with anything interfering with the labor their ideals and the wilderness conditions necessitated. Thus, while the fiddle or the jew's harp might be found enjoyable, they were nevertheless subordinated to the ax and the plow.

By the eighteenth century conditions had changed considerably. Seaboard New England had become dotted with towns in which a thriving commercial class was much in evidence. While urban Puritans were no less devoted to utilitarianism and the work ideal than their rural contemporaries, their existence was less tentative, less dependent upon the vagrancies of the frontier. The merchant class, as a rule, also enjoyed greater wealth and increased leisure. Since the manner in which they demonstrated this wealth and leisure often had direct bearing on their social position, a cultivated use of leisure among the urban *nouveau riche* took on practical overtones. Eighteenth-century Puritan city dwellers not only had the time to enjoy a more diversified musical life, but also found an increased cultural awareness essential to their social standing. As the colonial cities grew more sophisticated, and consciously sought to offset their rustic beginnings with a facade of gentility, the Puritan elite had no choice but keep pace or be left behind—socially and, more importantly to them, economically. Although the Puritans were generally willing to leave the arrangement of most secular musical events to their more urbane Anglican neighbors, they attended concerts and gradually became increasingly involved in their city's cultural life, as both their interest and their aesthetic image matured.

But in the realm of religious music, the Puritans were more involved and, therefore, more capable of assuming roles of leadership. As the trend toward refinement became evident, those Puritan congregations where the cultural impulse was strongest were able to substitute singing by note for the "lining-out" method, establish choirs, accept anthems and hymns, and eventually even install organs, because they realized that not to have done so would have placed them in a category with the uncivilized. As the secularization of colonial society became more widespread throughout the eighteenth century, Puritan leaders were able to accept these musical innovations with a minimum of conscience pangs, their sense of practicality overshadowing religious conservatism. Along these same lines, Puritan leaders realized by the early 1800s that with the secularization of society a splintering of Puritan ranks was likely. To keep this to a minimum a more liberal doctrine would have to be assumed, and yet if the clergy were to maintain its influence over their congregations, some sort of discipline and order was essential. In this sense the insistence on singing by rule is a reflection of a larger movement in which the Puritan clergy attempted to reestablish control over its fragmenting urban congregations.

Although the Puritan influence would remain strong in America until well into the twentieth century, the semblance of a unified Puritan theology was severely shattered by the 1750s. Intellectual historian Perry Miller has demonstrated that the Puritans were never as homogeneous a group nor as stereotyped in their attitudes as writers once thought. Certainly this is no less true of their musical experiences. With the maturation of city life diversity became the keynote; the contrast between the folk tradition of the backcountry and the genteel, often artificial, patterns emerging from urban sophistication appeared more sharply drawn.

CHAPTER

II

The Middle Colonies

Although the population of colonial New England, particularly by the eighteenth century, broadened to include other than Calvinist elements, the Puritan viewpoint served as a focal point for the region at least until the eve of the Revolütion. The Middle Colonies, on the other hand, presented no such initial unity, contained no such common denominator in their intellectual development. By far the most heterogeneous section of colonial America, the Middle Colonies—aside from the British core—embraced Germans, Dutch, Swedes, Finns, and French, while the index of religions ranged from Anglican to Quaker, Calvinist to Catholic, Mennonite to Dutch Reformed. In musical tastes these colonies were no less diverse, encompassing the Quakers, who deplored musical entertainments and opposed the use of music in their worship even more staunchly than the Puritans; the Catholics, who welcomed both vocal and instrumental music into their religious services and enjoyed it on secular occasions; and the Moravians, who adored music in a variety of forms, both inside the church and out, and probably had the highest musical standards of any group in colonial America.

To the Quakers, members of other religions tended to substitute sensual pleasure for spiritual perception, even in their worship services, while they themselves found God in the simplicity of an Inner Light. The Friends worshipped God through the plainness of quiet waiting and adoration, unhindered by hymns, instrumental music, stained-glass windows, or religious images. Since art and music was considered by Quakers as concessions to worldliness and distractions from religious devotion, they excluded the arts almost totally from their lives. Dancing particularly was viewed as frivolous and idolatrous, and the Quaker's war against the theater was unrelenting. Yet, while members of the Quaker community were repeatedly urged to shun musical diversions, their leaders were tolerant enough to accept the musical needs of others. At William Penn's insistence Pennsylvania became a haven for members of oppressed religions, where the various sects could sing God's praises and amuse themselves in any way they saw fit. By the middle of the eighteenth century, as life along the coast grew more urbane, progressive Quakers, particularly in Philadelphia, began to enjoy a gayer existence, relaxing their restrictions on musical activities even for members of their own faith.

By contrast the Catholic Church saw no conflict between music and religion and in fact found music a particularly effective aid to its ritual. The Church in the English colonies was never as wealthy as in the larger Spanish provinces and therefore could not compete with the lavish musical presentations given by cathedrals in viceregal cities like Mexico and Lima. Still, John Adams and others attest that music was not only important, but given careful preparation by Anglo-American Catholics. When the future president visited St. Joseph's Church in Philadelphia in October, 1774, he recorded that the Gregorian chants were "exquisitely soft and sweet," and added that, "The scenery and the music are so calculated to take in mankind that I wonder the Reformation ever succeeded."

But the most knowledgable musicians in colonial America, although definitely limited in their cultural impact, were the Moravians, who maintained close ties with musical developments in Europe, supported highly trained choirs, orchestras, and organists, and produced a number of composers. The Moravians were the spiritual descendants of Bohemian Protestants dating back to John Hus, but had gradually spread from Bohemia into Germany. Left in dire straits by the Peace of Westphalia, since they had no princes to represent them, fugitives of the Moravian Brethren were welcomed onto the estate in Saxony of Count Nicholas von Zinzendorf, a recent convert. In 1735 a small group of Moravians migrated to Georgia, planning to take up missionary work there among the Indians. Five years later, they moved to Pennsylvania, settling first at Nazareth on land owned by evangelist George Whitefield and later purchasing a tract of land on the Lehigh River, near Philadelphia. This settlement, which the Brethren called Bethlehem, was shortly visited by Count Zinzendorf and populated with additional recruits. So great was the Moravian zeal that Bethlehem almost at once showed signs of becoming a thriving community.

Unlike the New England Puritans, who found little time for music, the Moravians' way of life was permeated with musical sounds. They saw no need to separate work from music, no conflict between religion, art, and amusement. Labor was part of their devotion, while music was an aid to labor. The Moravians sang in the fields, in their shops, at meals, while traveling, wherever they were, often with instrumental accompaniment. They felt that music not only helped make arduous tasks more pleasant, but assisted in bringing work to a speedy conclusion while simultaneously arousing human ambition and kindling the imagination. Each occupation had its special hymns, often composed by the workers themselves. Nor was music any less an active part of Moravian devotion, for vocal and instrumental music filled every observance, and a knowledge of the hymnal was considered as essential as a knowledge of the Bible. Religion to the Moravians was a matter of deep emotion as well as something to be enjoyed; music played no minor role in arousing both emotion and pleasure. Religious festivals, therefore, were highlighted by fine congregational singing, most frequently accompanied by an organ, although all of the orchestral instruments available were welcomed into the church. When one zealous young minister asked about the propriety of using the same instruments in church that had been used the night before for secular purposes, an elder reputedly answered, "Will you use the same mouth to preach with today which you now use in eating sausage?" For the Moravian, religion, life, and music were enmeshed in a continuum.

Although the Moravians were better schooled in music than their Puritan contemporaries, a changed American environment also played a part in permitting their musical standards to remain at such a high level. The frontier of eighteenth century Pennsylvania which received the Moravians was far less severe than the wilderness into which the seventeenth century Puritans had come. Faced with conditions less harsh than those experienced by the earlier arrivals, the Moravians were able to continue their life much as it had been in Europe. Certainly their dedication to established cultural traditions was important, but Moravian workers could indulge in the luxury of taking up the violin, cello, or flute in the evenings not only because they loved music, but also because frontier conditions were not so extreme that their entire energy was taken up with taming the wilderness. The Moravians came to America after the urbanization process along the East coast was relatively advanced, the trend toward sophistication already begun.

At the same time the initial settlers at Bethlehem knew loneliness, and music helped comfort them, serving as a reminder of home and linking them with their Old World heritage. Singing was an important part of life at Bethlehem from the beginning, and the town early became a musical center of a magnitude far beyond its size. In 1742 the first *Singstunde* was held, at which eighty voices were heard. Later that same year musical instruments were imported, and on Christmas Day, 1743, violins, violas, flutes, and French horns were played in the church for the initial time. A month later the first harpsichord arrived, looking somewhat dilapidated from the voyage, but it was quickly repaired and used in the worship service the next day. By 1746 the church had a small organ, brought from Philadelphia and installed by Johann Gottlieb Klemm, a Moravian organ builder. Meanwhile something approaching an orchestra had been formed, playing from manuscript the simpler works of recent European composers. In December, 1744, a musical society, or *Collegium musicum*, was organized, patterned directly after a European example. The *Collegium* held weekly rehearsals and shortly began giving performances of chamber music and eventually symphonies. Works by such renowned composers as Mozart, Haydn, Graun, and Johann Christian Bach were presented, and later, when a choir was added, oratorios were included, among them portions of Haydn's *The Seasons* and Handel's *Messiah*.

The community at Bethlehem was made up of varied nationalities, for brotherhood and the universality of the church were Moravian ideals. As if to emphasize this point, polyglot singing was practiced in Bethlehem for a few years. A love-feast, for example, was held in September, 1745, during which the old German carol *In dulci jubilo* was sung simultaneously in thirteen languages by settlers, scholars, missionaries, and Indian converts—the languages including German, Bohemian, English, French, Dutch, Greek, Irish, Latin, Mohawk, Mohican, Swedish, Welsh, and Wendish.

Trombones were brought to Bethlehem from Europe in 1754, becoming one of the community's favorite instruments. A trombone ensemble, consisting of treble, alto, tenor, and bass instruments played in four-part harmony and performed on most of the town's special religious occasions. The ensemble at times was even used to welcome distinguished visitors. The trombonists normally announced festivals from the belfry of the church early on the morning of the event, and from this same belfry announced the death of a member of the congregation. A special function of the trombone quartet was to lead the procession to the graveyard for the sunrise Easter service. The trombones were almost always played in the open air—from the belfry, in the cemetery, or outside the church door—rarely inside the church or in concerts. Tradition has it that the brass ensemble saved the village from Indian massacre during the French and Indian War. Early one morning in 1755 Indians were supposedly hiding nearby, awaiting the moment to attack. Right before the signal was given, the assailants heard the sound of the trombones, as they announced the death of one of the Brethren. Startled and confused, the Indians quickly stole away, convinced that the Great Spirit must be protecting the whites.

Benjamin Franklin, who in 1756 was a lieutenant-general fighting Indians, temporarily made Bethlehem his headquarters. He records in his *Autobiography* that while in Bethlehem he "was entertained with good music, the organ being accompanied with violins, hautboys, flutes, clarinets, etc.," and in a letter to his wife he wrote, "Heard very fine music in the church." Martha Washington passed through Bethlehem in 1779, and George Washington stayed there three years later; both were favorably impressed with the musical entertainment.

By 1789 the orchestra at Bethlehem had grown and reputedly included all of the instruments used by European orchestras. The choirs were more difficult to muster, partly because so many male voices were taken up in the orchestra. Women singers were more easily come by. Between a third to half of the town's population is estimated to have taken part in the community's musical life, although all of the members of the *Collegium musicum* were amateurs in the sense that they pursued other vocations or held full-time professional positions—as teachers, ministers, craftsmen, or whatever. But their knowledge of music, their taste and skill, and their awareness of the musical progress abroad seem to have been astonishing. New instruments and compositions were constantly being imported by the Pennsylvania Moravians, and the claim is made that the first copies of several Haydn quartets and symphonies to reach America were brought to Bethlehem. In the Moravian Archives in Bethlehem are collected several hundred songs, arias, cantatas, and instrumental compositions, including manuscript copies of six trios and three symphonies by Mozart, dated 1785. The composer would have been a mere twenty years old at the time. The last decade of the eighteenth century and the first of the nineteenth constitute the golden age for Bethlehem's *Collegia musica*; thereafter it disbanded into the Philharmonic Society. The new organization, led by David Moritz Michael, reached a pinnacle in 1811, when Haydn's *The Creation* was partially performed— believed to be the first performance of this work in the United States.

Nowhere else in America could congregational singing and religious anthems be heard on such a high level. The Moravians delighted in singing their prayers and praises to God, and in sharp contrast to the Puritans sought to give vivid, sensual form to their religious convictions. To the Moravian, religion came from the heart, and music expressed those emotions in the most faithful way. Rather than singing all or several stanzas of one hymn, they preferred to sing selected stanzas from a number of hymns, interspersed with prayers and testimony, depending on the nature of the service. As a result of these "hymn-sermons," hymnals were arranged by subject matter, and estimates indicate that as many as 70,000 hymns were known to the Moravians, although many of these were undoubtedly variations of the same hymn, probably additional verses. Good singing was insisted upon, and certainly a high degree of skill was essential to cover this large amount of complex music. Organists were required to know hundreds of tunes, since the minister generally began singing a hymn without announcing it first. The organist and congregation were expected to join in as soon as they recognized the verse.

Musical presentations within the Moravian church often approached Catholic mass proportions. Separate male and female choirs existed, each complete in itself; boys customarily sang the soprano parts in the male choir. Some pieces were sung by the males, others by the women; when performing more complex compositions the choirs responded to one another or sang together. The beauty of Moravian singing rested not so much in the melody as in the harmony, usually four-part harmony.

At the close of the eighteenth century not even Philadelphia could approach in either quantity or quality the musical standards set by Bethlehem. But these Moravian musicians did not limit themselves to the classics, nor to works of religious expression, for music of a lighter vein was also popular. Groups of young men were fond of serenading visitors or members of the community on birthdays, and orchestral concerts were frequently given out of doors on summer evenings.

Musical education for children was stressed in Bethlehem, both for boys and girls, and instruction was normally given without charge. At the same time Moravian missionary zeal extended both to Indians and blacks brought to the New World and included musical training for converts. In 1763 the Brethren even published a collection of hymns in the language of the Delaware Indians, illustrating once again the universality of their religious outlook.

But in addition to conserving the Old World musical traditions through instruction and performance, the Pennsylvania Moravians also produced a number of composers. Most of their work was modeled after that of contemporary Central European composers, rather than containing anything particularly American, although it is natural that this should be the case, steeped as the Bethlehem musicians were in the renaissance, baroque, and early classical styles. The list of Moravian composers in America is substantial, but Jeremias Dencke, John Antes, and John Frederick Peter are among the best examples.

Jeremias Dencke possibly wrote the first sacred music in America. Himself a fine organist, Dencke arrived from Europe in 1761, settling in Bethlehem. His compositions show superior craftsmanship; his choruses are melodious and effective, while his use of instruments is in the best pre-classical style. Dencke's contemporary, John Antes, may well have written the earliest chamber music by a native-born American. Born in Montgomery County, Pennsylvania, Antes was schooled at Bethlehem, then sent to Egypt as a missionary. Most of his writing was done in England after 1781, although Antes remained technically an American. His compositions are those of a gifted amateur, consistent with the Moravian philosophy that music was an important part of life, but always a supplement to God's work. Antes was a clergyman first, a musician second.

But the most gifted of the American Moravian composers was John Frederick Peter. Arriving in Bethlehem in 1770 as director of music for the community, Peter brought with him large quantities of manuscripts which he had copied while studying in Germany, among them some of the early works of Haydn. Shortly after taking up his duties at Bethlehem, he began composing music for the church, eventually writing more than forty anthems. His only secular work is a set of six string quintets dated January 9, 1789, the first chamber music actually written in America. Although his technique is strongly reminiscent of Haydn and Stamitz, Peter's compositions are considered among the finest written in eighteenth century America.

Yet, while the Moravians maintained the highest musical standards in colonial America, an indigenous element was almost totally lacking. Their whole culture pattern was consciously derived from Europe, more particularly from Germany and Central Europe, invigorated by repeated contact with the Old World. The Moravians implanted in America a genuine love for "serious" music and their level of performance was unexcelled, but their influence on their English-speaking neighbors and their impact on the development of an American musical tradition were negligible. Until the beginning of the nineteenth century, the Moravian settlements were officially directed by the central administration of the church in Germany, forcing them to remain essentially European in orientation. While the Moravians are an interesting curiosity, presenting as they did the initial performances in America of major oratorios and symphonic works as well as producing the first chamber music written in America, they were essentially isolated from the mainstream of American life.

The same is largely true of earlier Pennsylvania Germans, although their degree of musical accomplishment was less than the Moravians'. Most German immigrants were cognizant of a deep musical tradition, including two centuries of Lutheran hymnody. The majority settled in areas where the frontier was partially tamed and where transportation facilities to the Old World were fairly extensive. Consequently, musical instruments and scores could be imported fairly easily, and the German folk heritage remained relatively unthreatened by wilderness conditions. But the music of these German immigrants was foreign to the surrounding English majority, if not actually alien to their religious philosophy. Most of the Germans settled in small, self-contained towns, closely bound together by blood ties, customs, and religious ideology. Relations with the outside world were minimal, not the least of the barriers being a language which most neighboring communities could not understand.

In 1683 a small group of Mennonites led by Francis Daniel Pastorius settled at Germantown, joined a generation later by a colony of Dunkards, or German Baptists. These settlers brought along with them their hymns and folk tunes, and Pastorius himself was an amateur composer. A band of German pietists settled on the Wissahickon River, eight miles outside Philadelphia, in 1694. Having sworn themselves to celibacy, these hermitlike religious mystics believed that the end of the world was near and that the only love should be a love for the Lord Jesus Christ. Led by Johann Keplius, the son of a minister at Dendorf, Germany, these pietists came equipped with musical instruments and trained voices; soon they acquired a reputation as fine musicians. In 1700 they were asked to provide the music for the dedication of the new Swedish Lutheran church, called *Gloria Dei*, in Philadelphia. Verses to nineteen of the hymns performed at the service were written by Keplius. Sometime before 1703 the Wissahickon Valley pietists acquired a small organ and formed an orchestra, since both were borrowed that year by the *Gloria Dei* church to assist in ordaining a new minister. A few months later, Christopher Witt, an English craftsman, joined the Wissahickon hermits and built for them the first organ constructed in the colonies, apparently for household use.

In 1732 another group of German pietists settled at Ephrata, Pennsylvania, in present Lancaster County, about fifty miles west of Philadelphia and southwest of where Bethlehem would later be located. Envisioned as a retreat where members could shut themselves off from the world, the community was originally called Ephrata Cloister and early took on an eccentric character. Musically, the settlement was always a maverick, expressing some fairly original—if not to say curious—features. Much of the community's peculiar personality could be traced to its founder, Johann Conrad Beissel, also organizer of the town's musical life. Born in Eberbach, Germany, of poor parents, Beissel first learned the baker's trade, but later became a weaver. He left Germany at age thirty because of his heretical religious views, immigrating to Pennsylvania. After living a while in Germantown, Beissel was struck by a fresh impulse of religious fervor and shortly forsook his fellow man for a brief residence as a wilderness hermit. Before long he had attracted a group of followers who sought to imitate his way of life, and Beissel suddenly found himself the leader of a self-styled religious community.

Fond of music since childhood, although scantily trained in that area, Beissel grew increasingly involved in musical activities throughout the rest of his life, finding music a relief from the world's burdens and a superior means of self-expression. Eventually Beissel took over the direction of the choir at Ephrata, following a quarrel between members of the group and the regular singing master. As leader he not only directed the choir's singing, but their lives as well. Beissel insisted that music was a reflection of theology and moral righteousness, and that behind the celestial sounds of the choir must be celestial lives. He therefore demanded the strictest of moral codes. His approach to vocal training was anything but orthodox, even going so far as to prescribe diets for his singers. Meat and animal products—such as milk, cheese, butter, and eggs—he felt were a hinderance to the cultivation of an angelic voice. Likewise, beans were too filling and stimulated impure passions. Wheat, potatoes, and turnips, on the other hand, preserved the purity of the voice and were strongly recommended. Sexual intercourse he also considered harmful to the voice, straining the soul and enfeebling the body.

Beissel also developed a special technique for singing in which all voices assumed a muted falsetto quality, the singers barely opening their mouths and scarcely moving their lips. The result was a delicate instrumental tone, supposedly evoking an otherworldly mood in its listener. A contemporary tells of visiting the Ephrata chapel, where he heard some girls singing concealed behind a curtain: "We were first entertained with a solo which I and every other person who had not been there before took for a wind instrument of some sort; I could almost have sworn that it had been the lute-stop of an organ, and could not be satisfied that it was not, till the curtain was drawn, and I was shown the performer." Most of the singing at Ephrata Cloister, in fact, was done by women. The sisters were organized into three different choirs, each of which sang in four-part harmony—women taking lower as well as higher parts. When the men did sing, they also harmonized; the combined choirs often sang in as many as seven parts. As there is no record of instruments being used, the assumption is that all of this singing was unaccompanied. Beissel believed that music was derived from nature and therefore sought to keep the harmonic pattern and rhythm simple. Harmony became merely a matter of consulting a chord table which Beissel made for each key, while rhythm simply followed the cadence of the text. Accented syllables were long, unaccented ones short. Since there was no fixed relationship between the duration of long and short notes, considerable latitude was permitted, resulting in a free, variable tempo. Members of Ephrata sang from large, handwritten books copied by the women and illuminated in the fashion of medieval monasteries. The official songbook of the community was Beissel's own *Song of the Lonely and Forsaken Turtledove, the Christian Church*, the very title of which indicates something of the author's mysticism. Only the singing of psalms and hymns was permitted at Ephrata; secular music was not tolerated. Visitors to the community were invariably impressed by the quality and peculiar beauty of the singing there. Beissel and his followers considered that they had recaptured the music of the angels.

Most of the church music imported from Europe in Beissel's mind was too complicated and artificial for his followers. He wanted melodies that would reflect the plainness of life at Ephrata and the simplicity of its religious ideals. To obtain the music he wanted, Beissel in 1743—then a man well along in his fifties—took up composition. Less than twenty-five years later, he had written a variety of pieces numbering into the thousands; words to several of these were printed by Benjamin Franklin on his press in Philadelphia. In addition to composing hymns and anthems, Beissel set whole chapters of the Old Testament to music. He knew little about the church music of the Reformation and cared less. His music was as personal as his religion, containing elements of mysticism. Inspired by the success of their leader, other members of Ephrata Cloister tried their hand at composition, the number swelling to a sizeable portion of the community within a few years and most following Beissel's simplified harmonious formulas. Music at Ephrata became paramount in the community's religious experience, much of it as singular as it was unconventional, as primitive as it was picturesque. Sonneck in his study of early American concert life goes out of his way to take a swipe at "that exotic musical weed reared by Conrad Beissel," although the accomplishments at Ephrata Cloister have been more kindly treated since. Yet while Beissel's compositions and his musical theories are fascinating relics of an esoteric faith, they had little or no effect on the development of an American music. Even more isolated from the enveloping Anglo-American culture than the Moravians, Ephrata, despite its uniqueness and charm, is of slender importance in terms of cultural impact. Held together largely by the force of its founder's personality, the community fell apart shortly after his death, its legacy as cloistered as the life it idealized.

The music of the less exclusive forms of German pietism may not have been as original as Ephrata's, but it was heard by a larger public and did exercise some influence over Anglo-American hymn writers. In this sense the Germans contributed an indirect element at least to an emerging American folk tradition, more particularly to the evolution of the white spiritual.

And certainly the religious music of early eighteenth century Philadelphia was strongly enriched by the city's large German population. Most of the Pennsylvania Germans entered the New World through the port at Philadelphia, some times numbering as many as 5000 in a year. While most of these German settlers moved on west to one of the smaller frontier communities, some of them located in the city. By the middle of the century the German population of Philadelphia had increased to such proportions that the British colonists became alarmed that Pennsylvania might actually be alienated from the English crown. The Philadelphia Germans were no less enthusiastic about music as a part of their worship than their contemporaries farther west, with the result that much of the city's early church music stemmed from German sources. Although the Quakers still had reservations about the use of music in church—or anywhere else, for that matter—they became increasingly tolerant of religious music and the more restrained forms of secular music as the eighteenth century progressed, allowing the Germans to sing their hymns and to build their organs without serious obstacle.

From 1750 on, however, Philadelphia assumed an increasing air of elegance, just as Boston was doing in New England. As the city grew in sophistication, secular music began to overshadow religious music as the dominant feature of the city's musical life. The first really fancy ball held in the city was probably given in 1726 in honor of the Prince of Wales' birthday, although dancing and fiddle playing had been a part of festive occasions long before. As early as 1728 Philadelphia had a dancing school, while in 1730 Thomas Ball's sister, "lately arrived from London," began teaching "singing, playing on the spinet, dancing, and all sorts of needle work." The number of music teachers, most of them coming from London, increased throughout the next two decades, and undoubtedly they brought with them a knowledge of Handel and the other baroque composers then so popular with the London music circle. The guiding spirit behind much of Philadelphia's early concert life was Francis Hopkinson. At age eighteen (1755) he is known to have been acquainted with arias by Handel, as well as with compositions by Scarlatti, Vivaldi, and Corelli; he was probably exposed to these masters by the London music teachers who settled in America around the middle of the century.

Trailing Boston, Charleston, and New York by several years, the first concert in Philadelphia was not recorded until January 25, 1757, when music under the direction of a John Palma was presented in the Assembly Room in Lodge Alley. The concert began at six o'clock, tickets selling at the London Coffee House for a dollar each. As in Boston and elsewhere, most of the early concerts in Philadelphia were supported by Anglicans, since the German mystics were scarcely more interested in secular music than the Quakers. Colonial newspapers seem a dubious source for judging the frequency of concerts, as they often did not record such events. For example Sonneck found no mention of a concert in Philadelphia between 1757 and 1764, although it seems unlikely that absolutely none was given. An Orpheus Club, supposedly a musical society, existed as early as 1759, and it is believed that amateur musicians were heard under the club's sponsorship. Within another decade evidence of concerts becomes more substantial and Philadelphia's musical life gives indication of having grown fairly lively. A series of subscription concerts, most likely managed by Hopkinson, was presented; programs consisted mainly of chamber music. Hopkinson, a harpsichordist himself, also gathered around him a group of amateur musicians, including Governor John Penn. This group would meet at Hopkinson's home to play their instruments; perhaps occasionally they gave public hearings.

Another of Hopkinson's friends dabbled in music, as he did in almost everything else—printing, poetry, politics, economics, literature, philosophy, science, invention, religion, diplomacy. This, of course, was Benjamin Franklin, who somehow found time to learn to play the violin, the guitar, and the harp and delighted in entertaining his friends in London and Paris with his musical versatility. He also impressed the music world of both Europe and America by inventing an instrument, known as the glass harmonica. The inventor became so fond of his instrument in fact that he believed it would eventually replace the harpsichord and the piano. Resembling the *Glasspiel* or musical glasses already in use in Germany, Franklin's instrument used specially blown glasses in the shape of hemispheres with holes in their middle, rather than beer glasses set on a table, as was the practice in Europe. The glass hemispheres employed by Franklin totaled thirty-seven and were graduated in size from nine inches in diameter to three. The resulting instrument was capable of producing three octaves of sound including half-tones. The glasses were mounted on an iron spindle, run through the holes in their center, each half sphere partially within the next larger one, but not touching it. The spindle was then placed horizontally in a long case mounted on four legs, somewhat resembling a xylophone. The player sat in front of the instrument, revolving the spindle with a treadle like a spinning wheel and rubbing the edges of the rotating glasses with his moistened fingers. The tones produced were, in Franklin's words, "incomparably sweet beyond those of any other [instrument]."

Franklin first heard musical glasses played in London during his second visit, but it was he who developed the idea into a working musical instrument. Nothing seems to have absorbed the inventor more between 1757 and 1762 than his glass harmonica. In a letter to Beccaria in Turin, July 13, 1762, he thanked the Italian for supporting his observations on electricity and proudly added a description of his instrument, which he felt was "peculiarly adapted to Italian music, especially that of the soft and plaintive kind." The harmonica did enjoy a considerable vogue in Europe for a number of years, particularly in Germany and Austria, where Franklin became as famous for his accomplishments in music as for his findings in electricity. Mozart and Beethoven both wrote works especially for the American's instrument, as did any number of lesser composers. Philadelphia first heard the harmonica in 1764, when Stephen Forrage incorporated the instrument into one of his concerts. After several unsuccessful attempts to apply a keyboard to the glasses, including an effort by Francis Hopkinson, the glass harmonica passed out of favor early in the next century, largely because its sound was too monotonous and its playing technique was too inflexible to meet the needs of a maturing romantic tradition that emphasized variety of expression.

Franklin even tried his hand at composition, writing at least one string quartet. He also penned ballad verses, and the musical tastes of this American Leonardo da Vinci are known to have run along the lines of simple airs rather than toward the ornateness of Handel's music. Consistent with his Enlightenment principles, Franklin felt that music should be simple and natural, as opposed to the grandiose artificialities that titillated high society. In this respect Franklin was one of the first Americans to appreciate the beauty and integrity of folk tunes in their primeval state.

While Franklin represents a minor protest in America against the elaborateness of the baroque style, London had recently experienced a virtual revolution in its musical taste, at least in opera and music for the stage. With the premiere performance in 1728 of John Gay's *The Beggar's Opera*, London suddenly turned away from the florid Italian opera that had heretofore been so fashionable and embraced a native product, the ballad opera. Tired of superficial elegance and dismal, sentimental plots, English theatergoers found the realism and earthy bawdiness of Gay's satiric opera refreshing. Told in the everyday speech of the London streets, *The Beggar's Opera* was a robust comedy with winning, familiar songs interspersed with spoken dialogue. Most of the tunes were popular seventeenth or eighteenth century ballads, although a few were more sophisticated, coming from the art songs of Purcell and others. The plot caught the spirit of the moment, caricaturing as it did Sir Robert Walpole, and depicting with considerable precision the crime, corruption, and poverty of London while making lowbrow fun of stilted Italian opera. Almost overnight baroque opera was temporarily driven off the English stage, while the era of the ballad opera entered to mass acclaim.

Within less than a decade after Gay's triumph, the ballad opera was introduced into the British colonies in America, the first produced in Charleston in 1735, but heard in New York by 1750 and in Philadelphia no later than 1759. By the middle of the eighteenth century Philadelphia was ready for theater, encouraged largely by the city's growing Anglican population. By then the Quaker opposition, while still vocal, had been reduced to minority status, as the Anglican element gained in number and wealth and came to play a greater role in local administration. From 1750 on Philadelphia assumed more and more the character of a little London, imitating the current English vogues in theater and music only slightly less closely than it did in dress, furniture, and architecture. The rage for ballad opera in London lasted from 1728 until about 1750, although classics like *The Beggar's Opera* continued to be staged with some regularity. The American Colonies caught only the last phase of this excitement, but remained enthusiastic about the ballad opera for another quarter century or more, when native American efforts began to supersede the British prototype. Much of the satire that London enjoyed was lost on American audiences, while the world of rebellious daughters and intriguing chambermaids, depicted so often in the ballad operas, was fairly alien to the American experience. And yet the ballad operas were popular because of their familiar tunes, their use of the vernacular, and their lusty comic plots. At the same time Americans felt they were seeing the theater favored by the London social circle, and in the colonial search for sophistication, timeliness was important.

A condensed version of the popular *Flora* or *Hob-in-the-Well* was given as an afterpiece during the Hallam company's initial Philadelphia season in 1754; this piece was more farce than ballad opera. Lewis Hallam's company, which began its American career in Williamsburg in 1752, but was later reorganized into the American Company, virtually monopolized theatrical activity in the English colonies, including the production of ballad opera. In fact the earliest recorded full performance of a ballad opera in Philadelphia was the American Company's staging of the classic *Beggar's Opera* on August 24, 1759, two years after the city's first known concert. By the time of the Revolution ballad opera had grown to tremendous popularity throughout urban seaboard America. Among others Philadelphia had heard *Damon and Philida, The Contrivances, Love in a Village, The Maid of the Mill* (based on Richardson's *Pamela*), and what proved the most popular work in colonial Pennsylvania, *The Padlock*.

Even straight dramatic offerings at this time were followed by a comic afterpiece, often including singing and dancing; it was not uncommon for popular ballads to be sung between acts—even of Shakespearean tragedies. Actors in the colonial days had to be versatile, capable of singing or dancing as well as acting. They were expected to assist with building scenery, making costumes, rewriting scripts, and anything else that necessitated their help.

By 1769 the American Company on its visit to Philadelphia gives evidence of having formed a regular orchestra, made up largely of Philadelphia musicians—probably the same ones who were providing the music for the subscription concerts. The local press, however, found it necessary to state that the musicians "have no View but to contribute to the

Entertainment of the Public [and] certainly claim a Protection from any Manner of Insult." Exactly what form of insult might occur is not mentioned. Perhaps social ostracism was feared, since anyone associating with actors in those days was looked on with suspicion. More likely the injury would come in the form of vegetables and debris thrown by the gallery crowd, since this segment of the public persistently came to the theater supplied with oranges and carrots and seemed to find the target presented by local gentlemen playing away in the orchestra pit especially difficult to resist.

Although the cities of colonial America maintained some of the distinctions of their varied heritage—Boston its Puritan element, Philadelphia its Quaker and German, New York its Dutch—the striking feature from about 1720 until the Revolution is their similarity. As each fell increasingly under the domination of the Anglicans and as the urge for sophistication grew with ascending prosperity, the major cities of Anglo-America all began a parallel effort to imitate the cultural life of the mother country. As they came more closely to approach their ideal, life in urban colonial America became more cosmopolitan on the one hand, more alike on the other.

In each case the wealthy merchants or planters and the officials of the colonial government were the chief supporters of the early concert life, and most often concert patrons were "Tory" Anglicans. Secular concerts were therefore closely linked with the colonial aristocracy, often held in conjunction with a grand ball or a society party. The programs were modeled after the English chamber variety, and the selections were essentially those heard in London, particularly the compositions of Corelli, Scarlatti, Vivaldi, Purcell, and Handel. The ballad operas, on the other hand, while attended by the social circle, were largely mass entertainment, containing as they did street tunes and strong doses of theatrical vulgarity. The delight of Anglicans and the more liberal religious element, ballad operas were attended by a fairly wide segment of the colonial population; sometimes theater managers found it necessary to bill the operas as "lectures, being a mixed entertainment of Representation and Harmony," to bring out the desired crowd.

The third major form of art music know to colonial America, the oratorio, was primarily the property of the churches, particularly members of the Anglican, Catholic, and German pietists. Originally designed as Lenten substitutes for opera, oratorios in abbreviated form were among the earliest choral offerings heard in the colonies, aside from psalms and hymns. In 1753 William Tuckey, the man responsible for the first presentation in America of parts of Handel's *Messiah*, arrived in New York. Previously Vicar Choral of the cathedral in Bristol, Tuckey was brought to America by Trinity Church. He quickly established himself in New York as an organist, choirmaster, concert artist, and composer. In all probability he gave the former Dutch city the best performances of organ music ever heard in the colonies—outside the Moravian settlements. On January 16, 1770, Tuckey conducted the overture and sixteen selections from *The Messiah*, two years before the work was performed in Germany.

Although New York in the eighteenth century was not the music and theater center it later became, and in many respects was less active than Philadelphia, the first recorded concert in New York predates the earliest known concert given in the Quaker city by over twenty years. The occasion was a benefit for Charles Theodore Pachelbel given in 1736. For the next several decades, however, concert life in New York was no less sporadic than that of early Philadelphia. A benefit for John Rice, the organist of Trinity Church, took place in 1745, the program consisting of a mixture of vocal and instrumental music. Tickets to the function were sold at *both* New York's coffee houses; the concert was announced to begin at five o'clock in the afternoon. Another musical program was offered on October 19, 1749 in the Court Room of the City Hall; but not for another four years was a similar event advertised. Then early in 1753, Charles Love, the harpsichordist for the Hallam company, gave a concert, assisted by his wife, one of the Hallam's ballad singers. In 1774 a Harmonic Society was formed in New York, its members becoming actively engaged in the city's growing concert life, which by this time included foreign musicians who were occasionally imported to give virtuoso performances.

The first ballad opera given in New York was the perennial *Beggar's Opera*, staged at the Nassau Street Theater on December 3, 1750. The Hallam troupe came later, providing not only drama and ballad opera, but considerable incidental music as well. Several of the musicians with the company supplemented their income by giving concerts or music and dancing lessons. William Hulett, a dancer with the troupe, opened a school on Wall Street for instruction in the violin, the German flute, dancing, and fencing, while Charles Love advertised lessons in the violin, viola, hautboy, bassoon, French horn, and flute. On its last tour of the colonies the Hallam company gave a total of fifty-eight plays, twenty of which were of a musical nature. Obviously the link between secular music and the theater had become a close one in pre-Revolutionary America.

On October 20, 1774, with the Revolution near, the Continental Congress, meeting in Philadelphia, temporarily curtailed the development of drama and music in America by issuing the resolution, "That we will in our several stations encourage frugality...and discourage every species of extravagance and dissipation, especially all horse racing, and all kinds of gaming, cock fighting, exhibition of shews, plays, and other expensive diversions and entertainments." The reason for this cutback in amusements was not so much the old moral question as the feeling that such diversions would interfere with the serious political business at hand.

Much of the theatrical fare presented in colonial America had been sheer entertainment, sometimes approaching the variety show level with an abbreviated drama serving to link the assorted acts. Most of the music presented in the theater was light and familiar, geared to popular appeal. But occasionally catchy lyrics were set to classical tunes—most commonly to melodies by Handel and Arne—with the result that Americans became aware of a certain amount of European art music without realizing it. Efforts to encourage "serious" music on a more elaborate scale, however, were the prerogative of the wealthy and suffered from the stodginess of an artificial environment as well as from being restricted to the upper social stratum. A symbol of sophistication and gentility, concert life in early America enjoyed a precarious existence, rarely seeming to be more than a feeble flicker struggling to exist in a rarefied atmosphere.

The individuals who supported art music in colonial America were essentially gentlemen dilettantes. Francis Hopkinson in Philadelphia is an excellent example. An amateur musician and composer who enjoyed the social limelight, Hopkinson gathered around him a group of influential friends, inviting those with a knowledge of a musical instrument to play together at his home. Hopkinson also served as the focal point of the city's concert life in the years preceding the Revolution and later would be one of the leaders in the movement for political independence. At the same time he unwittingly helped lay the groundwork for America's continued cultural dependence. Hopkinson's aim was to acquaint Americans with the best of European art, thereby implanting the model for later development. But by accepting European cultural archetypes as absolute, Hopkinson and his fellow dilettantes inadvertently fostered an attitude that eventually would retard the new nation's artistic development along independent lines.

Although less intrigued with the foibles of society and a man of superior intellect, Benjamin Franklin nonetheless was much the dilettante when it came to music. In addition to composing a few selections, Franklin was a publisher of music, the inventor of a musical instrument, a patron of the arts, and a frequent performer at home recitals. Unlike Hopkinson, however, Franklin was adverse to Italian opera and the oratorios of Handel, finding them contrived and artificial. In this respect he was an accurate image of the pragmatic American character. Likewise, his preference for ballad and folk tunes, although too isolated and premature to have any real effect upon the development of an American music, foreshadowed a stripping away of superficial gentility that was essential before America's music could bear serious resemblance to her national temperament.

Church music, at least of the psalm-hymn variety, was a more integral part of the early American musical tradition largely because it was less calculated and more tightly woven into the American experience. And yet much of the church music of the Middle Colonies was too grandiose to be consistent with the American spirit. The Catholic and Anglican efforts for all their urbanity and gentility stayed rooted in European tradition and far afield from the American ideal of pragmatic simplicity. Similarly the Moravians, astonishing though their musical accomplishments were, had little bearing on the American pattern, simply because Bethlehem and the later Moravian communities never really ceased being European, bound to the Old World as they were by church government and a cultural heritage nourished by repeated immigration. Ephrata, on the other hand, was too eccentric and too much the recluse to make a significant impact. The hymnody of the less cloistered heirs of the Lutheran musical tradition did have an influence on American hymn writing and would emerge at least as an indirect ingredient in the later white spiritual.

No group in the Middle Colonies, however, played as influential a role in shaping either the American mind or an American music as did the New England Puritans. The Quakers, the Anglicans, the Catholics all contributed their part in refining the American character, as did the Dutch, and Swedes, and Germans. And all but the Quakers added a dimension to the American appreciation of music. But the Puritans made the indelible mark both on the American temperament and on an embryonic American music. The music of the Puritans was certainly less spectacular, less cultivated, than much of that in the Middle Colonies; but the psalms and hymns sung in New England were more relevant to a broader and more influential segment of American life, their very simplicity in close harmony with American ideals. While the Moravian *Collegium musicum* may stand as the splendid ornament adorning the colonial patchwork, Puritan hymnody remains the constant strand woven into the fabric of music in American life.

CHAPTER

III

The Tidewater South

In the colonial South, where the Church of England was the established religion, few reservations about music and entertainment existed, unlike the more fundamental northern sects. The Anglicans did oppose dancing on Sunday, and the Virginia court records indicate that a number of fines were levied against persons who were found guilty of such Sabbath breaking. But for the most part southern Anglicans viewed musical diversions as an indispensable part of their social life. In their worship services the congregations of the Church of England found few musical expressions objectionable, so long as they were dignified and in good taste. Congregational psalm singing was practiced, but anthems and trained choirs were much desired, and organs were incorporated into the larger churches whenever the congregations could afford them and could acquire an organist. Since most of the American clergymen were either English by birth or English-trained, they naturally wished to imitate the Anglican ritual as closely as possible. And yet frontier conditions often necessitated simplification, with the result that music in the more isolated Episcopal Churches differed little from that among the Puritan congregations of New England. The lining out method was frequently employed, particularly where there were few psalters. A clerk would read the lines of the psalm aloud, just as in the New England churches, although he might be assisted by a gallery choir if the congregation were large enough. In the smaller chapels frequently there was no singing at all, simply the reading of the Prayer Book by the minister.

As tidewater conditions became less rustic and as the Anglican congregations grew in size and wealth, the folk way of singing was gradually replaced by singing by note, paralleling the similar development in urban

New England. Among the Virginia gentry regular singing became the only respectable method early in the eighteenth century, although as late as 1710 there was still dissension over the matter. William Byrd of Westover wrote in his diary that year, "In the afternoon my wife and I had a quarrel about learning to sing Psalms in which she was wholly in the wrong." But a week later he recorded, "We began to give in to the new way of singing Psalms." As in the North, singing schools were established, and instructional guides such as John Playford's *A Brief Introduction to the Skill of Musick* began to circulate. By the Revolution only the backwoodsmen still clung to the lining out tradition.

In the South the singing school developed in two directions and continued well into the nineteenth century. The urban schools, like their northern counterparts, taught regular singing and paved the way for the formation of choirs and choral societies and eventually for the presentation of the more complex European oratorios. But the rural schools that came later inculcated a homespun hymnody and a folk way of communal singing that became known as the "fasola" system. In remote communities these institutions also kept alive many of the old tunes, later fostering the revival spirituals and camp-meeting songs peculiar to the American frontier. Folk hymns were particularly adapted to the out-of-door services for which the southern climate was so conducive, while their unsophisticated and uninhibitive nature satisfied both the musical and social needs of the provincial folk. Thus, while folk hymnody continued to lose ground in the urban North, it spread throughout the rural South, entrenching itself as a southern tradition.

Among the wealthy planters a more secular musical pattern prevailed, one oriented toward gentility and Europe. Trained musicians had been present in the South since 1620, when John Utie sailed up the James River aboard the *Francis Bonaventure*. Utie, who had been "a fidler in England," quickly discovered that Jamestown could not support a musician and became a planter. Five years later he was elected to the House of Burgesses, although he still amused himself and his friends with his fiddling. That same year an opponent, William Tyler, referred to Utie as a "theefe" and a "Rogue and Rascall," with the result that Tyler was hauled before a Jamestown court. His offense was made all the greater because the term "Fidlinge" had entered into the name-calling. At this time most Virginians regarded professional fiddlers as rogues and rascals almost by definition and perfectly capable of theft or most any other unscrupulous act.

By the turn of the century, however, it had become a mark of social distinction for members of the gentleman class to be appreciative of good music and if possible play an instrument themselves. String instruments were preferable to wind, because the latter "puff out the face in vulgar fashion." Thomas Jefferson, for example, used to rise at five o'clock in the morning to practice the violin, and although Patrick Henry was said to have been the worst violinist in Virginia next to Jefferson, the two enjoyed performing duets together. Music was the special delight of Robert Carter, and his son Benjamin was tireless in his practice on a variety of musical instruments. At the Carter mansion in Virginia, Nomini Hall, could be found a guitar, a harpsichord, a pianoforte, a harmonica (or musical glasses), a violin, and a German flute, while their house in Williamsburg contained a fine pipe organ—all of which were played by members of the Carter family. A different type of gentleman musician is depicted by the British officer Thomas Anbury, who was held captive near Charlottesville during the Revolution. Anbury described the Virginia planter who, when not riding around his plantation, spent his day sprawled on the porch floor playing at the fiddle, drinking peach brandy, and counting his illegitimate mulatto children as they ran about the yard.

Even more essential to the planter's social image than playing an instrument himself was for his daughters to display some ability at singing or performing on the harpsichord, piano, or guitar. Accomplished ladies of the colonial South could play some sort of instrument, although the violin and flute were reserved for southern gentlemen, and it was considered unladylike for girls to learn to play them. The Carters spent many an evening at Nomini Hall listening to chamber music and to the vocalizing of daughters Betsy and Fanny, the girls often accompanying themselves as they sang. Jefferson professed to be "vastly pleased" with Jenny Taliaferro's playing of the spinet and singing, while the one thousand dollar harpsichord that George Washington bought for his adopted daughter, Nellie Custis, still stands in the drawing room at Mount Vernon.

Splendid spinets and harpsichords were imported by the planters from London, sometimes made by such master craftsmen as Plenius and Kirkman, the latter the Queen's instrument maker. These instruments were not inexpensive in London, but packing charges, freight, and commissions added considerably to the price paid by Americans. Jefferson and others gathered together fine music libraries, consisting of pieces by Corelli, Bach, Handel, Haydn, and other European masters, and William Byrd's extensive library at Westover included a number of examples of English and Italian opera.

An indispensable symbol of high breeding was the southern gentleman and lady's ability to dance. Balls were frequently held in the halls of the great plantations, and the larger planters often had servants trained as fiddlers who could supply the music for dances, although for a really elegant affair a small orchestra might be brought in. Dancing gave the southern lady an opportunity to demonstrate her dignity and skill at moving gracefully—a feat made all the more impressive dressed as she was in skirts of rich fabric, with cinched waist, and a coiffeur ornamented with jewels. A gentleman was expected to be a good dancer, but not an excellent one. If he proved too proficient in executing fancy steps, his masculinity might be called into question. The ideal, patterned after the Renaissance concept of the well-rounded cavalier, was for the southern gentleman to keep proportion in all things—always the adept amateur, never the professional. Still the planter gentry spent no little time polishing their steps. A typical entry in William Byrd's diary, for instance, reads, "I rose about 6, read Hebrew only. I prayed and had coffee. I danced."

To provide instruction for their children in dancing and playing instruments the patrician southerners acquired the services of a tutor, preferably importing him from Europe. Often several neighboring plantations would join resources in employing a music master. On a day designated as "dance day," for example, young people from several estates would gather together at a chosen home for lessons from an itinerant dancing master. Philip Fithian, a Princeton graduate who in 1774 became the tutor of the Robert Carter children, was highly impressed with his charges' dancing ability: "Mr. Christian, in the dancing room, teaches the children country dances and minuets. There a number of young persons are moving easily about to the sound of well-performed music, and with perfect regularity. Again in the evening, when candles are lighted, they repair to the drawing room. First, each couple dances a minuet, then all join, as before, in the country dances."

Music masters normally rode a circuit between the wealthy rice and tobacco estates of the colonial South. One German master traveled a monthly route that included stops at the homes of the Carters, the Lees, and other Potomac gentry. Elizabeth Lucas at Wappoo was given a harpsichord lesson every Monday morning by an itinerant musician. Historian Thomas Wertenbaker pictures Cuthbert Ogle, one of the more colorful southern music masters, as going "from plantation to plantation, violin and folio of music in hand, in his French gray coat and breeches, black silk waistcoat and flowing wig," peering "through his 'temple' spectacles at his notes" and keeping "time for his pupil at the harpsichord." Riding a circuit was time consuming and not without its dangers. Francis Russworn, who gave lessons on the violin and is said to have "played such a sweet fiddle," was drowned while crossing on a ferry in Virginia. Sometimes the planter would send a carriage to bring the music master from a neighboring estate, and the musician's visit was looked upon as a welcome relief from the monotony of rural life. The itinerant professor usually stayed for two or three days at each plantation—devoting his mornings to giving lessons, his evenings to discussing music with the family or perhaps joining the planter in a duet. The professor dined with the family, during which he brought his host up to date on local news and gossip; he was normally accepted by the tidewater gentry as a social equal.

Until late in the eighteenth century Charleston was the only southern city capable of supporting a permanent music master, although Annapolis and Williamsburg could usually be counted on for fairly lengthy stays. The most sought after masters came from abroad, usually from London but occasionally from Germany or Italy. Even when the professor hailed from the Continent, he generally entered America by way of England. Most of the masters had studied in Europe, had performed in concert halls and theaters there, and were quick to point out—and often exaggerate—their European experience to the American clientele. The majority of these musicians were frankly second or third-rate talents who had come to America expressly to escape the serious competition in Europe. The professor assured his public that he was capable of teaching "by the most approved methods." By his "easy" system an eight or nine year-old boy could surely play the violin within a few weeks, and a girl could be turned into a potential harpsichord virtuoso. The master claimed a knowledge of the latest techniques and newest works, understood the Italian style of singing, and could teach the violin by "the new Italian method." Above all he must prove a versatile musician, capable not only of teaching, but of giving concerts, planning musical programs, and even composing selections for special events. Dancing masters, aside from teaching the latest minuet, were also expected to instruct young gentlemen in the art of fencing.

In the cities these professors of music—in addition to playing church organs, selling music and instruments, and conducting theater orchestras—frequently arranged the ever-popular balls. At colonial Williamsburg grand balls were customarily held either in the palace ballroom or in the Apollo Room of the Raleigh Tavern, Williamsburg's famous inn. A sedate minuet usually opened the affair, followed by a series of lively cotillions and Virginia reels, interspersed with the dignified gavotte. This essentially followed the British pattern of alternating formal and country dances, and even the Virginia reel, which normally closed the ball, was danced to English tunes. William Byrd tells of a dinner in Williamsburg in 1711 at the Governor's home where he and some convivial friends located a couple of fiddlers, gave them some candles, and sent them ahead to the Capitol, where the party proceeded to hold an impromptu ball until midnight. Thirty years later Byrd still enjoyed dancing, confessing to his diary, "At night the women got me to quadrille." So popular in fact did the balls become in colonial Williamsburg that the Reverend Hugh Jones recommended that the College of William and Mary provide dancing classes for its students, and by 1755 a John Kello could write a London friend from Virginia: "Dancing is the chief diversion here."

Williamsburg was naturally the theatrical and musical center of Virginia in the eighteenth century. In fact the first theater in the English colonies was built there in 1716; and when the Hallams and other English actors began making tours of the colonies the little Virginia city became a major stop. George Washington was a regular attendant at the theater in Williamsburg, enjoying both the plays and the musical numbers between acts. In 1768 *The Beggar's Opera* was staged in the Virginia capital with Peter Pelham, the town's leading musician, conducting.

Brought to America from England at age five by his portrait-painter father, Pelham first lived and studied in New England. From 1743 to 1750 he was organist at Trinity Church in Boston. Then in 1752 he settled at Williamsburg, a few years later helping to install the city's first organ. For almost half a century Pelham was the organist and choir director of the Bruton Parish Church, tuning, repairing, and even building musical instruments on the side. At odd moments he gave lessons, attended the local jail, served as clerk for the House of Burgesses, and performed concerts. In his recitals he presented selections from Handel, Vivaldi, Felton, and probably a number of his own compositions.

"One might walk down a Williamsburg street," Richard Beale Davis writes in his *Intellectual Life in Jefferson's Virginia*, "and hear tooting and scraping of strings all the way. Spinets, harpsichords, violins, flutes, violincellos, trumpets, and French horns were everywhere." Governor Fauquier, a great lover of music, gathered about him three or four amateur musicians—including John Tyler, Sr. and young Thomas Jefferson—with whom he held weekly concerts in the drawing room of his palace at Williamsburg. The professional chamber concerts given in the ballroom of the Governor's palace were considered the epitome of aristocratic elegance. The selections and formats of these programs were cautiously patterned after similar functions in England. As with most of urban colonial America, Williamsburg's musical life reflected its inhabitants' desire to "live in the same neat Manner, dress after the same Modes, and behave themselves exactly as the Gentry in London."

That the Virginia planters were musical dilettantes there can be little question, capable perhaps of appreciating good music, but equipped to create very little. The colony produced no musical genius, no significant composer, not even a brilliant performer. While every community had its fiddlers, these preferred to play English tunes, which according to a contemporary, they murdered "ten times worse than the country fiddlers" of England. Even Jefferson admitted in a letter to the Italian Giovanni Fabbroni in 1778: "If there is a gratification which I envy any people in this world, it is to your country its music. This is the favorite passion of my soul, and fortune has cast my lot in a country where it is in a state of deplorable barbarism."

Had Jefferson lived in Charleston, he might have been less harsh in his evaluation of his country's musical climate, although the ground for musical creativity was scarcely more fertile there. Nevertheless, Charleston was the major city of the colonial South and by all odds the most sophisticated city in Anglo-America. Present were a substantial element of wealth, a well defined social structure, sufficient leisure, and a desire for refinement and elegance. Absent were most of the puritanical moral restrictions that governed the cultural life of the cities to the north. Plenty of good books could be found in the libraries of Charleston gentlemen, and the sons of the wealthier members of the community were educated at British universities. The city's social whirl was kept in motion by gala balls and dinners, while the cultural order was modeled after that of London. Charleston swarmed with coaches, household slaves in livery, and men and women dressed in the latest European garments. Since the city was relatively free from malaria, during the summer months it attracted planters from the mosquito-infested rice swamps. They came to the city looking for diversion, a chance to display their affluence, and an opportunity to indulge themselves in the social graces.

Eighteenth century Charleston then contained the population and most of the social requisites necessary for supporting theater and musical offerings on a fairly grand scale. The first recorded concert in the city was presented in April, 1732, just a few months after the earliest known concert in Boston. The event took place in the Council Chamber and consisted of a recital by John Salter, an organist from one of the local churches. That summer a concert of vocal and instrumental music was heard, after which there were country dances for the amusement of the ladies—a custom which prevailed in Europe. Mrs. Cook gave a recital of English and Scotch songs the following February, while Theodore Pachelbel, who had performed in Philadelphia's first recorded concert, offered a program on St. Cecilia's Day, November 22, 1737, promising a cantata suitable for the occasion. After that, at least until 1760, public concerts virtually appear to have died out in the city, in favor of ballad opera, private soirees and balls held by socialites, and dancing assemblies arranged by music masters.

The first ballad opera given in America was staged in Charleston in 1735, when Colley Cibber's *Flora, or Hob-in-the-Well* was produced at the Courtroom. A whimsical little farce about a fairy in a well, *Flora* was one of the more successful imitations of *The Beggar's Opera* and remained an American favorite for many years. Although the piece lacked the proportions of true ballad opera, its initial production in Charleston launched the mania for English opera in the colonies, and by the time the Hallam company arrived on the American scene in 1752 a taste for this type of musical drama was well developed.

Meanwhile professional musicians and teachers arrived in the city in steadily increasing numbers. Theodore Pachelbel began giving vocal lessons to young ladies in 1749, while Benjamin Yarnold, who came to Charleston from London in 1753, first served as organist at St. Philip's Church and later opened a music school. Within twelve to eighteen months Yarnold guaranteed to teach both the theory and practice of singing for twenty-five pounds a year. By the eve of the Revolution Charleston supported more professional musicians than any other city in the English colonies.

Beginning in 1736 the new Queen Street Theater was the stage for most of Charleston's early plays and musical activities. Peter Valton, Yarnold's successor as organist at St. Philip's Church, gave a concert there on November 13, 1765, which included a concerto on the harpsichord and the musical debut of Miss Hallam and Miss Wainwright, both of the American Company, who sang two songs. More and more, as the Revolution approached, resident musicians began finding competition from members of touring theatrical troupes, particularly as the latter started giving musical benefits of their own. On a more popular level, the Vauxhall Gardens opened nearby in 1767, serving tea, coffee, and liquors, and presenting "Private Concerts of Vocal and Instrumental Music" on Thursday evenings, in imitation of the famous English resort.

But the crowning achievement in the musical life of colonial Charleston was the founding in 1762 of the St. Cecilia Society, the oldest musical society in America. Named, of course, for the patron saint of music, the St. Cecilia Society was the first group in British America to support a paid orchestra, made up primarily of professional musicians but rounded out by talented amateurs. In 1771 the society advertised in northern newspapers for violin, hautboy, and bassoon players, offering them a one to three year contract and apparently sparing no expense in acquiring the best musicians available. The society itself was made up of 120 gentlemen, each of whom contributed twenty-five pounds a year for the privilege of attending concerts and of bringing "as many Ladies as he thinks proper." The number of concerts sponsored by the St. Cecilia Society seems to have varied from year to year, since the seasons opened and closed at irregular dates. As long as the season lasted, concerts were given fortnightly, and the bylaws stated that a yearly concert must be given on St. Cecilia's Day, November 22.

Backed by some of the wealthiest members of the colony and well patronized by its members, the society was a success almost from the beginning. The concerts presented were without doubt among the most impressive in colonial America, combining professional musicianship with an aura of social elegance. When Josiah Quincy of Boston attended a St. Cecilia concert as a guest in March, 1773, he found the occasion brilliant. "The music was good," he recorded in his *Journal*. "The two bass-viols and French horns were grand. One Abercrombie, a Frenchman just arrived, played a first fiddle, and a solo incomparably better than any I ever heard. He cannot speak a word of English and has a salary of five hundred guineas a year from the St. Cecilia Society." The chief defect in the concert, Quincy felt, "was want of an organ," although he also found Pike's Long Room, where the musicians played, "a large inelegant building." Upwards to two hundred and fifty ladies were present for the event, and "it was called no great number." Of the audience Quincy writes: "In loftiness of headdress, these ladies stoop to the daughters of the north,—in richness of dress, surpass them. In taciturnity during the performances, greatly before our [New England] ladies; in noise and flirtation after the music is over, pretty much on a par. . . . The gentlemen, many of them dressed with richness and elegance, uncommon with us: many with swords on. We had two macaronis present, just arrived from London."

Foreign artists were not infrequently imported by the St. Cecilia Society for special concerts. Maria Storer, probably the finest singer to perform in colonial America, was heard in a concert in Charleston in February, 1774, on a program which included vocal selections by Misses Hallam and Wainwright and a violin solo by the Frenchman Abercrombie, Storer had a remarkable voice and vocal technique and, aside from concerts, she also appeared in America in ballad opera. The repertoire offered by the St. Cecilia Society was most often music by living composers, since that was what colonial audiences seemed to prefer. Timeliness, scarcely less than fashion, was a major concern of the provincial gentry.

The St. Cecilia Society remained in existence until 1912, although its character changed greatly. As the years went by, musicians became difficult to obtain, and gradually the orchestra was reduced to a quintet. By the end the organization was frankly nothing more than a vehicle for giving balls and a means for differentiating the old wealth of Charleston society from the new.

From the beginning, however, the St. Cecilia Society had had a strong social orientation. Its musicales were open only to subscribers and their guests, while the ordinary people of the city heard none of the superb offerings which the wealthy enjoyed. Nor was the exclusiveness of the St. Cecilia Society unique, for most of the art music in the South was reserved for the upper classes. When Charleston's Thomas Pike, for instance, directed a concert in 1765, "performed by the Gentlemen of the place," he threatened to prosecute any ruffian who climbed over the fence and interrupted the music. And the guest lists for the balls and suppers were no less selective. While on his visit to Charleston, Bostonian Josiah Quincy dined with the Sons of St. Patrick. During the dinner music was provided by six violins, two hautboys, and other instruments, while after dinner six French horns played in concert—music which Quincy described as "most surpassing." But only the social elite ever heard anything like this. Art music was the special ornament of the wealthy, who hovered over it and smothered it like the dilettantes they were.

A socioeconomic barrier, therefore, separated the bulk of the southern population from the best of European classical music. For the most part this musical tradition was grafted onto an aristocratic social image, rather than becoming an integral part of the American colonial experience. While the common people had their music, which even the wealthy might enjoy in less guarded moments, the concept of gentility denied the presence of a folk element in the enriched environment with which the cultivated classes sought to surround themselves. At the same time what had been a vibrant musical tradition in Europe was in America reserved for and overindulged by such a select clientele that it suffered from artificiality on the one hand, risked stagnation on the other.

There were pockets within the South where European art music was a more integrated part of life. The southern colonies, like Pennsylvania, had their Moravian settlements, most notably Salem, North Carolina, which dated from 1766. At Salem musical festivals, organ building, the perfection of choral singing, and the formation of a trombone ensemble developed along lines similar to those in Bethlehem. Other German immigrants brought with them to the South their love of music, along with vast collections of scores and instruments. The Huguenots came with some knowledge of French music, although probably of the more popular genre. In each case, however, these communities were isolated from the mainstream of colonial life, with the result that the German and French impact on the development of a nascent American music was negligible. And despite their skill and devotion to preserving European music on a high level, the Germans of the South were no more successful than those of the Middle Colonies in transferring their appreciation of art music to the Anglo-American majority around them. Even the Moravian settlements were content to preserve their musical heritage existent within themselves, while the southern majority was almost as unmindful of their very presence as they were ill-equipped to grasp the depth of their musical accomplishments.

By contrast the ballads and psalms sung in the colonial South, probably from the settlement of Jamestown on, were no less a product of the Old World than the art music, but their popular nature tied them more closely to life in America. British folksongs were sung by artisans, merchants, and servants, as well as by planters in the tobacco fields—not to buttress their social position, but for pure enjoyment. While many of these songs dated back to Elizabethan times or before, their very relevance to the people meant that the songs evolved with the lives of their singers. In the hands of the common folk particularly this music began absorbing elements from the American environment. Eventually, gifted singers tried varying tunes and creating verses of their own, so that the embryo of a creative process slowly emerged. Meanwhile the individualistic nature of the rural southern singing schools also contributed to the development of an indigenous folk tradition, since they condoned the flexibility necessary for change.

The very lack of flexibility, however, prohibited the upper classes from approaching anything like musical creativity. Patterning their social and cultural ideals after European standards which they only superficially realized, the southern gentry's concept of artistic propriety was nevertheless molded by precedents set abroad. Hemmed in by a multitude of intricate rules of protocol, the tidewater aristocracy approached cultural matters with a self-consciousness and predetermined viewpoint that was calculated for social effect. The result was a regimentation diametrically opposed to the spontaneity and freedom essential for artistic innovation.

This restrictive atmosphere probably explains why the most original musical tradition to emerge out of the South came from that segment of society least affected by the European concept of gentility. So far outside the pale of social respectability were the black slaves that the airs of cultural refinement hardly concerned them at all. Consequently blacks enjoyed a freedom in their music that their masters' social image rarely permitted. Caught in the crosscurrents of two conflicting social milieus, the slaves were no more at liberty to create an absolutely new music than they were capable of cutting themselves off completely from their native customs or of denying the cultural environment surrounding them in America. In the early days of slavery particularly, blacks clung tenaciously to their African heritage, in music as in other areas. Later, as they became acculturated into the Anglo-

American tradition, they were expected by their white masters to adopt the musical folkways of the dominant race. And yet the distance between the African and the European musical patterns was sufficient to allow Afro-Americans considerable latitude for embarking on fairly inventive paths. Blending elements of their African background with selected ingredients from the Anglo-American civilization in which they were now expected to function, blacks of the colonial South implanted the beginnings of an amalgamated music that in its mature stage would be hailed as a distinctly American expression.

Just how much early Afro-American music owed to African origins, and how much was borrowed from the whites, has been the subject of impassioned controversy. To a great degree the argument has been linked with the broader racial issue, and the varying viewpoints have coincided in large measure with the racial attitudes of their proponents. White supremists have tended to take the position that blacks had to steal heavily from the white man's music, since Afro-Americans lacked the creative talent within their own race for composition. Blacks and champions of the black cause have counterbalanced this stand with the supposition that the black Americans originated a distinctive music, rooted in their African heritage—a music that the whites admired and imitated. All in all a highly complex question has been grossly oversimplified; the truth clearly lies somewhere in between. A mingling of the African and European musical traditions definitely took place. Which element predominated is an elusive matter, depending on a number of factors, not the least of which is the time under consideration and the form of musical composition involved.

A complicating aspect of this problem is that there is not one African music, but many. Africa is among the largest continents, containing a greater variety of peoples and linguistic groupings than any other land mass. The music of Africa differs more sharply than that of any two European countries has ever differed in recorded history. Therefore, to discuss African music as if it possessed a common denominator is again to be guilty of oversimplification. The slaves were brought to America from all over West Africa; they came from all levels of the West African social hierarchy. Consequently blacks arrived in America with differing customs and with diversified musical backgrounds.

Among the native peoples of West Africa music ranks as one of the most important aesthetic expressions, permeating virtually every phase of life from birth to death. Singing and dancing accompany many daily routines, and one of the primary concerns of music is to recount the past of the people. The most commonly employed musical form is the song, both with and without instrumental accompaniment. These songs range from lullabies and religious tunes to dance and work songs, while the principal instruments used are the xylophone, zithers, harps, guitars, and flutes.

The music of West Africa is some of the most complex, subtle unwritten music known, involving complicated scales, rhythms, and thematic organization. All of the major ingredients of western music—melody, harmony, rhythm, and timbre—are present in West African music; the difference lies in the relationship between these factors. While the western tradition strives for regularity—in time, pitch, timbre, and vibrato—the West African strives for the opposite. The songs of West Africa are usually antiphonal, while their rhythm assumes an indirectness that not only emphasizes syncopation, polyrhythm, stop time and multiple bar divisions, but also shifted accents—all of which adds up to chaos to the untrained western ear. In language the West African preference is for circumlocution rather than the direct statement, which is considered unimaginative and crude. The veiling of meaning in changing paraphrases is, on the other hand, considered a mark of intelligence and sophistication. In music the same tendency holds true. No note is attacked directly; instead the instrument or voice approaches it from below or above, revolving around the implied pitch without ever lingering on it for any length of time.

The people of the western world have tended to limit their concept of African music to the dance and the use of drums as rhythmic accompaniment. Actually the instrumentation associated with dancing is not considered by native performers as music at all, but merely sound effects. Dances, nevertheless, are highly significant in the culture patterns of West Africa and may be found in a multitude of forms. Some play recreational or social roles, while others serve ceremonial and religious functions.

Undoubtedly, Africans came to the New World bringing much of their musical heritage with them. Even aboard ship, music was encouraged to keep up the morale of the captives, who were customarily transported amid conditions of squalor and misery. Once in America, slaves were urged to sing and dance largely because their masters found watching them amusing and since overseers were aware that the blacks would do more work if they were permitted to enjoy themselves. A musical ability was often a valuable skill for the slave, winning for him prestige and occasionally preferential treatment. And apparently many of them were remarkably talented in this area. Jefferson at least thought so, observing in his *Notes on Virginia*: "In music they [the blacks] are more generally gifted than the whites, with accurate ears for tune and time, and they have been found capable of imagining a small catch. Whether they will be equal to the composition of a more extensive run of melody, or of complicated harmony, is yet to be proved." Jefferson also mentions that the slaves brought with them from Africa the "banjar," or banjo, an instrument which subsequently would become immediately associated with the sentimentalized view of the southern black.

How much of their African background the slaves retained in their new surroundings depended to a large degree upon the circumstances in which they found themselves. Household servants, for instance, who had intimate daily contact with their masters, were often encouraged to learn to play European instruments so that they might entertain plantation guests at social functions. Field hands, whose lives were less intertwined with those of their owners, were much freer to continue their native music, at least in the secular areas. Inevitably those African songs and dances that had no relevance to life in America died out, while those adaptable to the new environment survived. Among the songs to quickly fade from the American scene were those associated with tribal initiation rites, those dealing with African legends and famous ancestors, battle songs, ballads of past victories, and any others having no parallel in the American experience. Conversely, work songs, lullabies, love songs, game songs, and occasionally songs related to voodoo and magic endured, because they continued to serve a function in the New World, although these gradually incorporated Anglo-American features as the years went by.

The work songs of the plantation field hands probably adhered most closely to the African archetype, remaining similar in tune and intonation and differing in rhythm only so far as the rhythm of the work differed from that in Africa. The blacks were known to have sung as they worked before coming to America, and neither the plantation owners nor their overseers objected to the slaves' singing in the fields, so long as their tasks were performed. For the black the work songs were often an attempt to relieve the agonies of slavery by integrating hardships with music and recollections associated with better days. The field shouts and "hollers"—thin, wailing cries by which the slaves communicated with one another—were borrowed directly from African sources and in the early days must have been uttered in African dialects—that is, when actual words were used.

The Africans necessarily brought few native instruments with them from their homeland, although they quickly devised comparable ones from materials at hand in the New World. Makeshift drums were improvised out of kegs, boxes, and kettles, while the "banjar" and other instruments were relatively simple to reconstruct. Eventually the making of drums was discouraged because of fear of their being used as signals in uprisings, but the clapping of hands, the stamping of feet, and swaying bodily movements continued to accentuate the vigorous rhythm characteristic of much of the slaves' music.

From whites, both the gentry and the poor whites, blacks slowly picked up the ballad and the hymn, frequently adding their own touches and from time to time injecting African ingredients. And yet the pressure began early for the slaves to turn away from their old traditions and accept totally those of the Anglo-American majority. Far more than in Latin America, the slaves of the British colonies were regarded as persons of inferior quality, whose cultural background was barbaric. By insisting that the blacks give up their "primitive" customs, the slave owners considered they were furthering a humanitarian cause that would advance the black up the path toward civilization. With time and repeated attack, the slaves gradually learned to feel ashamed of their African origins and eventually became willing to embrace the white man's culture pattern. In music, much of what the slaves remembered from Africa was driven underground, emerging now and then when the blacks felt they were not being observed, but suppressed in the presence of whites.

This is particularly true of the spiritual. Until the middle of the seventeenth century the colonial churches of all denominations consistently discouraged missionary activity among the slaves. Since the Christian concept of brotherhood and slavery were difficult to reconcile at best, the incompatibility would obviously become even sharper should the blacks cease being heathens and become converted members of the Christian flock. But in the latter part of the seventeenth century this attitude lost ground, as the more evangelical faiths launched an active campaign to proselyte the blacks. Amid the religious fervor of the Great Awakening this missionary zeal grew to such intensity that by 1750 the original position on the slaves' spiritual needs had been reversed. The prevailing attitude now held that the only justification for slavery was the opportunity to convert the blacks to Christianity.

As the religious transformation took place, the slaves absorbed the obvious trappings of Protestant Christianity, including the singing of psalms and hymns. In contrast to the Roman Catholic colonies in South America, blacks who were converted into the Protestant creeds of Anglo-America were unable to assimilate African religious concepts with those of Christianity. The old ideas, such as the hierarchical polytheism practiced in Africa, had to be repudiated before the fundamentals of Protestantism became intelligible. As the religion of the blacks shifted, so did their music, for the native songs and instrumentation were no longer appropriate. Incidental elements of the old chants prevailed for a time, and certain rhythmic qualities perpetuated themselves; but most of the old African percussion instruments disappeared, along with the multimetered polyrhythms so characteristic of West Africa.

Instead blacks assumed—with some modification—the white folk method of hymn singing, which with its emphasis on improvisation and variation was not altogether dissimilar from the musical tradition the blacks were expected to reject. The white spirituals, especially when sung in the rural southern style, lent themselves to a personalized emphasis on feeling over meaning. Especially when coupled with an intensified rhythm, this emotionalism also was sympathetic with the blacks' native concept of singing. The sorrow of the southern blacks found ample expression in the borrowed spiritual without offending the whites, since the grief was couched in Christian terms. With the passage of time the slaves began composing their own spirituals, infusing them with their own distinguishing musical traits and not infrequently altering Biblical references to suit their own message and reflect their own experience.

In rendering the spirituals blacks continued from their earlier heritage certain singing conventions outside the American folk tradition. One was the tendency to break into falsetto tones, sometimes for a note or two, sometimes for an entire phrase. Falsetto singing had not only been practiced in Africa, but was held in high aesthetic esteem there. Another characteristic of Negro singing involved humming and "moaning and groaning"—the latter suggesting ecstasy, rather than grief or anguish. "Moaning" exploited full freedom of melodic improvisation and was achieved either with an open throat or, if a humming effect was desired, with closed lips. The vocal response was also deeply rooted in the blacks' past, although it quickly became a common feature of the black spiritual.

These spirituals came into existence only on the Protestant plantations of the Anglo-American South; black music in the Catholic colonies was a different matter entirely. Although much has been written about the importance of the Negro spiritual in southern life, black secular songs far outnumbered them. The work songs alone, if an accurate count could be made, would probably overshadow the spirituals numerically. The problem is that so few contemporary accounts exist from the early period of the nonreligious slave songs. And yet if the spirituals alone are considered, the percentage of European elements is far higher than when the entire spectrum of Afro-American music is taken into account. Religious music was handed to the slaves by whites with much the same urgency as Christianity itself was, while the pressure to adapt in the secular areas was less immediate, since continuing the native dance and work songs seemed less an affront to the majority culture.

In no other section of colonial America was the gulf between the emerging folk element in music and the strict conformity to European artistic standards so conspicuous as in the South. The relatively larger role played by a minority race is part of the explanation. The distance between the cavalier image and the folk reality, however, is much more to the point, coupled with the close economic and religious contact between the southern colonies and England. Although the cities of New England and the Middle Colonies had their sophisticates by the eighteenth century, the gentlemanly ideal and the dilettante psychology never reached the intensity in the North that they achieved among the southern gentry. At the same time the "fasola" tradition harbored by the common people and encouraged by the singing schools of the rural South represented a highly dynamic musical force, one that was relevant to the American experience and an integral part of the lives of its champions. Likewise the fusion of musical idioms paralleling the acculturation of the black American resulted in a genuine and virile music that was intensely meaningful to the slaves. Nevertheless both the white-folk and Negro traditions—despite their legions of participants—were placed in defensive positions by the devotees of style and respectability. Consequently the most independent musical expressions to emerge in the colonial South remained equated with the lower social classes, and originality became branded as inferiority. The cook who sang as she went about her work in the Georgian mansion in Charleston, the stable boy who played a homemade instrument after tending his master's horse, or the black mother who sang the plantation children to sleep might be voicing a developing American spirit. But the upper classes, while they were instrumental in formulating this American spirit in their economic and political activities, were dedicated to preserving the traditions of Europe in their cultural life. For them the European masters wrote the only music compatible with their concept of elegance, while the ballads and dance music of the English aristocracy were looked upon as the only tunes appropriate for their public amusements.

CHAPTER
IV

Hopkinson and Billings

While the musical tradition of Anglo-America doubtlessly goes back to the founding of Jamestown, the earliest composition in the English colonies did not appear until the latter half of the eighteenth century, virtually on the eve of the Revolution. Before music could be written in the New World, an urban base of leisure and cultural sophistication had to be achieved. Just who the first American composer was is difficult to establish, although Francis Hopkinson is generally awarded the distinction. Whether this genesis is justified or not is ultimately of less significance than Hopkinson's approach to music, which was that of the aristocratic amateur steeped in the genteel English tradition. Hopkinson's songs, so cherished by the pre-Revolutionary elite, assume an artificial, stilted quality that reflects the self-conscious atmosphere in which the composer dwelt.

His contemporary William Billings, on the other hand, wrote music that is now considered more important—music that is crude, if not downright gauche, but nevertheless vibrant and alive, bearing little resemblance to what the colonial gentry coddled and admired. A man of modest circumstances, Billings was a product of the Puritan heritage, yet demonstrated himself an individualist of the highest order. His music was written with virtually no formal knowledge, and he broke rules he had never heard of or with which he was only casually acquainted. His compositions, however, are as genuine and original as Hopkinson's are pallid and imitative. The contrast between them well illustrates the parallel trends already developing in American music—the one spontaneous and distinctive, the other contrived and mannered.

Francis Hopkinson was only incidentally a musician, for he dabbled in practically everything. Like his friend Benjamin Franklin, Hopkinson was an American Renaissance man, versatile in his interests and abilities. Although his enthusiasm for the arts ran deep, he approached art with a social rather than a professional attitude, always remaining the adept gentleman. Born on September 21, 1737, Hopkinson lived his entire life in and around Philadelphia. He was enrolled by his father, the lawyer Thomas Hopkinson, in the College of Philadelphia (later the University of Pennsylvania) supposedly as the school's first student. During his last year as an undergraduate a group of classmates staged *The Masque of Alfred the Great*, which the English composer Thomas Arne had set to music. Young Hopkinson is thought to have been the harpsichordist for the production. Certainly his interest in music and writing verse became evident during his college days, although after receiving the bachelor's degree in 1757 he studied law under Benjamin Chew, the attorney-general of Pennsylvania. Shortly after completing his legal training, Hopkinson began a long career of public service, first acting as secretary to an Indian commission.

Already Hopkinson had developed something of a local reputation as a man of letters, for he was frequently asked to compose verses for recitation on public occasions or to commemorate a birth, marriage, or death in one of Philadelphia's important families. He became a regular contributor to the *American Magazine*, although most of the poems found there are of more interest to the historian than to the literary critic. In May, 1766, he left for a year abroad, where he continued writing, mostly trivial verses complimenting ladies and flattering benefactors. While in London he spent some time improving his musical skills and is thought to have studied painting with Benjamin West, the noted American artist who had become the darling of the British court.

Soon after his return to Philadelphia, Hopkinson set up a shop as a retail merchant and married Ann Borden. Something of a dawdler before marriage, he now became more serious about economic matters and more ambitious. Either late in 1773 or early in 1774 Hopkinson moved across the Delaware River to nearby Bordentown, New Jersey, probably because he felt the chances for political advancement were better there. His friend William Franklin was governor of that colony, and his father-in-law, Joseph Borden, was a leader in provincial affairs there. In New Jersey Hopkinson began a law practice, was appointed collector of customs and provincial councilor, and quickly emerged as a prosperous man of affairs. His literary interests continued, although his writing became less directed toward poetry and more toward essays—for which he showed greater talent—modeled after the writings of Joseph Addison. After 1775 he contributed regularly to the *Pennsylvania Magazine* or *American Monthly Museum*, a new but highly influential Philadelphia periodical.

As the Revolution approached, Hopkinson became increasingly

alarmed over what he considered British abuses. He protested loudly in 1774 against the punishment of Boston and two years later came out boldly in favor of separation from England. As a member of the Second Continental Congress he was one of the signers of the Declaration of Independence. During the war he served as chairman of the Navy Board, successfully administering naval affairs during an extremely difficult period. He was also treasurer of loans, a job involving infinite detail and demanding painstaking accuracy, and was appointed Judge of the Admiralty from Pennsylvania. Most historians now agree that Hopkinson rather than Betsy Ross designed the first American flag, a design which the seamstress merely executed. He was later active in the convention of 1787 that framed the Constitution of the United States.

Despite his official duties Hopkinson found time during the Revolution to complete a sizeable amount of writing. He wrote articles, poems, and pamphlets ridiculing the British and encouraging the patriots. He penned a series of incendiary ballads aimed at destroying the legend of British invincibility, the most famous of which is "The Battle of the Kegs." Set to music, possibly by Hopkinson himself, and republished as a broadside, "The Battle of the Kegs" became one of the most popular songs among the armies at the front. Hopkinson apparently was fairly pleased with the ballad, for he sent Benjamin Franklin a copy of it in his own handwriting.

After the war Hopkinson continued an active life in public affairs, remaining a civic leader of Philadelphia, and serving as a federal judge until his death in 1791. At the same time he enjoyed sufficient leisure to write on subjects ranging from political "squibs" to learned articles on education. He developed a fascination for science, became active in the American Philosophical Society, and found time to work out a number of inventions, most of them more interesting than practical. He experimented with the principles of aviation and designed a dirigible. He developed a spring block to aid in sailing, devised an instrument for measuring distances on the high seas, found an improved way to grease the wheels of carriages, invented an improved form of candlestick, and even discovered a method for coloring artificial pearls.

But Hopkinson's major personal interests lay in the arts. In addition to his prolific writing, he tried his hand at painting and even before his trip to Europe had established a reputation in Pennsylvania as an authority on music. Having grown up in a family that was fond of the arts, Hopkinson began to study the harpsichord at age seventeen. He became quite proficient on the instrument and shortly wrote an "Ode to Music." His first song, "My Days Have Been So Wondrous Free," was composed in 1759, just two years after his graduation from college. Before leaving on his European tour Hopkinson made a metrical version of the Psalms for the Dutch Reformed Church in New York, using the payment to help finance his trip. He later studied the organ with Joseph Bremmer, an English musician who had arrived in Philadelphia in 1763, and with Bremmer's departure from the city Hopkinson succeeded him as organist of Christ Church.

Recognized as a musical light of Philadelphia before the Revolution, he became a member of a group of amateur and professional musicians who met in one another's homes to play the popular chamber works of their day. By Hopkinson's day subscription concerts had made their appearance in the seaboard cities of colonial America, and the composer became an active force in organizing Philadelphia's early concert life. London music teachers who had settled in the colonies around the middle of the century had introduced wealthier townspeople to arias by Handel and compositions by Scarlatti, Vivaldi, Pergolesi, and Corelli, preparing the way for public concerts. Hopkinson's familiarity with the works of these European masters is evident from his extensive music library, most of which has been preserved by his heirs and much of it transcribed in the musician's own hand.

Following the Revolution Hopkinson does not appear to have played as vital a role in Philadelphia's musical life, although he continued to serve as patron to most of the city's cultural events. With the growth of his interest in science, he began working on an improved method of quilling the harpsichord, which he eventually achieved by substituting tongues of sole-leather and cork for the quill picks previously used to produce the vibration of the strings. The invention received much attention in Europe and was considered to have improved the tone of the instrument and lessened the difficulty of keeping it in repair. Hopkinson corresponded at length with his Virginia colleague Thomas Jefferson over his new quilling technique, and Jefferson responded with considerable enthusiasm. The modification failed to make the impact its discoverer had hoped, in part because the harpsichord was fated to be pushed aside within a few years by the piano. Hopkinson's inventive mind led him to other musical experiments in his later, less politically active years, including an attempt to adapt a keyboard to Franklin's glass harmonica and a design for a metronome.

His most ambitious undertaking as a composer was the oratorio *The Temple of Minerva*, for which Hopkinson wrote both the libretto and music. Performed privately in Philadelphia on December 11, 1781, before a fashionable gathering that included General and Mrs. George Washington, General and Mrs. Nathanael Greene, and the minister from France, so far as it is known the work never received a public hearing. The complete libretto was published in the *Freeman's Journal* a week after its presentation in Philadelphia, but the music has not survived. Blatant in its postwar patriotism, the piece consists of two scenes in which the goddess Minerva and her high priest join with the Genius of America and the Genius of France to laud General Washington and the French-American alliance. Referred to on occasions as the first American opera, *The Temple of Minerva* was more dramatic cantata than opera, since it lacked a plot and consisted merely of a series of musical declamations on a political theme.

In 1788 Hopkinson published his *Seven Songs for the Harpsichord or Forte-Piano*, definitely his best music. The collection was dedicated to the composer's friend, George Washington, then about to enter his first term as President. Actually the volume consisted of eight songs, since another was added while the title page was being engraved. An announcement in the *Pennsylvania Packet* stated that the *Seven Songs* "are composed in an easy, familiar style, intended for young Practitioners on the *Harpsichord* or *Forte-Piano*, and is the first Work of this kind attempted in the United States." While the music is limited in originality, the lyrics are far superior to Hopkinson's earlier lyrics and sporadically show glints of poetic beauty.

In his dedication to Washington the composer wrote, "With respect to this little work, which I have now the Honour to present to your Notice, I can only say that it is such as a Lover, not a Master, of the Arts can furnish. I am neither a profess'd Poet, nor a profess'd Musician." But farther on in the dedication he conspicuously ventured his claim as America's first writer of music: "However small the Reputation may be that I shall derive from this work I cannot, I believe, be refused the Credit of being the first Native of the United States who has produced a Musical Composition." Washington replied from Mount Vernon: "I can neither sing one of the songs, nor raise a single note on any instrument....But I have, however, one argument which will prevail with persons of true taste (at least in America)—I can tell them that *it is the production of Mr. Hopkinson.*"

Certainly Hopkinson's esteem as a gentleman of the arts was assured among his contemporaries, particularly with the wealthier classes. John Adams met the versatile Philadelphian in 1776 at the studio of the painter Charles Willson Peale. In a letter to his wife Adams gave a candid impression of the meeting with Hopkinson: "He is one of your pretty, little, curious, ingenious men. His head is not bigger than a large apple. I have not met with anything in natural history more amusing and entertaining than his personal appearance, yet he is genteel and well bred, and is very social." Adams was impressed, too, with Hopkinson's delight in "those elegant and ingenious arts of painting, sculpture, statuary, architecture, and music."

In many respects Hopkinson was the epitome of the colonial concept of the well-rounded, urbane sophisticate. His cultivation of music as one of the "polite arts" reflected a viewpoint shared by most of the genteel quarters of eighteenth-century America. Like most of the devotees of taste in his day, Hopkinson looked to Great Britain for cultural models and sought to mirror in his music the grace of the aristocratic tradition. As early as "My Days Have Been So Wondrous Free," the composer's admiration for the style of Thomas Arne was evident. In imitating Arne Hopkinson produced a faint little pastoral song of "birds that fly with careless ease," prettified and polished, but as lacking in honesty and originality as it is artificially charming.

Although his technique both as lyricist and musician had improved by the time the *Seven Songs* were published, the depth of his expression and his artistic spontaneity had advanced only slightly. Again lyrics and melody each show strong influences of the sentimental style currently in vogue in Europe, as do the titles of the songs themselves: "Come, Fair Rosina," "Beneath a Weeping Willow's Shade," "See Down Maria's Blushing Cheek," "The Traveller Benighted and Lost." Hopkinson himself particularly liked the last, considering it to possess genuine pathos, although the mawkish element is obvious.

> *The traveller benighted and lost,*
>   *O'er the mountains pursues his lone way;*
> *The stream is all candy'd with frost*
>   *And the icicle hangs on the spray,*
> *He wanders in hope some kind shelter to find*
> *"Whilst thro' the sharp hawthorn keen blows the cold wind."*
>
> *The tempest howls dreary around*
>   *And rends the tall oak in its flight;*
> *Fast falls the cold snow to the ground,*
>   *And dark is the gloom of the night.*
> *Lone wanders the trav'ler a shelter to find,*
> *"Whilst thro' the sharp hawthorn still blows the cold wind."*
>
> *No comfort the wild woods afford,*
>   *No shelter the trav'ler can see—*
> *Far off are his bed and his board*
>   *And his home, where he wishes to be.*
> *His hearth's cheerful blaze still engages his mind*
> *"Whilst thro' the sharp hawthorn keen blows the cold wind."*

The composer sent a copy of his *Seven Songs* to Jefferson in Paris. The statesman, referring specifically to "The Traveller Benighted and Lost," replied, "while my elder daughter was playing it on the harpsichord, I happened to look toward the fire and saw the younger one all in tears. I asked her if she was sick? She said, 'No, but the tune was so mournful.'"

If the new nation was strongly under the influence of the Age of Reason, it also enjoyed lapses into sentiment. A rational man like Francis Hopkinson might be perfectly reasonable in his politics and business matters, but he found nothing inconsistent with letting his emotions drift into ecstasy in the arts. Music particularly was viewed by the seaboard aristocracy as something separate from the realities of life, an ornament on an otherwise pragmatic existence. The songs Hopkinson wrote were composed with relaxed gentlemen, ladies at harpsichords, and candle-lit drawing rooms in mind. Their gentle music and genteel lyrics were meant to be reminders of a placid civilization far removed from the turmoil of revolutionary America. Their quaint, innocuous strains enhanced the image of a cultivated leisure which wealthy Americans sought to attain and longed to feel was within their grasp.

The originality which later generations found lacking in Hopkinson's music bothered his contemporaries scarcely at all. Since music was looked upon by eighteenth-century connoisseurs of culture as a bond with the past, innovation would have been more suspect than admired. Hopkinson wrote his songs using the European masters as his model, and while posterity would find him no genius of expression, he reflected well the dreams and ideals of the society in which he lived. If his songs lack vigor, it was not vigor he sought. Strength and vitality for him had their place in economic matters and in securing the foundations of a new country, but the arts were the reserve of delicacy and refinement. Music to Hopkinson was a polite luxury, a symbol of good breeding. To have injected the utilitarian impulses of the workaday American experience into his songs would have been to debase his concept of art and strip music of its gentlemanly qualities. Hopkinson's musical world, observes Oscar Sonneck, his first biographer, "was an untrue Arcadia, populated with over-sentimental shepherds and shepherdesses, or with jolly tars, veritable models of sobriety and good behavior, even when filling huge bumpers for drinking-bouts."

The composer represented the social and intellectual establishment of America, and his contact with the common man, both in the city and on the frontier, was limited. Before his death on May 9, 1791, his patrician notions had received public criticism from more democratically inclined spokesmen. By working to create a cultured climate in Philadelphia, Hopkinson certainly played a significant role in establishing drama and concert life in colonial America. Yet as a composer, he exerted virtually no influence on later American music. His songs began no trend, laid no foundation on which future composers could build, but merely perpetuated a dilettante tradition rooted in the past. When the democratic impulses of the new nation swelled in the next century, Hopkinson's way of life would vanish. As it passed, his music remained a fragile reminder of a colonial aristocracy that time and an industrializing social system had left behind.

The essentially comfortable world enjoyed by Francis Hopkinson bore little resemblance to that of the more inventive colonial composer William Billings. Born in Boston on October 7, 1746, Billings was the son of a middle-aged, yeoman shopkeeper. His rudimentary common school education was cut short at age fourteen when his father died, leaving young Billings to be apprenticed to a tanner. The foul smells and dirt of the leather business held but slight fascination for the youth, while his interest in music, curiously enough, seems to have appeared quite early. During his adolescence Billings may have received brief musical instruction from John Barry, for a time choral director at New South Church, and who is thought to have acquired a copy of Tans'ur's *Musical Grammar*. So inflamed did Billings' passion for music become that tradition has it that he whiled away spare moments at the tannery by chalking tunes on sides of leather and over the walls of the shop.

The extent of Billings' formal training in music is uncertain, although he is considered to have been primarily self-taught. He doubtlessly participated in some of the early Boston singing schools, usually church-sponsored classes designed to teach young singers the fundamentals of reading music, and he apparently became associated with leaders in the movement toward regular singing, or singing by note. That Billings was active in the community's budding concert life or was intimately acquainted with the compositions of the European masters is doubtful. His interest in music largely emerged out of a religious atmosphere, and he remained basically a product of a folk heritage descended from Puritanism. He saw music in terms of the psalms, hymns, and anthems he had grown up with, while music as conscious art rarely entered his mind.

Little is known about the details of Billings' life. In 1774 he married Lucy Swan, a member of his singing class at Stoughton, and the couple had six surviving children—five girls and a boy. Sometime before 1770 Billings opened a music shop near the Boston post office, although he continued to practice the tanner's trade throughout most of his life. The plight of the professional musician in eighteenth-century America was at best financially precarious, and Billings especially seems to have been viewed by fellow Bostonians with mingled respect and curiosity. Surely he was vulnerable to more than his share of bantering, for a social dandy in appearance he was not. Blind in one eye, with one leg shorter than the other and a considerably withered arm, he possessed a raspy voice that became less offensive when he sang. To add to nature's afflictions, he was uncommonly slovenly in his dress and had a propensity for taking incredible quantities of snuff, which he carried around in his coat pocket. Every few minutes he would pull out a handful of snuff, and instead of taking it in the usual manner, daintily with thumb and finger, he would snuff it from his clenched fist. At the same time he manifested an infectious personality, appeared unlimited in vitality and enthusiasm, and displayed an aggressive drive approximating the Yankee Peddler stereotype.

All of this made Billings the frequent brunt of pranksters' jokes. The musician, for instance, was startled one evening by a loud screeching outside his door. Upon checking he discovered two cats, their hind legs tied together, unceremoniously thrown across the sign of his shop reading "Billings' Music." On another occasion the ungainly music master was asked by a wag whether he considered snoring vocal or instrumental music!

At his music shop Billings sold instruments and tunebooks, but his major interest was in organizing and teaching singing schools in and around Boston. Billings' aim was to teach musical notation without robbing his students of the joy of singing, and he represents the peak of the singing school tradition. Unlike his Puritan ancestors, who prized solemnity above everything else in sacred music, Billings assumed a downright playful attitude. He looked upon hymns and anthems as an amusement, rather than a sober duty to God. Singing schools lasted something like three months, with two or three meetings a week. Students were mostly teenagers and young adults, and Billings viewed these occasions as social as well as instructional. As his fame spread, his classes became so large that rehearsal rooms could not hold all those wanting to attend. Some had to content themselves with crowding outside the door to listen. Locally printed tunebooks were published for singing school use, and by the Revolution a growing proportion of the music included originated in America.

Billings himself would publish six tunebooks, the first of which was the *New England Psalm Singer*. Issued in 1770, the collection contained 120 hymns and several anthems, all composed by Billings. It was the first tunebook produced of entirely American music. Barely twenty-four years old at the time the compilation was published, Billings sought to invigorate the old psalm-settings, add variety to hymns like Watts', and create religious music that would be interesting and fun for his singing school participants. He wrote his compositions "as plain and simple as possible," and yet wanted his music to be "most majestic" and "so exceedingly grand" that the floors would tremble when choirs sang it. The composer later claimed that the pieces contained in the *New England Psalm Singer* were "more than twenty times as powerful as the old slow tunes." Possessing little more than a rudimentary knowledge of music, he professed breezy disregard for accepted rules. "I think it best," he declared with youthful brashness, "for every *Composer* to be his own *Carver*." He insisted, *"Nature is the Best Dictator,* for all the hard dry studied Rules...will not enable any Person to form an Air...without Genius. It must be Nature, Nature must lay the Foundation, Nature must inspire Thought."

And yet in practice Billings does not seem to have stood in open rebellion against the musical canons of his time, for certainly his works were influenced by the British models he knew. Within pre-existing forms, however, he was able to add variety and find a highly personal tone. Nor was his originality confined to music. He possessed a sensitivity to words, enjoyed wordplay for its own sake, and was not reluctant to alter even Biblical texts to suit his purpose. The composer held up publication on the *New England Psalm Singer* until he could have it printed on American paper, while its frontispiece was engraved by Paul Revere. The tune titles—several of them named after local places or referring to recent events—help give the collection a native flavor. Billings had a penchant for combining politically inspired texts with sacred music that was unprecedented. But above all it is the composer's energy that shines through, animating the words and invigorating their meaning.

His second collection, *The Singing Master's Assistant,* issued eight years later, showed the musician's talent and imagination to have advanced considerably. Often referred to as "Billings' Best," *The Singing Master's Assistant* reflects the composer's growing self-confidence, firmly established his reputation, and went through four editions. Published about the time the British were beginning to feel the determination and strength of the colonial armies, *The Singing Master's Assistant* was far more nationalistic than any American tunebook to date, containing several texts dealing with the war. The composer reworked "Chester," his most famous tune, adding four stanzas in which the references to British tyranny were made more specific. This revision captured the defiant spirit of the moment and was sung around campfires and played by fifers all along the Atlantic coast, becoming almost a battle cry for the Continental Army.

Let tyrants shake their iron rods
And slav'ry clank her galling chains
We fear them not—we trust in God.
New England's God forever reigns.

Howe and Burgoyne and Clinton too,
With Prescott and Cornwallis joined,
Together plot our overthrow
In one infernal league combined.

The foe comes on with haughty stride,
Our troops advance with martial noise.
Their vet'rans flee before our youth,
And gen'rals yield to beardless boys.

When God inspired us for the fight,
Their ranks were broke, their lines were forced.
Their ships were shatter'd in our sight
Or swiftly driven from our coast.

The Singing Master's Assistant also included Billings' famous paraphrase of the 137th Psalm, in which he refers to the British occupation of Boston. The composer penned the lament a few miles away, in Watertown, claiming to have "sat down and wept" when he heard of Boston's fate. The parody perhaps has even greater emotional force than a wholly new text would have had, since the familiar Biblical passages place current events within a religious setting. Billings knew several of the revolutionary leaders, including Samuel Adams, himself a music lover, and there are indications that the composer worked for the patriots' cause as a noncombatant.

Music in Miniature, published during the war, was Billings' only tunebook to include music other than his own. The *Psalm-Singer's Amusement*, which appeared in 1781, caught the sense of exuberance that followed the wake of the Revolution. The collection shows Billings at his most flamboyant. His maturation as a composer has continued, particularly evident in his anthems. And yet he has lost none of his jauntiness, and in pieces like "Modern Music" his imagination seems virtually unrestrained. He audaciously mixes the worldly and the spiritual without negating an atmosphere of genuine piety.

As was customary with compilers of singing books, Billings, undaunted by lack of formal education, undertook to explain the rules of music in the introductions to his various collections and expound his views on a variety of musical subjects. His prose proved as eccentric, homespun, and personal as his music. He later recounted his excitement while the *New England Psalm Singer* was at press: "Oh! how did my foolish heart throb and beat with tumultous joy." He could scarcely wait, he said, for the sheets to be stitched together and the cover put on. When the book emerged at last, he cried, "Go forth, my little book, go forth and immortalize the name of your Author; may your sale be rapid and may you be a welcome guest in all companies, and what will add tenfold to thy dignity, may you find your way into the Libraries of the Learned."

A man of Billings' spirit and self-confidence was not about to be hemmed in by established musical laws any more than he was to be intimidated by precedent or authority. Gentility was so far removed from his spectrum that cultivating the airs of refinement seldom entered his head. He wrote songs that grew out of his experience, music that to him was exciting. Billings wanted not only to supply the New England singing schools with American tunes, he also wanted to delight them with music that was fresh and alive, inviting a greater degree of involvement than the old psalm books permitted. The psalters and hymnals that had been used in New England for the past century and a half Billings considered monotonous and dull.

His major vehicle for enlivening vocal music was the fuging-tune, which he neither invented nor introduced to America, although he did become New England's most successful exponent of the fuging style. The fuging-tunes composed by Billings had almost nothing in common with the formal fugues of Bach and the European masters. Instead they were a form of hymnody in which, after an introduction, the usual homophonous technique of harmony is forsaken in favor of polyphony, the voices entering one after the other in round-like fashion, but at the close returning to the more conventional homophony. "The parts come after each other, with the same notes," Billings himself said of the fuging-tune. Then with a characteristic burst of color and enthusiasm he explained:

> Each part striving for mastery and victory. The audience entertained and delighted, their minds surprisingly agitated and extremely fluctuated, sometimes declaring for one part and sometimes for another. Now the solemn bass demands their attention; next the manly tenor; now the lofty counter; now the volatile treble. Now here, now there, now here again! O ecstatic! Rush on, you sons of harmony!

The fuging-tunes that Billings became so identified with had definite antecedents in England. They were actually survivals of the polyphonic motets sung in British cathedrals during the Elizabethan period. For a brief time in the eighteenth-century English fuging-tunes appeared as a temporary union between metrical psalmody and the contrapuntal technique, achieving considerable popularity in the rural sections of Great Britain but very little in the cities. By the 1760s the fuging-tune was out of favor in England, although emigrants in America undoubtedly brought some knowledge of it to the New World. By the time Billings arrived on the scene the fuging method had been incorporated into an amalgamating folk tradition, and the Boston tanner merely injected his ideas into a musical vernacular that provided him the flexibility he desired.

Three of Billings' fuging-tunes appeared in his *New England Psalm Singer*, and they evoked protests from the beginning. Samuel Holyoke argued early in the 1790s that the fuging style produced "a mere jargon of words." A generation later the method had come to symbolize for sophisticates all that was crude in the Yankee singing tradition. Billings had no notion that he was writing an American version of a Bach fugue, and those who have viewed his fuging-tunes as raw attempts to imitate the Baroque masters have missed the point. Billings' concern was with devising effective hymns for his friends and neighbors; he made no pretense at anything more aesthetic. As with much of colonial culture, the fuging-tune in America represented not so much an innovation as an adaptation of an English folkway. Billings was not unique in his method of composition, but in writing music that he felt would be meaningful to common people he was sensitive to the pulse of the New England environment and aware of changing currents in the American folk experience. Unlike Hopkinson, Billings was not patterning his songs after a rigid British concept of art nor striving to enhance his gentlemanly image by creating mirages of elegance. Whereas Hopkinson's approach to music was static, imitating as it did a formal English archetype, Billings' tunes were based on a less crystalized tradition that permitted the freedom for growth.

At the same time Billings was adamant in his opposition to the old lining-out method. "As all now have books, and all can read," he wrote, "'tis insulting to have the lines read in this way, for it is practically saying 'we men of letters, and you ignorant creatures.'" He particularly objected to the slow, fitful tempo that resulted from the lining-out arrangement and the lack of momentum possible when phrases of text were interjected between musical passages. Then too, the lining-out method had employed only a handful of tunes, and Billings loved variety.

Since his fuging-tunes had no stopping places, they were almost impossible to line-out. Much of their appeal seems to lie in the independence they provided the different vocal parts and in the excitement and sense of rivalry they stimulated among these parts. During sections of the songs all four parts would be singing different words simultaneously, making it difficult for the entire congregation to participate. Only those with books and training could hope to sing the fugues effectively, and yet most listeners, particularly the young people, seemed to delight in the music as much as the singing school members, who gradually evolved into a formal choir. For the first time in colonial New England, church music really became entertaining. Although conservatives found little in the fuging-tunes to induce an atmosphere of worship, the fugues continued to soar in popularity, reaching a peak in America about 1790.

That Billings possessed his limitations as a composer there can be no doubt. Even his supporters admit that he committed grave contrapuntal errors and that his understanding of the relationship of keys was vague. Certainly his musical language must be judged awkward and rough, and his harmony has been the focal point of prolonged controversy. The harmonic effects of the different vocal parts in motion at the same time were often distressing to hearers, for the tones sometimes combined in startling discords. The conflict of voices that so exhilarated Billings was found bewildering and chaotic by more tradition-bound listeners.

Rather than too much discord, however, Billings felt his music, if anything, lacked sufficient dissonance, and he set out to demonstrate just what he could do if he put his mind to it. In a tune called "Jargon," a dissonant musical joke, the composer twitted his critics and once again revealed his engaging sense of humor. The song began,

> *Let horrid jargon split the air,*
> *And rive the nerves asunder.*

Then Billings gave directions on how the piece should be presented:

> Let an ass bray the bass, let the filing of a saw carry the tenor, let a hog who is extremely weak squeal the counter, and let a cart-wheel, which is heavy loaded, and that has long been without grease, squeak the treble; and if the concert should appear to be too feeble you may add the cracking of a crow, and howling of a dog, the squalling of a cat, and what would grace the concert yet more, would be the rubbing of a wet finger upon a window glass. This last-mentioned instrument no sooner salutes the drum of the ear, but it instantly conveys the sensation to the teeth; and if all these in conjunction should not reach the cause, add this most inharmonious of all sounds, "Pay me what thou owest."

While his harmony might be unorthodox and controversial, Billings' undisputed strength was his remarkable feeling for melody. Drawing heavily from folksongs, Billings refined these folk melodies, added variation, and embellished them with personal touches. Into all his music he injected a vitality and cheer that even his opponents have found difficult to ignore, and his anthems particularly were filled with dramatic contrasts that result in emotionally exciting performances. And woven into the sweep of Billings' work was an integrity and a natural expression that remains unmatched in early American music. While his composition at times seems shockingly illiterate, he met the needs of the New England singing groups of his day by producing complex choral selections that were, nonetheless, within their grasp.

To judge Billings by the standards set by the European masters is, of course, to find him lacking. Cyclone Covey, in his argument that the Puritan environment in Massachusetts stifled the creation of truly notable music, insists that Billings' songs are intolerably crude "in light of the all-pervasive music of Handel in the eighteenth century." The fact that Billings wrote in the age of Haydn and Mozart, several years after Handel's death, is to Covey further proof that "the heights of Puritan music that we see in Billings are certainly stunted." On the other hand, critics more willing to accept the American composer on his own ground have assessed him more generously. Certainly the impression that Billings was at heart a musical barbarian is diluted if one looks beyond his early works. Many of the anthems of his middle and later periods, pieces like "I Am the Rose of Sharon" and the "Easter Anthem," musicologist Ralph T. Daniel concludes, "have the charm of enthusiasm and originality, but, more important, they are intrinsically attractive as music and compare very favorably with reputable English products of the same period."

Billings' last two songbooks, the *Suffolk Harmony* (1786) and the *Continental Harmony* (1794), were in neither case a commercial success. The latter particularly is dominated by longer pieces. In its introduction the composer admitted publicly his earlier ignorance of music. "I was fool enough," he confessed, "to commence author before I really understood *time, tune,* or *concord.*" In all Billings is credited with more than three hundred compositions, only two of them specifically calling for instrumental accompaniment. The immediate popularity of this music stems in large measure from the forcefulness of the composer's personality and from his effectiveness as a teacher. While Billings confined his instruction to Boston and the neighboring towns, his tunebooks came to be used all over New England and eventually spread into the South and West.

The musician apparently never learned to play the organ, violin, or harpsichord, and there is little evidence that he involved himself in organizing the secular concert life of Boston, except perhaps to sell tickets to musical events in his shop. Yet within his own realm, Billings was something of a perfectionist, demanding from his singers the highest standards. He is credited with being the first to use a pitch pipe to set the tune, is said to have devised an instrument similar to the metronome for establishing and maintaining tempo, and supposedly introduced the bass viol into the church as an aid to singing.

That Billings' method of training the voice was unconventional and quaint seems only consistent with his unique personality. "The Grace of Transition is sliding; not jumping, from one note to another," he wrote in the *Singing Master's Assistant,* "therefore, it is called a Grace because it is doing the work gracefully." And on the subject of embellishment, he observed:

Many ignorant singers take great license with these trills and without confining themselves to any rule, they shake all notes promiscuously and they are apt to tear a note to pieces, which should be struck fair and plump as any other. Let such persons be informed that it is impossible to shake a note without going off it, which occasions discord.

Eccentric though he may have been, Billings was the pacesetter for the New England music masters of the late eighteenth century. In 1783 he assumed the editorship of the *Boston Magazine*, a short-lived literary periodical, but was ousted as editor after a brief time. Billings was temporarily embittered by the episode, which serves to illustrate something of the cultural climate in post-Revolutionary America. Essentially the vernacular vigor represented by Billings was coming under strong attack from the forces of respectability. As a more stuffy, rarefied concept of art grew in strength, Billings' reputation began to eclipse. The composer suffered severe economic reverses in the middle 1780s, much as the newly independent states themselves. But when the broader economic picture started to improve around 1788, Billings' financial distress did not. In 1785 he was appointed to inspect trade in Boston, and a year later he became the street cleaner in the Eleventh Ward. In 1787 he was given the job of enforcing the law that hogs must be "yoked and ringed" and kept out of certain sections of town. About that same time he was named Sealer of Leather for the City of Boston, a position his skill as a tanner equipped him for and one that he kept for almost a decade.

While his musical activities had clearly declined, the composer did continue to teach singing schools, for which he received about two dollars per evening. A new anthem by Billings was sung at the opening of a meeting-house for Boston's First Church in 1785, the city's first Congregational Church to install an organ permanently. But still the musician's financial condition grew worse, to the point that in the early 1790s he was forced to mortgage his house. Already he had had to accept patronage from friends. Contemporary newspapers disclose that a "concert of Sacred Musick" was given in 1790 "for the benefit of Mr. William Billings whose distress is real and whose merit in that science is generally acknowledged." Two years later, a notice referred to "the distressed situation of Mr. Billings' family." The musician fathered his last child in 1794; his wife died the next year, leaving Billings at forty-nine with a large family to support alone. He himself died on September 26, 1800, by then virtually penniless. Following a funeral in the home of his eldest daughter, Billings was buried in an unmarked grave in Boston Common. The official death record gave his occupation as a tanner, since music was really considered no profession at all.

By the time of Billings' death the new nation had turned away from the singing schools toward the more sophisticated choruses of Handel, the anthems of Arne and Purcell, and eventually the compositions of Mozart and Haydn. In the urban East the old tunebooks were replaced by the more "correct" hymns of Watts and later Wesley and Mason, although in the rural sections of the country folk hymnody continued throughout the nineteenth century. In the southern shape-note collections Billings' music was well represented long after the northern advocates of taste had denounced the fuging-tunes as "a sort of musical horse-race."

Then beginning in the 1930s Billings' significance as a composer was restored, and he is now considered the foremost American musician of the eighteenth century. Once released from a European standard, Billings was recognized as an unconventional genius, often unconcerned with and hence unhampered by propriety. It is perhaps a fitting symbol of a democratic society that a Boston tanner was America's first great musical talent. Surely it was a mark of his century that Billings was able to do the variety of things he did. But he was a practical musician, whose tunes touched his countrymen in a personal way, revealing to them a musical energy they had almost forgotten they possessed. This was Billings' real triumph. His songs are as individualistic as the frontier spirit, consistent with the life he knew, an instinctive expression of the American experience.

Like most Americans Billings was impatient with theorizing; he learned by doing. Echoing the frontiersman's self-reliance and love of freedom, the musician wrote, "I don't think myself confined to any Rule for Composition laid down by any that went before me." And yet his devotion to music is evident throughout. "When we consider the many wonderful effects which music has upon the animal spirits," he exclaimed in the *Singing Master's Assistant*, "we are ready to cry out in a fit of enthusiasm!—Great art thou O MUSIC! and with thee there is no competitor."

Whereas Hopkinson and the foreign musicians migrating to America held to a single European-modeled standard for art, Billings seemed to accept that Americans were different. Music to be honest would have to incorporate that difference. For him no gap existed between life and art. Consequently Billings' works possess a spontaneity and an integrity that Hopkinson's lacks. As early as 1797 William Bently had stated in his diary that Billings composed with "more genius than Taste." But his music survives as a unique expression of early American culture, in much the same way as Cape Cod cottages, the silver work of Paul Revere, and the colonial portraits of John Singleton Copley.

The New Nation

1776-1865

CHAPTER

V

The Search for a National Identity

Although the American Revolution temporarily retarded the musical development of the emerging nation, the winning of independence almost immediately served as the focal point of a nascent patriotism evident throughout the country and mirrored in the arts. Even during battle patriotic airs could be heard, and the sentiments of the rebellion quickly became manifest in song, generally new words sung to familiar British melodies. Nevertheless these songs were considered symbols of America's struggle for freedom. "God Save the King," for instance, was transformed into "God Save the Thirteen States." Samuel Adams organized singing groups around Boston that learned political tunes like "The Liberty Tree," for which Thomas Paine had written words, while the Sons of Liberty adopted "The Liberty Song" as their official anthem, its lyrics by patriot John Dickinson set to the popular English tune "Hearts of Oak" by William Boyce. The verse was inspired by the Circular Letter distributed in 1768 denouncing unfair taxation, and according to John Adams' diary, the Sons of Liberty joined in a chorus three-hundred and fifty strong at their banquet in 1769, commemorating the anniversary of the Stamp Act riots, to sing Dickinson's words:

In Freedom we're born and in Freedom we'll live,
Our purses are ready,
Steady, Friends, Steady.
Not as slaves, but as Freemen our money we'll give.

These lyrics and others were placed on broadsides (handbills printed from woodcuts) and distributed in the streets of colonial cities and villages for a penny apiece, a custom practiced in England since the early sixteenth century. Broadsides were bought with enthusiasm in revolutionary America, since singing at home and during public meetings remained, after the closing of the professional theater and the suspension of civic amusements, among the few recreations available during the war.

After 1770 march music was common in Anglo-America, played mostly in jigtime. The military bands of the patriots were normally limited to drums and fifes, while their British equivalents were often supplemented by oboes and sometimes bassoons. Both camps drew from essentially the same repertoire, one of the more popular marching selections being the fife tune "The Girl I Left Behind Me." "My Dog and Gun" and "On the Road to Boston" also became favorites with Americans at the front.

The most celebrated of all the revolutionary fife songs, "Yankee Doodle," actually had become popular in colonial America some years before the outbreak of hostilities with England. The origins of "Yankee Doodle" are extremely vague, eluding even such meticulous researchers as Oscar Sonneck and John T. Howard. Most probably the melody began as an instrumental tune, arriving in this country from England, Ireland, or Scotland around 1755. One of the more logical theories regarding the origin of the song holds that "doodle" stems from "tootle," which in turn comes from the "tooting" into the German flutes so characteristic among eighteenth-century gentlemen. The supposition, therefore, is that "Yankee Doodle" began as a Yankee air that was "tootled" on the flute. The various texts of the song were added later, although the verse "Yankee doodle came to town riding on a pony" seems to have been in fairly common usage by 1767. The song was apparently used first by the British to taunt and belittle the colonials, but later was taken over by the Yankees as their special air. One of the favored pastimes of the British soldiers was to congregate outside New England churches and sing "Yankee Doodle" as the worshippers inside were singing their psalms. When Lord Percy's troops marched out of Boston bound for Lexington on the night of April 18, 1775, to assist in the capture of John Hancock and Samuel Adams, they kept step to the tune of "Yankee Doodle." With the routing of the British troops at Concord, the colonials seem to have appropriated the song as their own. While General Burgoyne surrendered his sword at Saratoga, American fifers were playing "Yankee Doodle," and Lord Cornwallis reportedly implored, "I hope to God I'll never hear that damned tune again!" Tradition has it, however, that as Cornwallis surrendered at Yorktown, the British band played "The World Turned Upside Down," and while the defeated general and his men left the field, the Americans responded with the strains of "Yankee Doodle."

After the Revolution "Yankee Doodle" continued virtually synonymous with a crystallizing American nationalism. By the time the tune was first printed in 1782 there were already a number of variations in the melody, and the words were being sung all along the Atlantic seaboard in several versions. With the production of Royall Tyler's play *The Contrast* in New York in 1787, the song became even more popular, for an unsophisticated character named Jonathan, the symbol of the New England Yankee in early American theater, sang "Yankee Doodle" from the stage, claiming it was the only tune he knew besides "go-to-meeting" songs. On a visit to a Cincinnati theater in 1827 Frances Trollope was appalled by boorish cries and the thumping of feet from the audience. When "a patriotic fit seized them," Mrs. Trollope wrote in her caustic account, "'Yankee Doodle' was called for," and "every man seemed to think his reputation as a citizen depended on the noise he made."

The young United States was indeed sensitive to its nationalism, sought desperately to flaunt its recently won freedom, saw its future as unlimited, and yet was uncertain as to just what being an American involved. Republican institutions were viewed as tangible manifestations of the new country's superiority over the Old World monarchies, and an elation over a government that espoused maximum freedom for the individual was discernible even to the most casual foreign observer. Americans talked enthusiastically among themselves of equality, of their democratic society, and of a liberty they felt was unique. And yet, despite America's pride in her social and political institutions, the United States remained essentially a country without a past. It had no history, few heroes, and only a nebulous set of national characteristics. It was an infant among nations with scarcely more than a superficial identity. The materialistic, utilitarian strain already apparent in the American temper seemed a dubious thread from which to weave a national fabric, and Americans preferred to look toward the grandiose—to find if possible some link with the ages, some tie with the great civilizations of the past.

Born in the Age of Reason, nurtured on the Enlightenment principles of rationalism, harmony, and natural order, the United States early identified with the ancient world, paraphrasing in American terms the democracy of Greece and the republicanism of Rome. Once symbolically anchored to classical ideals, the young country urgently sought a post-war personality and culture that was distinctive. In the years following the Treaty of Paris of 1783, a fervent search began for an American literature and a sense of historical depth. Above all else, political liberty was held as the distinguishing American trait—praised in poetry, dramatized in painting, lauded in song.

Lacking history, Americans made the most of its revolutionary heroes, particularly George Washington, who became the embodiment of America's love of liberty. Lionized by painters and sculptors, Washington served as a unifying figure around which thirteen varied states could rally, emerging in the popular mind as something of a democratic Caesar or a secular Zeus. Odes were written to Washington's greatness, and music was dedicated to his honor. Francis Hopkinson wrote "A Toast to Washington" in 1778, which was quickly followed by a legion of tunes known either as "Washington's March" or "The President's March." The most lasting of these "President's Marches" was written sometime before 1789 by Philip Phile, a Philadelphia violinist, and is thought to have been played at Washington's first inauguration in New York City. Originally written as an instrumental piece, Phile's melody was initially published in 1793, although the tune reached a greater popularity after words had been added and the title changed to "Hail Columbia."

The lyrics of "Hail Columbia" grew out of the conflict with France during John Adams' administration. France had gone to war in 1793 with England and Prussia, while American sympathy stood divided—the Federalists remaining friendly with England, the anti-Federalists favoring the support of France. Washington managed during his presidency to keep the United States neutral, but shortly after Adams' inauguration the issue reached a crisis when the French government insulted and attempted to bribe three American ministers. By 1798 a state of undeclared war actually raged on the seas, as Americans began fortifying harbors, building ships, and enlarging the army for increased hostilities.

During this tension with France a young Philadelphia singer and actor named Gilbert Fox asked Francis Hopkinson's twenty-eight-year-old son, Joseph, to write some patriotic verses to Phile's "President's March" for his coming stage benefit. Young Hopkinson, later a distinguished jurist and congressman, dashed off the words to "Hail Columbia" hurriedly and had them ready for his friend the next afternoon. Fox sang the song accompanied by a chorus and brass band at the New Theatre in Philadelphia on April 25, 1798, just as the war fever was reaching a peak. His success was unqualified. The actor was asked to encore the number six times, and the audience ended by jumping to its feet and roaring out the refrain in chorus. A few evenings later President Adams and his cabinet attended the theater expressly to hear the new song, and within the week Benjamin Carr published the stirring lyrics under the title "The New Federal Song." By the War of 1812 "Hail Columbia," as it became more commonly known, was looked upon as a national anthem, almost as familiar as "Yankee Doodle." Joseph Hopkinson, who never expected his lyrics to enjoy lasting renown, insisted the song was written "to get up an American spirit. . . . It was truly *American* and nothing else."

Even the most conscious efforts at expressing American nationalism, however, were ardently embraced by the young republic, whose very survival seemed far from assured. Hostilities with France melted into a series of naval skirmishes with Tripoli, which in turn were overshadowed by a second war with Great Britain. To teach the upstart Americans a lesson, the British,

August 24, 1814, attacked and easily captured Washington, burning a number of public buildings, including the Capitol, and wounding the sensitive American pride deeply.

On their way to Washington British officers had been entertained by a Maryland physician, Dr. William Beanes, a collaborationist who had extracted from the British a promise that his property would not be damaged. After the main body of invading troops had begun the march back to their ships, Dr. Beanes ordered three of their stragglers arrested. The British, learning of these arrests, sent a detachment back to release the three captives and to take Dr. Beanes prisoner. Despite efforts on the part of friends to secure his pardon, the Maryland physician was seized and held on board an enemy ship in Chesapeake Bay, where plans were being made for a British attack on Baltimore.

In desperation Beanes' friends asked Francis Scott Key, a young lawyer with known connections in Washington, to intercede. On September 2, Key left Washington, armed with a letter for Colonel John S. Skinner, the United States' cartel agent in Baltimore. Five days later, Key and Skinner were taken on an unidentified sloop out to the British fleet near the mouth of the Potomac. The two Americans eventually convinced the British to release Beanes, although all three were retained on board an enemy ship, for fear they might reveal plans for the attack on Baltimore. The British fleet started up the bay on September 8, nearing Baltimore harbor three days later. Troops, ordered to attack the city from the side, were landed on the north shore, while a number of small bombing vessels worked their way up the harbor for a frontal assault on Fort McHenry.

Francis Scott Key and his associates meanwhile were put under guard aboard their own ship-of-truce with orders not to attempt a landing. All during the night of September 13, Key—who had experienced the burning of Washington—stood on the deck of the American sloop watching the rockets arching over Fort McHenry and exploding in mid-air. He knew that the group of small boats was going to attempt a capture of the fort, and when the firing stopped around one o'clock in the morning, he had no idea whether the enemy's mission had succeeded or not. Through the early morning hours the tension grew, and as dawn crept out of the East, Key gradually was able to discern the outlines of the fort through the drizzle and mist. Suddenly he caught sight of the tattered American flag still flying over McHenry, and in a moment of emotional excitement he pulled an envelope from his pocket and feverishly scribbled the lyrics to "The Star-Spangled Banner."

As he wrote, Key most surely had the tune of "To Anacreon in Heaven," a popular English drinking song of the period, running through his head, for the melody was associated with "The Star-Spangled Banner" from the beginning. In fact Key himself had earlier written a parody on the British song, calling it "The Warrior's Return," and had even sung these lyrics at a dinner in December, 1805, honoring Stephen Decatur's return from Tripoli. Many of the ideas Key used in his earlier song were incorporated into "The

Star-Spangled Banner" that morning of September 14, as he stood aboard ship outside Baltimore harbor.

The next day a broadside was printed of Key's poem, bearing the title "The Defence of Fort McHenry" and the suggestion that the words be sung to the tune of "To Anacreon in Heaven." That night the song was sung in a public tavern, and a week later the lyrics were printed in a Baltimore newspaper. Throughout most of the nineteenth century "The Star-Spangled Banner" shared honors with "Hail Columbia" as the national anthem. Then during the Spanish-American War, Admiral Dewey designated "The Star-Spangled Banner" as the approved anthem of the armed forces, although the choice of the civilian population remained divided. To end this confusion Congress early in 1931 passed a bill making "The Star-Spangled Banner" the official national anthem, a bill which President Herbert Hoover signed the day before he left office.

The popular songs of the early republic emerged not only from wars and foreign conflict, but out of domestic storms and triumphs as well. Americans seems to enjoy best singing about events of current interest, political issues, and the heroes in their struggle to gain freedom and governmental solidarity. Milestones like the signing of the Declaration of Independence, the ratification of the Constitution, and the opening of the Erie Canal were all echoed in a number of popular tunes of the day. Songs were written about the demise of the Federalists, the death of Washington, the inauguration of Jefferson, the issue of imprisonment for debt, virtually every presidential election, and a host of lesser events, many of them patriotic in nature.

Unique among these national airs, since it was inspired by no war or any immediate political action, is the song "America." In 1831 Lowell Mason, the distinguished music educator and hymn writer, brought several volumes of tunes to twenty-three-year-old Samuel F. Smith, a student of theology at Andover, Massachusetts, and suggested that the clergyman use one of the melodies for a new patriotic hymn. A few afternoons later Smith was looking through Mason's books and happened to notice the tune "God Save the King." He immediately took up his pen and wrote the words to "America." "It was struck out at a sitting," Smith later insisted, "without the slightest idea that it would ever attain the popularity it has since enjoyed." The song was first sung publicly at a children's celebration of American independence on July 4, 1831, at the Park Street Church in Boston, employing the tune of the British national anthem.

While political and patriotic themes dominated the popular music of the nation's formative years, tunes were consistently either British or copies of current British styles. Desperately wanting "American" songs, eager young patriots set about creating in verse paeans to political ideals they were incapable of exalting in music. Far more literal and utilitarian than lyrical in temperament, Americans clearly found recording the verbal substance of their patriotic bliss easier than providing the musical form. Desiring distinctiveness on the one hand, yet wanting to remain within the bounds of conventional taste on the other, Americans found an expedience in adhering to the British tunes that were both a part of their heritage and a substitute for melodies they lacked the ability to produce themselves—at least with the rapidity at which the major American patriotic hymns were written. Rather than creating new musical forms, early American songwriters for the most part simply reordered British airs, superimposing New World concepts of liberty on traditional Old World melodies.

In many instances, of course, British songs were kept intact. A good example is "Drink to Me Only with Thine Eyes," which became immensely popular in late eighteenth-century America, both with the tune used now and others. Ben Jonson's lyrics, however, were employed fairly consistently. Folk ballads like "Barbara Allen," "Chevy Chase," "Lord Thomas and Fair Eleanor," and "Derry Down" were all borrowed from England, but gradually absorbed American variants as they evolved in the new environment. Since singing was a major form of entertainment in early America, songsters were widely circulated for use at home, public meeting houses, men's social clubs, quilting bees, and political rallies. These songsters were generally pocket size and modestly priced, contained lyrics only, and were filled with songs on political subjects. They were hawked on the streets, entire editions often selling out within a few days after publication.

Aside from William Billings' "Chester" and the adaptation of Phile's melody to "Hail Columbia," one of the few early American patriotic songs not set to a British tune was "The American Hero," more commonly known as "Bunker Hill." Both words and music were written in 1775, shortly after the colonial's defeat at Bunker Hill and the demonstration that the war for independence was to be grim and of uncertain outcome.

> *Why should vain mortals tremble at the sight of*
> *Death and destruction on the field of battle*
> *Where blood and carnage, Where blood and carnage*
> *Clothe the ground in crimson, sounding with death groans.*
>
> *Life for my country and the cause of freedom,*
> *Is but a trifle for a worm to part with;*
> *And if preserved, And if preserved,*
> *In so great a context, Life is redoubled.*

These stark lyrics were written by Nathaniel Niles; Andrew Law composed the tune, melancholy rather than rousing and clearly patterned after the English ballad.

Composer Andrew Law was considerably more at home writing psalms than political tunes, as he had originally trained at Rhode Island College for the ministry and always saw music chiefly as an appendage of theology. In 1777 Law, nevertheless, abandoned his plans to become a minister, proclaiming himself a singing master instead. He admired the work of

Billings and included six of the Boston musician's tunes in his *Select Harmony*, a song book compiled by Law in 1779. Unlike Billings, Law viewed music largely as a means to intensify the meaning of a devotional text. He traveled throughout seaboard America, teaching singing and distributing his tunebooks in the major cities from Boston to Charleston. The latter part of his career Law devoted to developing a systematic vocal method, published first in 1794 as the *Art of Singing*. Much a part of the genteel tradition that was characteristic of so many early American sophisticates, Law grew disturbed by the crudity of singing in the United States at the turn of the century and revised his *Art of Singing* in 1803 to include shape-notation, which he hoped would bring about the reform he desired. Among his other accomplishments Law is thought to have introduced the custom in America of placing the melody of a song in the soprano range.

Although Law's tune for "Bunker Hill" achieved immediate fame, sung in camps, public meetings, and churches throughout the young republic, it marked a departure from the wholly religious context of most of the composer's melodies. Much awed by the beauties of European music, Law wrote psalms and hymns comfortably within the simpler British pattern and worked mightily to bring American musical standards up to those of his foreign contemporaries. He was made increasingly aware of European prototypes by contact with the scores of foreign musicians that appeared in the coastal cities of the United States following the close of the revolutionary war, musicians which Law met on his peregrinations through Federalist America.

Of this stream of talented foreigners who came to dominate American music during the last fifteen years of the eighteenth century, none made a more profound impact than Benjamin Carr. Arriving in Philadelphia from England in 1793, just as concert life was reawakening after its colonial beginnings, the versatile Carr quickly won acclaim as a composer, pianist, organist, singer, chorus master, concert manager, and music dealer and publisher. Born on September 12, 1768, young Carr studied music in England with Dr. Samuel Arnold and Charles Wesley, both outstanding church musicians, and participated in a number of London concert ventures. At age twenty-four he migrated to America, followed a few months later by his father, Joseph Carr, and brother, Thomas. The Carr family had long been associated with the music publishing business in England and came to the United States for the express purpose of transplanting that tradition here. The Carrs presently set up music dealerships in three different American cities—Joseph and Thomas in Baltimore, the energetic Benjamin dashing between projects in New York and Philadelphia.

In musical taste, however, the Carrs never really ceased being British, for their imprints consisted primarily of English compositions. They paid little heed to the growing taste for French music that followed the influx of French musicians after the revolution in France and the Santo Domingo bloodshed. Their only major departure from the prevailing English repertoire consisted of the publication of American patriotic songs, such as Francis Scott Key's lyrics for "To Anacreon in Heaven," which the new nation demanded in such quantities. In 1800 Joseph Carr founded the *Musical Journal*, edited by his son, Benjamin; the publication included instrumental and vocal music both of foreign importation and native inspiration.

In spite of heavy commitments in widely scattered areas, Benjamin Carr managed time to compose several selections of his own. Among his more ambitious works is the *Federal Overture*, a patriotic potpourri performed first in Philadelphia on September 22, 1794. The composition consists of nine tunes, beginning with "Yankee Doodle," then moving into the "Marseilles," and including "The President's March" and "Oh, Dear, What Can the Matter Be?". While the overture is scarcely a musical masterpiece, it does reflect on a somewhat elaborate scale the close connection between music and politics during the formative years of the United States. "Viewed against the backdrop of its own exciting era," Irving Lowens concludes, "the piece tells us a good deal about not only specifically musical matters, but more particularly about the manner in which citizens of the infant nation felt and acted in regard to the issues of their day." Evidently commissioned by the managers of the Old American Company, the *Federal Overture* was published in 1795, containing the first known printing of "Yankee Doodle" on this side of the Atlantic.

Carr also made a major step in the direction of Americanizing the ballad opera, still a popular theatrical form in the years immediately following the Revolution. In 1796 Carr wrote a piece called "The Patriot, or Liberty Obtained," based on the legend of William Tell. A few months later he expanded the idea into a full-length musical drama, setting his music to a libretto by William Dunlap, one of the more distinguished and versatile of the young nation's men of the theater. Entitled *The Archers*, or *The Mountaineers of Switzerland*, the production adhered to the typical ballad opera pattern, combining spoken dialogue, choruses, solos, duets, and trios; included between acts were dances and specialty numbers. It was atypical only in its American origin and its stress on political liberty rather than romantic love. Although the story was set in Switzerland and dealt with William Tell, audiences equated the Swiss fight for freedom with the recent American struggle for independence, and therefore the play took on patriotic nuances. First performed by the Old American Company at the venerable John Street Theater in New York City, April 18, 1796, *The Archers* is considered the first musical production professionally performed in the United States written by Americans. Only two numbers from the work have been preserved, however—the Rondo from the overture and the song "Why, Huntress, Why?"—both published in Carr's *Musical Journal*.

Formal musical tributes to American nationalism by late eighteenth century immigrant composers were more consciously grandiose. A prime illustration is James Hewitt's *The Battle of Trenton*, published in 1797 and dedicated, as usual, to George Washington. Hewitt was born in Dartmoor, England, on June 4, 1770. As a young boy he entered the navy, but resigned as midshipman when his sensitive nature rebelled at the harsh treatment of sailors on board his ship. Since the youth had earlier demonstrated a talent for music, Hewitt's father decided to sponsor the boy in a musical education. The lad's progress was rapid, and he eventually became the leader of the court orchestra of George III. In 1790 Hewitt married a Miss Lamb, but his wife and child died the following year. It was at this point that the tempestuous young musician decided to move to America. He arrived in New York late in 1792, just twenty-two years old at the time.

Shortly after landing Hewitt and a group of his friends presented a concert in New York City, the program including one of Hewitt's own compositions, an "Overture in 9 movements, expressive of a battle." The work was doubtlessly inspired by Kotzwara's *The Battle of Prague*, an insipid piece enjoying high fashion in Europe at the moment, and was probably written before Hewitt left England. The overture successively depicted:

Introduction
Grand March; the Army in Motion
The Charge for the Attack
A National Air
The Attack Commences, in which the Confusion of an
            Engagement Is Heard
The Enemy Surrender
The Grief of Those who Are Made Prisoners
The Conqueror's Quickmarch
The Finale

The piece exemplifies the more banal program music in vogue among social sophisticates of the late eighteenth century, in both Europe and America, and reveals Hewitt as a composer closely tied to the musical tastes of his day.

Hewitt lived in New York until 1812, continuing to give concerts (particularly on the violin), conducting theater orchestras, and for a time directing all of the city's military bands. He became active in promoting subscription concerts and in 1798 purchased the New York division of Benjamin Carr's publishing business. Meanwhile he married a second time, now to Eliza King, an accomplished young woman who had been in school in Paris during the French Revolution. The Hewitts had six children, the most renowned of whom was the eldest son, John Hill Hewitt, later a popular composer of sentimental ballads. The family moved to Boston in 1812, where James Hewitt assumed the musical supervision of the Federal Street Theater and later was appointed organist of Trinity Church. After 1818 the Hewitts alternated irregularly between New York and Boston, apparently overseeing musical enterprises in both cities.

In 1797, about the time he was becoming recognized as New York's leading professional musician, James Hewitt wrote his most lasting composition, *The Battle of Trenton*, a "military sonata" for piano. The work is a quaint period piece, highly stylized and artificial, and contains most of the cliches of contemporary European art music. The sonata may have been an entirely fresh work, although the programmatic resemblance to the composer's "Overture in 9 movements, expressive of a battle" is so striking that it appears likely that American events were simply substituted for the more general references of the earlier piece. In *The Battle of Trenton* Hewitt attempted to represent:

Introduction
The Army in Motion
General Orders
Acclamation of the Americans
Washington's March (at the Battle of Trenton)
The American Army Crossing the Delaware
Ardor of the Americans at Landing
Trumpets Sound the Charge
Attack
Cannons
Bomb
Defeat of the Hessians
Flight of the Hessians
The Hessians Begging Quarter
The Fight Renew'd
General Confusion
The Hessians Surrender Themselves Prisoners of War
Grief of the Americans for the Loss of their Comrades Killed
        in the Engagement
Yankee Doodle
Quickstep for the Band
Trumpets of Victory
General Rejoicing

For a ten-minute composition this is an ambitious program indeed! The music is slight and highly melodramatic, sprinkled with showy passages calculated to appeal to young ladies of the period who entertained at the keyboard during salon gatherings.

Although *The Battle of Trenton* may readily be mutilated on aesthetic grounds, as an historical document it discloses much of the cultural dilemma and artistic preferences of the early United States. The theatrical effects of the piece are characteristic of the popular art of the late eighteenth century, echoing an heroic tendency found similarly in painting, music, and literature. While the precedent had clearly been set abroad, Americans had a particular penchant for the exaggerations of the heroic school, since that approach magnified great moments of the past to epic proportions. Having few historical moments to draw from, Americans delighted in making the most of what they had, and the heroic excesses fit their needs nicely. Looking principally to the American Revolution, painters of the young United States depicted select scenes from their country's brief history with Homeric majesty, however contrived. Canvases were filled with neoclassical detail, overstated drama, inflated heroism, and death in defense of liberty—all linked whenever possible to Greek and Roman analogies. Typical of this school are the works of John Trumbull, "The Battle of Bunker's Hill" or "The Death of Montgomery," for example—huge canvasses that almost burst with calculated histrionic particulars of one of American history's pivotal moments. In much the same way in music James Hewitt's *The Battle of Trenton* is packed with dramatic effects symbolizing one of the crucial engagements of the American Revolution.

To argue that either Trumbull or Hewitt had created truly American pieces would reveal great gullibility, for the nationalism of both artists was clearly surface, a mere superimposition of American themes onto commonplace European art forms. Having studied in London with Benjamin West, Trumbull's first independent work was based on a subject from Homer, "Priam Returning with the Body of Hector." But he had served as Washington's aide-de-camp during the Revolution, knew most of the major figures of that war, and shortly abandoned Greek themes in his painting for the American War for Independence. Hewitt, on the other hand, knew the Revolution only indirectly and probably had the outline for his *The Battle of Trenton* already in hand when he left England. In any event Kotzwara's *The Battle of Prague* definitely remained the musical model onto which Hewitt grafted American incidents. Yet in the United States' search for a national identity such deliberate patriotism added measurably to the country's psychological security as well as to her sense of historical dimension.

Hewitt wrote other nationalistic pieces, of no greater depth. His *The 4th of July*, a "grand military sonata" for piano, was probably composed the year before *The Battle of Trenton*. The work was another involved program piece, containing the strains of "Hail Columbia" near its conclusion. In 1794, while arranging music for the Old American Company, Hewitt wrote a ballad opera, which he called *Tammany*. Produced by nonprofessionals in New York under the auspices of the strongly anti-Federalist Tammany Society, the work combined American Indian lore with a contemporary political theme. The libretto, written during the heat of the controversy between Federalists and anti-Federalists, was by Mrs. Anne Julia Hatton, a sister of Mrs. Siddons, the actress, and wife of one of New York's leading manufacturers of musical instruments. Since Mrs. Hatton's drama was blatantly anti-Federalist, it stirred up no little controversy and was freely condemned by Federalists as a "wretched thing" and "literally a melange of bombast." Neither the complete libretto nor the score of *Tammany* are thought to have been published, but one of Hewitt's instrumental numbers, known as the "Tammany Quickstep," did become quite familiar around the turn of the century.

As the careers of Hewitt and Carr illustrate, the political theme so prevalent in the popular songs of the new nation appeared more elaborately, if less spontaneously, in the formal compositions of the Federalist years. The immigrant musicians often caught the patriotic mood of their adopted country, although they chose to express this patriotism in terms quite traditionally European. Yet even in their musical conservatism these foreign musicians aptly suited the aesthetic taste of late eighteenth century America, for despite political independence Americans still wanted assurance that they had not left the bounds of civilization. Of political radicalism American patriots might be guilty; of artistic innovation they were almost wholly innocent. Americans subsconsciously wanted their conscious expressions of nationalistic fervor phrased in conventional language. They produced patriotic declarations that were obvious, superficially spectacular, calculated for emotional effect, often pretentious. But once the surface nationalism of these works was stripped away, beneath the conspicuous tribute to liberty, was invariably a European cultural prototype currently in vogue.

Less synthetic musical manifestations of an evolving American spirit were present, but were considerably more subdued. Genuine, inherent aspects of America's musical identity clearly came neither from the pens of established patriots like Joseph Hopkinson and Francis Scott Key nor from the notebooks of foreign professionals. Instead, those elements intrinsically American in the nation's music were essentially rooted in the common experience of the country's expanding population, black and white. Within the Anglo-American community a native musical tradition sprang from the spontaneity of the "lining-out" system, from the eccentricities of the singing school masters—particularly Billings, since he more than any other was willing to break with the musical protocol of Europe—and from the frontier camp meetings, where spiritual devotion took precedence over both the established hymnody and recognized concepts of art.

The folk heritage associated with the "lining-out" method was never completely suppressed, although the early eighteenth century New England singing masters worked feverishly to rehabilitate the musical standards of northern seaboard America. The music masters themselves, despite their insistence that singing must follow strict notation and established rules, often implemented their reforms through highly individualistic means and thereby added to an incipient American folk tradition in the process. John Tufts' system of teaching students to read music by using letters and punctuation marks to indicate tone and tempo, while not entirely original, is a classic illustration of the quixotic methods of the early New England singing instructors. Following Tufts' example, William Little and William Smith devised the popular "shape-note" system, first published in their tunebook, *The Easy Instructor*. Since the folk tradition used only *fa-sol-la-mi* notation, Little and Smith simply designated a differently shaped note to represent each of these four syllables. A triangular note stood for *fa*, a round note for *sol*, a square one for *la*, and a diamond-shaped one for *mi*. The advantage of this system was that the singer with minimum training could distinguish the notes of a piece almost instantaneously and was spared the mental computations made necessary by changes in key.

By the 1780s, as the northern urban areas fell increasingly under the spell of professional foreign musicians and grew too sophisticated for the methods of the self-styled Yankee singing masters, the shape-notes were denounced as "dunce notes" among the cultural elite of the New England and Middle Atlantic cities. Leaders of the large urban choirs would have nothing to do with such a form of notation or the unassuming music affiliated with it, preferring instead the more complex works of Handel and Haydn. On the other hand, country people throughout the rural South and frontier West were less concerned with genteel graces and continued to enjoy the shape-note system until the twentieth century.

Although the singing schools lingered in New England as an anachronism only in the more isolated villages, after 1800 the singing masters began expanding into Kentucky, Tennessee, and the valley of the Mississippi, exerting no little impact. With them went the "fasola" system, the fuguing-tune, and the folkhymn or spiritual folk song. The latter, essentially a secular folk tune sung to a religious text, dated from the "Great Awakening" of Jonathan Edwards and George Whitefield in the 1730s, but had quickly been incorporated into the singing school repertoire. As the second wave of religious revivals swept the country in the early 1800s, this folk hymnody became increasingly identified with rural America, gradually becoming enmeshed with the Yankee fuguing-tunes and the old New England psalm tunes.

At the opening of the nineteenth century two conflicting musical traditions were evident on the American scene. In the urban North the way had been prepared for "scientific improvement" in singing. The newer European system of solmization came into use, whereby a different syllable was assigned to each note of the scale (that is, do-re-mi-fa-sol-la-ti-do). The custom of having the women sing the melody in the soprano range was adopted, and the old tunes were being replaced by more sophisticated compositions, preferably those of the European masters. By the time Lowell Mason initiated his program of music education in the public schools in the 1830s, these "scientific improvements" were recognized as an established part of the musical heritage of the Eastern seaboard.

In the rural South and on the frontier the "fasola" system continued, employing only four syllables in singing the notes of the scale: fa-sol-la-fa-sol-la-mi. Although this practice had its origins in Shakespearean England, it became identified early on with the singing school movement in America and the common way of singing. Associated with the "fasola" tradition was the custom of placing the melody in the tenor range, while a restrained folk hymnody largely devoid of harmonic lushness continued to be characteristic.

By the time the "fasola" system reached the frontier, however, the singing schools fostering it had become appreciably more secularized than they were in their early days in New England. Many of the songs used were still nominally "sacred," but the aura surrounding the schools grew increasingly social. Instruction was frequently offered in a room of a local tavern, which the owner willingly rented for a token fee, knowing full well that his bar would enjoy a healthy patronage during recess and afterwards. The singing master himself was often a man inclined to steep "his talents in spirit," and any number of his pupils demonstrated the conviction that vocal ability improved proportionately with the amount of liquor consumed. While singing, members of the school sometimes beat out the time with their hands, giving the occasion an even more festive air. After the Revolution an increasing number of newly composed American tunes came into use among the singing schools as a conscious antipathy toward melodies of British origin. When traditional English tunes survived, they gradually absorbed New World features, reflecting an Americanization process at work during the primitive stages of the frontier.

But the musical tastes of the western frontiers evolved much as those of colonial New England had. In the early years the common method of singing and folk hymnody were not only welcomed, but preferred. In areas of sparse population itinerant circuit riders traveled through the countryside on horseback, bringing both the gospel and folk hymns to the scattered pioneers. As settlement increased, seasonal camp meetings were held, where frontiersmen of several denominations could come together for spiritual rejuvenation. The religious experience at these camp meetings was intense, often wildly emotional, aimed at mass conversions. Hours of preaching and prayer climaxed in great soulful outpourings in song, building the spiritual delirium of the crowd even higher. Worshipers clapped their hands, jumped and screamed, patted and thumped the ground, agitated their bodies, sometimes barked and howled. As the hysteria mounted, the din of the singing grew louder and more disorderly. At times several hymns might be sung at once, with each group attempting to outsing the other. Samuel Asbury, a descendant of one of the early circuit riders, recalled this revival singing from his youth: "at a hundred yards it was beautiful; and at a distance of a half mile it was magnificent." No musical instruments were used, and the men carried the melody. The women sang their harmony an octave higher, as Asbury says, "singing around high C with perfect unconcern because they didn't realize their feat."

Many of the lyrics to the camp meeting hymns were never recorded. Congregations relied largely on preachers to furnish both the words and the tune essentially in the old "lining-out" manner. Some of the folk hymnody was taken down, however, and shortly after the Kentucky Revival camp meeting hymnals began to be printed. Traditional English hymns, like those of Isaac Watts and Charles Wesley, survived in the West, but folk hymns became an increasingly significant part of the evangelical experience on the frontier. Religious ballads, hymns of praise, and revival spirituals all emerged as integral facets of the camp meeting hymnody, as worldly tunes became joined to sacred texts, much like John Wesley had done in England years earlier. As Charles A. Johnson writes, "Any worshiper who had gone to a social affair and raised his voice in song could be equally exuberant at the camp meeting. His old favorites now carried a religious message, but the musical score remained the same."

Camp meetings were also held in the rural South and attended there by substantial numbers of blacks. The spread of religious instruction among the slaves basically coincided with the second "Great Awakening," of which the camp meeting movement was a dramatic part. The blacks sang many of the same songs at these meetings as the whites, although a definite Negro spiritual eventually appeared. In frequent cases the Negro spirituals were simply adaptations of white folk hymns, or were similar to them, but at the same time reflected certain characteristics unique to the American slaves' experience, or were loosely analogous to their African heritage. The uninhibited emotional quality of the camp meeting songs, for instance, was sympathetic with the native musical tradition of the blacks, and the "lining-out" system was not unlike the call and response pattern present in African singing. In all likelihood blacks in America created folk hymns by much the same process as whites, adding personalized religious texts to tunes that had gradually become familiar. As the years went by, singing differentiation and textual variations produced songs that at first glance seemed distinctive.

The folk hymns of the South and West were not restricted to religious meetings, for they quickly found their way into the cabins and everyday life of the backwoods. Both blacks and whites sang spirituals as accompaniment to routine work of all types, often interspersed with ballads. "Springfield Mountain," perhaps the earliest truly American folksong, and one of the more popular ballads, appeared in many forms, originally as a lament over the death of a young man bitten by a rattlesnake.

For the first three decades of the nineteenth century the folk singers, with their "fasola" shape-notes and local singing schools, largely had their own way in the rural South and West. But as the frontier regions matured, as cities appeared and the urge for sophistication developed, a "better music" movement spread through the West much as it had along the Atlantic coast a half century before. In the larger cities like Pittsburgh, Cincinnati, Cleveland, and St. Louis, the "fasola" system became anathema to the devotees of propriety and gentility, who began insisting that the do-re-mi solmization, by then standard in Europe and the eastern United States, was the only "correct" method of notation.

In the Old Northwest the "better music" movement is well illustrated by the career of Timothy B. Mason, the brother of the great eastern music educator Lowell Mason. In the early 1830s Timothy Mason left Boston, the center of music reform in the East, and made his way to Cincinnati, just emerging as the cultural center of the Ohio Valley. Mason was horrified to find singers in the Ohio city still enjoying the "fuguing-tunes" of Billings and the rest of the old-time singing school repertoire and using hymnbooks printed with the common shape-notes. Determined to elevate the musical level of the area, he quickly set about compiling an instruction book, the *Ohio Sacred Harp*, that would acquaint westerners with the orthodox method of singing. Mason's book, following the pattern set by the New England manuals, included a twenty-page "Introduction to Vocal Music" and 220 pages of song, originally published in shape-notes. "The most correct method of solmization," Mason nevertheless declared in his introduction, "is to apply a distinct syllable to each note of the scale.... Indeed, by pursuing the common method of only *four* syllables, singers are almost always superficial. It is therefore recommended to all who wish to be thorough, to pursue the system of seven syllables, disregarding the different forms of the notes."

In addition to working to make the indigenous singing schools out of date, Mason introduced orchestral instruments into the church services of the Old Northwest and was largely responsible for the installation of an organ in Cincinnati's Second Presbyterian Church, thought to be the first organ west of the Alleghenies. He was also active in a music education program for young people, which went a long way toward preparing the community for the active concert life that came later.

Similar reforms were championed throughout the maturing frontier. No sooner had the larger western communities achieved a level of urbanity than indigenous cultural forms were supplanted by hallowed European ways. Musical preferences clearly reflected this shift from rusticity to calculated sophistication, as the frontier cities exhibited the desire to appear culturally established. An insistence on "correct" singing was but a first step, shortly followed by the importation of professional musicians as teachers and concert artists. Music of proven artistic worth was as coveted as the classics in literature and the tragedies of Shakespeare on the stage, while folk traditions were derided and hidden as far as possible from public view.

Despised though the "fasola" system may have been by urban cultural leaders, it nevertheless provided a more solid foundation for building a distinctly American music than did the self-conscious efforts at formal composition. Crude and artless as the homespun method of singing may have appeared, it served the needs of the frontier well, was comfortable in its primitive surroundings, and thereby simulated the spirit of rural America far more honestly than did the conspicuous efforts at musical grandiloquence that later ensued.

Understandably, the early years of the United States were permeated with zealous nationalism, only somewhat more tentative than that of Italy and Germany in the late nineteenth century. Unlike the unification movements of central and southern Europe, the American experience had been so brief that a cultural identity was almost entirely unrecognized. To make up for the lack of a heritage that only time could provide, Americans amplified their scant past, at the same time clinging to select traditions from their British origins. Political superiority was confidently asserted, while economic progress was praised with only slightly less certainty. The highly nationalistic *American Museum*, for example, offered piano making in Philadelphia as support for the magazine's contention that American manufacturing by 1790 was correctly preferred over foreign imports. Native workmanship was better, the publication insisted, while home manufacturers used a higher grade wood in their pianos and screws rather than glue.

Of their artistic priority Americans were less confident and therefore ungrudgingly permitted patriotic themes to substitute for art forms of intrinsic originality. The folk art taking shape about the time America was discovering its nationality in other fields, when considered at all, was looked upon as too ordinary to be of either artistic value or national pride. Ignoring the vernacular tradition that would later be hailed as the roots of American music, the newborn United States chose instead to gratify its nationalistic urges with contrived outpourings of musical patriotism, frequently as extravagant in form as they were sparing in beauty and aesthetic content.

CHAPTER

VI

Early Concert Life

The influx of skilled musicians from Europe at the close of the Revolution accelerated the pulse of concert life in America. Steeped in the tradition of the European classics, these immigrant musicians quickly assumed the guardianship of the new nation's formal musical affairs and established the standard of taste among the young country's cultural elite. Professional musicians increasingly came to replace amateurs in the larger seaboard cities; subscription concerts were resumed on a broadened scale once the war was over. Opposition to theatrical performances decreased, reflecting the secularization of American society that had evolved over the course of the eighteenth century. Philadelphia repealed its laws against theaters in 1789, and Boston allowed similar restrictions to lapse by default four years later.

Enlightenment, a belief in progress, and faith in man's ability to control his own destiny—ideas planted before the Revolution—continued to swell in the American mind. God was transformed from a narrow-minded taskmaster into a vague, detached First Cause, while theological concern for the details of human behavior declined. By 1820 the lingering prejudice against organs in churches had paled, although the most austere Protestant faiths still tended to look upon the instrument as an "infernal box of whistles with the devil inside." Congregational singing generally improved following the achievement of independence, at the same time that the secular music available was both deepening in quality and becoming more complex and varied in form.

Following the Revolutionary War the center of concert life in the American states shifted from Charleston to New York, Philadelphia, and

Boston, as more and more professional musicians began drifting into the northern cities. Since most concert artists in late eighteenth-century America came from the theater, songs and scenes from ballad opera were frequently performed on the concert stage. Actors in theatrical troupes were still expected to do some singing, while singers were customarily assigned small roles in dramatic presentations. All four leading ladies of the Old American Company in 1793 were singers, and all four appeared regularly in the concert life of the coastal cities. Concerts were generally given in the same theaters as plays, although if singers and instrumentalists from touring theatrical companies made side trips to smaller towns for concerts, they often performed in coffee houses, taverns, court houses, or even warehouses. Singers were expected to render several different kinds of songs—ballads, patriotic airs, French and Italian operatic arias, solos, duets, and glees. Two or more singers from a theatrical troupe normally appeared together in these programs, since concert appearances by single individuals had not yet become fashionable. Vocalists by the 1790s were occasionally provided orchestral accompaniment, but concert orchestras even in the larger cities were fairly small.

The approach of the nineteenth century found the United States with a burgeoning concert life. Music lovers in the principal cities had a choice of attending concerts of five different types: individual public concerts, subscription concerts, concerts of the various music societies, outdoor concerts, and, if one was part of the privileged elite, private concerts held in the homes of the wealthy. As both theater and concert managers discouraged paying admission at the door, tickets were generally bought in advance, often at a tavern. The normal charge was around one dollar, although prices for an entire series or for women with male escorts averaged less. Most concerts began during the hour between six and seven o'clock in the evening. Programs consistently blended serious music with lighter works, vocal pieces with instrumental. It was not uncommon for conversation to persist through an entire performance, while the audience found food and refreshments readily available. Since a ball followed most concerts in the larger cities, dress was appropriately elaborate.

Music for dances after plays and concerts was provided by the theater band, and stage performers were often on hand to demonstrate new steps and suggest their abilities as dancing instructors. Audiences frequently adapted stage choreography to their own pleasure, while popular dances were as likely to find their way to the stage. The most popular urban dances toward the close of the eighteenth century were the gavotte, the minuet, the allemande, the sarabande, and the waltz, although reels, jigs, quadrilles, and country dances were also enjoyed.

By 1794 so many amusements had appeared on the American scene that a plea was made for tastefully planned programs as a means of counteracting "lower" forms of entertainment. Gradually the theater was coming to be looked upon as a means of spiritual uplift, and the musical stage was steadily growing in importance. Almost all stage attractions contained some musical numbers, many of them interpolated. The repertory of the Old American Company, flourishing in the 1790s as never before, consisted of between fifty and sixty tragedies, comedies, and farces, balanced by an equal number of musical presentations. Ballad operas continued to thrive in the United States long after their decline in popularity in England, but gradually became relegated in shortened forms to afterpieces and "ballad farces." Shield's *Rosina*, Victor Pelissier's *Edwin and Angelina*, and Sir Henry Bishop's *Clari, or The Maid of Milan* (with its libretto and familiar air, "Home, Sweet Home," by New York dramatist John Howard Payne) were favorite ballad operas of post-Revolutionary America, as were revivals of scores of works given before the war.

Theaters which a few years prior to the Revolution had provided only rows of benches in the pit and straight chairs in the boxes were being replaced by the turn of the century with structures of beauty, style, and comfort. Wignell and Reinagle's "New Theatre" on Chestnut Street in Philadelphia was the last word in elegance in 1774, featuring pit seats with backs that were arranged in curved rows, and tiers of boxes partitioned off from the gallery. In New York a corresponding landmark in theater design, the Park Theater on Park Row, opened in 1798. Managers in both cities went to considerable lengths to assure patrons that their theaters would be warm and properly lighted. Although gas lighting was introduced into Boston in 1822 and the New York Gas Lighting Company was begun the next year, for several years to come candles were still used to illuminate theaters. As late as 1845 people were enticed to a musical performance by an advertisement announcing that the concert hall would be lighted by a thousand candles.

Outdoor summer concerts grew in popularity after 1766, combining music and entertainment with food and dancing. Late eighteenth century New York had its Ranelagh Gardens and Vauxhall, favored both by commoners and the fashionable set, while Philadelphia, Charleston, and Savannah enjoyed *al fresco* amusements amid arbors, near mineral springs, as well as in various other picturesque locales. Niblo's Garden, at the corner of Broadway and Prince Streets in New York, first opened in 1823, served food and drink, and later offered recitals and opera in a quaint setting that was enhanced by fountains and foliage-lined paths. Niblo's was the last of the great concert gardens, although in its beginning years the grounds were situated so far outside of town that William Niblo arranged to transport audiences from Bowling Green to his out of the way facility.

By the end of the eighteenth century most of the larger seaboard towns had at least one concert society, in which amateurs and professionals met to play and periodically perform for social gatherings. As early as 1759 Philadelphia had its Orpheus Club, and Charleston formed an Orpheus Society in 1772. Boston's Music Society was flourishing after 1786, while similar societies had been organized before 1800 in Concord, Baltimore, Fredericksburg, and Newport. New York by this time had four such groups, all actively providing the city with musical programs and occasionally presenting guest artists. While a certain social prestige was associated with an invitation to attend a music society program, concert societies in America, like the New England singing societies, were far less aristocratic than those in Europe. By the turn of the century the larger American music societies had become semiprofessional and were attempting the more complex works of Handel and Haydn.

Meanwhile, the flood of immigrant musicians from Europe continued. In 1795 a German-born instrumentalist named Gottlieb Graupner arrived in Charleston, where he married a successful singer and shortly moved to Boston. Graupner had lived for a time in London, and while there had played under Haydn. He taught oboe, flute, and violin, and in Boston opened a music store and music publishing house. In 1810 Graupner organized a small orchestra, the Philharmonic Society of Boston, consisting of professional and amateur musicians who met regularly to practice Haydn symphonies and other contemporary works for their own pleasure. Sometimes called "the father of the American orchestra," Graupner worked to whet Boston's appetite for the foreign classics and set the tone for the city's musical life in the early nineteenth century, much as the less sophisticated Billings had done a generation before.

In 1815 Graupner was a guiding force behind the formation of Boston's Handel and Haydn Society, one of the genuine landmarks in the history of music in America. Composed of both instrumental and vocal members, the Handel and Haydn Society presented its first concert on Christmas night, 1815, and shortly became the hub for the appreciation of serious music in Boston. The society's chorus numbered between 100 and 150, while its orchestra consisted of from fifteen to twenty members, most of whom came from the Philharmonic Society. For the dignified Graupner, Haydn and Mozart represented the culmination of musical art, and while he dominated the Boston musical scene, the repertory of the city's music societies remained limited. With Graupner's gradual retirement from public life after 1820, however, the Handel and Haydn Society became more progressive in its programs, even offering a commission to Beethoven for an oratorio in 1823.

In Philadelphia Benjamin Carr continued to play a leading role in musical affairs until his death in 1831. After several years of Wednesday night meetings in private homes during the winter months to practice string quartets, Carr and a circle of his friends formed the Musical Fund Society in 1820. The organization's double purpose was to assist needy musicians and advance Philadelphia's musical taste. Its first concert was presented to the public on April 24, 1821, and included what was probably the initial American performance of a Beethoven symphony, the First in C major. To make the composition more palatable to the audience, it was interrupted at the end of each movement and a light vocal or solo number was inserted. The following year the Society gave a performance of Haydn's *Creation*, in which over a hundred musicians took part, a number of them recruited for the occasion from the Moravian community at Bethlehem. In 1824 a site was purchased on Locust above Eighth Street for the erection of the renowned Musical Fund Hall. For forty years the best musical talent in Philadelphia gravitated to the Musical Fund Society, although it never regained its prominence after the Civil War. The Society staged its first opera on February 8, 1841, the American premiere of Mozart's *The Magic Flute.*

With the opening of the Erie Canal in 1825 New York, which before the Revolution had bowed to Boston and Philadelphia in size as well as cultural significance, became the major port in America. Doubling its population within a decade, New York by 1840 was a thriving, cosmopolitan commercial center, far larger than either of its colonial rivals. All types of entertainment began to flourish there, as the city developed a substantial middle class, a secure economy, and an organized social life. While a noticeable dearth of instrumental musicians had been apparent during the years before 1830, in 1842 the New York Philharmonic Society, the nation's oldest extant professional orchestra, was organized through the combined efforts of Ureli Corelli Hill, formerly conductor of the New York Sacred Music Society, and Anthony Reiff, a tenor in the St. Patrick Cathedral choir and a music teacher at the local Blind Institute.

What the Handel and Haydn Society had done in Boston with oratorio, the Philharmonic Society of New York accomplished for orchestral music. The orchestra was large enough to do justice to the breadth of the symphonic repertory, numbering over fifty members, and dedicated to quality performances. The group was organized on a cooperative plan by which each musician contributed twenty-five dollars to the general treasury during the initial year and thereafter shared in the profits. The first season netted $1,854 in receipts, bringing each musician about a twenty-five dollar gain. Only conductors were paid a contract salary. Fifteen years later the orchestra's income amounted to $4,810, or approximately $143 for each member.

The Philharmonic Society presented its opening concert on December 7, 1842, at the Apollo Rooms on Broadway. The program included Beethoven's Fifth Symphony, the overture from Weber's *Oberon*, a scene from *Fidelio*, and a Mozart aria. Three different conductors officiated, a practice that continued over the next ten years. Members of the orchestra, except for the cellists, performed standing, while those who did not own dress clothes were permitted to wear dark trousers, a cravat, and a frock coat. As an economy measure, ushers were members of the orchestra, "selected by the governors because of their appearance and address." Holding a long, thin rod as a symbol of their office and wearing white gloves, the ushers escorted subscribers to their places, then hurriedly ascended the platform to their allotted concert positions. At the group's first rehearsal the proprietor of the Apollo Rooms displayed so little confidence in the orchestra's chances for success that he demanded the rental fee on his hall *before* the session began. As each musician entered the auditorium, he was asked to contribute twenty-five cents toward the rental charge.

For sixteen years the Philharmonic Society offered four concerts a season.

Programs were consistently ambitious, presenting the great classical orchestral music interspersed with vocal selections from oratorio and opera. The execution of such difficult works at times left much to be desired in the early years, as conductors often directed them without having heard an adequate performance and with no particular insight into the subtleties of interpretation. Yet while the aspirations of the New York Philharmonic Society sometimes exceeded its accomplishments, the level of performance steadily improved through the years and came to serve as a model for orchestras in other American cities.

Other than the New York Philharmonic, the standard of precision among early nineteenth century American orchestras was distinguished principally by its mediocrity; they were found lamentable especially by European observers. One German musician wrote that orchestras in this country were "bad, as bad as it is possible to imagine, and incomplete. Sometimes they have two clarinets, which is a great deal; sometimes there is only one first instrument. Of bassoons, oboes, trumpets, and kettledrums one never sees a sight. Oboes are totally unknown in this country. Only one oboist exists in North America and he is said to live in Baltimore." As a result, the composer's original orchestration had to be repeatedly rearranged to conceal the absence of essential instruments. An early New York performance of Beethoven's *Eroica* Symphony, for instance, is recorded to have been played by an ensemble of seven instruments! Concerts were seldom adequately rehearsed, although the musical sophistication of the new nation's audiences was such that crudities in performance sparked minimum comment. The premiere playing of a Haydn symphony in New York supposedly brought such enraged responses from the audience that members of the orchestra were pelted with eggs and vegetables. The quality of playing, it seems, was not the objection; what the indignant listeners wanted was "Yankee Doodle" or any tune equally consistent with their cultural tastes.

In 1848, precipitated in large measure by the European revolutions of that year, a score of well trained, but financially distraught German musicians banded together for a concert tour of the United States. Calling themselves the Germania Orchestra, the group made a profound impression on American audiences and eventually played a considerable role in the maturation of the country's symphonic movement. Their first few concerts in New York and Brooklyn, however, were so poorly attended that lack of funds almost compelled them to break up. A benefit concert by the New York Philharmonic finally made it possible for the tour to continue. The Germania Orchestra ventured to Philadelphia, where the profit on one concert totaled a bare $9.50. Fairly responsive audiences were found in Baltimore and Washington, but in Boston the orchestra played to full houses and enthusiastic crowds. The remainder of the tour, which extended as far west as St. Louis, was generally successful. Since many listeners had never heard symphonic works before, the musicians found it expedient to follow the custom of mixing Mozart, Haydn, and Beethoven with popular waltzes, polkas, and quadrilles. The Germania Orchestra even included a novelty on a number of their programs called "The Railroad Gallop," during which a toy locomotive circled the stage, puffing smoke.

While the Germania Orchestra had this lighter side, its playing of the classics remained exceptional and embraced the most complex works—including, in a joint concert with the Handel and Haydn Society, Boston's first hearing of Beethoven's Ninth Symphony. The orchestra's success, limited though it may have been in the beginning, stimulated considerable interest in instrumental music among the American public and provided an example of quality playing. When the group disbanded in 1854, many of its members stayed on in the United States, assuming positions from Boston to Chicago, further shaping the development of the country's musical taste. Carl Bergmann, for example, one of the leaders of the Germania Orchestra, later became the conductor of the New York Philharmonic. With continued immigration from Germany, art music in the United States came increasingly to be built on the German model. American music students swarmed to Germany for study between 1850 and 1870, and the German romantic tradition was sanctioned as the epitome of beauty and musical refinement. By the outbreak of the Civil War, New York's musical life was not appreciably different from that of a good-sized German town, while German settlers in Cincinnati and Milwaukee formed their *Saengerfest* and *Musikverein* and otherwise played formative roles in their cities' musical experience.

Dance in America, on the other hand, remained much more under the influence of the French. Ballet had received a marked impetus early in the 1790s, when the French Revolution and the uprisings in Santo Domingo sent troupes of refugee dancers to American shores. Most professional dancing in the period following the Revolution was associated with the theater, although even the pastoral ballets given on the early American stage were patterned after the dance traditions of the Paris Opera. John Durang, the first American dancer of note, performed classical dances, enacted Harlequin roles, and offered variations of his famous "Hornpipe" (on tightropes and even eggs) with the Hallam company and other theatrical troupes throughout his long career. Presumably self-taught, Durang made his debut in Philadelphia in 1784, attracting significant attention simply because he *was* a native American. Fifteen year-old Augusta Maywood, two years after a successful appearance in her native Philadelphia, became the first American engaged as *premiere danseuse* by the Paris Opera and for the next two decades won critical acclaim throughout Europe. Of the European dancers to tour America, none made a greater impression than Fanny Elssler, the beautiful Viennese ballerina who visited the United States for two years, 1840-42. Wine was drunk from her slipper, Congress adjourned so that its members might watch her perform; and Elssler concluded her trip having made a fortune.

Although early nineteenth century Americans often lacked the ability to judge musical performance, they were masters at manufacturing. By 1789 "joiners" in the major seaboard cities were making excellent pianos, essentially copied after English models of the time, and within a few years

Boston and Philadelphia particularly were supporting an active piano trade. Jonas Chickering, the great name in early American piano building, began as a cabinetmaker in Ipswich, New Hampshire. In 1818, at age twenty, he moved to Boston to seek his fortune, apprenticing himself to one of the town's leading piano makers. Meanwhile he joined the choir of the Park Street Church and became a member of the Handel and Haydn Society. Within five years Chickering had learned the details of the piano trade and devised a number of improvements in construction. In 1823 he and a partner entered business for themselves. Seven years later Chickering was engaged in manufacturing the recently developed upright piano, a superior product in design and quality to anything available before. A combination of fine workmanship, awareness of improved mechanical developments, solid business methods, and ample capital enabled Chickering's firm to ride the ante-bellum wave of prosperity to national preeminence. The company held together through the panic of 1837, and in the next decade was essentially without competition or fear of fluctuations in the business cycle.

Amid great advances in commerce and technology and despite far-reaching changes in their social pattern, cultural leaders in mid-nineteenth century America continued to look to established European standards for aesthetic guidelines. Alarmed by the shallowness of musical appreciation in their young country, guardians of the genteel tradition grew determined to preserve and spread an artistic heritage in a rustic land whose natural inclinations leaned more toward the material, the practical, and the mundane. "Good taste" and "correctness" became watchwords in the larger urban centers, just as "singing by rule" had a hundred years before. But the sophistication admired by cultural spokesmen in early nineteenth century America went far beyond the homespun methods of standardization championed by the singing schools. Musical improvement to the later generations, as with progress in other areas of life, was felt to come most effectively through science. Consequently the "better music" movement of the pre-Civil War era, while linked to hallowed European traditions, was repeatedly couched in modern scientific terminology.

The distinguished leader of the new reform movement was Massachusetts-born Lowell Mason. Although he had demonstrated unusual musical talents at an early age, Mason was sent to Savannah, Georgia, in 1812, where for fifteen years he worked as a bank clerk. His leisure time, however, he devoted to teaching singing classes, composing, and leading church choirs. He delighted in taking themes from various renowned compositions and harmonizing them into hymntunes for his church services. In 1822 his *Handel and Haydn Collection of Church Music* was published in Boston, under the auspices of the Handel and Haydn Society, and was an immediate success, bringing its author instant recognition. Five years later, Mason was invited to Boston to supervise the musical endeavors of three churches, one of them being Lyman Beecher's. Reflecting the decorous taste of the time, Mason degraded the old-fashioned anthems of Billings and insisted on "up-to-date" music that took advantage of "modern improvements," which in many instances meant fairly colorless imitations of the European classics. Yet for a nation bubbling with optimism and whose faith in progress on all levels was undaunted, the appeal of the "better music" movement was great, and Lowell Mason became its very symbol.

For Mason the most efficient means of raising the musical taste and proficiency of the American public was through the instruction of children. Shortly after coming to Boston, he began a singing school for boys and girls and demonstrated with a series of concerts that children could be taught to sing well. He added a children's choir to his church services and launched a ten-year campaign to introduce music into the Boston public school system. Mason's method of teaching was based primarily on Pestalozzian principles, which were enjoying a considerable vogue among educators at that time. Accepting Pestalozzi's process of gradual instruction, Mason taught his pupils a song phrase by phrase, rather than starting them off with the complete tune and thereafter correcting mistakes as they occurred. He insisted that this procedure of *"building* up rather than *patching* up" was a more natural method than the old plan, and he quickly became identified as the most progressive teacher of music in the United States.

In 1833 Mason and a group of influential associates founded the Boston Academy of Music, the first school of music pedagogy in America, which was responsible for the earliest music appreciation courses in this country. Mason realized the value of training music teachers, and although the plan spread throughout the country, the Academy of Music in Boston remained the movement's center. Hundreds of teachers attended annual conventions, where discussions and lectures on teaching problems and techniques were offered over a four day period. In 1834 Mason issued his *Manual of Instruction,* which became the handbook for music teachers across the nation. Finally, in 1838 music instruction was accepted into Boston public schools. Lowell Mason was given charge of this program by being appointed the first Superintendent of Music in an American school system, a post which he held until 1845. With Boston as the example, school systems in cities all over the United States began adding music study to their curricula; more and more participants of the Mason-inspired music conventions were becoming imbued with a missionary zeal.

Mason held that music was not an end in itself, but an effective benefit to man's moral nature. "Music's highest and best influence," he once wrote, "is its moral influence." Much like Pestalozzi, Mason believed that "the highest, ultimate end of all that can be drawn out of the kingdom of tones," works toward "the perfecting of man's emotional or moral nature." For Mason the great music of the classical masters not only provided cultural refinement, but an uplifting ethical experience as well. By combining a conservative devotion to the European musical tradition with a belief in science and progress, Mason caught much of the spirit of early nineteenth century America as it looked ahead and backwards at the same time.

Blending a lingering Puritan heritage and such cherished Enlightenment ideals as progress and social reform with elements of European
romanticism, the New England Transcendentalists sought to bridge the gap
between eighteenth and nineteenth century American thought. John
Sullivan Dwight, whose *Journal of Music* set the artistic standard during
much of the nation's formative period, reflects best Transcendentalist
attitudes on music. A Bostonian, Dwight graduated from the Harvard
Divinity School in 1836, planning to become a Unitarian minister. Upon
leaving Harvard, he read a great deal of German literature, translated German
poetry, and became absorbed in music. On a trip abroad he met several of the
leading German musicians of the day and became a particular admirer of
Beethoven. In 1840 he was chosen pastor of a church at Northampton,
Massachusetts, but left the church after one year and returned to Boston,
convinced that he lacked the personal qualifications necessary for the
ministry. A friend of Emerson's, Dwight had grown enthusiastic about
Transcendentalist ideas, and in November, 1841, joined the short-lived Brook
Farm experiment, where he taught Latin and music.

While Dwight's instinct for music was good, it is doubtful that he ever
studied the technical aspects of the art seriously, certainly not intensively. His
experience in listening to music was limited, for he rarely heard performances
outside Boston. Nevertheless, he may justly be considered America's first
great critic, possessed of fine literary style and an intuitive sense of quality.
His *Journal of Music*, launched in 1852 with the support of the Harvard
Musical Association, was the first American periodical of national
importance to attempt critical reviews of musical performances. The
circulation of Dwight's *Journal* was always small, partly because it devoted
itself to the best in music and fought a determined battle for excellence in an
age that doted on gimmicks and musical curiosities.

Even before leaving Harvard, Dwight had expressed the root of his
Transcendentalist attitude toward music. Essentially his idea was that while
words are the language of thought, music must be considered the language of
feeling. Since not everything can be communicated in words, the person who
cannot perceive the emotional message of music is denied a knowledge of
some of life's profoundest mysteries. "Music," Dwight wrote, "stands for the
highest outward symbol of what is most deep and holy, and most remotely to
be realized in the soul of man." The moral, spiritual and aesthetic qualities
present in music, he held, were readily available through the great European
masterpieces as performed by superior artists. He therefore was impatient
with inferior composition and technical inadequacy. The greatness of music
itself was sacred to Dwight, not its association with a religious text or ritual.

Time and again Dwight suggested that music could provide the bridge to
a better world. A society which extolled only money and power was a defective
one, and it was music's holy mission to correct this blemish by "familiarizing
men with the beautiful and the infinite." Music's divine purpose was to
"excite common feeling, create common associations, and unite individuals

in common sympathies found in things eternal." Americans in particular could benefit from the transcendental qualities of music, as Dwight indicated in 1870 in the *Atlantic Monthly*:

> We as a democratic people, a great mixed people of all races, overrunning a vast continent, need music even more than others. We need some ever-present, ever-welcome influence that shall insensibly tone down our self-asserting and aggressive manners, round off the sharp, offensive angularity of character, subdue and harmonize the free and ceaseless conflict of opinions, warm out the genial individual humanity of each and every unit of society lest he become a mere member of a party or a sharer of business or fashion.

Music to Dwight was the great unifying link, since it was the one language that men all over the earth could comprehend. Accepting man to be most nearly united in spirit, he concluded that the language of emotions most closely approached a universality. Like Beethoven, his idol, Dwight had a vision of music's unification of mankind into a great social brotherhood, held together by an appreciation of the world's musical masterpieces. The utopian socialist ideals that enamored the critic so deeply in his youth appeared less in his lectures and writing as the years went by, but he never abandoned the conviction that music served humanity as a tremendous ethical force.

More immediately, Dwight's objective was to plant the works of the great classical and early romantic composers in the hearts and concert halls of the American public. His aims for music were incontestably high, but his own musical shortcomings at times clouded the critic's ability to distinguish between genius and superficial skill and identify real greatness. Insisting that music must lift its hearers from the "hard and hapless prose of daily life," Dwight dismissed much contemporary music, both foreign and American, as missing its purpose. At the same time his own inadequacies and conservative preferences led him to disparage the later works of Wagner and the relatively complex structure of Brahms. For Dwight the musical masters remained Handel, Bach, Mozart, Haydn, and Beethoven.

Yet Dwight, like Mason and the music educators, contended that the art should embrace the breadth of American democracy. "A true idea of music," Dwight said, "forbids the thought that it is anything exclusive." If mankind were to reach the ideal moral realm and transcend into a social Utopia, music—the unifying link—clearly would have to extend to the entire community. On the other hand, with the emergence of a more distinct American middle-class in the decades before the Civil War, an expanding segment of a socially mobil population began assuming aspirations formerly reserved for the upper classes. Attending concerts and opera not only became a means of deepening one's cultural, and therefore spiritual, dimension, but a convenient avenue for demonstrating a newly achieved economic station and implying a graduation in social standing. The theater and concert hall for most nineteenth century Americans connotated moral benefits to be had beneath a visage of respectability and affluence.

"Music," the *Message Bird* concluded in 1852, "belongs democratically to all who desire it, or are moved by it." Consistent though such views might have been with American ideals, mass appeal in the arts often involved sacrificing quality to quantity. "A concern for the amateur and the naive layman in music," James H. Stone has written, "was a counterpart to faith in the amateur officeholder and the farmer-patriot of democratic politics. The idea that music was most valuable when it produced the widest social response matched the dominant faith that equalitarian and democratic social and political institutions gave American life its most lasting significance." While cultural spokesmen like John S. Dwight viewed music as "the TRUE and *ever* Beautiful, the Divine," concert life in early nineteenth century America seldom attained such heights. To gain the popularity harmonious with democratic sentiment, concert artists directed themselves to the crowd, employing gauche theatrics and an array of musical tricks ranging from novel to monstrous. Although an elevation of the human spirit remained the goal of Dwight and cultural idealists, a spectrum of unsophistication formed a pattern for mid-nineteenth century American concert life that was in keeping with the character of its patronage.

Soloists and featured artists were rare in the United States before 1825, since native talent was scarce and the long, often dangerous voyage from Europe made foreign musicians of distinction reluctant to undertake the adventure. Primitive conditions in the New World joined with limitations in the cultural climate of the young country to further convince European musicians that a tour through the scattered American cities would be neither tolerable nor profitable. As concert activity quickened during the second quarter of the century, artists of some reputation began visiting the United States, limiting themselves initially to the Eastern seaboard, but gradually venturing out into the trans-Appalachian urban frontier. The response they encountered was often longer on enthusiasm than taste or intelligence. As Stone suggests, "The soil for an esthetic culture was thin," while theatrical emotionalism, on stage and off, was "characteristic of popularized Romanticism."

American audiences preferred that their musical entertainment be grandiose. The bigger the display, the more the concert was likely to be appreciated. Recitals by single artists generally were considered a bore. An evening of chamber music had only limited appeal, but a program featuring sixteen pianists on eight pianos could count on reasonable success. Americans even in the early nineteenth century displayed a special penchant for variety and wanted concerts featuring as many artists as possible. Events offering an assortment of soloists, both vocalists and instrumentalists, supplemented by a chorus and orchestra, were preferred. Combinations were sometimes curious. Henri Vieuxtemps, the great Belgian violinist, for example, once appeared on the same program with a concertina artist who titillated his audience by crushing his instrument on his forehead or nose.

"Music at the time," David Ewen insists, "appealed to American audiences for the very reasons that circuses did." The public thrilled at the unexpected, the sensational, and the eccentric, while music alone held little real fascination. Teresa Carreño was advertised across the country as "the greatest woman pianist in the world," more like a freak of nature than as an artist. "Master March," one of the musical wonders of the early nineteenth century, was a four year-old child prodigy who could play on two drums at the same time. Hatton, another pianist, delighted audiences by appearing on stage with a string of sleigh bells attached to his right leg. When he came to appropriate passages in a composition describing a sleigh ride, he would shake his leg, while an assistant imitated the cracking of a whip. "And this thing," Dwight reported in his *Journal*, "aroused a storm of applause which had no end until it was repeated several times *da capo*." The Polish pianist Volovski induced capacity houses by promising to play four hundred notes in a single measure, while the singer De Begnis claimed the ability to sing six hundred words and three hundred bars of music within four minutes. Leopold de Meyer publicized that he could perform melodies on the piano with elbows, fists, and even a cane.

French pianist Henri Herz, who came to America on an extended tour in 1846, was largely responsible for establishing the vogue of excessive ornamentation in piano playing, including spectacular runs, arpeggios, trills, and much arm waving and head bobbing. Following a series of concerts in Charleston, the pianist concluded that southern audiences were more knowledgable and appreciative of music than those in the North. After winning acclaim in Boston, Philadelphia, and New York principally as the composer of variations on "Home, Sweet Home," Herz was pleased to discover that southerners "enjoyed compositions more elevated than the simple fantasies and variations on popular airs that crowded my earlier programs." The musician found that in the United States artistic appreciation in general, but music appreciation in particular, left much to be desired, "in spite of several good philharmonic societies and the efforts of a number of good musicians to popularize the works of the masters." Herz recounts observing one lady in a music store testing pianos by poking the keyboard with her parasol.

The atmosphere of mid-nineteenth century American concert life is probably captured best through the New World careers of three significant European musicians: violinist Ole Bull, soprano Jenny Lind, and conductor Louis Antoine Jullien.

Ole Bull was born in Bergen, Norway in 1810, studied in Christiania and later in Paris, and won much of his early acclaim as a violinist in Italy. Far more self-taught than any of the other famous violinists of the nineteenth century, the tempestuous Norwegian grew impatient with the rules and restraints imposed by his teachers and largely developed his own technique. Even as a youth his playing assumed a technical brilliance and a warm, lyrical melodic line that remained characteristic throughout his long career. He spent hours alone mastering the mechanics of his instrument and experimenting with new methods of playing. By flattening and lowering the bridge of his violin, Bull discovered he could play on all four strings at the same time. Later in his career this *quartetto* playing caused a great sensation, and Bull even wrote a Quartet for solo violin. For Ole Bull musicianship was highly personal, and he looked upon the violin as a means for individual expression.

During the 1830s Bull achieved a renowned European reputation, although one tinged with controversy. Chopin, Spohr, and Malibran all praised him, and most listeners were impressed by the perfection of his staccato and arpeggio. His lack of sound theoretical training, however, was apparent to any professional musician, while conservative critics often objected to his unorthodox techniques and were suspicious of his reluctance to perform the classical repertoire. As the years went by, the violinist was increasingly accused of indulging in musical tricks and cheap concert theatrics.

By 1843 Bull had grown tired of touring Europe and was convinced by his friend Fanny Elssler, the dancer, that a fortune awaited him in America. He sailed for the United States on November 4, arriving in Boston. Proceeding directly to New York, the musician found that the city awaited him enthusiastically while the press somewhat sweepingly hailed him "the world's greatest violinist." Bull's love of freedom and his belief in the common man of his own country evoked a curiosity about the American democratic system and an eagerness to meet a people who governed themselves. New York in the 1840s was excited at the prospect of having within its midst the world's greatest anything, but after suffering the lampoons of such foreign observers as Frances Trollope and Charles Dickens, a European celebrity known to have expressed sympathy for American institutions was welcomed with special favor.

If the reportage of the times was correct, Ole Bull was not only an exciting artist, but a romantic figure as well. He was said to be a handsome man with a fine physique, looking like some Viking god. Biographical information was gleaned from European newspapers and circulated to the New York press, much of it more fiction than truth. The musician was reputed to have attempted suicide by jumping into the Seine, dueled in Germany, and enjoyed a thrilling debut in Bologna. Stories of his physical prowess were particularly relished. As the *New York Herald* reported the day after Bull's arrival in Boston, "Ole Bull, the prince of violinists, from Europe, is expected here tomorrow, by the steamer. He is the greatest and best of the lot in the old world—is a fine looking young man, and fights like a tiger."

The violinist gave his first American concert on November 25, 1843, before an immense crowd at New York's Park Theater. The audience included the cream of the city's social and cultural elite. Ladies wore decollete gowns, long curls, and that look of genteel sadness which was a feminine affectation of the time. Gentlemen came dressed with flapping collars and large cravats. As the tall figure of Ole Bull strode confidently to the center of the platform, a hush fell over the house. For a moment he stood before the sea of faces, his violin loosely hanging from his arm, a slight smile gracing his expression. As he tucked his instrument under his chin and lifted his bow, a sigh swept through the theater. When he played his body swayed widely, his long hair fell over his eyes, while his face assumed a look of rapture. In the middle of one number a string snapped, but without loss of dignity he transposed the rest of the selection and finished on three strings. The effect on his listeners was electric, and the concert ended with great applause. The musician acknowledged the compliment with such polished stateliness that the audience began to clap and cheer even louder.

Within a few days Ole Bull's name was on the lips of virtually the whole town. Excited ladies, whose hearts had been set fluttering by the handsome young genius, deluged the violinist at his Astor House suite with flowers, poems, and invitations to tea or dinner. Parents named children after him, the eighty year-old John Jacob Astor entertained him at his home, and newspapers were filled with interviews and daily accounts of Bull's activities. Without question, the Norwegian enjoyed the most fantastic acclaim of any European musician to date.

Early in 1844 the violinist embarked on his first tour of the American hinterland, encompassing in less than two years practically every city of any size east of the Mississippi. Bull himself was invigorated by the rough, brawling life on the frontier, and he rapidly became the common people's ideal of a great musician. Audiences were delighted by his exaggerated movements, his public baring of his soul through music, and the playing of his own compositions. The performer accepted the American public for what it was, and unlike more austere classical artists, willingly mixed serious selections with the claptrap entertainment he knew audiences wanted. These unsophisticated concertgoers liked narrative music and went wild over imitations of bird calls, waterfalls, and other sounds of nature; Ole Bull gave them what they enjoyed. Audiences were astounded by his pyrotechnics, his skill with melody, and his ability to endow simple folk tunes with life and feeling. Thomas Ryan, an early member of Boston's Mendelssohn Quintette Club, recalls hearing Bull play "The Arkansas Traveller":

I shall never forget it. The piece opened with a short introduction— a quiet, plaintive air—at the conclusion of which he gently lifted up his right foot, much in the old-grandfather manner of beating time; then he suddenly brought down that foot with tremendous force on the uncarpeted stage and dashed off into the most reckless, mad, and intoxicated jig any dancer ever heard to start the fever of dancing within him. It was startling.

The average American was no less delighted by Bull's manliness and lack of artistic pretentiousness. An anecdote from one of his southern visits was widely publicized, winning new admirers for the violinist as the report spread. Supposedly the Duke of Devonshire had given the musician a large diamond with the request that it be placed in the bow of his violin. A river ruffian noticed the gem and demanded that Bull relinquish it. The Norwegian replied that the stone had been a gift and that he had no intention of either selling it or giving it away. "But I am going to have that stone!" the assailant allegedly insisted and began to draw a bowie knife. With one quick movement of his arm, Ole Bull felled the thief with a blow across the throat. "The next time I would kill you," the violinist warned, his foot pressing down on the man's chest, "but you may go now." As he got up, the fellow expressed admiration for the musician's adroitness and strength and asked Bull to accept the knife he had intended to use against him.

Fables of the performer's good looks and personal courage, along with his reputation for fiddle magic, had preceded him into the American back country. On days he was scheduled to give a concert, the roads into town teemed with horses or ox-carts carrying whole families to hear him. The violinist symbolized high-sounding music, yet presented it in the exalted terms that an artless populace could comprehend. Although Ole Bull's natural talent was considerable, it was his robustness and human touch that attracted most American listeners. As Mortimer Smith, Bull's biographer, explains, "to his admirers he was not an interpreter of abstract music but a man writing his biography with a fiddle-stick, revealing a 'noble' and a 'pure' soul." To the lowly he represented success and culture combined with modesty and virility. For others the musician's flamboyance alone captured their imagination, while one old rustic professed admiration for Bull, insisting simply that listening to his music had cured his rheumatism.

Ole returned to Europe in the winter of 1845, after farewell concerts in Boston, Philadelphia, New York, and Baltimore. The *New York Herald* estimated that the violinist had traveled 100,000 miles, performed over 200 concerts, and earned a net profit of nearly $100,000—proof to most Americans that he was indeed a great musician. Bull visited the United States many times over the course of his long career, on his second excursion including California on his tour. It was also during this second American trip, 1852-54, that the violinist was teamed with conductor Maurice Strakosch and little Adelina Patti, the eight year-old sister of Strakosch's wife. Billed as "the infantile prima donna," the young Patti sang bravura arias written for the mature voice and by the Civil War had developed into one of the foremost sopranos of the nineteenth century.

Concert artists in mid-nineteenth century America were a stalwart breed, for the conditions they experienced on their travels surely left much to be desired. The caliber of orchestral accompaniment Ole Bull was able to obtain even in the larger cities was inferior, and a passably good pianist was frequently hard to come by in the smaller towns. Halls in the South and West particularly were often makeshift, ranging from hastily constructed "opera houses" to storerooms over shops. Audiences were characteristically boisterous, curious, enthusiastic, sometimes intrusively familiar.

Yet Ole Bull enjoyed traveling through frontier America and admired the heartiness of the people he met. Frontiersmen in turn appreciated the violinist's roaring laughter and powerful slaps on the back. "The artist from Europe's great concert halls," Mortimer Smith writes, "the gentleman who had graced London and Paris drawing rooms, became to them 'boss' and 'partner.'" Bull's own temperament personified much of the idealized American spirit, and he shared many of the country's cherished dreams and aspirations. Like most nineteenth century Americans, he was an idealist, willing to sink a fortune into a Utopian community for Norwegian immigrants in Potter County, Pennsylvania. Formed along the lines of Fourier socialism, the settlement, called Oleana, was plagued with difficulties from the start and failed in less than four months. The experiment meant heavy financial losses for Ole Bull, but endeared the violinist more than ever to Utopian-haunted Americans. Here was an artist with whom young America could identify, who spoke their thoughts if not their language, symbolized the height of European culture but enjoyed playing "Yankee Doodle" as an encore, and blended a natural artistic talent with a romantic image and a practical showmanship.

Unlike Ole Bull, Jenny Lind—another Scandinavian—was neither flamboyant nor physically attractive. Instead, she was a plain, narrowly pious, introverted woman, lacking practically all of the idiosyncrasies of a prima donna. Born out of wedlock in Stockholm, Sweden, on October 6, 1820, she was fourteen years old before her parents married, spending her childhood branded as a bastard. Raised in an atmosphere of extreme poverty and devout Protestantism, feeling unloved and persecuted, Jenny reached maturity marked with an inferiority complex and an aggressive morality. She also suffered from a mouth that was too wide, a "potato" nose, and dun-colored hair, none of which enhanced the girl's self-image. She did possess a remarkable voice, however, and at sixteen appeared in her first opera. She made her real operatic debut two years later as Agatha in Weber's *Der Freischutz*, remaining in Stockholm until 1841. Then, dissatisfied with her progress in Sweden, she left for Paris, where she sought instruction from the Spanish tenor Manuel Garcia.

With the assistance of Meyerbeer, the soprano appeared in Berlin, as Norma, on December 15, 1844, winning a resounding success. She made her Viennese debut in the same role on April 22, 1846, and went on to general European acclaim. Her voice was soft and glowing—"all *piano* and sweet," as Queen Victoria described it, while Frederic Chopin said, "Her singing is pure and true; the charm of her soft passages is beyond description." By 1849 Jenny Lind was at the peak of her artistic development and widely considered the leading soprano of her day. Early that year, somewhat shy of her thirtieth birthday, she announced her intention of retiring from the operatic stage. The reasons for this decision are not altogether clear, but it was reported that the singer considered the theater morally tainted and no longer wished to be a part of it. She would devote herself henceforth solely to concert engagements and oratorio.

Following a sequence of triumphant appearances in London, the great American showman P. T. Barnum heard of Jenny Lind and began toying with the notion of luring the singer to the United States. Emerging from humble origins, Barnum had become renowned as an entrepreneur of freaks and oddities. After a number of experiences with traveling shows of various sorts, Barnum's first major step up the ladder toward success came in 1835, when he bought a withered, crippled slave named Joice Heth and exhibited her about the country. The woman was claimed to be a hundred and sixty years old and was said to have been George Washington's nurse. In 1841 Barnum purchased Scudder's American Museum in New York City, renaming it "Barnum's Great American Museum." Bewitched by the exhibitor's clever publicity and advertising magic, the public flocked to see Barnum's collections of curiosities and hoaxes. A special favorite, although viewers were invariably disappointed, was the Fejee Mermaid, consisting of the head of a stuffed monkey and the body of a large fish. In 1842 the showman acquired perhaps his biggest success, a live boy midget whom he called General Tom Thumb. Shortly becoming a household word in the United States, Tom Thumb later enjoyed a triumphant tour of Europe, which included a command appearance before Queen Victoria.

The Barnum reputation, however, had been built on humbuggery, and while this had been profitable, it had not brought the producer the dignity and prestige he wanted. He harbored the ambition of becoming an impresario of genuine artists and sought an attraction that would link his name with refinement and civilization. In the fall of 1849 his attention focused on Jenny Lind, whom he had never met nor heard. She came to represent to Barnum all that was cultured and genteel. If he could convince the soprano to come, she would be the first great European singer to visit America at the peak of her fame. To bring this celebrated prima donna to the United States at a time when all of Europe clamored for her would not only advance Barnum's fame, but would raise America's cultural status as well. The showman doubted that he would make much money off the venture, although this was not his major consideration. "Inasmuch as my name had long been associated with 'humbug' and the American public suspected my capacities did not extend beyond the power to exhibit a stuffed monkey," he wrote in his memoirs, "I could afford to lose $50,000 in bringing to this country, in the zenith of her life and celebrity, the greatest musical wonder in the world, provided the engagement was carried out with credit to the management."

With this purpose in mind Barnum sent a spokesman to visit Jenny Lind in Lubeck. The showman's notorious luck held again, for at that moment the Swedish soprano was recovering from an unfortunate love affair and eagerly welcomed a change of scene. She had also become decidedly money-conscious, for while her earnings had been considerable, she now looked forward to retirement and to acquiring sums large enough to endow schools and hospitals in her native Stockholm. Barnum's offer seemed to provide a ready means of realizing these charitable aims. In addition, the singer was frankly curious about America and vaguely intrigued with what she knew of Barnum. On January 9, 1850, after several sessions with Barnum's representative, Jenny Lind signed an agreement to come to America for as many as 150 "concerts or oratorios" at a fee of $150,000. She maintained the right to end the arrangement after seventy-five appearances and to sing for charity whenever she pleased. She was also granted expenses and salary for a maid, a secretary, a valet, and a traveling companion. She would be accompanied by Giovanni Belletti, the Italian baritone, and Sir Julius Benedict, a German-born pianist and conductor.

Notified that the contract had been signed, Barnum was impatient to learn what the American public knew of his singer. He recalls how he informed a train conductor of his plans to present the diva in this country. "Jenny Lind?" the conductor asked. "Is she a dancer?" Barnum informs us that the question, "chilled me as if his words were ice." It suddenly became apparent to the manager that while the soprano might be the toast of the European capitals, she was virtually unknown in the United States. A handful of musical sophisticates were aware of her, a few American travelers had even heard her sing, but the thousands upon whom Barnum must depend, if he were at least to break even on the undertaking, were almost totally ignorant of the singer's European fame. The seriousness of the situation was driven home still farther when Barnum attempted to secure financial backing from a New York bank. "Mr. Barnum," the bank president spoke gravely, "it is generally believed in Wall Street that your engagement with Jenny Lind will ruin you."

Aware of the financial risk ahead, the showman set out to put Jenny Lind's name on the lips of a nation whose gullibility and naivete he perhaps understood better than anyone else of his day. Barnum realized that the soprano's personal virtue and deep religious conviction would appeal strongly to mid-nineteenth century America. But he also played on something else—the fact that the singer was planning to use much of her income for charity rather than self-indulgence. Knowing full well that a woman with the voice of an angel and a benevolence to match would prove irresistible to young America, Barnum began referring to Jenny Lind in the press as "a lady whose vocal powers have never been approached by an other human being, and whose character is charity, simplicity, and goodness personified." Capitalizing on the mood of his time, the manager built the Jenny Lind legend carefully emphasizing the note of purity. As Irving Wallace puts it, in his biography of Barnum, the Swedish soprano was turned into "a chaste, unblemished, virgin creature using God's gift of voice in the repelling sink of hell that was the theater, to raise money for the poor and unfortunate."

The promoter acquired a romanticized portrait of the singer from a

European artist for fifty dollars and had it reproduced in American newspapers, journals, and handbills. He secured the services of an English writer who had heard Lind sing and paid him to turn out weekly stories, released under a London date line, pointing up her piety, generosity, and European triumphs. An innocent American public was barraged with accounts stressing the soprano's sterling character and Victorian moral standards; her name grew to mean something transcendental. With his inimitable flair for advertising, Barnum succeeded in igniting the public's imagination to an extent that Jenny Lind's arrival was viewed as practically a Second Coming. "Never, in the history of music or in the history of entertainment in America," Joel Benton, a friend of Barnum's, later wrote, "has the advent of a foreign artist been hailed with so much enthusiasm."

When the prima donna arrived in New York City on Sunday, September 1, 1850, an estimated thirty thousand people were at the dock to greet her. Barnum had been rowed out to the incoming ship, where he met Jenny Lind for the first time. The manager, carrying a large floral bouquet, found the soprano on deck chatting with the owner of the steamship line. The showman took the singer's hand, observing that she was not beautiful. She stood no more than five feet four, possessed an almost peasant face, wore no make-up, but disclosed lively, expressive blue eyes and a figure that was almost perfect. As the steamer made its way to the dock, hundreds of people cheered and shouted from piers and anchored ships. The wharf was lined with screaming humanity, eagerly awaiting a glimpse of the exalted "Swedish Nightingale." A number of Barnum's employees were among the crowd, dressed in black broadcloth and each holding a huge bouquet of red roses. When the singer appeared at the top of the gangplank, her Pekinese dog under her arm, the mob began to press forward. In the confusion several persons were injured, and one man was edged off the dock into the water.

The soprano descended the carpeted gangplank, escorted by the ship captain and followed by P. T. Barnum. She was placed in a private carriage and driven through two triumphal arches covered with flowers and greenery. Atop one of the arches was an eagle and the legend, "Welcome to America!" while on the other was inscribed, "Welcome, Jenny Lind!" As the singer passed, the crowd pelted her carriage with flowers, while the police cleared a path to the Irving House, the Broadway hotel where she was to stay. Hundreds followed the carriage, and outside the hotel entrance a reported five thousand awaited the singer. Even after she was safely in her suite, the noise from the street continued. The diva appeared on her balcony, waved her handkerchief, but the din only grew louder. By evening Broadway was completely blocked, for the crowd had swelled through the afternoon to a reckoned twenty thousand. Around midnight three hundred firemen in red flannel shirts, grey helmets, and black pants marched up Broadway carrying burning torches, followed by two hundred members of the local Musical Fund Society. Again Jenny Lind appeared on her balcony, as the musicians serenaded her with "Hail Columbia" and "Yankee Doodle."

The next day the mayor and civic leaders came to call. "Her rooms," Barnum later wrote in his autobiography, "were thronged by visitors, including the magnates of the land in both Church and State. The carriages of the wealthiest citizens could be seen in front of her hotel at nearly all hours of the day, and it was with some difficulty that I prevented the 'fashionables' from monopolizing her altogether." But the press was making sure that the common people were involved too, and newspaper reporters kept up a constant vigil in her hotel corridor. Dressmakers, milliners, and accessory shops inundated the soprano with gifts, as gloves, bonnets, mantillas, riding hats, shawls, chairs, and sofas were named after her. Restaurants served dishes *a la Jenny Lind*, while poems and songs were dedicated to her. There was a Jenny Lind pancake and a Jenny Lind cigar. All sorts of gossip began to circulate. A New Yorker who supposedly found one of the singer's gloves was said to have amassed a tolerable sum, allowing people to kiss the garment, inside or out, for a fee. The soprano's peculiar manner of dressing her hair, coiling it as she did on either side of her head, aroused curiosity and eventually gave rise to the widely believed rumor that she had no ears.

With difficulty Barnum succeeded in getting his singer, heavily veiled, and her fellow artists out of their hotel to inspect possible sites for the Lind concerts. It was finally decided to hold her debut at Castle Garden, an abandoned brick fortress at the foot of Broadway, set out in the water some 200 feet beyond the Battery. Converted into an auditorium in 1822, the island structure was reached by a wooden bridge connected with the mainland and was vast enough to seat between six and seven thousand persons. Jenny Lind, baritone Belletti, and conductor Benedict took turns speaking and singing from the stage and concluded that the acoustics of the cavernous hall were adequate. Eight days before the initial concert Julius Benedict auditioned musicians for the sixty-piece orchestra that would accompany the soprano; most of them were chosen from the New York Philharmonic Society.

Four days later, Barnum held a public auction of tickets for Jenny Lind's opening night. Despite inclement weather, over three thousand people gathered in Castle Garden to participate, paying a twelve-cent charge to cross the bridge from Battery Park. Bidding on the first ticket was furious. The prize finally went for $225 to John N. Genin, the owner of a hat store next to Barnum's museum. The showman had advised Genin to purchase the ticket, no matter what the price, assuring him that the publicity value would be well worth the cost. As usual in such matters, Barnum was right. Newspapers across the country picked up the story, while customers flocked to Genin's store prepared to pay a higher price for his hats. A Genin product shortly became a symbol of prestige, and within twelve months the proprietor had sold 10,000 more hats than the year before. As bidding for tickets continued, the price leveled at around twenty dollars for a time and then dropped to between six and seven. By the morning of the concert Castle Garden was completely sold out.

The much-heralded Lind debut took place on September 10, 1850. An impatient crowd gathered so early that it was necessary to open Castle Garden three hours before the concert was to begin. The wooden bridge leading to the auditorium was lighted and covered with an awning, while the house inside was divided into four sections, each section lighted in a different color. On the stage was a painted arch from which the flags of the United States and Sweden hung. Suspended from the balcony was a bank of flowers spelling out the words, "Welcome, Sweet Warbler."

People continued to arrive all through the first selection, the overture to Weber's *Oberon*. By the time Belletti had finished his solo, the hall was filled, the audience overwhelmingly male. A hush fell over the house, as Julius Benedict led Jenny Lind through the orchestra. She was dressed in white, except for a blue belt and a small corsage. As the *New York Tribune* recorded the moment:

> It is impossible to describe the spontaneous burst of welcome which greeted her. The vast assembly rose as one man and for some minutes nothing could be seen but the waving of hands and handkerchiefs, nothing heard but a storm of tumultuous cheers. The enthusiasm of the moment, for a time beyond all bounds, was at last subdued...and the divine songstress, blending a childlike simplicity and half-trembling womanly modesty with the beautiful confidence of Genius and serene wisdom of Art, addressed herself to song.

She sang the *"Casta diva"* from *Norma*, her voice appearing to tremble a bit at first, but shortly brought under masterful control. As she sang, the soprano's appearance became something celestial and sublime. "Towards the last portion of the cavatina," Barnum recalled, "the audience was so completely carried away by their feelings, that the remainder of the air was drowned in a perfect tempest of acclaim."

Following a number for two pianos, Belletti and Lind joined in a duet from Rossini's *Il Turco in Italia*. The only disorder at the concert came during the intermission, when a group of rowdies in boats, on the water side of Castle Garden, yelled and shouted and at one point attempted to force an entrance. After several minutes of noise and confusion, the police succeeded in driving the troublemakers away. With quiet restored the "Swedish Nightingale" returned to sing a Meyerbeer trio for soprano and two flutes, a number of Scandinavian folk songs, and a special "Greeting to America," the words written for the occasion by Bayard Taylor. The press reflected the excitement of the event, describing everything from the timbre of the soprano's voice to the color of the badges worn by ushers. "Jenny Lind's first concert is over," the *New York Tribune* reported, "and all doubts are at an end. She is the greatest singer we have ever heard, and her success is all that was anticipated from her genius and her fame."

After six performances in New York City, Barnum took his "musical saint" on the longest musical tour yet arranged in the United States. The Swedish soprano gave sixty concerts within a period extending from November through late May. Beginning in Boston, Philadelphia, and Baltimore, the excitement at Castle Garden was repeated wherever she sang, and in the larger cities the practice of auctioning off tickets was continued. A record high was reached in Boston, when Ossian F. Dodge, a minor vocalist, paid $625 for the first seat sold there. Henry Wadsworth Longfellow, on the other hand, spent $8.50 and contented himself with a place in the gallery. An enterprising owner of a livery stable near the Boston concert hall set up a limited number of chairs outside his establishment and for a fee of fifty cents allowed patrons to station themselves in the vicinity, on the chance that a favorable wind would waft some of the melody their way. In Washington, D.C., President Millard Fillmore visited Jenny Lind at her hotel. Finding her out, he left his card. The next day the soprano, escorted by Barnum, returned the call, spending the entire evening at the White House with the Chief Executive and his family. It was also in Washington that the diva initiated the custom of including "Home, Sweet Home" on her programs, a song that quickly became her hallmark. Throughout the rest of her tour, she could not finish a concert without singing the number at least once, while music publishers were unable to print copies of the tune fast enough to fill the demand. She appeared in Richmond, Charleston, and Havana, and then prepared for a trip up the great river system of the Midwest.

When the singer arrived in New Orleans, the crowd at the waterfront was so dense that sailors had to make room for the gangplank. For the excursion up the Mississippi, Barnum chartered one of the most sumptuous river steamers, the *Magnolia*. Concerts were presented in the major cities along the way, including Natchez, Memphis, St. Louis, Louisville, Cincinnati, and Pittsburgh. The opening in Pittsburgh seems to have been one of the few occasions on which a Lind concert aroused hostility rather than more chaste emotions. The concert was set for a Friday evening, which was also payday for the city's miners. Since many of these workers headed for the saloon as fast as they received their wages, the local taverns were teeming with laborers in fairly high spirits by the time the well-dressed townspeople made their way to the hall to hear Jenny Lind. Curious about the formal attire, a number of the miners fell in behind the fashionable set, until the streets around the concert hall were eventually filled with tipsy workers. As the orchestra began to play inside, the men set up such a jeer that the music was almost drowned out. Jenny Lind herself could barely be heard over the noise from the streets. When the police attempted to drive the miners off, the latter started shouting louder and hurling missiles against the walls of the auditorium. Even after the concert the musicians were afraid to leave, waiting for several hours with the lights turned off before venturing through alleys to their hotel. A second concert for Pittsburgh was cancelled, and Barnum and his troupe left the next day for Baltimore.

Repeat performances in Baltimore, Philadelphia, and New York were as successful as Lind's earlier appearances had been, while Barnum was able to cut his advertising to a minimum since manufacturers and shopkeepers had so largely taken over publicizing his soprano. Then, in June, 1851, on the eve of her ninety-third concert for Barnum, Jenny Lind decided to terminate her contract with the showman. Considering the differences in personality, the two had gotten along remarkably well, but the manager's crude ways and lack of artistic taste had grated on the singer for several months. The vulgarity of much of his publicity had particularly come to annoy her, and she later complained that Barnum "exhibited me just as he did the big giant or any other of his monstrosities." After traveling almost twelve thousand miles, the soprano was both physically tired and vocally exhausted. She wanted free from the contract with Barnum so that she might pursue her American career at a more leisurely pace. The series of concerts for Barnum had grossed $712,161, earning the "Swedish Nightingale" a net share of $176,675. It had been by far the most profitable musical venture yet undertaken in the young country, and Barnum's grandiose and exaggerated methods, though frequently gauche, were fundamental to the conquest.

Jenny Lind remained in the United States for almost another year, giving forty concerts in some seventeen cities with Barnum's assistance. For a time the magic of her name brought audiences clamoring to hear her, but she never again attracted the same crowds she had under Barnum's direction. Business details bothered the singer, and without Barnum's showmanship to generate enthusiasm, interest in her concerts gradually subsided. On February 5, 1852, while in Boston, the soprano married a young German pianist named Otto Goldschmidt and shortly initiated plans for returning to Europe. Her farewell appearance took place four months later, on a rainy night in New York City. The scene was again Castle Garden, although box office receipts were less than half what her debut there had produced. Barnum was given a complimentary ticket and came backstage to say goodbye. The soprano, accompanied by her new husband, departed on May 24, on the same ship that had brought her, leaving behind a lore that enthralled Americans for generations to come.

"It is a mistake to say the fame of Jenny Lind rests solely upon her ability to sing," Barnum later cautioned in his memoirs. "She was a woman who would have been adored if she had had the voice of a crow." True though this may be, the showman himself had been the greatest single factor responsible for the extent of the Swedish soprano's American success. It was he who ignited the nation's curiosity about the singer by spreading stories of her goodness and generosity; it was he who circulated the information that she neither smoked nor drank, wore no make-up, and preferred simple clothes. As a result the diva endeared herself to hundreds who normally cared little for operatic music and others who essentially considered the theater the devil's domain. Le Grand Smith, who knew Jenny Lind well, later wrote her American courier, "Well, Mr. Barnum, you have managed wonderfully in always keeping Jenny's 'angel' side outside with the public." But while Barnum had accentuated her sterling characteristics, the singer was admittedly an unusually virtuous woman, who particularly when she sang, projected an aura of purity and high-mindedness. With Barnum's publicity as a catalyst, she understandably came to symbolize to an innocent American public, far more than to Europeans, a harmonious embodiment of beauty, piety, and simplicity. Probably in no other age could this particular approach have awakened quite the response it did in the United States of the mid-nineteenth century. Jenny Lind was welcomed as a personification of America's basic Romantic ideals in music, representing a union of art and religion.

The triumph of the Lind tour opened new horizons for European art music in America. Stimulated by the "Swedish Nightingale's" dazzling success, voice instructors across the country began to prosper as never before, while pianos were being sold faster than manufacturers could produce them. Singing societies, patterned after those in Germany, increased in number and membership, and the pulse of the nation's concert life quickened noticeably. With the trail now blazed, other great European singers followed in Jenny Lind's path. Grisi, Mario, and Alboni all made plans to visit the United States, and Henriette Sontag arrived in New York about the time the Swedish soprano was preparing to leave.

A year after Jenny Lind's departure, Americans heard their second major European orchestra. Its conductor was the talented, but eccentric Antoine Jullien, who carefully selected the more than forty musicians he brought to the United States with him. Born in 1812, the son of a French bandmaster, Jullien had grown up with band music and as a child had learned to play a number of musical instruments. He studied for a time at the Paris Conservatory, but left before graduating to form his own dance band. At twenty-eight he went to London, where he became the summer conductor of the Drury Lane Theatre. His success was so complete that he shortly was made conductor of the theater's winter season as well. Cutting something of a rakish figure, with his stylish mustache and whiskers, Monsieur Jullien soon developed into the rage of London society and was dubbed "the Mons."

A superb showman and organizer, the conductor arrived in New York during the summer of 1853 and launched a promotional campaign worthy of P. T. Barnum. The walls of the city were plastered with posters, printed in black and flaming scarlet; large amounts of handbills and pictures of Jullien and his soloists were circulated. The Frenchman put on display "the world's largest bass drum," advertising that it would play a prominent role in his forthcoming musical spectacles, and leased Castle Garden, sending in a platoon of carpenters, painters, and decorators to make the hall suitable for his orchestra's debut. On the evening of Jullien's first American concert, the middle of the Castle Garden stage was adorned with a conductor's platform covered in crimson and edged with gold. Upon the platform was a gilt figure supporting a rack for the maestro's music. Behind the stand was a carved, thronelike armchair, tapestried in crimson velvet and decorated in white and gold. Monsieur Jullien appeared, resembling a reigning monarch, dressed in an immaculate waistcoat, an elaborate shirt front, and a cravat that one observer could only describe as "unutterable."

The conductor's musicianship was often quite remarkable, and his performances generally were more than competent. He was able to extract from his orchestra a fire and zest that American audiences had seldom heard. But Jullien's primary desire was to entertain and win the public's applause. He adored pomp and ceremony and indulged in ritual whenever possible. Before conducting a composition by Beethoven, the Frenchman would stand solemnly beside his music stand, facing the audience. He would then ceremoniously turn the white, lacy wristbands attached to his short sleeves back over the cuffs of his black coat. In a moment an assistant would come forward, carrying a silver tray. On the tray was a pair of white kid gloves and a jeweled baton. The maestro would pick up the gloves and put them on with deliberate movements. As he took the baton, the assistant would bow and walk from the stage. In an atmosphere of reverence, Jullien majestically lifted his gloved hands and jeweled baton, and after an effective pause, motioned for the great Beethoven's music to commence.

In conducting his own quadrilles, the musician would often become so impassioned that he would seize the concertmaster's violin and bow or, at other times, draw a piccolo from the breast pocket of his velvet jacket. Then, with much swaying, exaggerated motion, and ecstatic facial expressions, he would join in playing with the orchestra. At the conclusion of the piece, the conductor would sink with exhaustion into the huge, ornate chair on stage, wiping his perspiring brow with a silk handkerchief. His most famous number was the "Fireman's Quadrille," which began slowly and quietly, depicting a town peacefully asleep on a moonlit night. Suddenly a discordant phrase entered the music, as the tempo grew faster, the volume louder. The brass gradually blared forth; the piccolo screeched above the din. Then the piercing clang of real fire bells reverberated through the hall, as simulated flames burst from the ceiling. In the initial New York performance, three companies of actual firemen dashed in at this point carrying ladders and dragging hoses. With firemen shouting commands here and there, real water streamed from the nozzles of their hoses, false wood panels were splintered with axes, and glass was broken. Members of the bewildered audience stood at their seats in alarm, while women screamed and some fainted. All this time the orchestra continued undisturbed in an amplified, agitated manner. Ushers, realizing that the house was about to panic, ran up and down the aisles insisting that the commotion was all part of the show. Jullien, glancing at the audience and surveying its excited state, quickly led his disciplined orchestra into the sedate strains of the "Doxology." As the firemen withdrew, order was restored, while the audience, first timidly, then vociferously, joined in singing the venerable hymn. Once all was calm, the audience cheered Jullien's exhibition and pronounced the "Fireman's Quadrille" a thrilling musical experience. For years to come orchestras and bands throughout the country performed the piece, although never so elaborately as the French conductor had staged it.

Jullien presented nightly concerts in New York for some two months before embarking on a nine month tour of the United States. He traveled from Boston to New Orleans, giving over two hundred performances. Returning to the East, he instituted the first of America's sententious "festival" concerts, assembling 1500 instrumentalists and sixteen choral societies to perform selections from the great symphonies and oratorios before an audience of 20,000. In June, 1854, Jullien gathered together his extensive American profits and sailed for England. Three years later, he would suffer heavy financial losses on an unsuccessful opera venture. To escape creditors he left London for France, where economic difficulties persisted. Spiritually and mentally broken, he died in 1860 confined to an insane asylum near Paris.

Probably in no other artistic area was mid-nineteenth century America as awkward and immature as in her musical tastes. Uneducated in the subtleties of European art music, lacking well defined standards of artistic excellence, a guileless public clamored for the obvious and sensational, preferably covered with thick coatings of sentiment and virtue. The blatantly exquisite, the excessively genteel, the overstatedly pure, the theatrically banal were readily construed as proper expressions of the cultural veneer being superimposed on American society. European artists like Ole Bull, Jenny Lind, and Antoine Jullien represented the desired link with established civilization, yet appealed to New World audiences for a variety of reasons only indirectly associated with musical proficiency. An untutored American public wanted its refinement communicated in exciting, straight-forward, ostentatious, moral terms, and the performers who succeeded in the rustic nation were those who were able to envelop their art in an attitude consistent with vernacular ideals. They were able to project, or have projected for them, an image sympathetic with popular values. European celebrities came to the United States primarily to make money; their appeal to a mass audience, however, was not merely essential to their own designs, but harmonious with a society emphasizing the least common denominator. In this context Barnum's supersalesmanship, while inordinate, was consistent with the aesthetic climate of the country at this time. Musical marvels presented in a posture of glamor and spiritual uplift offered special enticement, since the spectacular delighted amusement seekers and the sublime was cherished by sophisticates inclined to look upon art as a branch of ethics. But the public was not alone in its naivete, for early critics in the United States were scarcely better informed. As a consequence of these combined limitations, European art music throughout the vast reaches of Anglo-America was artificially embraced and remained tentative in standing until well after the Civil War.

CHAPTER

VII

European Opera and a Crystallizing Social Order

Since mid-nineteenth century Americans rarely graduated beyond super-ficiality in their grasp of serious music, they were easily diverted by the trumpery surrounding musical presentations. The excitement of the crowd, the occasion for donning formal attire, and the visage of high society that was associated with early concert life was heightened by the appearance of grand opera. Exceeding what concert soloists could supply to the people in the way of cultivation and pomp, opera provided a supreme social and cultural experience for a budding commercial elite, embellished with theatrical spectacle, melodramatic action, and visual opulence. For an untutored public the scenic splendors of European opera ranked second only to the genteel aura of the event itself, explaining the art's appeal among the young country's parvenu leaders. The intrinsic musical qualities of an operatic performance, while glimpsed by exceptional individuals and groups, particularly islands of French, German, and Italian immigrants, were eclipsed for most Americans by the more obvious visual and social aspects.

The great exception emerged in New Orleans, where a cultivated musical life dated back to the eighteenth century. Balls, concerts, light theater music, and grand opera all thrived in the Louisiana city; as did street performers, singers, black dancers, and instrumentalists, as well as marching bands—all of which joined to make New Orleans by far the most musical city in antebellum America. But the city at the mouth of the Mississippi was exceptional in many regards—cosmopolitan, strategically located at the crossroads of the American interior, and essentially Latin in heritage. New Orleans became the musical center of early nineteenth century America primarily because she was a French-Spanish city rather than Anglo-American. The puritanical restrictions and the Protestant work ethic that had limited musical development in the colonial North did not affect New Orleans, and the French particularly transferred to the city the love of music they had known in Europe.

Dancing appeared as the earliest sustained musical activity in New Orleans but later was frequently presented in conjunction with the opera. Nearly every traveler who passed through the city during the early nineteenth century commented on the New Orleanians' passion for balls. Boleros, cotillions, gavottes, gallops, waltzes, reels, mazurkas, minuets, and quadrilles were all popular, reflecting the polyglot nature of the city's population. The public balls in fact played an important role in blending national differences in New Orleans, encouraging tolerance and understanding, and converting the city into a cultural confluence at an early date. Balls ranged from elegant social affairs with sizable orchestras to the disreputable quadroon balls, where free women of color came escorted by white males. The quadroon and lower class white balls especially were common fields of operation for prostitutes and scenes of constant brawling. The disorder was intensified by the fondness for masquerades, as well as by the low-cut gowns then fashionable for women. Fights were so frequent and so taken for granted that they rarely even interrupted the dancing. A visiting actor, George Vandenhoff, observed that a fatal stabbing not only failed to stop the music, but inconvenienced the victim's girl merely until she could find another partner. Gun fights were more disruptive, since shootings were noisier than stabbings. Quarrels begun in the better ballrooms were often settled on the dueling ground. Yet despite the mayhem and complaints from officials, dancing continued as one of New Orleans' favorite pastimes and followed most of the city's major theatrical events.

Opera, however, was the city's cultural glory throughout the nineteenth century. The first operas to depart from the English ballad tradition given in America were staged there—of course, sung in French. Whereas other cities of the United States supported operatic presentations sporadically after 1825, antebellum New Orleans maintained a continuous resident opera company, offering the best integrated performances found in this country. On occasion as many as three companies operated in the city simultaneously. "At its prewar height," Henry A. Kmen maintains, "opera in New Orleans represented a cultural flowering in the old South that differed only in kind, not in degree, from the vaunted flowering of New England." Viewing itself as an American Paris, the river city sought to import the same singers that were performing in France, presenting them in the latest operas.

The first recorded opera in New Orleans was Andre Gretry's *Sylvain*, given on May 22, 1796, at the St. Peter Street Theater, although there is every reason to believe that earlier productions had been staged. Sometime between the summers of 1804 and 1805 Louis Tabary arrived in the city from Santo Domingo, and with his arrival, opera in the Crescent City began in seriousness. The town's population at the time was a bare twelve thousand, over a third of whom were blacks. During the months from June, 1805, to February, 1806, at least twenty-three operatic performances were presented at the theater on St. Peter Street, among them works by Gretry, Boieldieu, Mehul, Dalayrac, and Monsigny—all stalwarts in Paris. On December 10, 1805, Giovanni Paisiello's *The Barber of Seville*, among the earliest works still occasionally produced, was heard, probably for the first time in America.

Four years later the *Theatre d'Orleans* was built by gambler-impresario John Davis and rapidly became the city's cultural center. The theater burned in 1813, but was shortly rebuilt more splendid than ever, at a cost of $180,000. Its interior contained a parquet, two tiers of boxes, and *loges grillees*, or latticed boxes, where persons in mourning, pregnant women, or illicit partners could sit and not be seen. It was at the *Theatre d'Orleans* that an operatic tradition was firmly planted in the river city. Each season John Davis visited Paris, where he recruited artists for his company at the Paris Opera House and gleaned ideas for future productions. His troupe gradually enlarged, the quality of the orchestra improved, and a professional ballet was introduced. As the French nucleus of the city became increasingly threatened by the swelling tide of Anglo-Americans, the French theater and opera became patriotic symbols, conspicuous rallying points for a national group eager to preserve its cultural identity. After visiting the river city in the late 1840s, Henri Herz noted, "I believe myself about in France itself when I was in the French quarter of New Orleans. Indeed that quarter is like a portion of France which has succeeded in avoiding being swallowed up in the rushing torrent of American civilization."

Opera became an integral part of life in the French Quarter, not just for the wealthy and social elite, but for humbler citizens as well. Annually the townspeople awaited the announcement that was a major event—the list of operas and singers to be presented that year. On the day the notice was issued, excitement ran throughout the Latin section of the city. Men stopped one another on the streets, and women visited their neighbors to discuss plans for the coming season. By the 1820s New Orleanians heard three or four opera performances a week during the winter season. Lafayette, the French revolutionary, visited New Orleans in 1825 and attended a performance at the *Theatre d'Orleans*, after which he declared that the theater, the singers, and the audiences compared favorably with those of the famous opera houses of Europe. "Certain it is," wrote a contemporary music critic, "that an evening passed at the *Theatre d'Orleans* is an era of delight for anyone with a musical ear."

After John Davis' retirement, his son Pierre took over the management of the New Orleans opera house for twenty-five years. The masterpieces of Rossini, Spontini, Mozart, Gretry, Gluck, Cherubini and the other great operatic composers of the time were presented in lavish fashion, although often with marginal financial results. Rossini's *The Barber of Seville* was first heard in the city on March 3, 1823, just seven years after its premiere in Italy and almost three years before its first authentic staging in New York. Meyerbeer's *Les Huguenots* and Donizetti's *Lucia di Lammermoor* were just two of the many operas to receive their American premieres at the *Theatre d'Orleans*. The five act, five hour *Les Huguenots* became the special favorite of the Crescent City, staged time and again, year in and year out, while music stores sold Meyerbeer's score arranged for piano, voice, and even guitar.

James Caldwell's Anglo-American theater on Camp Street was also musically active between 1827 and 1833, boldly competing with the French theater by offering over a hundred performances of opera during that six-year period. On March 30, 1835, Meyerbeer's *Robert le Diable* was staged for the first time in the United States in Caldwell's theater—a decided affront to the French, since the Americans had beaten them in mounting one of the significant French operas. Later in 1835 Caldwell opened a magnificent new theater, the St. Charles, where he continued his production of opera. He imported an Italian troupe in March, 1836, which initiated its season at the St. Charles with the American premiere of Bellini's *Il Pirata*. New Orleans now had three theaters presenting opera in operation at the same time. Of the city's 60,000 population, about 25,000 were whites, 20,000 were slaves, and 15,000 were free Negroes. Since the St. Charles Theater alone seated between four and five thousand people, it is obvious that blacks formed an essential part of the city's operatic audiences. The St. Charles reserved a section for free blacks, while slaves could sit in another section if they had written permission and fifty cents from their masters.

No other city in the United States could match either the consistently well rounded opera productions given in New Orleans or the breadth and sophistication of that city's audiences. Not only were the French determined to preserve their opera, but the river city genuinely came to love the lyric drama as nowhere else in antebellum America. There was to be sure a social element, and "the fashion and beauty of New Orleans" could be counted on to make regular appearances at the opera house. Newcomers into town, who desired to establish themselves socially, quickly found it advantageous to rent a box and be seen in it on the nights when the music was most difficult. The balls held after special performances enhanced the enjoyment of traditional European culture by extending the evening to include the popular dances of the day.

On December 1, 1859, the famous French Opera House on the corner of Bourbon and Toulouse Streets was opened, soon emerging as "the lyric temple of the South." Built in a record 233 days, after the *Theatre d'Orleans* had raised its rental, the French Opera House quickly became the crowning achievement in the city's operatic history, overshadowing both the *Theatre d'Orleans* and the St. Charles Theater. Designed in an Italian Renaissance style, the new house contained four curved tiers rising one above the other, each gradually receding. Two broad staircases led up to the boxes, while impressive chandeliers were strategically placed. On either side of the stage, a huge mirror added to the sweeping effect of the interior. The French Opera House was formally instituted with a gala production of Rossini's *William Tell*, featuring a mammoth all-star cast. When interest in the second season began to falter, as a result of the intensifying sectional conflict, young Adelina Patti, soon to become the toast of the operatic world, was engaged for a series of performances. The soprano sang *Lucia di Lammermoor, Martha, The Barber of Seville,* her first *Il Trovatore* and *Rigoletto,* and the American premiere of Meyerbeer's *Dinorah.* Her success was one of the brightest moments in the city's rich musical history. During the four years of Civil War, the French Opera House was dark, but activities resumed as soon as the combat was over.

Particularly in the French Quarter was opera a coveted institution among broad segments of the population. Premieres and opening night performances at the Opera House found the humblest workers rubbing shoulders with the city's most prosperous gentlemen. By three-thirty in the afternoon on the day of a special opening, a few enthusiasts could already be seen standing in line for seats in the third and fourth tiers. Opera among the Creoles was a serious matter—not a luxury item, but one of life's basic essentials. "The housekeeper," says Harnett Kane, "planning her week, might omit meat from a meal or two; tomorrow, soup and nothing else. But seldom would she fail to set aside the twenty-five-cent pieces for her family's visits to the temple of music." Young men with ambition rarely hesitated to borrow formal dress from wealthier relatives for gala performances, or they might mortgage their salaries or even borrow money from friends in order to rent a tuxedo.

On premiere occasions the proscenium boxes were filled by the regular occupants, along with their guests, and were the center of attention. The horseshoe on the first tier, according to Andre Lafargue, was occupied with "the most beautiful girls of New Orleans and the vicinity, in *decollete* and wielding fans of rare plumage and variegated colors, wearing in their hair or around snowy white delicate throats dazzling pieces of jewelry." The second tier was also filled with spectators in formal dress, and up in the third and fourth tiers, the *paradis*, as it was often called, sat people in business suits or unassumingly dressed. Most of the residents of the *Vieux Carre* walked to the theater, in fair weather or foul, and on the way home after an exciting performance, one could hear snatches of the opera's melodies being hummed or whistled by the young men as they walked along the dark streets. For days after a premiere the city bustled with talk concerning the Opera House's latest triumph. "One would have thought that the very existence of the city hung in the balance," Lafargue insists, "as these discussions went on...sometimes degenerating into fights or acrimonious remarks."

A favorite anecdote among New Orleanians concerns a Creole belle who came dangerously close to being born in one of the boxes at the French Opera House. It seems that not until the middle of the third act of *Faust* did her mother, Mme. Blanque, turn to M. Blanque and somewhat excitedly inform him, "Pierre, I do not think I can wait for the ballet!" Another frequently told story centers around a small, middle-aged woman who lived in the French Quarter and had long ago reconciled herself to a life of spinsterhood. For years the little lady had earned her modest living at one service or another, sometimes clerking, sometimes working in a millinery shop, sometimes making Mardi Gras masks, but she never met a man who would show her the least attention. Then a cousin gave up her concession stand at the French Opera House, allowing her spinster relative to take it over. Suddenly the pallid little woman was besieged by a horde of eager suitors, and within a month she had become a bride, taking her choice of several marital proposals. The explanation lay in the fact that the man who married her would get free admission to the Opera House, a boon worth most any sacrifice.

As one walked about the *Vieux Carre* in the days of the French Opera House, he found himself in a world enchanted with music. "Melody showered the streets," Harnett Kane writes. "From the window of this galleried house rose the notes of an aria; Madame was repeating a second act number from last night's opera. Over there, carrying a basket of crabs on her head, a *marchande* sang still another solo." The baker from Lyon and the grocer across the alley both boasted of not having missed a week at the opera house in the past fifteen years. The little sewing woman who lived in the cubbyhole down on St. Anne Street with her husband, the barber's assistant, were as poor as could be, but they loved music and attended the French Opera House regularly. The Creoles knew their opera, were severe and quick in their criticism, and demanded productions on the highest level.

But New Orleans *was* the exception. No other community in America could approach the depth of the river city's operatic tradition. Ballad operas, of course, had been heard consistently throughout the northern coastal cities during the last half of the eighteenth century, yet not until late in that century were modified French and Italian works, by such relatively sophisticated composers as Rameau, Gretry, Cimarosa, Pergolesi, and Paisiello, presented in the North. From the 1790s on, light operas of this genre were occasionally sung in foreign languages in the larger cities of the Atlantic seaboard, although generally in abbreviated forms. The Park Theater, after its opening in 1798, became the first home of foreign opera in New York, and a condensed English version of Rossini's *The Barber of Seville* is known to have been staged there as early as 1819.

Six years later, the Rossini masterpiece became the first opera given in New York in its original language and form by a professional company from Europe. By that time the English ballad opera had lost favor, and as the cultural break with Great Britain widened, Americans increasingly turned to the Continent for artistic inspiration—in painting, architecture, and sculpture, as well as in music. In 1825 the cultural scene in New York was far more cosmopolitan than it had been in the days of Carr and Hewitt, and with the opening of the Erie Canal that year, the city's wealth expanded sharply. Ocean travel improved with the clipper ship, prompting a growing number of Americans to travel abroad. When Manuel Garcia's troupe opened its season of Italian opera at the Park Theater on November 29, 1825, New Yorkers welcomed the foreigners as representatives of the more sophisticated musical culture they now sought to emulate. Ballad opera had become too much a part of the vernacular and was considered too vulgar to carry the proper social distinction. Grand opera, on the other hand, gradually became looked upon as the special ornament of a crystallizing commercial society— an art whose sentimental and extrinsic qualities made it all the more desirable to an affluent minority for whom artificiality was the greatest luxury.

Manuel Garcia, the Spaniard who eventually came to be Jenny Lind's teacher, had been one of the greatest tenors of his day. When he brought his Italian opera troupe to New York, he was fifty years old and past his prime. Garcia had created the role of Almaviva in Rossini's *The Barber of Seville* and repeated it at the Park Theater on his company's opening night in America. The part of Rosina was sung by his eighteen-year-old daughter, Maria—later to become the distinguished Maria Malibran. On the day after the Italians' debut, the *Evening Post* wrote, "We were last night surprised, delighted, enchanted; and such were the feelings of all who witnessed the performance." In the months to follow Garcia's troupe presented *La Cenerentola, Semiramide, Tancredi, Il Turco in Italia,* and *Don Giovanni* on a reasonably high artistic level, but with frequent deletions in text. The company remained in the United States for almost a year, presenting in all seventy-six performances of eleven operas, then left for Mexico. Although the venture failed financially, it opened the way for a veritable flood of foreign operas in their original languages.

At the time of the Garcia family's visit to America, Lorenzo da Ponte, Mozart's librettist for *The Marriage of Figaro* and *Don Giovanni,* was a professor of Italian literature at Columbia University. Inspired by Manuel Garcia's acclaim, da Ponte dreamed of establishing Italian culture in the New World. In 1832 da Ponte and a French tenor named Montressor collaborated to bring opera to the Richmond Hill Theater in New York, gathering together remnants of the Garcia troupe. The group failed after thrity-five performances, in part because the ladies in his potential audience hesitated to frequent the neighborhood in which the theater was located. Undaunted, da Ponte the next year persuaded a group of the city's wealthy to finance the building of an Italian Opera House at Church and Leonard Streets. The house opened on November 18, 1833, with Rossini's *La Gazza Ladra,* attracted fairly large and fashionable audiences, but closed the season with a deficit of over $30,000. After another year the project was abandoned.

In 1844 Ferdinand Palmo, a prosperous restaurant owner, reconditioned Stoppai's Arcade Baths, on Chambers Street, for the purpose of staging opera.

Since the theater was in a highly disreputable section of town, Palmo arranged for a special car with police protection to run from his opera house to Forty-second Street. The impresario's hope was to democratize opera, but he failed miserably. Opening with Bellini's *I Puritani*, Palmo's Opera House within a year was in the throes of bankruptcy. Palmo even lost his restaurant and was forced to be a cook in an effort to regain his operatic losses.

A more elegant attempt to plant opera permanently in New York occurred in 1847 with the building of the Astor Place Opera House. The emphasis here was on opulent dress and high society. "At this time," critic Grant White wrote, "the common enjoyment of a great and refined pleasure made the opera at Astor Place a very delightful form of society." The repertoire consisted primarily of Bellini, Donizetti, Rossini, and early Verdi. Solo voices were often good, but the ensemble, chorus, and orchestra—as was typical in New York—were notoriously limited. Acting was minimal, while sets were conspicuously made of cardboard. But all of this was subordinated to the ritual surrounding the opera. "Opera hat, cane and gloves, hansom cab, the clop of horse's hooves on cobblestone, flickering gaslight, the murmur of conversation in the glittering lobby, the cozy tête-à-têtes in the lounge chairs while the orchestra tuned up"—these were the dominant characteristics, according to Ray Ellsworth, of a night at the Astor Place Opera House.

Despite its refinement, however, Astor Place shortly faced the same financial difficulties that Ferdinand Palmo had encountered earlier. As the operatic deficits mounted, the directorship of the theater passed into the hands of William Niblo, the proprietor of the city's famous outdoor theater, Niblo's Garden. Guided by his astute business sense, Niblo largely dispensed with opera and substituted entertainment that he knew would have general appeal.

One of the more laudable operatic companies to play New York City in these years was the celebrated Havana Opera Troupe of Señor Francesco Marty y Tollens, which presented well integrated performances of Italian opera. The group's chief asset was its conductor, Luigi Arditi, composer of the perennial coloratura favorite "Il Bacio." The Havana Opera was first brought to the United States in 1847, primarily through the combined efforts of Niblo and actor James Hackett. Its initial season was presented in the Park Theater, after which a number of extra performances were staged at Castle Garden. The repertoire included Verdi's *Ernani* and *I Due Foscari*, Bellini's *Norma* and *La Sonnambula*, and Rossini's *Mose in Egitto*. Senor Marty returned for the next three seasons with a company which Max Maretzek insisted was the finest ever heard in America. Among the later operas produced were Verdi's *Attila* and *Macbeth*, Meyerbeer's *Les Huguenots*, and Donizetti's *La Favorita*.

To fill the void left by the demise of grand opera at Astor Place, the Academy of Music—the great predecessor of the Metropolitan Opera House—was opened on October 2, 1854, at Fourteenth Street and Irving

Place. For an inaugural production, the Academy presented Grisi and Mario in a performance of *Norma*. Luigi Arditi served both as conductor and general director. The Academy of Music, a great white and gilt palace of a theater, emphasized beauty and stateliness off stage and was shortly sanctioned as the favored social arena by the Astors and the established wealth of the city. In large measure patterned after the fashionable Paris Opera, the New York Academy rapidly emerged as the pacesetter for opera houses throughout the country and became recognized as the foremost monument to the art of *bel canto* in America.

In its second season the Academy of Music presented the American premiere of both Rossini's *William Tell* and Verdi's *Il Trovatore*, while in the years ahead other operatic staples were heard there for the first time in this country—including *Aida*, *L'Africaine*, *Lohengrin*, and *The Flying Dutchman*. The New York Philharmonic played in the opera house after 1856, and on Thanksgiving Day, 1859, sixteen-year-old Adelina Patti made her operatic debut at the Academy in Donizetti's *Lucia di Lammermoor*, nearly seven years after her concert appearances with Ole Bull. While the Academy of Music was distinguished by islands of glory in the pre-Civil War years, these were most frequently stellar performances from individuals rather than well integrated, balanced productions. There was no resident company at the Academy, and the quality of troupes leasing the house varied widely. There was no permanent director, no overall planning. Little time was allotted to rehearsal, while scenery and properties were carelessly pulled together, with bits from several operas indiscriminantly mixed in the staging of another.

Financial disaster was often close at hand at the Academy of Music, and from time to time the house was even forced to close as a result of difficulties precipitated by capricious or inexperienced visiting impresarios. Violinist Ole Bull, for instance, became seized with the desire to try his hand at producing opera and in 1855 took a lease on the Academy of Music. The experiment was brief and ended in calamity. *Rigoletto* was given four times in succession, then *Favorita*, and *Lucia* was announced. On the morning when *Lucia* was slated for production, a notice was posted on the Academy's door: "In consequence of insuperable difficulties, the Academy of Music is closed."

On the whole the Italian works dominated the New York repertoire, and unlike New Orleans, where even Rossini and Donizetti were customarily sung in French, the Italian operas after 1825 were normally performed in their original language. Wagner was not heard in the city until 1855, when twelve nights were devoted to German opera at Niblo's Garden. Neither the public response nor the financial results of the occasion left much room for encouragement. The singers, in fact, were accused of "inexorable shrieking," and when the conductor took his benefit, the program consisted mainly of Italian selections.

By comparison with New Orleans, opera in New York was on far more provisional ground. While the spectacle of the art held definite appeal and star performers commanded special attention, New Yorkers looked upon the opera primarily as an expeditious means of enhancing at the same time their social position and their cultural image. Lacking the Creole's depth of musical appreciation, New Yorkers tended to find the exclusive air surrounding the opera more exciting than the productions themselves, the visual effects on stage more captivating than either the score or the performances. With such cursory interest in the opera itself, attendance remained erratic, and underwriters easily grew discouraged. Not until the establishment of the Academy of Music, forty-five years after the first *Theatre d'Orleans*, did New York maintain anything approaching a permanent home for grand opera, and even then seasons were sporadic and perennially harassed by artistic and fiscal limitations.

The operatic climate in other northern cities was even more tentative. Philadelphia's first real season of grand opera was provided by John Davis' French opera troupe from New Orleans, which launched its beginning tour of the Northeast in New York in July, 1827, played three weeks in Philadelphia's Chestnut Street Theater, and returned more or less annually until 1842. The Havana Opera Troupe initially appeared in the Quaker city in July, 1847, repeating the visit for the next five years. In 1856 the city opened its Academy of Music, larger and more sumptuous than the one in New York. On the troupe's later excursions into the Northeast Boston and Baltimore were both given their first taste of professional opera by the New Orleans company.

West of the Alleghenies operatic beginnings were far more humble, usually involving small itinerant groups of indefinite artistic merits. Operas were often shortened and sometimes drastically mutilated. St. Louis' first operatic performance, in 1837, consisted of a curious potpourri of tunes assembled from several Rossini operas and externally applied to a version of the Cinderella story (although not Rossini's own *La Cenerentola*). The audience was remarkably unimpressed. "Cut out the music," was the candid plea of one observer; "it is tedious." Midwestern audiences were even less knowledgeable than those of the East and tended to grow impatient quickly. "The fact is," a Missourian confessed after the 1837 Rossini conglomeration, "the people of St. Louis had very little taste for music in any form."

Chicago's first opera was presented on July 29, 1850, when a company of four singers arrived by boat from Milwaukee, singing a performance of *La Sonnambula* at Rice's Theater that same evening. Since the troupe brought with it neither orchestra nor chorus, the theater band played the accompaniment, while local singers undertook the choruses and some of the minor roles. Admission prices ranged from fifty cents in the boxes to twenty-five cents in the pit. When the curtain rose, Rice's Theater was crowded with the cream of Chicago's bucolic society. A number of gentlemen came dressed in swallowtail coats, while some of the ladies carried lorgnettes. The audience was enthusiastic, if somewhat at a loss as just how to express this enthusiasm.

As a result, the first-nighters managed to applaud in most of the wrong places, and cheers went up here and there as friends and neighbors were recognized among the local singers. At the conclusion of the opera one fellow sitting near the front hesitated a moment, then with a laconic "Well, well!" began applauding profusely.

During the repeat performance of *Sonnambula* the audience was less numerous, but scarcely less agreeable. The ensemble "*O Mio Dolor*," in which Amina pleads her innocence was soundly applauded, although the ovation was not for the soprano, but for the villagers—the Chicago chorus—as they tiptoed into the Count's room. The second act had no more than begun when cries of "Fire!" rang out from the street below. Suddenly through the windows a reddish glow became discernible. The house was safely cleared, but not without some mad scampering. When everyone was apparently outside, a party of visiting Englishmen missed one of their friends. Thinking he might have been injured, one of the group burst into the theater, bumping into manager John Rice on his way out carrying a piece of scenery over each shoulder. The missing Britisher was discovered sitting on the front row of the empty house, in a pleasant state of inebriation, applauding frantically, and declaring that it was the best damn imitation of a fire he had ever seen! He had to be dragged to safety.

In October, 1853, an Italian opera company headed by Luigi Arditi visited Chicago for three performances. Rosa Devries was the featured prima donna, while *Lucia di Lammermoor, Norma*, and *Sonnambula* were the works presented. Five years later, the Durand English Opera Troupe staged a two-week season at McVicker's Theater—with a *Miss* Georgia Hodson singing the tenor leads, including Manrico in Verdi's *Il Trovatore*. Local critics were hostile. "*Il Trovatore* was shrieked, screamed, groaned, and killed," the *Journal* wrote. "The properties were miserable, the action tame, the music inharmonious, false, and discordant. *Il Trovatore* is far beyond the capabilities of the troupe, and we trust that they will not again allow the charge of murder to rest upon them." The following year Chicago heard three separate opera seasons, presented by three different companies, the most notable one directed by Maurice Strakosch. During the middle of the Civil War, Jacob Grau visited the city, producing a variety of interesting works—among them, *Sicilian Vespers, Un Ballo in Maschera, La Juive*, and *Moses*. But Chicagoans indicated they would rather spend their time down at the Court House steps, listening to the Lumbards or John Hubbard or Charley Smith sing war songs. In January, 1865, Leonard Grover brought the city its first German opera company for fifteen performances, including mountings of Wagner's *Tannhauser* and Beethoven's *Fidelio*. Chicago's German population was highly pleased with Grover's productions, but the town as a whole remained noticeably passive.

At the end of the Civil War opera in Chicago, as in the other major cities of the American hinterland, was a long way from being an integral part of the community's cultural life. A normally unassuming social circle attended the brief, sporadic seasons with some aplomb, mainly because they felt it the thing to do, but the wealth and fashion, though growing, was not yet marked enough to support such conspicuous leisure for very long. Chicago's middle class was not prosperous enough, sophisticated enough, nor sufficiently educated musically to court the opera with much passion, and for the laboring people the whole experience was largely out of the question. German immigrants made a special effort to turn out for Wagner and Beethoven, but this was considered a patriotic obligation and was highly exceptional.

Basically, Chicago and her sister cities of the Midwest were still too rustic, the frontier legacy of utilitarianism too strong, for opera to find a particularly comfortable home there. An occasional stopover was fine. If times were good, the city was a gracious host. Yet the guest could easily overstay its welcome, particularly as costly a guest as grand opera. For Chicago especially the Civil War produced changes in the economic and social fiber of the city that would permit the support of opera on a steadier basis. In April, 1865, Maurice Grau's Italian Opera Company from the New York Academy of Music was brought to the Illinois city for the opening of Crosby's Opera House, the nucleus of the city's operatic life until the great fire of 1871.

Throughout the larger towns of the Far West, the frontier opera house appeared as a mark of cultural distinction and urban solidarity, although a minimum of grand opera was actually presented there. As the western communities grew in population and wealth, an enterprising civic spirit developed, coupled with a deepening cultural inferiority complex. Partly to compensate for the primitive environment that enveloped them, partly as a reaction against the crime, violence, gambling, prostitution, and drunkenness so prevalent during the earlier years of the western cities, frontiersmen as well as growing numbers of women and children, yearning for the trappings of established civilization, surrounded themselves whenever possible with ostentatious manifestations of traditional high culture. Merchants and land speculators, realizing an advantage in projecting an element of permanence and stability, began encouraging cultural activities in the hope of attracting prospective settlers and industries into town. Parvenu rich, sensitive about a lowly background too recent to ignore, sought from the arts a facade of cultivation and an avenue for social acceptance—differing in degree rather than kind from the parallel impulse in the East. And yet in the convulsive western societies in which everything must be done quickly—amid the work of establishing an economy, maintaining law and order, and building homes and schools and churches—time was at a premium. Cultural symbols, therefore, must be tried and sure, potent with civilizing influence, and guaranteed to produce immediately the desired aura of stability and refinement. What urban frontiersmen wanted was a hypodermic filled with a cultural concentrate to ward off the barbaric influences of the untamed environment into which economic opportunities had lured them. In this search for instant culture the frontier opera house emerged as perhaps the most coveted of cultural symbols, conspicuous in its elegance and a visible tie with the past and the best of European civilizations.

While the early frontier theaters were generally crude and makeshift— often no more than a loft over a saloon—attempts at sophistication in this matter soon became the order. For example, inside the American Theatre of San Francisco, built in 1851, the carpets were soft and thick, the paintings were gilt-framed, and the boxes had red velvet curtains and seats of red plush. Over the sides of the proscenium, close to the top, two eagles spread their wings, with chandeliers hanging from their beaks. Never mind that the edifice was built in such haste and on a foundation so flimsy that its walls sank an inch or two on opening night!

By the time the western opera houses appeared, baroque ornateness had become the ideal, with decorations either imported from or modeled after Europe. When Thomas Maguire's Opera House opened in San Francisco in 1856, its stage boasted a characteristic drop curtain representing the city of Venice, with its palaces, domes, and towers. On a canal in the foreground floated gondolas bearing aristocratic ladies and gallant cavaliers, flanked by a Venetian porch with columns and tapestries.

The dramatic and musical offerings at these frontier opera houses, regardless of their real worth, was generally praised by local critics, whose reviews were characteristically short, filled with rococo phrasing, often strained, sentimental, and moralistic. Describing an aria from *La Sonnambula* sung by a Señora Abalos, the *Alta California*, December 23, 1850, wrote:

> We almost thought we could see those exquisite notes taking wings like angels, and float aloft, or, converting themselves into wreaths of evergreen memory, festoon each pillar or cornice, chaplets to tell how the heart may be softened and all the avenues of the soul laid open and the feelings born captive by the witching power of the most divine of all our enjoyment, Music.

More than a monument of civic pride, the frontier opera house, far beyond its eastern equivalent, was held as a place of beauty and spiritual uplift, taking on an almost religious air. The assemblage gathered there was repeatedly identified by the local press as the "beauty, taste, and fashion of the city," or "the better class, the most refined and intelligent of our citizens." When Catherine Hayes sang a concert in San Francisco in 1854, the audience was described as "the high minded, the pure and virtuous." The feeling seemed to exist that the beauty of the nobler arts somehow contained the power to combat the evils of the saloon and gambling den. At its best the stage was looked upon as a companion of the pulpit in the fight to bring civilization and spiritual rejuvenation to communities surrounded by wilderness and permeated with moral depravity.

Since the opera house particularly was viewed in the West as an ennobling temple of art and refinement, the personnel associated with these frontier theaters often seemed to sense an obligation to maintain a genteel image in their own lives. Thomas Maguire, the theatrical lion of the west coast, had been an illiterate hack driver and ruffian in New York, a gambler and saloon keeper in his early days in San Francisco. By the time he had become the leading impresario of the California-Nevada mining region, however, he was suave in his manners and fashionable in appearance, wearing an enormous diamond in his scarf, a large solitaire on his finger, and a heavy gold watch chain and charm across his waistcoat. His first three theaters Maguire called the Jenny Lind, although the Swedish Nightingale herself never got near any of them. Be that as it may, following her successful American tour, Jenny Lind's name suggested all that was august and beautiful, and Tom Maguire was expedient enough to capitalize on it. Imbued with the gambler's fascination for impossible odds, Maguire was intrigued with producing grand opera and was personally enthralled with the operatic spectacle. Shrewd and opportunistic in virtually everything else that he did, Maguire's grandiose illusions lured him away from the practical path on this particular subject, for his experiments with opera invariably resulted in heavy financial losses. After a series of early flirtations with the lyric theater, Maguire opened his opera houses in San Francisco and Virginia City, Nevada, preferring in both cases the term *opera house* to *theater*, since it implied refinement and avoided the tainted connotation that *theater* carried with it at the time. At his opera house in San Francisco, Maguire presented opera on a grand scale, imported the best companies available, paid lavish prices, and halted only when faced with bankruptcy. Nothing in his early experience seems to indicate that Maguire was a lover of grand opera before coming to California, but once there he appears to have felt that the loftiness of the lyric art was the surest way to implant civilization on the west coast and win for himself a gentlemanly reputation.

To hear the local press describe the audiences attending the frontier opera house, they were refined, enthusiastic, and knowledgeable in the extreme. In repeated instances these reports became blatant examples of civic boosterism. "There are few cities in the world, or any of its population," wrote the *Alta California*, April 25, 1853, "that affords so liberal a support to the same number of artists, of every class and order, as San Francisco." Seven years later, reviewing a season of Italian opera at Maguire's Opera House, the *Golden Era* insisted, "In the large Atlantic cities a season of fifteen nights is regarded as a wonderful musical achievement, but here in San Francisco—where dollars are as plentiful as are dimes elsewhere—we can keep up a 'run' for at least forty nights, and still ask for more." A few days later, carried away by the success of the current season, the exaggeration grew still farther. "In California," the newspaper declared, "the *habitues* of the Opera are particularly exacting. They possess, in the aggregate, a higher degree of musical apprehension than audiences on the Atlantic side. . . . There is not a city in America where the Opera would be sustained for one hundred nights in uninterrupted succession, except San Francisco."

Yet even during this generally successful 1860 season at Maguire's, public enthusiasm for opera began to wane after a few repetitions. Try as the frontier press might to show the opera house as a popular institution, in less guarded moments critics would admit to frequent poor attendance. Even in San Francisco, the undisputed culture center of the American West, poor attendance plagued the opera house unless the repertoire was constantly being changed and presented with fresh voices. As a result, it was not unusual for a successful company touring San Francisco to present from twenty to thirty operas within a ten-week period, generally with fairly marginal artistic results. A good percentage of the urban frontiersmen after all came to the opera, as their eastern counterparts did, for spectacle rather than vocal artistry; once the novelty of the spectacle had worn off, audiences either demanded new visual delights or their interest dwindled.

Although the frontier opera house was a symbol of refinement and civilization and often spoken of as a fortress at war against barbarism, most of its patrons were either already culturally astute or were more interested in social display than in the art of the lyric theater. The most dedicated supporters of the opera in the West, much like their equivalents on the east coast, appear to have been the new rich, who found the dress circle an ideal arena for parading their latest finery. A report in the San Francisco *Daily Evening Bulletin*, July 1, 1859, is typical: "While the dress circle was well filled last night, the other portions of the house were poorly attended— indeed, the two upper tiers of boxes were almost empty." San Francisco, nevertheless, had the added advantage of possessing a substantial foreign population, which turned out for the opera in force, especially the Italians and Germans. Evidence is slight, on the other hand, that ordinary frontiersmen attended the opera with any consistency. With rare exceptions miners, trappers, and soldiers on a spree into town far preferred the entertainment of the saloon and variety hall to the offering at the opera house, which in most cases they were simply not educated enough to appreciate.

Contemporary accounts from the frontier areas are filled with allusions to the civilizing influences of the performing arts, but the facts rather suggest that the less genteel element was discouraged from attending. In addition to being a shrine of beauty and culture, the opera house in the mind of urban frontiersmen was a place of social grace and elegance. The more provincial inhabitants of the West clearly did not fit into the grandiose image civic leaders were striving to establish. Even the foreign population, while welcomed at the opera as a reliable boost to attendance, was at the same time viewed with some suspicion. Most foreigners were considered superior judges of music, but in their enthusiasm they often indulged in behavior and expressions of emotion that the Anglo-American majority deemed questionable. The Italians particularly disturbed the sense of propriety of San Francisco's social elite with their practice of throwing flowers to a favored prima donna or tenor, and there were eventually pleas to have these demonstrations stopped.

With such a strict sense of etiquette enforced, the opera house affected an artificial air, becoming something of the special playground for a town's social aspirants. The foreign population persisted in attending in fairly appreciable numbers out of genuine devotion to the music, but members of the community with more tentative musical interests were frequently intimidated by the formalism superimposed by parvenu leaders, and visiting miners or workers were not likely to feel comfortable amid such synthetic surroundings. In the smaller towns of the western back country ordinary citizens and casual visitors might occasionally pass through the opera house, but in the larger, more urbane communities the chances were unlikely.

An obvious indication that the opera house was more a *symbol* of culture than a real cultural force is the relatively little amount of grand opera that was actually performed. In more cases than not frontier opera houses were such in name only, and certainly more melodrama was staged in these theaters than opera. San Francisco enjoyed more opera than any other community of the American West—wealthy, cosmopolitan city that it was, strategically located on the California coast close to the mining activity—but even here Maguire's Opera House staged more minstrel shows, burlesques, melodramas, farces, and magic acts than grand opera. In fact Maguire relied heavily on the popular forms of theater to help pay for his costly operatic ventures.

If the frontier opera house was not all it was alleged to be, it nevertheless reflected the image of a civilization left behind. In most cases products of boom conditions, western communities longed for a tie with the past, some tangible indication that the wilderness had indeed been pushed aside. The old operatic warhorses, even more than Shakespearean tragedy, represented high culture in conspicuous, spectacular terms. The opera house, therefore, emerged as a western community's finest decoration, representing all that was opulent, genteel, and decent. Built after the city had attained a degree of size and wealth, usually by the self-made entrepreneurs nineteenth-century Americans admired so much, the frontier opera house became a rallying point for civic pride, signifying progress, permanence, and stability. Rejuvenated in their basic optimism as the wilderness was brought under control, people of the urban frontier considered the appearance of an opera house—even more than a school, churches, or a hotel—an indelible mark of the town's maturity. With the opening of the opera house, western townspeople viewed an unlimited cultural future and contemplated artistic triumphs that were far beyond their means to realize.

Throughout mid-nineteenth-century America the opera house was looked upon with reverence and awe, regarded as a cultural cathedral that would infuse a community with some aesthetic spiritualism, paralleling what seemed would be unlimited commercial advances. For the new rich particularly the opera house brought social distinction and an aura of sophistication, more imaginary than real. While frontier practicality, the

Protestant ethic, and blatant materialism remained central to the thinking of the developing United States, the ornaments of civilization—which European opera came to symbolize—were desired as a security that wealth alone could not provide. Outside the French section of New Orleans, grand opera was rarely more than artificially embraced by antebellum America, and yet the operatic experience etched itself in the urban mind as an index of a community's social and cultural standing.

CHAPTER
VIII

The Roots of Serious Composition

The last years of the eighteenth century found Americans exhilarated by the success of their Revolution. The inauguration of a republican government under the head of respected, conservative leadership, an anticipation of unlimited economic possibilities provided by a wilderness teeming with natural resources, and the Enlightenment optimism amid which the United States had been spawned, melded to form a confident new country. Represented was a democratic experiment commanding the attention of the entire western world. Convinced of her political, military, and material security, the fledgling nation extended her enthusiasm to include a naive assumption that a domestic art would accompany governmental solidarity. Painters Benjamin West and John Singleton Copley were both in London, but their work nevertheless demonstrated that Americans were capable of producing visual art. William Billings was being hailed in New England as a composer of considerable genius, while Francis Hopkinson's music was highly regarded in the more exalted social circles along the Atlantic coast. Immigrant musicians like Benjamin Carr and James Hewitt were providing the young nation with compositions lauding by their titles at least the victories of the Revolution and the formation of sound government.

Apart from Billings, however, the "new man" heralded by Crevecoeur—
a man "who acts upon new principles"—was slow to emerge in American
music, even more belated in this area than in painting or literature. Not until
over a hundred years after Yorktown would the United States glimpse its
musical equivalent of Emerson, Melville, or Whitman. Yet this is not to
suggest that early American art music is uninteresting, for some of it is
remarkably adroit, with pieces occasionally holding moments of charm,
spontaneity, and excitement. Although pre-Civil War America produced
neither a Handel nor a Beethoven, her people did not live in a musical
vacuum. Certainly the struggles of the serious composer are an interesting
reflection of the artistic milieu of those years, if not always resulting in works
that are aesthetically satisfying or emotionally stirring.

Before the turn of the nineteenth century art music remained essentially a
prerogative of the wealthier, intellectual classes of eastern seaboard America.
What compositions were written grew out of urban social contexts and were
primarily aimed at the traditional tastes of the cultural elite who subscribed to
the concerts and attended the city's theaters. "This was essentially the
honeymoon period of American civilization," Irving Lowens maintains, "an
era of exquisite balance between equalitarianism and libertarianism." While
Lowens insists that the impulse toward social equality was vital to the
development of American popular music, social conditions emphasizing
individual patronage and guidance were fundamental for the growth of art
music. During the early years of the American republic, Lowens feels, "a
leaning in the direction of equalitarian excess was tempered by patrician
leadership of the state and patrician direction of thought." In this regard
serious music encountered a more receptive environment in Federalist
America than it would later, after the "democratic revolutions" of Jefferson
and Jackson had taken place.

Among the professional musicians to come to the United States from
England in the wave with Carr and Hewitt was Alexander Reinagle, probably
the most gifted immigrant composer of the eighteenth century. Reinagle was
born of Austrian parents in Portsmouth, England, in 1756, the year of
Mozart's birth in Salzburg. The boy acquired his love of music from his
father, who had been a musician in Austria. Sometime prior to the youth's
eighteenth birthday the family moved to Edinburgh, Scotland, where
Alexander studied piano and harpsichord with Raynor Taylor, who later
followed his student to the New World. Before journeying to America,
Reinagle was selected to be a member of the Society of Musicians in London
and had visited Carl Philipp Emanuel Bach in Hamburg. On October 23,
1784, he appeared in Lisbon with his consumptive brother, Hugh, a cellist.
The following January Alexander gave a solo concert in the Portuguese
capital, and followed up his concert a week later with a performance before
the royal family of Portugal. Upon the death of his brother, Reinagle
returned to Portsmouth and migrated to America the next year.

He arrived in New York before June 9, 1786, promptly announced that he was prepared to offer instruction on the piano, harpsichord, and violin, and hired the Assembly Room of City Tavern for a concert. Here, on July 20, in this two-story building featuring long windows extending to the floor that overlooked the bay and river, Reinagle performed his first American concert. He appeared as pianist, cellist, and vocalist, his program including one Piccini number, three Haydn selections, and five pieces by Handel. He was assisted by the charming actress-singer Maria Storer, who had sung Handel oratorios in Bath and Salisbury and performed ballad operas with the American Company. Since New York's response to Reinagle was far from encouraging, the musician shortly decided to move to Philadelphia, which he understood was more advanced culturally.

Within a few months he was in Pennsylvania, participating in a benefit concert for Henri Capron on September 21, 1786. In October Reinagle announced a benefit of his own, which he opened and closed with works by Haydn. His reception in Philadelphia was encouraging, both as a concert pianist and as a teacher. With the assistance of Capron, William Brown, and Alexander Juhan, Reinagle revived the "city concerts," a subscription series that demonstrated his musicianship and lofty standards. During his second year in Philadelphia, Reinagle introduced four-hand piano music to this country, playing with Juhan's assistance, a Haydn sonata for two artists. He continued managing the concert series until 1794, performing in the majority of the concerts himself, occasionally playing one of his own piano pieces. George Washington, who enjoyed concerts almost as much as he loved theater, heard Reinagle perform several times while he was attending the Constitutional Convention, and the musician eventually became the harpsichord teacher of Washington's step-daughter Nelly Custis. Another contemporary, John R. Parker, editor of the *Euterpeiad*, described Reinagle's style of piano playing as "peculiarly his own. He never aimed at excessive execution, but there was a sweetness of manner, nay, in the way he touched the instrument I might add, there was a sweetness of tone which, combined with exquisite taste and neatness, produced unusual feelings of delight."

Before leaving England Reinagle had composed "Six Sonatas for the Piano-Forte or Harpsichord, with an Accompaniment for a Violin," dating about 1780. Piano sonatas with violin accompaniment made for dilettante ensembles were much in vogue toward the end of the eighteenth century. Christian Bach, Johann Sebastian's son, who dominated the London musical scene at the time, much as Handel had earlier, had published ten such sonatas, and Reinagle's early compositions reveal the strong influence of the younger Bach, particularly in their formal construction and Italianate features. A musical world long enchanted with contrapuntal artificiality was in the throes of a revolution during these years, with the sons of Johann Sebastian Bach leading the movement to return music to a simpler, more natural expression.

Reinagle gradually became impressed with the piano writing of Carl Philipp Emanuel Bach, with whom he visited and corresponded. His four American sonatas, written during his first eight years in Philadelphia, clearly reflect this enthusiasm for Emanuel Bach, along with his devotion to Haydn. Yet Reinagle was no slavish imitator for, as Ernst C. Krohn observed, he possessed the capacity to assimilate "another man's style without losing his own individuality." While his "passage-work derives to a great extent from Christian and Emanuel Bach," Krohn contends, "there is ever in evidence a conscious striving for more effective, less hackneyed, and more individual technical figuration." His broad experience as a pianist and harpsichordist helped in this respect, giving the composer the confidence to explore new methods of expressing his individuality with greater chances of success and increasing effectiveness.

Reinagle's American sonatas are rich in harmony, melodic freshness, and rhythmic charm that doubtlessly endeared them to post-Revolutionary listeners. Composed for piano rather than harpsichord, they nevertheless betray signs of having been subconsciously conceived in terms of the older instrument. The repeated writing in two parts and the slight use of resonant chordal passages were earmarks of the harpsichord age and indicate that Reinagle had not made the full transition to piano writing. At the same time his four American sonatas are far better than his earlier London set and disclose Reinagle as "a thoroughly trained and exceptionally gifted composer." According to Krohn, "He may be characterized as one of the lesser masters of the preclassical school." Certainly when Reinagle's later sonatas are compared with those of American contemporaries like James Hewitt, they emerge superior, probably the finest instrumental works produced in eighteenth-century America.

After 1794 Reinagle became intensely preoccupied with music for the stage, and his more serious composition was largely curtailed. Thomas Wignell, the English actor, left the Old American Company in 1791 and shortly induced a group of Philadelphians to finance the construction of a new theater and support a resident drama company. When the stock company was formed, Wignell and Reinagle were appointed managers. Wignell then went abroad to recruit actors and singers, while Reinagle stayed in Philadelphia to supervise the building of the New Theater, located on Chestnut Street. The theater opened on February 2, 1793, with a "grand concert of vocal and instrumental music" presented by Reinagle, but in a few weeks, after two additional concerts, the house was closed because of the yellow fever epidemic that raged through the city that winter. A year later, much to the relief of anxious stockholders, the Chestnut Street Theater reopened with a performance of *The Castle of Andalusia*.

The interior of the theater was a copy of the Theatre Royal at Bath, while the facade—not finished until 1805—measured ninety feet. Reinagle, who had probably been a harpsichordist for the American Company for a while, was in charge of the New Theater's music, although George Gillingham, a violinist whom the director had known in England, was brought over to conduct the orchestra. The company gave regular seasons after 1794, both in Philadelphia and Baltimore, with Reinagle overseeing the music until his death in 1809. Musical standards remained high. The best singers available were attracted to the company, while the theater orchestra numbered around twenty. In its first six seasons the Chestnut Street Theater produced over seventy-five musical works. Reinagle developed a great facility for adapting current English ballad operas to the American stage, sometimes adding new music, rewriting the accompaniment, or composing new overtures. The manager also wrote entire scores of his own, such as those for *The Sicilian Romance* and *The Volunteers*, two ballad operas composed in 1795. He wrote original incidental music for pantomimes, like the French *La Foret Noire* in 1794; plays, such as *Slaves in Algiers* (1794), *The Mountaineers* (1796), *Columbus* (1797), and *The Italian Monk* (1798); and farces, like *The Savoyard* (1797).

For over twenty years Alexander Reinagle dominated the musical life of Philadelphia, composing prolifically throughout most of this time. Like his emigrant contemporaries Carr and Hewitt, he occasionally turned to patriotic themes, expressing the ardor he felt for his newly adopted country. In 1794 Reinagle composed the song "America, Commerce, and Freedom" for the ballet pantomime *The Sailor's Landlady*. This lusty tune—originally sung by Mr. Darley, one of the more noted singers of the Federalist period—is considered among Reinagle's best theater airs. A "Federal March" by the composer was performed in a "grand procession" in Philadelphia on July 4, 1788, celebrating the ratification of the Constitution by the nine states necessary to make it effective. Reinagle also wrote a "Monody on the Death of the Much Lamented, the Late Lieutenant-General of the Armies of the United States" (composed with his former teacher Raynor Taylor in 1799), a "Concerto for the Improved Pianoforte with Additional Keys" (1794), a "Masonic Overture" (1800), and two books of songs. His much admired song "I Have a Silent Sorrow" from *The Stranger* illustrates the composer's vigor and dignified melody. Toward the end of his life the musician was involved in the composition of an oratorio based on Milton's *Paradise Lost*.

Besides his concert activity in Philadelphia, Reinagle was responsible in September, 1788, for reviving New York's subscription concerts, essentially dormant since the Revolution. The following season, at which time New York was the nation's capital, he joined with Capron to give three more concerts in that city. Reinagle's superb musicianship, combined with his effective, forceful personality, did much to root an appreciation for the music of the German masters among the cultural leaders of Philadelphia and New York, as well as pave the way for later musical development.

In his theatrical work Reinagle achieved a standard in ballad opera production unmatched in early America. When Thomas Wignell died in 1803, the musician continued the management of the Chestnut Street Theater with his associate's widow. In his last years Reinagle managed a theater in

Baltimore, where he died on September 21, 1809. He had married twice and fathered two sons, Thomas and Hugh—the latter a painter of theater scenery and named for Alexander's brother, the consumptive cellist who had died in Portugal.

A few months after Reinagle's death, another emigrant musician appeared in Philadelphia who would greatly affect the musical development of early nineteenth century America and become the first composer to create an American expression in symphonic terms. His name was Anton Philip Heinrich; a Bohemian by birth, he was of German descent, as his name suggests. Born on March 11, 1781, at Schonbuchel near Schonlinde in northern Bohemia, just across the border from Germany, Heinrich in his early life was adopted by a well-to-do uncle. With the death of his adoptive guardian in 1800, young Anton became heir to a handsome house and a thriving business, a wholesale merchandising concern dealing in linen, thread, wine, and similar commodities. The youth shortly became recognized as one of the leading merchants in all Bohemia, and for a time Heinrich devoted himself industriously to the affairs of his business and even worked to enlarge its scope. Before long, however, his persistently restless spirit prompted him to travel—partly for commercial purposes, but primarily to indulge his own sense of adventure. He journeyed through Italy, France, England, Portugal, and portions of Spain. Then in 1805 he decided to visit America, as he later explained, "to take a peep at the new world."

Perhaps the genial young man spent too much time in travel and turned over too much of his business responsibilities to others, for shortly after returning home he began to learn that all was not well. The Napoleonic wars were inflicting widespread financial hardship to the Austrian Empire, and business in Europe was suffering in general. Unwise speculation and dishonesty within his own company made depressed economic conditions particularly difficult for Heinrich. With crisis at hand, the young merchant's thoughts returned to America, which had impressed him most favorably. He consequently consolidated what remained of his fortune, fitted out a merchant vessel with Bohemian glassware, and sailed again for the New World, this time to begin business anew.

His life in America seemed fairly prosperous at first, and in 1810 the carefree Heinrich was living in Philadelphia as a reasonably wealthy merchant. He apparently was none too absorbed with the operation of his business, but was happily directing the music at the Southwark Theater, simply for pleasure and completely without salary. Since childhood Heinrich had been profoundly devoted to music; he had studied piano and violin in Bohemia. On a trip to Malta the young merchant acquired a Cremona violin, which became his constant companion. His duties at the Southwark provided him with the opportunity he had dreamed of, and he eagerly assumed the gratuitous post, considering himself no more than a musical amateur. The Southwark Theater, built in 1766 by David Douglas, had been badly eclipsed by this time by the Chestnut Street Theater, and the management there was content to accept whatever talent it could find.

Heinrich's solvency, however, was short-lived, for in 1811 the financial crash came in Austria. The government went bankrupt, and the European investments on which Heinrich's prosperity was based suddenly became worthless. Although poverty was now dangerously close, the old wanderlust came over him again. In 1813 Heinrich and his new wife left for a visit to Bohemia, where a baby daughter, Antonia, was born. Shortly after reaching Schonlinde the couple made plans to return to America without delay, leaving the baby behind, oddly enough, with a distant relative. Almost immediately upon arriving in Boston, his wearied wife died, and Heinrich found himself not only virtually penniless, but alone.

He returned to Philadelphia, evidently having made arrangements to serve as the American agent for a large export firm in Trieste. This business connection lasted only a brief while, perhaps because of further economic difficulties within the Austrian Empire. At this point Heinrich decided to give up business and devote himself exclusively to music. Thirty-five years old, rich only in energy and enthusiasm, the former Bohemian merchant chose to launch a new career, accepting an offer to direct the music at the theater—the only theater—in Pittsburgh. The position would pay a regular salary and entitle him, in the minds of western Pennsylvanians, to be properly called "professor" of music. The journey from Philadelphia to Pittsburgh, through almost three hundred miles of wilderness, Heinrich made on foot.

He remained in Pittsburgh a very short time, since financial problems at the theater lost him his position there. Taking a boat down the Ohio River, Heinrich landed at Maysville, Kentucky, and walked overland some sixty miles to Lexington, in the heart of the bluegrass region. On November 12, 1817, the freshly arrived musician gave a "grand concert of vocal and instrumental music," undoubtedly as a benefit for himself. The occasion found him performing as violin soloist and pianist and conducting a small orchestra in compositions by Beethoven, Mozart, and Haydn. He immediately became active in teaching and directing both in Lexington and Frankfort, until some time that winter when he was taken seriously ill with a fever.

Still recovering his health in the spring, Heinrich also suffered emotional distress over his limited formal training in his newly acquired profession. His exposure to good music in Bohemia and Germany had imbued him with standards he realized he lacked the capacity to attain. Without "scientific" foundation as a musician, he remained an amateur, an uncultivated talent at best. Since there was no one on the Kentucky frontier to instruct him, Heinrich determined to effect his own development. The spring of 1818, consequently, finds him retired to a simple cabin in the forests near Bardstown, devoting himself strictly to his music. As he perfected his violin technique in the solitude of the Kentucky woods, haunted by thoughts of his wife and daughter, the musician became filled with a longing to express himself creatively. Gradually he began to improvise on his violin and eventually to compose pieces of his own.

As he became increasingly fascinated with free self-expression, he expanded his compositions to include selections for violin, piano, voice, and even chamber ensemble. By January, 1819, Heinrich had accepted an invitation to live on the estate of Judge John Speed, about six miles outside Louisville. He remained there for nearly two years, working diligently on the set of compositions that would be published in 1820 as *The Dawning of Music in Kentucky*. Although Alexander Reinagle may have produced more skillful music, Heinrich's selections are more individualistic and express a variety of moods. His consistent penchant for ornamentation is already in evidence, but overelaboration was a common failing at this time, in Europe as well as America. While his creative methods were not always dependable, Heinrich clearly shows himself in these initial works as a sincere composer of considerable natural ability. In name and setting his music was comfortably American; the accent, however, was unmistakably central European.

During the winter of 1821 the eccentric Heinrich returned to Philadelphia, where his melodrama *Child of the Mountain* or *The Deserted Mother*, most likely written in a contemporary ballad opera style, was first performed on February 10. He gave a concert at Masonic Hall on April 19, then traveled back to Kentucky, where he again became ill and suffered severe financial hardship. Early in 1823 a group of Bostonians, who had become acquainted with *The Dawning of Music in Kentucky*, invited Heinrich to perform a concert there. He appeared at the Boston engagement as conductor, song composer, pianist, and—surprisingly enough—organist. For three months he served as organist at Old South Church, but finding the demands of a full-time church position too confining, he resigned. The desire to see his daughter, still in Bohemia and now ten years old, had steadily grown stronger, and Heinrich vowed to return to Europe, earning his way as a concert artist. For three years he resolutely taught and performed to gather the funds necessary to launch his much-desired trip abroad. On April 29, 1826, he presented a farewell concert at Boston's Boylston Hall.

The musician envisioned himself returning home as the great American composer, and during his three years in Boston, he *had* been somewhat overzealously referred to as the "Beethoven of America." Heinrich planned to visit London before going to Bohemia, eager to submit his art to the critics there. He was anxious in fact to expose as many European cultural centers as possible to his American music, viewing himself as some sort of unofficial musical emissary. On the way to Europe, however, a shipboard accident resulted in personal disaster. Heinrich's priceless violin was crushed and—for a violinist the worst of fates—the index finger on his left hand was broken, leaving the finger permanently crooked. When he arrived in London, any possibility of his performing a concert was out of the question, and he resorted to teaching in the hope of earning enough money to travel to his daughter. Eventually he was able to play in the orchestra at the Drury Lane Theater, using a large share of his earnings to hire a piano and purchase paper to continue his composition—meanwhile living on bread and milk.

Heinrich remained in England for nearly five years; in 1828 he published the first of his London works, a little song called "The Absent Charm." His London compositions reveal such marked improvement over *The Dawning of Music in Kentucky* that his biographer, William T. Upton, speculates that he must surely have been studying there. "The Absent Charm" shows a close relationship with German Lied, but while Heinrich's tendency to over-embellish the melodic line is still evident, his early London songs are among his simplest. In 1829 he met and had dinner with Mendelssohn and two years later heard a concert by the great violinist Paganini, fresh from triumphs in Vienna and Paris. In April, 1831, Heinrich composed an orchestral fantasy entitled *Pushmataha: A Venerable Chief of a Western Tribe of Indians*, presumably his first piece for full orchestra. The composition is also probably the initial attempt by an American to recognize the Indian in music. *Pushmataha* was the first in a long line of monumentally conceived works, which, despite weaknesses in execution, likely form the truest expression of Heinrich's musical personality. "As a man he seemed ever simple and childlike," Upton writes, "as a musician, he was too often verbose and rhetorical."

Sometime during the fall of 1831 Heinrich sailed for America, without having seen his daughter, Antonia. He arrived in Boston, where on March 17, 1832, he performed a concert. He published a number of compositions that year, one of which, "Hail Beauteous Spring," he dedicated to his friend Jonas Chickering, the great American piano manufacturer. Early in 1833 he returned to London, again en route to Bohemia and once more playing with the orchestra at Drury Lane to secure funds. The next two years were among the busiest of Heinrich's entire career, for he continued in London, teaching and composing more than at any other time in his life. He became absorbed in writing for orchestra, probably broadening his orchestral horizons by attending concerts of the London Philharmonic. In May, 1834, he completed *The Tower of Babel*, or *The Languages Confounded*, which he called "a grand oratorical divertissement." A few months later he finished a still larger work, *Complaint of Logan the Mingo Chief, the Last of His Race*, a selection reminiscent of Heinrich's trip down the Ohio River, a journey he colorfully but somewhat pretentiously called a "Fantasia Agitato Dolorosa." As his interest in Indian themes continued, he produced *The Indian War Council* and *The Treaty of William Penn with the Indians*. In 1835 he composed the work probably nearest and dearest to his heart, *The Ornithological Combat of Kings*, or *The Condor of the Andes and the Eagle of the Cordilleras*.

Following another illness, Heinrich left London for the long deferred trip to Bohemia. When he arrived at last in the little village where his daughter had been residing for over twenty years, he discovered Antonia gone! Having wearied of waiting for her father to come to her, she had decided to sail for America, expecting to find Heinrich in Boston. The musician lingered in his native land for the better part of a year, visiting old friends and traveling to Prague, Vienna, and Graz. While in Graz, in June, 1836, he had the pleasure of hearing the first movement of his *The Combat of Kings* performed in a concert by a professional orchestra. Exhilarated by what was thus far the highlight of his career, he left Graz, again suffered ill health, then began a long trip through Italy and France. In Venice he practically drowned when he fell into one of the canals; in Milan a Bohemian count gave him a letter of introduction to the famous music publishing house of Ricordi; and in Bordeaux he completed another composition, *The Hunters of Kentucky*.

By the fall of 1837 Heinrich was back in the United States, living in New York City and finally reunited with his daughter. The financial panic that swept the country in 1837 affected Heinrich adversely, but he did publish a song, "Bonny Brunette." On his sixtieth birthday, March 11, 1841, he completed the score of *The Jubilee*, based on scenes from American history, and the sudden death of President William Henry Harrison prompted him to write "The President's Funeral March," originally composed for piano and organ, but later arranged for military band. Two other piano pieces— "Tyler's Grand Veto Quick-Step" and "The Texas and Oregon Grand March"—were published three years later, revealing Heinrich's awareness of current political issues. In April, 1842, when the Philharmonic Society of New York was formed in the Apollo Rooms, Heinrich was named chairman of the meeting. He was also active in teaching during these years and occasionally gave concerts.

The years 1845-47, from a standpoint of composition, were among Heinrich's most productive, comparable only to the 1834-35 period in London. When Jenny Lind came to America in 1850, the composer tried to call her attention to his work, hoping the diva might agree to sing some of his songs. By the time she arrived in New York he had written *Jenny Lind and the Septuagenarian*, "an artistic perplexity" that he suggested her orchestra play as a featured number. He also wrote *Barnum: Invitation to Jenny Lind, the Museum Polka*, but the singer remained unimpressed. After the soprano married Otto Goldschmidt, Heinrich attempted to see her husband and sent him a volume of his songs. Goldschmidt eventually returned the music without comment, enclosing instead a pair of tickets to one of his wife's concerts. Heinrich considered it the greatest insult of his professional life.

By this time the composer was looked upon in New York as the grand old man of American music, affectionately called "Father" Heinrich. He assisted at frequent concerts and was still writing at a prodigious rate, although much of this work remained unpublished. On April 21, 1853, a grand valedictory concert was held for Heinrich at Metropolitan Hall, honoring him before he was supposed to leave on another voyage to Europe. The program consisted primarily of Heinrich's own compositions, beginning with *The Wildwood Troubadour, a Musical Autobiography*, an overture in four parts representing the "Genius of Harmony slumbering in the forest shades of

America." Then came *The New England Feast of Shells*, which its creator called a "Divertimento Pastorale Oceanico." The piece, combining in Heinrich's special way the commonplace and the exotic, depicted nymphs departing for a maritime festival, mermaids frolicking in the ocean surf (off the coast of New England!), and a romantic love feast, more prosaically known as a clam bake. A quintet from Heinrich's *The Pilgrim Fathers* was included on the second part of the concert, and the affair closed with the concluding section of his *The Tower of Babel*, in which "the dispersion" was represented by "a gradual cessation of melodies and consecutive retirement of each individual performer."

The composer's anticipated departure for Europe, however, was delayed for over three years, while the septuagenarian painstakingly collected the essential funds. He rewrote and rearranged a number of his orchestral scores in the hope of hearing them performed abroad. Sometime late in 1856 the musician reached Prague, remaining there for an entire year. He seemed to arouse considerable interest among his former countrymen, who found both his personality and his life in America intriguing. Several of his major compositions were performed in Bohemia and received with widespread enthusiasm. Heinrich spent the spring of 1858 in Dresden, but by April, 1859, he had returned to Prague, where he continued to enjoy a moment of personal glory. He was back in New York in October, penniless and in extremely bad health. Although the illness lingered for several months, the composer lived to celebrate his eightieth birthday. He died two months later, on May 3, 1861.

There seems little question that Heinrich's enthusiasm for music far outdistanced his capabilities. Simple and sincere by nature, the musician maintained until the end a childlike optimism regarding his own creative capacity that those around him found endearing. Progressive in viewpoint, willing to attempt almost anything, the erratic Heinrich represents in his work a curious combination of the old world and the new, the formal and the vernacular, the grandiose and the bucolic. His compositions were certainly every bit as mercurial as his personality—crude, frequently deficient in technique, yet containing a refreshing spark of originality and at times remarkable refinement. The composer himself once characterized his music as "full of strange ideal somersets and capriccios," while the conservative John S. Dwight found these works "bewildering...wild and complicated."

Undoubtedly Heinrich's major limitation was his tendency to embellish his melodies to the point that the melodic line at times was practically lost. Most of his pieces would have benefited from vigorous pruning, for length, complexity, and repetition held an irresistible lure for him. Undisciplined and virtually untrained, he tended in his longer, more grandly conceived works to grow diffuse; his musical fabric was rarely closely knit, although his compositions came across most expressively in their slow movements. His harmonic skill showed definite limitations, and his melodies seldom rose above the conventional. His strength, on the other hand, was his sense of timing, his imagination in selecting appropriate material, and his ability to adapt that material to the mood he sought to express. His orchestrations, calling for an enlarged orchestra, were quite daring for the time, if habitually rough and clumsy. His instinct for orchestral coloring, nevertheless, demonstrated that Heinrich by temperament was best suited to writing for the orchestra.

The composer's primary significance in American music lies in his liberal handling of nationalistic material. "Although he made the eagle scream too loudly," Irving Lowens concludes, "he was our first, and by far the most enthusiastic, musical nationalist." His use of the Indian as a theme for orchestral works was truly pioneering, but he wrote *Indian Fanfares* for piano and later recommended its components—"The Comanche Revel," "The Sioux Galliarde," and "The Manitou Air Dance"—as quick-steps for military band. Most of Heinrich's orchestral music consists of descriptive tone poems in several rather pompously titled movements. Besides Indian and patriotic topics, he composed pieces treating the American landscape (like *The War of the Elements and the Thundering of Niagara*) and tributes to personal heroes (such as *Schiller, The Tomb of Genius: To the Memory of Mendelssohn-Bartholdy,* and *To the Spirit of Beethoven*). He consistently used foreign languages in names and descriptions of pieces based on American subjects, often confusing the tongues indiscriminately—for example, *Der Felsen von Plymouth, oder die Landung der Pilgrim Vater in Neu-England,* or the published *Storia d'un Violino of the Premier Violon to His Majesty Andrew the 1st, King of the Yankee Doodles.* Even his simpler titles—*Yankee Doodliad* and *The Columbiad,* for instance—were not without affectation.

When Heinrich died, he literally left trunks full of music, only a fraction of which had been performed. Eccentric though he may have been, the composer towered head and shoulders above his contemporaries. He had pondered American life from a variety of angles and was able to incorporate at least a portion of his New World experiences into his compositions. At the same time he remained very much a central European, desperately seeking the approval of his native countrymen. He managed to blend humble American subjects and a European grandiloquence of style into a musical composite that was uniquely his own. He could mingle simple dance tunes with elaborately chromatic melodies, classical harmonies with wildly modulating passages, producing an orchestral poetry as distinct as his own irregular disposition. Conventional though much of his work was, his imagination at times led him down unusual paths—requiring in his orchestration of *The Indian War Council,* for example, the glass harmonica invented by Benjamin Franklin. He was at the same moment a voice of the future and a profile of his own age, with his music uncomfortably caught between. "Himself of the time of Berlioz," William Upton maintains, "he wrote for the technical equipment of that impetuous French composer, and when the passing decades had finally met these extravagant technical demands, the ideas themselves were outmoded—the world had passed them by."

A few days before the grand valedictory concert was held honoring Heinrich in 1853, the New York critic William Henry Fry lamented that the public knew practically nothing about the merits of Heinrich's music. Such ignorance was understandable, Fry insisted, for "a composer in this country may as well burn his compositions for any opportunity he has for making himself heard. Our Opera Houses and Musical Societies are worse than useless so far [as] they foster American Art, that art which elevates artists here above the level of provincial beggars." Being a serious composer himself, Fry knew well the dilemma of the American artist in the early nineteenth century, and for over ten years he used his podium as critic to wage a militant crusade in behalf of the American musician.

William Henry Fry was born in Philadelphia on August 10, 1813, the year that Anton Heinrich and his young wife left for their visit to Bohemia. Fry's father, a man of some means, established the Philadelphia *National Gazette* in 1820 and provided his three sons with a cultivated domestic atmosphere, stimulating in them an interest in politics, a love of great literature, and a deep appreciation for music. Tradition has it that William Henry began writing orchestral overtures at the age of fourteen. When the French Opera Company from New Orleans performed in Philadelphia in 1827, young Fry was most impressed, and after he heard a season of Italian opera given by the Montressor Company in 1833, he vowed to become a composer of operas himself. He studied music with local teachers, most notably Leopold Meignen, and as a youth worked on his father's newspaper, covering theater, music, and art. He graduated from the University of Pennsylvania in 1830, stayed on for graduate work, and eventually was admitted to the bar.

Music, however, remained his absorbing interest, opera especially. An overture by Fry, written when he was twenty, was performed by the Philadelphia Philharmonic Society, and with the reorganization of that society in 1836, the young composer became its secretary. Two years later, he attempted to write an opera, *Christians and Pagans*, but never finished it. Early in 1840 the Fry brothers began preparing for a Philadelphia production of Bellini's *Norma*, to be given in English. Joseph Fry adapted the text, Edward served as general manager, and William Henry supervised the music. The first of some dozen performances took place on January 11, 1841, at the Chestnut Street Theater. Within a few months William Henry completed an opera of his own, *Aurelia the Vestal*, bearing marked similarities to *Norma* both in musical technique and dramatic situation. Although *Aurelia the Vestal* was not produced, Fry immediately embarked on a second opera, *Leonora*, finished in 1845.

Based on Bulwer-Lytton's perennial melodrama *The Lady of Lyons*, *Leonora* was the first grand opera by a native American composer to receive a public staging and, therefore, stands as Fry's most renowned work. The libretto was adapted by the composer's brother, Joseph, while the work's musical line continued to bear definite resemblances to Bellini. The opera was first staged, in English, by the Sequin opera troupe on June 4, 1845, at the Chestnut Street Theater. The production, paid for by Fry himself, was a lavish one, with elaborate sets and costumes, an orchestra of sixty, and a chorus of eighty. The leading roles were taken by Arthur and Anna Sequin, well known singers from England. The work was generously received and enjoyed a successful run of twelve performances. "*Leonora* improves with each subsequent repetition," claimed the Philadelphia *Public Ledger* on June 12, 1845, "and is now universally pronounced the most brilliant spectacle of the opera kind ever afforded in this city."

While the drama was set in Spain during the time of the early American conquests, the music was quite comfortably Italian. The score contained a long overture, the usual ornate arias, a number of effective choruses and ensembles, long recitatives not always advancing the drama, much vigorous orchestral writing, and a melodramatic climax. Fry's love of melody is evident throughout, and his music is always singable, if not strikingly original. *Leonora*'s major weaknesses are its length, the constant repetition, an overabundance of coloratura, a monotonous use of melodies cast in the same mold, and a tendency to fragment these melodies into metrical parts. It is evident that *Norma* still loomed large in Fry's mind, although there are touches of Rossini and passages strongly reminiscent of Donizetti.

Fry left Philadelphia early in 1849 for travel in Europe and to spend three years in Paris as foreign correspondent for the New York *Tribune* and the Philadelphia *Public Ledger*. He loved Paris from the start, continually referring to her as "that great center of beauty, art, and bold thinking." He enjoyed a great deal of music there, attended the premiere of Meyerbeer's *Le Prophete*, and heard Jenny Lind and Henriette Sontag sing, before either had appeared in the United States. Gregarious and an excellent conversationalist, Fry delighted in the outdoor cafes and constantly remarked upon the courtesy of the French people. The behavior of his fellow countrymen abroad he found less admirable, often pronouncing them oafish and coarse. He was greatly disappointed in the American showing at the London Exposition of 1851, feeling that our national reputation suffered a serious blow. "The exposition is judged by looks," Fry wrote. "It simply exposes exteriors, and the most splendid and artistic carry the day—and we do not." This was merely a reflection, the journalist felt, of America's general lack of artistic awareness.

He returned to the United States in 1852 as music editor of the New York *Tribune*, determined to teach his public to recognize and appreciate the best in art and music. He assumed his post as music critic—the first music critic of an American daily—ready to fight for the United States' musical independence from Europe. No sooner had he arrived in New York than he launched a series of ten illustrated lectures on the history and language of music. Delivered in Metropolitan Hall on successive Tuesdays, beginning November 30, Fry's lectures were unlike anything attempted before in this country. Assisting him were the Philharmonic orchestra and the Harmonic Society chorus, both under the leadership of George F. Bristow, and soloists from the Italian Opera Company, then performing in New York. These artists were assembled solely to illustrate, musically, points made by the speaker. Tickets for the course sold for five dollars, and although three thousand people are reported to have attended the final lecture, Fry still lost a great deal of money, something approaching four thousand dollars.

In his final lecture the composer-critic presented his ideas on native American music. His position was that American music should not remain subservient to foreign influence, following instead its own path, in whatever direction that might lead. By dauntlessly adhering to their own course Americans should eventually achieve an individuality in music consistent with their national ideals. As Fry himself said:

> Until this Declaration of Independence in Art shall be made—until American composers shall discard their foreign liveries and found an American School—and until the American public shall learn to support American artists, Art will not become indigenous to this country, but will only exist as a feeble exotic, and we shall continue to be provincial in Art. The American composer should not allow the name of Beethoven, or Handel, or Mozart to prove an eternal bugbear to him, nor should he pay them reverence; he should only reverence his Art, and strike out manfully and independently into untrodden realms, just as his nature and inspirations may invite him, else he can never achieve lasting renown.

The nation's musical societies should allot a portion of their rehearsal time to American compositions, performing the best of these in public. "I am always told that we are new," Fry objected. New York "is now twice as large and indefinitely richer than any Italian city was when Haydn and Mozart went there to perfect their art." Why should the United States lag behind in music, except for public apathy? In this country, the critic insisted, the politicians reap all the applause, while American musicians are ignored.

By the time Fry delivered his New York lectures, the musical life of the United States had come increasingly under the domination of foreigners, particularly the Germans. Following the revolution of 1848 the flood of immigration from central Europe swelled, as refugees sought political asylum and better labor conditions. The immigrants came, many of them with musical backgrounds, at a time when Americans were beginning to taste serious self-doubt. The post-Revolutionary confidence that an American art was in the making had been eclipsed by an attitude of condescension toward native efforts. Considering themselves especially limited in music, Americans were willing, even eager, to allow the German immigrants to assume the direction of the nation's formal music, since their artistry was clearly superior. By 1860 the *Journal of Commerce* counted nearly thirty German musical societies in New York alone, and a *Saengerbund* had been formed in practically every major city. Most of the nation's music teachers, conductors, and instrumentalists were German. The Philharmonic Society of New York was essentially a German orchestra, and the situation was similar with chamber groups throughout the country. If American musicians took themselves at all seriously, they hurried to Leipzig or Berlin to study in the shadow of the German masters. While Americans basically considered their native talents in music to extend little beyond hymns and minstrel tunes, the country's art music escheated into the Teutonic domain.

Fry hoped that his 1852-53 lecture series would set off the powder keg of revolution, and through his writing for the New York *Tribune* he continued his resolute Young America stance. Yet for Fry musical independence was not so much pursuing a new line of development as it was breaking away from the German mold. Certainly he did not exhibit in his own compositions the freedom he idealized in theory, indentured as he was to Bellini and Donizetti. To Fry the center of the musical world was Italy, and what he really seemed to want for America was the substitution of Italian influences for the German. Pugnacious nationalist though he might appear in rhetoric, his musical expressions remained firmly Italianate.

During his sojourn in Paris Fry had valiantly attempted to convince the Paris Opera to stage his *Leonora*, even offering to pay for the production himself. To add insult to injury, he was told by the director, "In Europe we look upon America as an industrial country—excellent for electric telegraphs, but not for art. . . . They would think me crazy to produce an opera by an American." Six years after returning home, Fry succeeded in getting his opera revived by an Italian company at the Academy of Music in New York. The score was considerably reworked, and the libretto was translated into Italian, since the singers knew only a little English. The first of two performances was mounted on March 29, 1858, and received mixed reactions from the critics. The *Express* found the opera "full of delicious, sweet music," but felt it constantly recalled *Norma* and *Sonnambula*. The *Times* confirmed the derivative nature of Fry's music, but insisted that Beethoven had not been altogether original in his first symphony. Several suggestions were made that Fry had used his prestige as music editor of the New York *Tribune* to secure a staging for his opera, which otherwise would have remained obscure. This second version of *Leonora*, however, shows a refinement of Fry's style, and the changes attest that the composer's musicianship had clearly advanced over the past thirteen years.

While opera was always Fry's first love, he also demonstrated a fondness for orchestral and choral writing. He wrote four tone poems, each based on a detailed program—*Childe Harold*, *The Breaking Heart*, *A Day in the Country*, and, probably the best, *Santa Claus: Christmas Symphony*. All four were performed several times by Jullien on his 1853-54 tour of the United States; the opportunistic Frenchman had realized that playing music by American composers was an effective way of gaining an audience. As a foreigner Jullien could conduct American works with greater popular success than the same renditions by domestic orchestras could achieve. Fry's reputation as a critic made his compositions a logical choice, and Jullien was undoubtedly aware of this. The imitation of snow storms, trotting horses, sleigh bells, and cracking whips in the *Santa Claus* symphony would also have appealed to the conductor's theatrical nature. Fry's fellow critics were less enthusiastic, however, and Richard Storrs Willis dismissed the piece in a few lines, finding it unworthy of serious comment. To Willis it was no more than a seasonal extravaganza that "moves the audience to laughter." Infuriated, Fry responded with a twenty-five page letter, arguing that *Santa Claus* was the longest orchestral work on a single subject written by an American and therefore deserved an extended review.

The conflict with Willis heightened over the years, with Willis referring to Fry in 1854 as a "splendid frigate at sea without a helm." When the composer published his Eleventh Quartet, Willis declared: "Fry is a bundle of genius and waywardness. He does not know himself whether he likes better to do the brilliant and clever thing, or the wayward and eccentric thing." John Sullivan Dwight, who opposed Fry's contention that American music must free itself from German influences, tended to second Willis' reservations, observing after Fry's lectures in 1853, "I should like him but disagree with him."

The decade of the 1850s proved the busiest of Fry's career, as he was heavily involved in newspaper work, lecturing, and composing. Aside from the revision on *Leonora*, he wrote a *Crystal Palace Ode*, performed in 1854 as part of the dedication ceremonies for the Crystal Palace in New York, and his only complete oratorio, *Stabat Mater*, probably Fry's most outstanding work besides his operas. He began another oratorio, *Moses in Egypt*, but left it unfinished. His work during this period reveals his prevailing tendency toward overelaboration. He seemed always to think in grandiose terms, writing large scale compositions for orchestra and chorus and showing practically no interest in songs or simple piano pieces. His biographer, Upton, suggests that he might almost be considered an American Berlioz. Not all contemporary critics disagreed with Fry, and some looked upon him as a dynamic pioneer, as well as national champion. A *Dispatch* article in 1861 stated: "Liszt, Wagner, Berlioz, and Fry have all created much and envenomed discussion on account of their peculiar views, scorn of established customs, and contempt for the well-worn paths of science. And why? Because innovations are always the longest in being understood, and old ears are like old dogs, and cannot (soon) be taught new tricks."

During the presidential campaign of 1860 Fry's political interests burst forth in unbridled enthusiasm for Lincoln, to the extent that he entered into a stumping tour on behalf of the Republican candidate. Never robust, the journalist overtaxed his strength in electioneering, with the result that his normally fragile health deteriorated. Tuberculosis soon developed, from which he never recovered. For four years he carried on his combined work as critic and composer, but only with considerable physical anguish. Toward the end, when illness prevented his attending opera performances he particularly wanted to hear, the invalid supposedly eased his disappointment by propping himself up in bed with the score, surrounded by photographs and sketches of the singers performing that evening.

Fry wrote two significant overtures in the early 1860s—to *Evangeline*, concluded on March 16, 1860, and the *Overture to Macbeth*, dated June 22, 1862. The latter, slightly reminiscent of Auber, represents perhaps the composer's best orchestral writing and is certainly one of his freshest, most spontaneous and finely scored pieces. His major work during this period, however, was another opera, *Notre Dame of Paris*, finished in 1863. The libretto, again written by Joseph Fry, was a four act adaptation of the Victor Hugo novel. Despite failing health, the composer wrote the music, all except the last scene, in thirty days. His melodies were now simpler and more direct, while a greater use of altered chords produced deeper harmonic richness. Dramatically Fry seemed to be developing toward a more impassioned realism—as, for instance, in his expression of the anger of the crowd in the first act.

The opera was elaborately staged at the Academy of Music in Philadelphia on May 4, 1864, as part of a musical festival held for the benefit of the United States Sanitary Commission, a Civil War equivalent of the Red Cross. Apparently no expense was spared on sets and costumes for the production, which included an orchestra of sixty, a military band of thirty, a chorus of one hundred, and a ballet of one hundred and fifty. At the height of the spectacle nearly three hundred people were massed on stage. It was conducted by twenty-eight year-old Theodore Thomas.

The premiere of *Notre Dame of Paris* aroused far more excitement than *Leonora* had some two decades before. "New York may for once envy Philadelphia," the New York *World* conceded. "A large number of artists, journalists, amateurs and amusement hunters are going to cross Jersey for the purpose of witnessing the production of a work which excites the greatest interest in musical circles throughout the country." After seven performances in Philadelphia the opera was taken to New York for a brief run.

Six months later, Fry left the United States for an indefinite visit of the West Indies, hoping to restore his health. The journey, urged upon him by friends and relatives, proved in vain, for the musician died in Santa Cruz on December 21, 1864. His last composition, *Mass in E Flat*, was completed just nine days before his death.

Fry was probably more gifted as a journalist than as a composer, and in all likelihood his greatest contribution to American music was his eloquent support of its independent development. He had returned from Europe in 1852 angry and bitter about the low regard shown the American artist at home and abroad. Over the next decade he persisted as the most articulate champion of the native composer—even attacking the New York Philharmonic for not performing American works. Aggressive, egotistical, opinionated, and on occasions as narrow in viewpoint as his adversaries, Fry nevertheless emerged as a magnetic personality, a skillful, broadly erudite critic, and an effective, if at times quixotic, spokesman for the American artist.

But his worth as a composer cannot be denied, especially when his works are viewed in historical perspective and in the social context in which they were written. Fry, to be sure, was a gentleman amateur whose mastery of technique generally exceeded his inspiration and genius. "If...we should fuse our mental pictures of Fry and his music into a single composite scene," Upton suggests, "it would certainly disclose high ambition, endless energy, technical mastery of many media, and ever increasing success in merging music and mood." He wrote prolifically and with notorious rapidity, although customarily with meticulous care. While his work is never great, his best rises beyond mediocrity and contains elements of distinction. Unlike his Russian contemporary Glinka, Fry ignored his country's folk tunes in his effort to create an indigenous music and rarely drew upon native legends or local history for his material, preferring to base his compositions on European themes. In subject matter at least Fry was less American than Heinrich, and while the earlier composer's style was oriented toward central Europe, Fry's leaned toward Italy and occasionally France. Fry may neither have written enduring music for the ages nor achieved the heights of his own ideals, but his mark on his own generation was nevertheless an indelible one.

Among those strongly influenced by Fry's credo was George Frederick Bristow, who had conducted the orchestra and chorus that had been engaged to illustrate the senior composer's famous lecture series. Twelve years Fry's junior, Bristow was born on December 19, 1825, in Brooklyn. His father, a native of Kent, England, had settled in New York about a year earlier, working for a time as a singing master and later serving as organist of St. Patrick's Cathedral. At age five George began music lessons, and at eleven he was playing the violin in the orchestra of the Olympic Theater. By the time he was fourteen he had published his first composition. When the New York Philharmonic Society was founded in 1842, Bristow became one of the original violinists and remained a member of that organization for nearly forty years. His first overture was performed by the orchestra at a public rehearsal, but never at a regular concert. Later he became one of the first Americans to have his music included on a New York Philharmonic program, and his Symphony in D Minor was played by the group in 1856, when Jullien visited as guest conductor.

Bristow was a more formally trained musician than Fry and more professionally experienced. He was a member of the orchestra that accompanied Jenny Lind during her initial American concerts and had played with Jullien's orchestra in 1853-54. In personality Fry and Bristow were almost totally different. Whereas Fry was forceful, Bristow was basically timid; Fry vain, Bristow modest; Fry flamboyant and learned, Bristow slow and plodding. Yet the two stand together as the major serious composers of their time, writing both symphonic works and opera. In craftsmanship there is a solidity in the best of Bristow's compositions that Fry never achieved; the greater dramatic sense, on the other hand, belonged to Fry.

Certainly Bristow was a no less dedicated fighter for the recognition of the American composer than Fry. W. J. Henderson described him as "a most earnest man, filled with real love for his art, and self-sacrificing in labor for its benefit; one of the earliest of the long-suffering band of American composers, who will be remembered always as one who strove to push American music into artistic prominence." When Bristow became director of the Harmonic Society in 1851, he did everything he could to present the works of American musicians, although they were not readily available. From 1854 until his death in 1898, he was a supervising teacher in the New York public school system, striving to lay the foundation of a music education program.

After writing several orchestral pieces, Bristow produced his most noted work in 1855, the opera *Rip Van Winkle*—the first American opera based on a native subject. The work was given its premiere at Niblo's Garden by the Payne and Harrison Opera Company, September 27, 1855, and was repeated sixteen times during the next month. Audiences were vastly enthusiastic, and William Henry Fry elated: "As it is by an American who depends on the verdict of his countrymen—there being no ready made opinion from Europe to be adopted parrot like, we have great pleasure in stating that Mr. Bristow's debut as a dramatic composer was equally successful with those of the established composers of Europe." While most of the critics praised the orchestration and staging, many of them complained of the opera's extreme length, its monotony of style, and the excessive use of solo rather than ensemble numbers. "The music," according to R. O. Mason, "was bright and taking, though not always in perfect keeping with the quaint old-time subject, and the orchestration was excellent."

Rip Van Winkle's libretto, by Jonathan Howard Wainwright, took certain liberties with the Washington Irving story, interjecting episodes from the American Revolution and a love affair between Rip's daughter Alice and a British officer. This revision provided Bristow with the opportunity for love duets, marches, and soldiers' choruses, sung by both the Continental and British troops. The opera was less derivative from the Italian than Fry's *Leonora*, although it was reported to be almost completely lacking in dramatic force. Bristow proved severely limited both in expressing a variety of emotions and developing musical characterization. At the same time *Rip Van Winkle* reveals the composer's solid grounding in contemporary German instrumental music and his technical proficiency.

Compared with other current theatrical attractions in New York, Bristow's opera did rather well at the box office, largely because it was a novelty. A week after its premiere *Rip Van Winkle* drew $700 in one night at Niblo's, whereas the Italian opera at the Academy of Music produced only $600. Wood's Minstrels and Buckley's Serenaders that same evening took in $300 and $250 respectively, although straight drama at the Metropolitan Theatre attracted receipts of $4500. *Rip Van Winkle* was revived at the Academy of Music in Philadelphia in 1870 and given in concert form in New York in 1898.

Bristow's first oratorio, *Praise to God*, was initially performed at Irving Hall by the New York Harmonic Society, March 2, 1861. His *Columbus* Overture was played by the Philharmonic Society in Steinway Hall five years later, and *Daniel*, Bristow's second oratorio, was heard there in 1867—performed by the Mendelssohn Union, with Parepa-Rosa as soloist and conducted by the composer. Altogether he wrote six symphonies, in an essentially polished style suggestive of Mendelssohn; as well as two string quartets. One of the symphonies, the *Arcadian* Symphony, attempted to utilize an American Indian melody, while his two cantatas, *The Great Republic* (1879) and *Niagara* (1898), both reflect Bristow's interest in native material. At the time of his death, December 13, 1898, Bristow was working on another opera, *Columbus*. Although less public in his testimony, Bristow remained as determined as Fry in his opposition to the German influence on American music. He once commented that by performing practically no native compositions the Philharmonic Society had "been as anti-American as if it had been located in London during the Revolutionary War."

Bristow was a less inspired composer than Fry, but a far more scholarly one. While neither his musical conceptions nor their executions were impressively original, his technical command was assured. His works were carefully constructed and then painstakingly revised for maximum precision. Undoubtedly the strongest feature of Bristow's music was his penetrating sense of harmonic color, which added a richness to American music heretofore unknown. What was lacking was spontaneity, a sustained emotional appeal, and a convincing embodiment of the life experience.

By the time of Bristow and Fry American art music had fundamentally lost contact with the realities of the social and cultural matrix supporting it. The techniques and apparatus of European serious music had been transported to the United States with some success, but the spiritual essence was missing. Native composers largely attempted to write American music, employing European tools and methods, without taking into account the substance of the American experience. They composed from European models, mastered European rules, but isolated their works from the vernacular spirit that might have injected them with the vitality to endure. When superimposed upon an incongruous American social structure, European formulas for art generally resulted in sterility, since the organic bonds were so slight between creativity and the existence from which these efforts nominally sprang.

Reinagle, to be sure, looked to the European masters for inspiration, but his formative years had been spent in Europe, where he became saturated with the musical traditions then in vogue. His reliance on Old World patterns was therefore more plausible, more natural, than for later American composers who had glimpsed only the surface of European culture—and that frequently secondhand. Then, too, Reinagle composed his serious works for an elite eastern seaboard audience whose artistic link with Europe was still quite pronounced. When he wrote for the theater, he was flexible enough to adapt his music to the momentary needs, although he was most often composing for plays, ballad operas, and pantomimes that looked to the Old World rather than America for inspiration. His European approaches here again were consistent with the design of his work, as well as with the musical tastes of his public.

Although Heinrich's central European orientation was unending, he experienced American life far more broadly than Reinagle. Through his concerts he knew the cultivated circles of the east coast, and his years in Kentucky and western Pennsylvania had taught him something of the frontier. While he might have liked to compose in a traditional manner and often harked back to the more grandiose European forms, his musical training was such that innovation, within his limited context, was frequently necessary. His works therefore became a singular composite of the cultures of central Europe, of homespun America magnified to epic proportions, of faltering eastern gentility, and of the special idiosyncrasies of Heinrich's unique personality.

With Fry and Bristow the individual element was meager, as human warmth was subordinated to mechanical proficiency. Both had studied music formally, learned their lessons adequately, and in Bristow's case particularly, acquired a rigorous sense of discipline. But in each case the composer's own experience remained noticeably outside his music. Fry approached his work from the vantage point of the critic—well versed in rules, abounding in theory. He attempted to bring to his compositions the musical skills he had studied as a youth and apply them to the cosmopolitan themes he admired as an adult. Despite pleas to the contrary, his music was not notably American, in large measure because it was not notably Fry. Although more native in his choice of subjects, Bristow was even more academic in his methods. A scholar by nature, Bristow looked at music through the eyes of a technician, as something separate from human feelings and mortal drama.

For Fry and Bristow writing music was to pen a set of ideals, rather than draw from the heart of life around them. Their works consequently stress the grandiose, often resulting in a hollow, artificial sound. The composers' select positions as critic and professional musician and teacher isolated them to an extent from the mainstream, much as Washington Irving and James Fenimore Cooper, for different reasons, had been isolated earlier. The dimension of American life was beyond their grasp, as was their ability to express the broad vernacular in terms of art.

While the literary figure could operate independently, exploring the reaches of the human existence in his search for meaning and modes of expression, the musician was more limited by structure, more closely tied to the established order. For the composer a mastery of instruments and a technical confidence were essential before the creative processes could flower. Then there was the problem of getting compositions before the public, a difficult chore indeed when symphony orchestras and opera companies were involved. Finally, the musician was dependent upon critical acclaim if his work was to gain a lasting reputation. Should composers' conceptions and creative integrity prove too advanced for the public, too at odds with the general taste, their compositions were likely to be shelved after an incidental hearing.

With the election of Jefferson in 1800, the leveling influences of the frontier began to temper the aristocratic facets of Federalist America. By the 1830s the country's enthusiasm for Jacksonian democracy was sharply undermining the presence of a defined cultural elite. While the impulse toward equality favored a keener interest in popular and folk music, it was at variance with the development of a native art music. In the late eighteenth century serious compositions could emerge now and then from the restricted concert life of the eastern seaboard, or from the more advanced singing schools; but the equalitarian ideals championed by Jackson and his supporters minimized the select social stratum on which art music has traditionally depended. With the social elite narrowing and an intellectual class still in its formative stages, the audience for an American art music was slender indeed. As Alexis de Tocqueville was soon to observe, the democratic spirit that might prove so admirable and beneficial in politics offered severe limitations to the growth of art—reducing American life to a common denominator, diluting its sense of excellence in the process, and further separating the artist from his society.

CHAPTER

IX

Louis Moreau
Gottschalk

By far the most remarkable art composer of early nineteenth-century America was Louis Moreau Gottschalk, who convincingly blended the European romantic tradition with characteristics of the black and Creole cultures he had experienced as a child. Less ambitious than either Fry or Bristow in the scope of his music, Gottschalk was the more successful in part because of his basic simplicity and directness of approach. His work possessed the individuality his New York contemporaries lacked, along with a spontaneity, a verve and excitement, and a special charm that drew listeners inside the music itself. At a time when the artistic climate of the United States, particularly for the musician, bordered on impotence, Gottschalk was fortunate in two regards: he possessed a personal genius and the affluence to cultivate it, and he was born and raised in New Orleans, antebellum America's most musical city.

The composer's father, Edward Gottschalk, was an English Jew, a native of London and a gentleman of considerable cultural dimension. He had studied medicine for two years in Leipzig, then at twenty-five years of age emigrated to New Orleans, where he became a successful broker and clothing store operator. Sophisticated, handsome, and prosperous, in the early 1820s Edward was admitted into the best of Creole society, entertained by the city's most aristocratic French and Spanish families.

In this inner social circle he met and fell in love with Aimee Marie de Brusle, a young Creole girl of extraordinary poise and beauty. She was the daughter of a titled French family that had fled to Louisiana during the slave rebellion on Santo Domingo. For twenty-five years her father had owned and managed the bakery that supplied the French Quarter of New Orleans with bread. Aimee was thirteen years younger than Edward, intelligent, musically talented, and imbued with exalted notions of greatness. The couple were married in St. Louis Cathedral on May 26, 1828.

The Gottschalks promptly identified themselves with the Protestants in the American section of the city, and within slightly less than a year, May 8, 1829, their first son was born. He was named Louis Moreau, after a maternal uncle, and called Moreau by his family. The boy inherited his mother's blue eyes and winning smile, his father's hair coloring and facial features, and even as a child was incredibly good looking. His family atmosphere was generously furnished with taste and finery and prepared him well for the cosmopolitan life he was to lead. While his father remained an English gentleman in speech, manners, and dress, he possessed a fluent command of Spanish and German, and the family generally spoke French at home. The boy grew up listening to his mother's singing and piano playing, and at age two was noticed patting his hands and swaying to the rhythm of her playing. A short time later she discovered him standing at her side, watching her hands as they moved over the keys.

One afternoon Aimee Gottschalk spent a couple of hours at the piano learning an aria from Meyerbeer's recent opera *Robert le Diable*. Her young son—so the story goes—stood fixed by her side. When she grew tired, she went into an adjoining parlor to take care of some mending. In a few minutes she heard someone playing the aria from *Robert le Diable*, exactly as she had been singing it. She dropped her sewing and went to the parlor door. There she found her son standing at the keyboard, playing the tune with his right hand. From this moment on little Moreau—barely four years old—was recognized throughout New Orleans as a child prodigy.

Within a year his parents decided he must have lessons. Francois Letellier, who had come from Paris five years before, was selected as the boy's teacher. Letellier, besides offering instruction in singing, piano, and organ, had sung minor roles at the *Theatre d'Orleans* and was director of music at St. Louis Cathedral. But never before had he encountered a talent quite like Moreau Gottschalk's. In practically no time Letellier was boasting that the boy could sight read any piece of music placed before him and play it on the piano.

When Moreau was seven and a half, he was supposedly sitting in the Cathedral with his grandmother Brusle one Sunday, waiting for the celebration of high Mass. Suddenly an usher appeared and told him that Monsieur Letellier wanted to see him immediately in the choir loft. As he approached his teacher, he observed Letellier's worried expression. The teacher informed his pupil that he had just learned that his bass soloist would not be able to sing that day. He would have to take the part himself, and Moreau would have to play the organ. While his teacher manipulated the pedals, the boy sight read the Mass, so creditably it was said that only those in the choir loft realized that Monsieur Letellier was not at the organ as usual.

That same year Moreau's parents took him to the St. Charles Theatre to hear his first opera. The work was Bellini's *Il Pirata*, being staged by the Montressor troupe for the first time in America. Although he had little idea of the story being sung on stage in Italian, the child was enthralled with Bellini's romantic music. As the final curtain fell, he expressed impatience to get home. Once there he ran to the piano and began pouring out the *Pirata* melodies, repeating those he especially liked over and over again, until his father finally sent him to bed. Later, at the *Theatre d'Orleans* the boy heard *Robert le Diable*, recalling as an adult, "This beautiful creation of Meyerbeer's colored my whole childhood." He also heard *Norma*, retaining the score vividly in his memory.

But Moreau's musical exposure in New Orleans was not limited to the refined forms. In the streets he heard vendors singing as they peddled their wares, and at home—in the garden—he would imitate the sounds from the streets. Sunday afternoons found him climbing up to the third floor gallery of the house to listen to the beat of the drums coming from Place Congo, a few blocks away. During these years the city's slaves were permitted to congregate in Place Congo on this one day of the week, generally under police supervision, for dancing and merriment. At other times the square served as a drill field for the local unit of the Louisiana militia, but the slaves were allowed to gather there on Sundays from noon until sundown. Much of the dancing was a remnant of a voodoo cult originating in Africa, in which ritualistic body movements were employed to induce "possession" by supernatural spirits. Drums made from hollow logs, covered with skin at one end and open at the other, were the principal instruments that provided the rhythm for the dancers. As the beats grew louder and faster, the blacks would break into impassioned shouts. Moreau Gottschalk, from the third floor of his home, would follow the rhythm, marching and dancing and repeating, when he could, snatches of melody.

By the time the boy was eleven Monsieur Letellier declared there was nothing more he could teach his precocious student. He must be sent to Paris to further his musical education. The lad was also studying violin with Felix Miolan, concertmaster of the *Theatre d'Orleans*, but it was decided that advanced work in Paris would be essential in the near future. On April 23, 1841, young Gottschalk gave a concert assisted by several adult musicians, and during the next year he participated in a number of musical soirees given by Creole society. After months of preparation the thirteen year-old youth sailed for Le Havre on May 17, 1842, aboard the *Taglioni*. The vessel, loaded with a cargo of cotton, hides, and ham, ordinarily carried no passengers, but Moreau was placed in the special custody of the ship's captain, George L. Rogers.

In Paris the boy came under the tutelage of his great aunt, the Marquise de la Grange. He was immediately taken to the Conservatoire, but was turned away without a hearing when the director discovered that Moreau had never before been outside the United States. The lad was then interviewed by Charles Halle, a young pianist from Westphalia, who agreed to teach the boy after hearing him play a single piece. Halle, however, wanted Gottschalk to practice Bach and Beethoven, and for a youngster raised in a city strong in the French and Italian operatic tradition this was a fairly heavy assignment. Impressed as Moreau might be with the music of the German composers, he was unaccustomed to their style and felt ill at ease playing their works. Within a short time Monsieur Halle informed his pupil that henceforth his teacher would be Camille Stamaty, a pianist known to lean more heavily toward the purely romantic school. Another of Stamaty's students, whom Gottschalk came to know, was the seven year-old prodigy Camille Saint-Saens. Later Moreau began studying harmony and composition with Pierre Maleden.

Meanwhile, through the connections of his great aunt, the boy's way was paved into the salons of the Parisian social circle. His aunt's aristocratic friends were enchanted both by Moreau's personal charm and his keyboard magic. By April, 1845, Stamaty announced that his pupil was ready for a private debut, to be held in Pleyel Hall. The principal selection on the program was Chopin's Concerto in E Minor, although the young pianist also performed Liszt's fantasy on Meyerbeer's *Robert le Diable* and Thalberg's transcription of arias from Rossini's *Semiramide*. Present in the audience was the great Chopin himself, who came backstage when the concert was over to congratulate the boy on his interpretation. Taking Moreau by the hand, the composer prophesied that he would one day be a great virtuoso.

Young Gottschalk also learned in Paris the gentlemanly graces—riding, fencing, as well as the Greek, Latin, and modern classics. By the time he was eighteen he had reached his full physical height, approximately five feet eight inches. He was slender, possessing delicate, yet manly features, a melancholy expression, and droopy, romantic eyelids. In dress, manners, and speech he was an aristocrat, little suggesting his provincial background.

Shortly before the Revolution of 1848 Moreau's mother and younger brothers and sisters came to France for an extended visit. With the outbreak of hostilities in Paris the family hastened to a village some forty miles north of the city. There Gottschalk wrote two of his earliest compositions, *La Bamboula* and *La Savanne*. Both were piano pieces, the first based on the dance rhythms he had heard as a boy from Place Congo, the second drawn from Creole folk music he had grown up with in New Orleans. Exhilarated by his work, the youth grew anxious to return to Paris to play his compositions for his aunt's friends. It was not safe to do so, however, until October.

His pieces received their first salon hearing early the next month at one of Madame Merlin's soirees. Moreau played *La Savanne* first, and it was applauded warmly by the guests. Then he played *La Bamboula*, and his listeners went wild with excitement. After a ten minute ovation the composer explained the origin of each selection and played both again. Soon invitations to perform his music for social gatherings poured in from all over the city. At one of these later gatherings Gottschalk played his pieces for the distinguished Victor Hugo, who was enthralled, as were sophisticated Parisians generally, with the music's exotic quality and rhythmic bravura.

Early in 1849 the young American composer signed a contract granting Leon and Maris Escudier exclusive rights to publish his works. Included in the publishers' list of composers were such names as Hector Berlioz and Giuseppe Verdi. A few days after negotiating the contract the Escudier brothers began publicizing Moreau's professional Paris debut. The concert was scheduled for April 17, 1849, again held in Salle Pleyel. All twelve hundred seats were sold a week in advance, while on the evening of the concert the hall was laden with flowers. The audience was an aristocratic one and included the now fourteen year-old Saint-Saens and eleven year-old Georges Bizet. The climax of the affair came with the playing of *La Bamboula*, which was repeated on demand. The Parisian critics devoted special space in their columns to the concert, and all were highly enthusiastic, some even comparing Gottschalk favorably with Chopin.

The prodigy continued to compose, producing in 1850 the charming *Le Bananier*, based on a French Creole tune accompanied by a marchlike beat common in the music of the New Orleans blacks. Like its predecessors *Le Bananier* was played with great success in the salons of Paris and shortly came to be called "a pendant to *Bamboula*." The major similarity between the two works was that the rhythm in each case was derived from the American black. The Escudiers published the new piece, and its immediate popularity resulted in a substantial royalty payment. *Le Banjo*, written a year later, was another success. It opens with a banjo imitation reminiscent of Stephen Foster, while the coda particularly recalls "Camptown Races." The selection is full of ingenious strumming, radiates tremendous verve, and is definitely among Gottschalk's finest compositions.

Probably the most interesting feature of the teenage composer's work was his ability to combine effectively Creole and Afro-Caribbean elements, casting them in a romantic piano virtuoso setting that was acceptable to the Parisian socialites. His pieces glitter with a rhythmic bounce and a melodic brilliance, blending the commonplace with the sophisticated. As English-man Wilfrid Mellers says of *La Bamboula*, "the Latin flavour of the music is modified by a Yankee swagger; the dancer wears his straw hat at a rakish angle," like the black in a minstrel show. At a time well in advance of Dvorak, Grieg, Rimsky-Korsakov, and Sibelius, Gottschalk took the lead with Glinka in producing music of a decidedly nationalistic tenor. By joining Negro idioms with Creole folk melodies the pianist accomplished in polished form what Anton Dvorak nearly a half century later would severely criticize American musicians for not doing.

Yet Gottschalk's nationalism is stated in cosmopolitan terms, the ornamental elaborations fitting comfortably into the climate of European romanticism with which the composer associated himself. Enveloping his American folk characteristics was a personalized expression of the romantic spirit, ranging in mood through the course of his compositions from Lisztian grandeur to Chopinesque morbidity. The pianist not only balanced a New World color and an Old World grace, but intimately phrased the union in terms of his own infectious charm. In the process he lifted humble slave rhythms and provincial folk tunes to a patrician level, at the same time manifesting a nostalgia for qualities the urbane man had lost. Unlike Chopin's mazurkas, which become internalized poetic commentaries on Polish folk material, Gottschalk's pieces are extroverted recreations for piano of the original energy of their prototypes, full of action and the composer's self-confidence.

In a review of one of Gottschalk's concerts in 1851, Berlioz wrote that "everybody in Europe now knows *Bamboula*, *Le Bananier*, *Le Mancenillier*, *La Savanne*, and twenty other ingenious fantasies in which the nonchalant grace of tropical melody assuage so agreeably our restless and insatiable passion for novelty." Of the American composer's ability at the keyboard Berlioz declared, "Gottschalk is one of the very small number who possess all the different elements of a consummate pianist—all the faculties which surround him with an irresistible prestige, and give him a sovereign power. He is an accomplished musician—he knows just how far fancy may be indulged in expression."

With his reputation in France secure, Gottschalk began to tour Switzerland and Spain. At Geneva in 1851 he became a favorite of the Grand Duchess Anna of Russia and flattered the Swiss with an arrangement of selections from Rossini's *William Tell*. In Madrid he was informed after a concert before the Queen that he could win the Spaniards best with flashy virtuoso theatrics. To appeal to Spanish patriotism and their love of sensationalism concurrently, Gottschalk composed *The Siege of Saragossa*, a "symphony" for ten pianos based on the country's national airs and folk tunes. The work possessed most of the standard effects of battle pieces so popular in concert halls and parlors since Kotzwara's *The Battle of Prague*— all of which delighted Madrid audiences. To celebrate Gottschalk's triumph, troops reportedly passed before him in review, and a famous bullfighter awarded the composer his favorite sword.

After spending eleven years in Europe, Moreau decided to return to the United States, influenced by reports of Jenny Lind's fantastic American success. He arrived in New York in January, 1853, and was met by his father. The musician quickly discovered that he had remained so long abroad that most of his countrymen considered him a foreigner. His first New York concert was a selective affair, given on Friday, February 11, in Niblo's Saloon, an intimate concert hall adjacent to the larger theater where operas were staged. His public debut came a few nights later in Niblo's Garden, where he was asked to repeat both *La Bamboula* and *Le Bananier*. In writing of his compositions, however, most of the New York critics focused on his *Jerusalem* fantasy (taken from Verdi's *I Lombardi*) rather than pointing to anything especially original about his Creole and Afro-American pieces. They spoke of Gottschalk essentially as they would speak of Thalberg or Liszt.

Within a few days P. T. Barnum called on the pianist at his Irving House suite, offering him a contract for an extensive tour of the United States. The manager proposed to pay Gottschalk $20,000 a year, besides expenses, for two or three years, depending on the length of the tour. The musician was tempted, but his father voiced strong opposition, arguing that the fee was much too low and that an alliance with the vulgar Barnum would be damaging to his son's public image.

Shortly after his New York debut Gottschalk left for New Orleans, playing concerts in Philadelphia and Louisville on the way. Philadelphia tried to outdo New York in greeting the young American, hailing him "the King of Pianists." During his second concert there Gottschalk performed a portion of his *The Battle of Bunker Hill*, which actually was taken from *The Siege of Saragossa*, the Spanish melodies having been replaced by "Yankee Doodle," "Hail, Columbia," "The Star-Spangled Banner," and two Stephen Foster tunes. The Philadelphians responded far more enthusiastically to this potpourri than to his more inspired piano selections. By April the musician was back in New Orleans, joyously greeted by Monsieur Letellier, his first teacher, and within a few weeks the pianist had presented several concerts for his native city.

He performed his first engagement in Boston in the fall of 1853, immediately meeting sharp criticism from John Sullivan Dwight. The critic had begun sniping at Gottschalk right after his New York debut, objecting mainly to his failure to play the classics. Gottschalk's flamboyant style obviously did not fit into Dwight's classical German mold. While the critic never denied the musician's brilliance at the keyboard, he insisted that a great technique was nothing unless placed in the service of great music. By limiting himself to operatic transcriptions and dazzling pianistic exhibitions, Gottschalk was denying—in Dwight's opinion—his own genius. The critic doubted, however, that Moreau could ever develop into a serious musician, since he had studied in frivolous, pleasure-loving France rather than reflective, industrious Germany. So staunchly had Dwight's *Journal of Music* censured the pianist that his initial concert at the Boston Music Hall was played to a half empty house, a fact which Dwight attributed to the public's "distrust of an artist who plays wholly his own compositions."

Certainly Gottschalk was no musical reformer, for he remained as much showman as artist, preferring to play romantic salon pieces instead of the classics. He might privately play Bach and Beethoven for friends, but he insisted on giving the public what it wanted. Gottschalk looked upon himself as an entertainer, not an educator, and he willingly met his audiences on their own level. As a result, he succeeded on the American concert stage at a time when the country's level of music appreciation was grossly underdeveloped. He was able to create an audience for piano recitals, even in areas where a grand piano itself was a rarity.

In addition, Gottschalk shied away from the German classics simply because he had been schooled in a different technique. Although he understood that sentimental salon pieces and opera transcriptions were a less lofty art than the great classical masterpieces, they nevertheless projected the style he knew best and mirrored his personal taste. The pianist also perceived the dangers of superimposing a mature German tradition upon a provincial people, neutralizing native characteristics in the process. Gottschalk found German musicians everywhere in the United States and viewed the stereotype with no little suspicion. In St. Louis he wrote in his journal:

> I was introduced to an old German musician, with uncombed hair, bushy beard, in constitution like a bear, in disposition the amenity of a boar at bay to a pack of hounds. I know this type; it is found everywhere. It should be time that the many great unknown musicians should be convinced that a negligent toilet is the maladroit imitation of the surly and misanthropic behavior of the great symphonist of Bonn.

Not all of the American critics were as intolerant as Dwight, and most of them found Gottschalk both an exciting performer and a sound musician. The New York *Herald* said, "He makes the keys all but speak," while the *Home Journal* claimed his playing had the effect of an orchestra. His colleague and friend William Mason later recalled:

> I knew Gottschalk well, and was fascinated by his playing, which was full of brilliancy and bravura. His strong, rhythmic accent, his vigor and dash, were exciting and always aroused enthusiasm. He was the perfection of his school, and his effects had the sparkle and effervescence of champagne.

When George Upton asked the musician why he did not attempt the classics, Gottschalk reportedly answered, "there are plenty of pianists who can play that music as well or better than I can but none of them can play my music half so well as I can. And what difference will it make a thousand years hence, anyway?"

The sudden death of his father in 1854 forced Gottschalk for the first time to concern himself over money, with the result that the pace of his concertizing was stepped up drastically. He gave some eighty concerts in New York alone over the next three years. He signed a profitable contract with Jonas Chickering agreeing to use the manufacturer's piano exclusively in public appearances, but still financial problems plagued him. Driven by economic necessity, the musician jumped from city to city, village to village, wooing the heart of America with his keyboard pyrotechnics and a repertoire that grew increasingly nostalgic and sentimental. He addressed himself essentially to the crowd—his handsome appearance, natural aristocratic bearing and French accent, acquired foreign mannerisms, and international reputation all working to enhance his popular appeal. Gottschalk was soon lionized as a matinee idol, especially worshipped by ladies. Stories abound of women in his audiences rushing to the platform, seizing the pianist's gloves and fighting for scraps of his clothing.

Such idolatry may have enlarged the musician's purse, but it proved deadly to his genius. "The virtuoso lived and prospered," Lowens contends, "but the manufacturer of skillfully mechanical, glittering salon pieces for sentimental misses gradually began to supplant the genuine creator." The dimension and verve of his earlier works vanished, as he began to cater to his feminine admirers by writing saccharine pieces of froth like *La Scintilla*, designated as a sentimental mazurka. Sentimental to the point of being maudlin was *The Dying Poet*, one of Gottschalk's best known selections. The piece proceeds slowly and soulfully, involving much languid handcrossing— ideal for young ladies to demonstrate their talent on social occasions in the family parlor.

In Cuba in 1854, following his father's death, Gottschalk wrote perhaps his most successful composition, *The Last Hope*, definitely among his most heartrending efforts. The musician claimed he improvised the tune to ease the deathbed melancholy of a prominent Cuban lady, and assuredly hundreds of young women soaked their handkerchiefs over the piece in the years ahead. The melody is slow and sweet, decorated by a profusion of rapid little tinkling effects in the high treble and later by ornamental runs and trills. For generations the selection remained the fond property of American girls who fancied themselves parlor virtuosos. By serious artistic standards *The Last Hope* clearly ranks as trash, much in the vein of Bardazewska's *The Maiden's Prayer*—a superlative example of the sentimental religious songs so much in vogue in the mid-nineteenth century, a piece that Gottschalk himself considered an abomination. *The Last Hope* later became familiar as a church hymn, called "Mercy," and the tune was a perennial favorite during the silent movie days.

Even in his tawdriest compositions, however, Gottschalk showed signs of craftsmanship. Potboilers though they may have been, his sentimental salon pieces possess a surface brilliance, a rhythmic vim, a melodious flow, a harmonic unity, and a poignancy that set them above the run of commercial songs in pre-Civil War America. Trivial and overembellished to be sure, these selections nevertheless maintain an aristocratic flair and an elegance that reflect the strivings of an evolving middle class without entirely sacrificing Gottschalk's native sense of taste. The composer was fully aware that he was writing in this instance for an America struggling for gentility and could even view the situation with some humor. When an engraver printed the title page of a later edition of *The Last Hope* as "The Latest Hops," Gottschalk laughed in delight.

The pianist's Havana debut in 1854 and the following tour of the Cuban interior were so successful that he decided to return to the Antilles three years later. He appeared in concert engagements throughout the Caribbean islands with fourteen year-old Adelina Patti and lingered in the West Indies almost six years, indulging himself in idle pleasures. He became increasingly desultory in his professional work, playing only when he felt like it or when local officials could convince him to take part in a festival. He later said, "The islands of the Antilles impart a voluptuous languor that is contagious. It is poison that slowly infiltrates all the senses and benumbs the soul with a kind of ecstatic torpor." And in his journal, he spoke of his years in the Caribbean as

> foolishly spent, thrown to the wind, as if life were infinite, and youth eternal; six years, during which I have roamed at random under the blue skies of the tropics, indolently permitting myself to be carried away by chance, giving a concert wherever I found a piano, sleeping whenever the night overtook me—on the grass of the savanna, or under the palm-leaf roof of a 'veguero'.

Gottschalk did manage some serious composition during these years, initially conceiving for violin and piano what would eventually become his *Grand Tarantelle* for piano and orchestra. The work was first played in Havana in 1860 by the composer and his friend Jose White; it was later revised for piano, violin, and cellos, and arranged for piano and orchestra a few months before Gottschalk's death. The *Grand Tarentelle* is far more theatrical than the musician's earlier compositions, but it is typical of the bravura showpieces so admired by keyboard wizards throughout the nineteenth century. The pianist's affection for the scenery and beauty of the Caribbean islands was incorporated into his orchestral poem, *A Night in the Tropics*, a colorful work somewhat in the tradition of Berlioz. Performed at the *Teatro Tacon* in Havana in 1861, *A Night in the Tropics* marked Gottschalk as a pioneer in the use of Cuban percussion in a symphonic piece.

In Cuba the pianist also engaged in the first of his "monster concerts," similar to those directed by Jullien and illustrating well the romantic penchant for the colossal. For a concert in Havana in 1860 an orchestra of 650 was assembled, along with a chorus of eighty-seven, fifteen soloists, fifty drums, and eighty trumpets—"that is to say," Gottschalk reported, "nearly nine hundred persons bellowing and blowing to see who could scream the loudest." The program of another Havana concert opened with a four-piano fantasy based on *William Tell*, a novelty that proved as exciting in Cuba as it had been in Spain.

In February, 1862, the spell of the tropics finally broke and Gottschalk was back in New York. Impresario Max Strakosch offered him a contract for another tour of the United States. The pace was arduous—traveling long hours, enduring all sorts of personal discomfort, playing for audiences chiefly interested in how fast his fingers could fly over the keys. "The devil take the poets who sing the joys of an artist's life," the pianist wailed. He toured across the entire eastern portion of the country, from Virginia to Wisconsin, and up into Canada, giving so many concerts he felt on the verge of becoming an automaton. At the close of his first season, December, 1862, he wrote:

> A few weeks more in this way and I should have become an idiot! Eighteen hours a day on the railroad! Arrive at seven o'clock in the evening, eat with all speed, appear at eight o'clock before the public. The last note finished, rush quickly for my luggage, and *en route* until next day to recommence always the same thing! I have become stupid with it.

During the combined seasons of 1862-63 Gottschalk gave more than eleven hundred concerts across the eastern United States and Canada.

He posed on these tours as the great romantic figure, making the most of the fiction that had come to surround his life. He usually wore white gloves to his concerts, keeping them on as he greeted his audience from the platform. Then, leisurely and with calculated indifference, he would remove them, a finger at a time, while he casually scanned the house and nodded to friends. In the back country he engaged in all kinds of subterfuge to titillate his audiences, even summoning patriotic sentiments by playing "Yankee Doodle" with his right hand and "Hail, Columbia" at the same time with his left.

The pianist's spell over women was widely proclaimed, and his erotic nature and countless love affairs had by now become legendary. His peculiarities were frequently embroidered to add mystery to the public image—as with his habit of visiting insane asylums whenever nearby. Meanwhile the weeks of touring stretched into months, the months into years, as the musician attempted to scratch out a living in an age when the solo recital was just coming into fashion. On the whole, however, Gottschalk found America's musical appreciation in the 1860s noticeably improved over what he had experienced a decade earlier. He observed during the Civil War:

> I am daily astonished at the rapidity with which the taste for music is developed and is developing in the United States. At the time of my first return from Europe I was constantly deploring the want of public interest for pieces purely sentimental; the public listened with indifference; to interest it, it became necessary to strike it with astonishment; grand movements, *tours de force*, and noise had alone the privilege in piano music, not of pleasing, but of making it patient with it.

Gottschalk traveled throughout the Civil War and, despite his southern background quickly became outspoken in his sympathy for the North. When asked to play "Dixie" in Canada, the musician stubbornly refused. He arrived in Harrisburg for a concert during the time that Confederate forces had invaded Pennsylvania, just before they were repulsed at Gettysburg, but the pianist agreed to perform despite the encircling danger. His journeys led him into the thick of the turmoil, and he often found himself surrounded by wounded soldiers and grieving friends and relatives. He played before Lincoln, whom he admired deeply, and wept when he learned of the President's death.

The musician sailed for the west coast, via Panama, in 1865, performing in San Francisco and traveling by stagecoach into the interior of California and Nevada. After touring the mining camps, Gottschalk returned to San Francisco for repeat engagements. At Maguire's Opera House on August 24, he and nine other pianists, each seated at a different instrument, played multiple piano arrangements of the "Soldier's Chorus" from *Faust* and the march from *Tannhauser*. The westerners greeted the piano ensemble with great enthusiasm—yelling, stamping their feet, and pelting the strings of the ten Chickering grands with pieces of gold and silver.

Amid hints of scandal, Gottschalk suddenly left California on September 18, 1865, for South America. A feeling of failure engulfed him, and in his state of depression he became more and more obsessed with the macabre, the bizarre, and the grotesque. Repeated concert successes in Lima and Santiago did little to relieve his disillusionment. He was disturbed by revolution in Peru, corruption almost everywhere, and tormented by an unrelenting sense of personal defeat. Still the concert treadmill continued, as Mexico, Bolivia, Chile, Uruguay, Argentina, and Brazil each in their turn came to idolize him. But while the performer's surface charm persisted, the inner anguish deepened.

In Rio de Janeiro he prepared another of his "monster concerts," dreaming of "eight hundred performers and eighty drums to lead," all under his direction. Musicians from the bands of the Brazilian National Guard, the Army, Navy, and War Arsenal were enlisted for the occasion, along with three professional orchestras. The festival began on November 11, 1869, with Gottschalk's *A Night in the Tropics* as one of the featured works.

A few days later the pianist awoke too ill to get up, suffering from a pain on the right side of his abdomen. By evening the pain had sharpened, but Gottschalk refused to call a doctor. A little past eight o'clock he was at the opera house, determined not to disappoint the thousands that had paid gala prices for tickets. The musician waited for the opening numbers of the program to terminate. Then, after a brief intermission, the curtain rose on an empty stage except for a grand piano and a table on which was placed a vase of flowers. In a moment Gottschalk appeared, acknowledged the applause, sat down at the piano, and slowly removed his white gloves. He was scheduled to play a group of his shorter pieces, beginning with the elegy *Morte!!*, one of his later piano solos. He had completed no more than a half dozen bars when he faltered and fell to the floor.

Even before the curtain was rung down a group of men and women standing in the wings were at his side. The pianist was shortly restored to consciousness and taken to his hotel on a stretcher. Later he was removed to Tijuca, a neighboring village, where he fell into a coma from which he never awoke. On Saturday, December 18, 1869, Gottschalk was dead—at forty years of age. His death had been caused by yellow fever, although—as with so many facets of his life—the details of his unexpected demise soon became buttressed with fabrication. Unconfirmed reports still linger that the pianist was assassinated, perhaps by a jealous lover. His body was eventually returned to New York and buried in Greenwood Cemetery, Brooklyn.

A young American music student, Amy Fay, lamented in Berlin when she heard of Gottschalk's death, "The infatuation that I and 999,999 other American girls once felt for him, still lingers in my breast." Without doubt the pianist was the most beloved and respected American musician of his day, both for his virtuoso abilities and his personal warmth and charm. Although he was American by birth, Gottschalk was the first musical figure from the United States to gain international recognition. At a time when the young country generally was viewed abroad as uncultured and barbaric, the polished Gottschalk captivated the European social circle with an unexpected urbanity. He was an American who curiously evidenced the attitudes and appearance of a sophisticated man of the world.

In many respects the career of Louis Moreau Gottschalk is one vast enigma. Fundamentally, he was a pioneer in the use of native folk materials in serious musical composition, emerging in this regard as America's first convincingly integrated nationalist. Concurrently, he distinguished himself as the earliest great American cosmopolitan in music, encompassing in his ornamentation a universal quality derived from the European romantics. But the best of the composer's work also displayed a special intangible ingredient that was uniquely Gottschalk. This fusion of local color, individual style, and mid-nineteenth century romantic embellishment formed the heart of the spirited piano selections the Parisian salons found so enchanting.

Gottschalk's earliest compositions remained his best, for never again would he achieve that original blend of simplicity and elegance, freshness and formality. *La Bamboula, La Savanne, Le Bananier*, and *Le Banjo* were all essentially boyhood works, written when his memories of Negro and Creole music were still vivid. Full of youth and exuberance, these colorful little pieces possess a direct, natural vigor only occasionally encumbered by showers of scales, arpeggios, and various types of florid passagework. Later, in response to the popular tastes of his home country, the composer wasted his genius on sentimental froth, writing for young ladies posturing before the family piano. Since death was a highly fashionable topic for poetic expression in the Victorian Age, Gottschalk entitled two of his more mawkish pieces *The Dying Poet* and *The Last Hope*. Whereas he had absorbed characteristics of the European romantic tradition honestly from his musical experiences in Paris, admitting these elements into his first selections with credibility, his efforts at reaching the emotions of the American masses resulted in synthetic pretenses at sentiment.

Neither do his Caribbean pieces come off with the same conviction as the piano solos of his youth. Although Gottschalk's New Orleans' upbringing had exposed him to Latin American rhythms and his own disposition responded amicably to Caribbean themes and tempos, his work in this genre is often self-conscious, the exotic atmosphere a bit strained. The folk ingredient in the orchestral compositions particularly becomes magnified to the point of artificiality. Again, the more intimate piano pieces are the most effective—like the *Souvenir de Porto Rico*, which combines a leisurely Negro theme with an intriguing cakewalk rhythm.

All together Gottschalk composed just under a hundred piano pieces, about a dozen songs, several works for orchestra, at least two operas—*Charles IX* and *Isura de Palermo*, neither apparently performed in public. The composer consistently proved a graceful melodist, skilled in harmony and engaging in tempo. He was a far better schooled musician than any of the other American composers of his day, although a much less academic one than either Fry or Bristow. Unlike Heinrich, whose American material was seldom more than veneer, Gottschalk succeeded in using his Creole and Negro material to form a solid entity. His romantic embellishments, in contrast to Fry's imitation of Bellini, were drawn from legitimate sources that he had come to know intimately as a youth, not patterned after an ideal he had glimpsed secondhand.

Gottschalk's tragedy was not that he had never been exposed to excellence, but that he failed to sustain it. While he maintained his patrician bearing in his personal life, he willingly diluted his art to comply with the equalitarian tastes of the American democracy. In his adult years he not only squandered much of his energy as a composer, but also exhausted himself as a pianist playing to the multitude. As the years went by, he became more and more the robot, performing the keyboard tricks he knew the public adored. The genius that had flickered so brightly in France gradually paled with the months of grueling travel and mechanical concertizing.

Rather than maturing into the poet of the piano as expected, the prodigy in later life resorted to theatrics and synthetic glamor to court the favor of the crowd, becoming something of a common man's Liszt. Although Gottschalk occasionally revealed private contempt for the coarseness and puritanical attitudes of the masses, he was driven by economic necessity to bend his talent to their level. He exploited the popular predilection for multiple pianos and, in Latin America especially, pushed the festival idea to ponderous lengths. Beneath the weight of battalions of musicians Gottschalk's instinctive genius was virtually smothered, much as his skill at composing for the piano was weakened in his more complex orchestral writing.

To assure his image as matinee idol, the pianist surrounded himself with a mythology highlighting his romantic predilections. Almost immediately he became regarded by the public as a paragon of finesse, a ladies' man without equal, and a grand, exotic idler. Gottschalk's life grew so entwined with fiction that even the more scholarly of his biographers have been unable to sort out fact from fancy. For instance, on his second trip to the Caribbean, the musician wanted to spend some time composing. He reputedly learned of an abandoned hut on the edge of a dormant volcano, and accompanied by a servant, went there to write. He had a piano moved to the sanctuary, where he devoted himself temporarily to art and beauty. "Every evening I moved my piano out upon the terrace," Gottschalk wrote, "and there in view of the most beautiful scenery in the world...I played, for myself alone, everything that the scene opened before me inspired—and what a scene!" Incidents like this permeate the pianist's whole life and are practically impossible to confirm. Certainly Gottschalk himself is not an altogether reliable source, for by the end of his life there is evidence that the musician too had become clouded in his ability to distinguish reality from press notices, eventually causing him a serious identity crisis.

Half believing his own publicity, aware that his genius had tarnished through the years, Gottschalk died despondent and confused. He had possessed the talent and the background to become the lion of early American musicians, and even with his limitations the pianist unquestionably stands as the extraordinary figure in the serious music of the United States during the mid-nineteenth century. At his best he was the forceful genius, while even at his most banal he remained a superb craftsman. In his composition he persuasively joined a cultivated tradition with the vernacular, invigorating an aristocratic style through personalized folk idioms. His music disseminated Creole, Afro-American, and Caribbean melodies and rhythms throughout the civilized world, while his ability as a keyboard virtuoso was greeted across the length and breadth of the Americas as a symbol of taste and quality. Although Gottschalk's standards were not always the highest, they were inferior largely in comparison with his potential. Had Gottschalk developed fully into a musician of depth, he would have been rejected by the untutored American masses. If he were to become their hero, the pianist sensed correctly, he must emphasize the flamboyant and adorn the obvious, at whatever expense to his creative art.

1. Tom Meeker as Captain Macheath in John Gay's perennial *Beggar's Opera* (Courtesy of Hoblitzelle Theatre Arts Library, Humanities Research Center, The University of Texas at Austin)

2. Eighteenth century printing of Alexander Reinagle's
"The Tars of Columbia" (Courtesy of Hoblitzelle
Theatre Arts Library)

3. Fanny Elssler
   Courtesy of
   Hoblitzelle Theatre
   Arts Library)

4. Catharine Hayes
   (Courtesy of
   Hoblitzelle Theatre
   Arts Library)

5. Ole Bull (Courtesy of Hoblitzelle
Theatre Arts Library)

6. Jenny Lind (Courtesy of Hoblitzelle
Theatre Arts Library)

7. Exterior of Castle Garden in New York (Courtesy of Hoblitzelle Theatre Arts Library)

8. First appearance of Jenny Lind in America, Castle Garden, September 10, 1850 (Courtesy of Hoblitzelle Theatre Arts Library)

9. Theatre d'Orleans (Courtesy of Hoblitzelle Theatre Arts Library)

10. The Academy of Music in New York, 1856 (Courtesy of
Hoblitzelle Theatre Arts Library)

11. Louis Antoine Jullien
    (Courtesy of
    Hoblitzelle Theatre
    Arts Library)

12. Louis Moreau
    Gottschalk (Courtesy
    of Hoblitzelle Theatre
    Arts Library)

13. Contemporary advertisement for the
Italian Opera Troupe at Niblo's
Garden (Courtesy of Hoblitzelle
Theatre Arts Library)

14. Pianist Henri Herz (Courtesy of Hoblitzelle Theatre Arts Library)

15. Composer George F. Bristow (Courtesy of Hoblitzelle Theatre Arts Library)

16. Songwriter Stephen C. Foster (Courtesy of Hoblitzelle Theatre Arts Library)

17. "Get Out" number, Moore and
Burgess Minstrels (Courtesy of
Hoblitzelle Theatre Arts Library)

18. Ethiopian Serenaders (Courtesy of Hoblitzelle Theatre Arts Library)

19. Minstrel Billy Emerson (Courtesy of Hoblitzelle Theatre Arts Library)

20. The Hutchinson Family, April 25, 1846 (Courtesy of Hoblitzelle Theatre Arts Library)

CHAPTER

X

Sentimental Songs in the Age of Innocence

By the close of the Revolution the social pattern of urban America had solidified to a point that the wealthier, more fashionable segment of the young nation's pliant population aspired to a popular music beyond the folk level. Erratically tutored in an appreciation of the European classics, a maturing nucleus of the coastal townspeople were nevertheless growing too sophisticated in their tastes to find continued satisfaction either in the songs of the singing schools or the commonplace ballads imported from England and Scotland. Even the hymns and anthems of Williams Billings were disparaged by the champions of the "better music" movement of the early nineteenth century, as the renewed impulse toward gentility turned American ears again toward Europe for propriety in style. While temporal songs continued to be patterned after the more refined popular airs of England, religious music tended toward simplified paraphrases of the works of the European masters.

In the decades following 1800 church music in the United States fell into the hands of musicians better educated than Billings, some of whom had studied abroad, but none were as inspired as the unorthodox Boston tanner or composed with his degree of originality. New England city churches particularly began demanding dignified, stately hymns, much like those found currently in formal Protestant collections, although Sunday schools and rural revival meetings remained loyal to the unassuming gospel tunes. The early pacesetter for a more "scientific" American hymnody was another Bostonian, the music educator and Congregational layman Lowell Mason. Mason's style of writing, while consciously simple, was nonetheless one of formal correctness, broadly within the European classical tradition. Yet by the mid-nineteenth century his hymns had reached a general popularity with Americans approaching that enjoyed by the country's most revered patriotic songs.

Beginning with "A Missionary Hymn" ("From Greenland's Icy Mountains") in 1823, Mason wrote and arranged sacred music with remarkable facility, eventually composing some 1200 original hymn tunes and adapting almost 500 more to melodies by other composers. Among his more familiar works are "Olivet" (based on Ray Palmer's "My Faith Looks Up to Thee"), "Bethany" ("Nearer, My God, to Thee"), and "Watchman" ("Watchman, Tell Us of the Night"). Although only a few of his hymns are remembered today, many of them gained wide recognition in the years after their publication, selling successfully enough to distinguish Mason as one of the few composers in early America to net appreciable profits on his work. Royalties from the sale of his collections, in fact, produced a comfortable fortune for the musician.

His hymns are characteristically uncomplicated in harmony, gentle in melodic thrust, bland in rhythm, expressing no great originality. Consistent with the simple words to which they are set, his tunes seldom exceeded the singing ability of congregations and reflect vividly the depth of Mason's own spiritual convictions. While he was no genius, the composer essentially recognized his limitations and rarely attempted to go beyond them. For the most part he wrote unaffected, straight-forward hymn tunes and short anthems, mirroring the rules of correct composition and capturing the evangelical religious sentiment that permeated the age.

Having grown up during the singing school era, Mason did not come into contact with professional musicians of note until he made a trip to Europe in 1830, at that time spending a year abroad in travel and study. His talent was the capacity to adapt what he had learned as a disciplined musician to the needs and faculties of a developing American public. A number of his tunes were modeled after music he brought back with him from Europe and others were direct paraphrases, stated in terms a callow urban populace could comprehend. While critics — even in Mason's time — would belittle his hymns as insipid appeals to emotion over reason, the composer's intention was to write for the sophomoric masses rather than produce music of a loftier vein. Estimates hold that Mason's collections have sold over a million copies, and without question they set the standard in sacred music for the more progressive American churches throughout the nineteenth century.

In compiling his *Spiritual Songs for Social Worship* Mason collaborated with his New York friend Thomas Hastings, most famous as the composer of the tune for Augustus Toplady's hymn "Rock of Ages." Next to Mason, Hastings probably contributed a larger portion of hymn tunes still in use than any other American musician. Unlike Mason, the New Yorker looked with skepticism on music not related to the church, felt that even religious pieces should occupy a subordinate place, and denied the role of music specifically to add beauty to the worship service. A less skilled musician than Mason, Hastings was a few years older and more narrowly devout, insisting that music's proper function was merely to exemplify the teachings of the Scriptures. Hastings supposedly wrote 600 hymns and 1000 hymn tunes in all, the more lasting of which include "Gently Lord, O Gently Lead Us," "How Calm and Beautiful the Morn," "Return, O Wand'rer, to Thy Rest," and "Come Ye Disconsolate, Wher'er Ye Languish." Often considered a better poet than musician, Hastings' sacred verses incorporate well the fundamental spirit of early nineteenth century American Protestantism. His tunes are homespun, yet distinguished by an essential correctness of harmony.

Largely self-taught in the rudiments of music, Hastings was leading a village choir at age eighteen and already had begun to assemble the first of his fifty volumes of sacred songs. Like Mason he was descended from generations of educated and professional men, and like his two brothers he was a complete albino, his hair absolutely white since childhood. Before moving to New York City in 1832, he taught psalmody in Troy, Albany, and other towns in the eastern portion of the state, devoting himself by 1816 exclusively to the profession of music. Although harboring a limited view of music as art, Hastings did much to promote correct singing among urban congregations through his collections of hymns and elementary books of instruction. A Presbyterian, he directed the choirs of several New York churches and for a number of years was choirmaster of the Bleeker Street Church. Many of his more appealing tunes appeared under foreign names, since Hastings realized early the impression European affectations made on the American public. "I have found that a foreigner's name went a great way," he once wrote, "and that very ordinary tunes would be sung if 'Palestrina' or 'Pucitto' were over them, while a better tune by Hastings would go unnoticed." The prolific hymnist died at age eighty-eight, having produced a body of highly regarded tunes for a generation whose middle class ideals were sheathed in an attitude of restrained Protestant piety.

Aside from sacred and patriotic music, the English ballad opera supplied young America with her first popular songs acceptable to the genteel urban classes. After Carr and Dunlap's *The Archers* appeared in New York in 1796 the ballad opera became increasingly Americanized along the east coast, paving the way for a more distinctly American musical stage and providing a foundation for popular music in the more commercial sense. The gamut from love songs to comedy numbers was spanned on the Anglo-American ballad opera stage, the mass of which was of a decidedly saccharine turn. Of the airs to acquire a permanent place in the song repertory, none has been more durable than "Home, Sweet Home" from the production *Clari, the Maid of Milan*, which opened in New York on November 12, 1823. The lyrics were written by the American actor John Howard Payne, the melody by Sir Henry Bishop, a prominent English composer and conductor.

English performers on tour in the United States also provided the nation with some of its earliest popular songs of lasting appeal. Baritone Henry Russell spent nearly nine years in America, 1833 to 1841, barnstorming the eastern section of the country as a recitalist, serving as organist of the First Presbyterian Church in Rochester, New York, and composing a host of celebrated songs. His greatest success came with "Woodman, Spare That Tree" (1837), to words by George P. Morris, which sang of the sentimentalized joys of home, symbolized in an aged oak, as it shamed and defied the despoiler's axe.

> *Touch not a single bough,*
> *In youth it shelter'd me,*
> *And I'll protect it now.*

Three years later Russell published one of the earliest "mother" songs, "The Old Arm Chair," its maudlin text, by Eliza Cooke, setting the pattern for household songs for decades to come. The narrator gazes at the homely armchair "with quivering breath and throbbing brow," remembering his mother in thoughts choked with religious ardor.

> *I almost worshipp'd her when she smiled,*
> *And turn'd from her Bible to bless her child.*

The chair itself is venerated as a tangible remnant of the poet's departed parent.

> *I love it, I love it, and cannot tear*
> *My soul from a mother's Old Arm Chair.*

Characteristic of nineteenth century sheet music, the cover page is adorned by a lithograph picturing mother and chair. The melody is simple, constructed of only five notes, in an essentially declamatory style.

A few years later, Russell wrote a companion to "The Old Arm Chair," entitled "Oh! Weep Not," copies of which sold for six cents. He also wrote during his American period "The Brave Old Oak," "The Ivy Green," "The Old Bell," "Our Way Across the Mountain, Ho," "A Life on the Ocean Wave," "I Love a Man with a Generous Heart," "Those Locks, Those Ebon Locks," and "The Old Sexton"—the latter about a grave digger who sings while he "gathers them in" to "their final rest," down in "the earth's dark breast."

As a singer Russell was a favorite with the public, benefited by curly black hair and a matinee idol appearance. He played his own accompaniment at the keyboard and won particular acclaim singing his own songs. His most pathetic numbers, like "The Maniac" and "The Gambler's Wife," which he rendered with a calculated look of sympathy and pity, invariably brought tears from his audience, who came expecting to be purged of plaintive feelings and exalted in the nobler sentiments. Dramatic human tragedy, realistically sung, was relished by an American public that sought escape from the workaday world by blubbering at the concert hall and theater, much as they enjoyed pouring over a barrage of mawkish novels penned by that bevy of "scribbling women" Nathaniel Hawthorne so deplored. Russell's song "The Maniac" provided the singer an opportunity to titillate this morbid public by describing a tormented soul, sinking into insanity, while the performer rolled his eyes, disheveled his hair, and screamed the refrain, "No, by heaven, I am not mad."

While his voice was not without limitations, Russell was well trained as a musician and at one time had been a student of Rossini in Naples. A master of theatrical tricks, much adored on both sides of the Atlantic, the singer made a fortune from his appearances in the United States. He nevertheless had severe critics among the cultural elite; Dwight's *Journal* recalled him in 1853 as "a great charlatan." His bathetic songs, however, were looked upon as becoming expressions of popular gentility and were imitated repeatedly throughout the rest of the century.

Often appearing on the same programs with Russell in New York was another English performer and ballad writer, Joseph Philip Knight, composer of "Rocked in the Cradle of the Deep." Knight spent one year in the United States, 1839, during which he wrote a number of his more famous songs, including "Oh, Fly on the Prairie" and "The Old Year's Gone, and the New Year's Come." Among Knight's greatest successes was "The Grecian Daughter," set to lyrics by Thomas Haynes Bayley, composer of "Long, Long Ago." These verses were prophetic of the approaching school of self-pity so much in vogue in the popular music of mid-nineteenth century America. Bayley also scored hits with "Oh, No, We Never Mention Her," its sequel "She Never Blamed Him, Never," and "She Wore a Wreath of Roses," in which the anguished heroine is presented first wearing roses, then orange blossoms, and finally a widow's cap.

Sometimes considered the "father of the American ballad" is John Hill Hewitt, the eldest son of the composer of *The Battle of Trenton*. Hewitt was born in Maiden Lane, New York, July 11, 1801, was admitted to West Point, toured the South with one of his father's theatrical troupes for a while, then taught music and studied law in Columbia, South Carolina. He later moved to Greenville, where he established a newspaper called the *Republican* and in 1825 composed his first song, "The Minstrel's Return from the War," which won him an immediate reputation. This was followed by "The Knight of the Raven Black Plume," "The Mountain Bugle," "Our Native Land," "Rock Me to Sleep, Mother," "Where the Sweet Magnolia Blooms," and the Civil

War ballad "All Quiet Along the Potomac." He taught music at the Chesapeake Female College in Hampton, Virginia, for nine years and remained in Virginia throughout the Civil War. An ardent supporter of the Confederacy, Hewitt volunteered for active military service, but was rejected since he was then a man in his sixties. Jefferson Davis eventually did appoint him drillmaster of recruits in Richmond, in part a recognition of his West Point training. After the war he composed "Take Me Home to the Sunny South," probably his strongest expression of Southern sentiment.

Hewitt enjoyed a varied, colorful career. He saw Fulton's first steamboat on the Hudson, was present when the initial message was sent over Morse's telegraph line between Washington and Baltimore, and once won a poetry contest over Edgar Allan Poe. But music was always his first love. "Since my earliest youth," he affirms in his reminiscences, "I have sought its gentle influence." His oratorio, *Jephtha*, was given successful performances in Washington, Georgetown, Norfolk, and Baltimore, although it was treated none too kindly by critics in New York. He also published several cantatas, wrote operas, poems, and plays, in addition to over three hundred songs. His greatest fame, however, rests on his narrative ballads, and in this capacity the composer exercised a decided influence in shaping the course of later American song writing.

The demand for a cultivated popular music grew during the early nineteenth century, paralleling the growth of city population, the rising standard of living, the gradual increase in wealth and leisure, and the expansion of professional musical performances. After a modest beginning in the eighteenth century and a slow development in the years before 1820, music publishing in the United States broadened steadily in the decades preceding the Civil War. Thirty-one new publishing firms appeared between 1830 and 1839, thirty-seven between 1840 and 1849, and sixty-six between 1850 and 1861—a score of them surviving for at least a half century. Music publishers and dealers both attempted, whenever possible, to place their songs in the hands of established performers, hoping the prestige of the singer or instrumentalist who performed the songs would help sell copies. Still it is estimated that three-fourths of the music sold in the country prior to the Civil War was distributed by teachers, who bought at a discount and sold to their pupils at retail prices.

The staples of the music publishing business remained instruction books, collections of exercises, hymnals, and albums of traditional and patriotic airs, in endless combinations, although quick profits increasingly came to be made off the sale of sheet music of popular songs and fashionable instrumental numbers. While the types of commercial songs diversified during the antebellum years, a languid, sentimental style persisted. Intense emotional values were attached to matters which, when viewed more rationally, paled before such exaggerated declarations of feeling and shrank in lasting significance. "Excitement, enthusiasm, nostalgia, wonder, grief, or euphoric love," James Stone concludes, "were meant to be represented or aroused by music and poetry which themselves, however, were so convention-bound to brevity and banality that they were emblematic of emotions rather the opposite of those presumably involved."

Topical songs expanded in importance, as a self-conscious people hungered for descriptions of American scenes and expressions of nationalistic attitudes from their informal arts. A reasonable chronology of the development of the United States in the nineteenth century could be constructed from the nation's popular music, as one by one the more colorful events came to be recorded in song. Technological and scientific advances were favorite subjects among ballad writers who focused on contemporary happenings, since these kinds of achievements were direct manifestations of the country's progress and invigorated the dominant optimistic mood. The completion of the Erie Canal in 1825 inspired the dramatic "The Meeting of the Waters," dedicated to Governor DeWitt Clinton and composed by Samuel Woodworth, better known for his classic "The Old Oaken Bucket." Three years later "The Rail Road" and the "Rail Road March" announced the completion of the Baltimore and Ohio line, while in 1856 Stephen C. Massett and Charles Mackay wrote "Clear the Way!" in anticipation of the projected Great Pacific Railroad.

Politics provided popular composers with timely themes, and songs about the President and national political figures were common in the early years of American independence. After the boisterous "Tippecanoe and Tyler Too" campaign in 1840, however, when the Whigs surmised the fate of Martin Van Buren in his bid for a second term by singing "Van Is a Used-Up Man," election songs became appreciably more important. The depression of 1837 resulted in a flood of critical numbers, among them "The Aristocracy of Democracy," "The Currency Song," and "The President's Conscience," while a later generation would sing a more positive note with "Lincoln and Liberty."

Battles and heroes were celebrated in a range of songs covering the sweep of events from Saratoga to the Alamo to Gettysburg. "The Boy Defender of Kentucky's Honor" recounted the exploits of sixteen year-old William F. Gaines, who carried the Second Kentucky Infantry's colors at the battle of Buena Vista during the Mexican War. Twice overpowered by the enemy, the boy regained the flag both times, promptly emerging as a national hero. "The Old Constitution, the Pride of the Navy," published in 1851, glorified the famous battle ship of the War of 1812 at the time of its retirement to a New York dock. Of a less martial nature, "Firemen, the Pride of the Nation" exalted a volunteer group of civic heroes in the early 1830s, when fire was a constant menace to city living.

The opening of the West was another frequent topic of songs in young America, as armchair pioneers sounded the call of "manifest destiny" and lauded life on the open prairie. Samuel Woodworth's "The Hunters of

Kentucky" told of that tough breed of Kentucky backwoodsmen, well skilled in the use of the rifle, who assisted Andrew Jackson in the victory at New Orleans in January, 1815. Ossian E. Dodge, who would later pay $625 for the first ticket auctioned in Boston for Jenny Lind's debut there, wrote a song depicting the virtues of the West, entitled "Ho, Westward, Ho!", while the glory of the Pacific coast was praised in Dr. M. A. Richter's "The California Pioneers," set to a slight bolero rhythm, and published in San Francisco in 1852. Around 1840 the Indian became the subject of a number of instrumental pieces, such as "The Osceola Quick Step," "The Keokuck Quick Step," and "The Nahmeokee Waltz," as well as vocal selections like "The Indian Hunter" and "The Song of the Red Man." The latter's plaintive lyrics begin:

> Oh! why should the white man hang on my path,
> Like the hound on the tiger's track!

Among the more sentimental songs dealing with the noble American savage was Alexander Lee's "Cora, the Indian Maiden's Song," in which Cora sings:

> Oh! The wild free wind is a spirit kind
> And it loves the Indian well,
> When its course it ploughs thro' the crashing boughs,
> Or moans in the ocean shell.
> When the Indian maid hath implored its aid
> The wild free wind is there.
> And it speeds her dart to the red deer's heart
> As he bounds from his secret lair.

Many of the pieces written in the 1850s related the misfortunes of southern slaves and their attempts to escape the persecution of harsh masters. "Underground Rail Car, or Song of the Fugitive," published in Cleveland in 1854, finds a fleeing black praying, "O Great Father! Do thou pity me, and help me on to Canada where the panting slave is free!" A host of songs followed in the wake of Harriet Beecher Stowe's Uncle Tom's Cabin, one of the more popular being "Eliza's Flight"; the problems of another growing minority group were viewed in "The Lament of the Irish Emigrant," published in 1840 by William R. Dempster and Mrs. Price Blackwood.

The temperance crusade, the fight for women's rights, and other social crusades of mid-nineteenth century America, as well as the nation's fads and follies, were reflected in the popular music of the day. The Bloomer Girl inspired all sorts of published pieces portraying fetching maidens sporting the new attire on the covers of music folios. One of these was "The Bloomer's Complaint, a Very Pathetic Song for the Piano Forte," whose composer elected to remain anonymous. A style-conscious public of the 1840s and 1850s seemed to enjoy laughing at themselves in song, frequently poking fun at their attempts at elegant dress and foppish mannerisms. "The Standing

Collar" in 1851, for instance, gently twitted one of the more uncomfortable features of contemporary men's fashion.

The patent medicine craze had begun its ascendency in American life, one of the early best sellers being a Buffalo, New York, nostrum called the "Wahoo Bitters." In 1856 John N. Pattison composed a musical tribute, a dance tune entitled "The Great Wahoo Polka." Mrs. Trollop's visit produced a deluge of songs, most of them as uncomplimentary to her as the Englishwoman had been of the United States. "Mrs. Trollop's March" was followed by "Mrs. Trollop's Quick Step," the latter described as "a new tune on an old subject," and dedicated to "all the Trollops," meaning the members of the world's oldest profession. Jenny Lind's arrival in this country was more favorably hailed in popular music, and the Swedish soprano's face probably appeared on more copies of sheet music than any other personality of the century. Ossian Dodge, who paid that exorbitant price for a ticket to the Lind concert in Boston, achieved national attention with a song named "Ossian's Serenade."

Songwriters of mid-nineteenth century America eagerly turned accounts of current disasters into song, relating harrowing details as melodramatically as possible. "The Snow Storm" narrated the sufferings of a mother who wandered over the Green Mountains with her child in 1821 in search of a husband already frozen to death. "The Great Railroad Wreck" and "The Ship on Fire" dealt with two famous calamities, the latter selection beginning by telling of a tremendous thunderstorm that has the ship's passengers and crew on bended knee; the song ends with the vessel bursting into flames. These events were so graphically told that in Canton, Pennsylvania, a Dutchman, upon hearing the song, supposedly forgot himself, rushed out of the performance into the street, and set off an alarm that brought fire engines racing to the theater. The sea gave popular composers special opportunities for conjuring human emotions with tales of drownings, stowaways, collisions, and heroic rescues. The sinking of the steamship *Golden Gate* in 1862 off the coast of Mexico resulted in the loss of nearly two hundred lives, including those of several women and children. But the gallant rescue of an eight year-old girl named Addie Manchester from the wreckage inspired the song "I Do Not Want to Be Drowned," published less than a month after the catastrophe took place. Two years before, Henry C. Work's "Lost on the Lady Elgin" preserved the memory of a disaster on the Great Lakes, in which three hundred passengers and crew were drowned.

Individual suffering and personal affliction of all sorts were garnished by popular composers into declamatory eulogies to human misery. Dead babies, crippled children, blessed old decrepit grandparents, dying sweethearts, and ascents into Heaven were frequently heralded in the lyric expressions of antebellum America; songwriters, in their determination to move audiences to tears, at times bordered on the vicious in the images they conjured. "The Lament of the Blind Orphan Girl," published in 1847 by W. B. Bradbury, composer of the hymn "He Leadeth Me," in skipping rhythms and a modest coloratura vocal line reminiscent of Bellini and Donizetti, told of a doubly afflicted heroine. As H. Wiley Hitchcock points out, the piece provided "a remarkable lesson in how to turn sentiment into sentimentality." And yet American tunes of this genre, no matter how dismal their subject, were almost invariably written in a major key, the minor mode apparently considered too potent a declaration of sadness for a society so basically unqualified in its optimism.

The genteel tradition in the United States spent its formative years cloaked in a shroud of mid-Victorian morbidity and grief. "Being sorry for yourself has always been one of the great American indoor sports," Sigmund Spaeth maintains, and this particularly tended to be true of the undeveloped sophisticates of the mid-nineteenth century. Edgar Allan Poe's dictum that the most aesthetic subject in the world was the death of a beautiful young woman was echoed as a fundamental tenet in refined popular music, although premature death in general came to be part of the penchant. "The Guardian of the Grave" was supplemented with "They Sleep in the Grave Together" and a succession of ballads that wound a tear-drenched path which seemingly extended to every burial plot in the country.

Yet if Americans in the age of innocence lived only to die, they were happiest when they were sad, at least according to much of the popular music of the day. The somber notes of "When Summer Flowers Are Withered" and "When Shall We Meet Again?" were resounded in "Last Year's Flowers" and "Oh! I'm in Sadness." A busy nation on the rise had little time for emotional development, so preoccupied were its people with essential physical and social growth. The blatant sentimentality of America's popular music is in part an indication of this emotional immaturity. The maudlin verses and solemn melodies of its songs served as a cataract over which the country's vernal feelings could surge, providing a release for pent-up anxieties phrased in terms a naive public could understand. "If to cry is to be happy," Philip Jordan and Lillian Kessler conclude, "then young America was exuberant."

A dynamic mobile society found emotional stability in nostalgic tunes of home and childhood. "My Trundle Bed" is a simple tale of one who wanders into the attic; finding the trundle bed of infancy, the narrator is overcome by a host of childhood memories. "Home of My Boyhood" and "New England Farmer" both reflect a longing for a rural past and the Yankee's continued dedication to Puritan ideals—hard work, thrift, love of God and family. Although lyrics occasionally dealt with children who ran away from an unhappy home or evil parents, especially fathers who drank and stayed out late at night, the more common theme concentrated on the heartaches of families who were separated. "My Darling's Little Shoes" pictures, for an age of high infant mortality, a mother holding the scuffed shoes of a child only recently in its grave, as her thoughts roam from recollections of the boy at play to dreams of the man who was to be. "The Mother Who Hath a Child at Sea" was a particularly pathetic narrative, although hardly more so than "What Is Home Without a Mother?" By the 1840s "mother" songs were being turned out by the scores, three of them special favorites: "Dearest Mother," "I Cannot Call Her Mother," and "My Mother's Bible."

"And then there were love songs," Meade Minnigerode asserts in *The Fabulous Forties*, "gloomy love songs, tearful love songs, unrequited love songs, peevish love songs, wonderfully self-pitying, luxuriously depressing, delightfully sad love songs with tombstones and weeping willows on the covers—little loose strings from Mr. Byron's lyre." Hundreds of these pieces melded to create the time-honored formula of boy casually meets girl, boy immediately loves girl, boy either marries girl or promises never to forget her. The kiss was viewed as the ultimate in human ecstasy, expected to be followed by holy matrimony. While no category of popular music was more clearly sentimental than the songs of love and courtship, the conclusion might be drawn from the ballads of the day that marriages in antebellum America were shamefully unhappy. Parental interference seems to have posed a recurring obstacle to marital bliss, although shiftless, wanton husbands caused their share of domestic turmoil. "The Married Woman's Lament" finds its heroine—with good reason—crying, "Oh! how I wish I was single again!" Not only is the woman herself ill-treated, but she is forced to,

> Take those children and put them to bed,
> Before their father curses them, and wishes they were dead.

At the same time that woeful songs of humble cottages, pastoral settings, and the simple joys of youth provided an unsettled American people with a psychological bond to their own idealized past, the melancholy emphasis of popular music in the mid-nineteenth century may indeed be evidence that Americans were extremely satisfied with life as they found it. According to Minnigerode:

> Sentimentality is primarily, perhaps, an outlet for superabundant contentment, and a romantic disposition the prerogative of dwellers in security and uneventful ease. Life was so pleasant and well ordered, so placid and comfortable, that they [Americans] were quite willing to warble delicately of death and misfortune, shipwreck, storm and disaster, confident that such catastrophes could only seldom touch them, in order to use them as a dark background upon which to contemplate the bright picture of their own well-being.

Or perhaps a solidifying urban population was merely bored. Having been nurtured in an active, often exciting, frontier environment, a rising industrial middle class may simply have found the more structured life of the city lackluster and routine. An uncomfortable American townspeople were possibly sublimating in song their still basically adventuresome nature, along with a spiritual and moral zeal only partly diluted from the intensity of the frontier camp meeting.

But while homely rural values were often exonerated in the popular music of the mid-nineteenth century and lyric outbursts of emotion considered vaguely divine, these sentiments were of necessity polished enough in their statement to comply with polite society's concept of refinement. If the commercial value of these songs was to be anything noteworthy, popular pieces had to conform to the bounds of the genteel tradition, since most of the sheet music sold by the 1840s was bought by the upper middle classes whose tastes had been molded by professional teachers and spokesmen of the "better music" movement. Musical life in most mid-Victorian homes centered around the parlor piano, usually a square model with heavy carved legs. While piano playing was considered a particularly becoming activity for young ladies, the whole family might gather around the instrument on special evenings, blending their assorted voices in song. On social occasions friends sometimes joined in singing or the daughters would entertain, either at the keyboard or with a voice solo or duet. In any event, domestic music, according to the ideals of the day, was a family affair, and only songs gentle enough for the ears of the entire family were considered in any way appropriate.

The humorous songs so integral a part of the country's popular entertainment were accepted with distinct reservations into the hallowed parlors of antebellum America. Whimsical numbers of the less boisterous variety were sometimes heard at family gatherings, but they were not considered to possess the same noble qualities that the delicate "heart" songs did, no matter how free of vulgarity. Clearly the desire to be emotionally moved did not extend, in a refined context, to being moved to laughter, since laughter was considered as basically undignified as the soulful tear was uplifting.

Traditional airs and European art songs were occasionally performed at more formal parlor affairs, along with selections from lighter operas like Balfe's *The Bohemian Girl*. But after the 1830s, a period of depressed activity, American music publishers expanded to meet an increased demand for popular ballads of native origin. The market was flooded with pieces styled in the contemporary vogue, as prices on sheet music leveled in the face of keen competition. Few of the songs published were of lasting interest, and successful compositions were imitated time and again. Publishers expected at least half of their works in the popular field to fail completely, while sales of 3000 copies for instrumental pieces, or 5000 copies for vocal selections, were considered appreciable. The demand was strongest, Stone insists, "where quality was nearest the prevailing level of banality, sentimentalism, and simplicity," and those composers who succeeded best adhered to this precept rigidly. Under great commercial pressure, publishers were reluctant to pay substantial royalties or bind themselves to composers through longterm commitments.

Although America's interest in music rose substantially during the two decades before the Civil War, the public's musical experience nevertheless remained limited, and popular taste stayed loyal to romantic lyrics and elementary tunes, occasionally spiced with titillating references to novel and stirring events. The sheet music trade being their major means of support, composers wrote for the readiest market, in a style within the grasp of the amateur musician. To encourage sales song covers were decorated with eye-appealing lithographs that illustrated in detail, and sometimes in color, the literal theme of the piece.

At the same time that the American mind was uncomfortable with the abstract, its concept of "correctness" was clearly associated with the more sedate human emotions. These feelings, however, were dealt with in the popular culture of the nineteenth century in specific, direct terms, seldom bordering on the philosophical and without much regard for the niceties of technique. In commercial music society's platitudes were consistently related to immediate experiences, while sentimentality entered in some form into virtually every song not frankly satirical. "The penalty of democracy in art," Sigmund Spaeth observes, "is that it teeters too dangerously on the tight-rope between the sublime and the ridiculous. Pathos is constantly in danger of descending to bathos. The simple, naive sentiment of a great folk song is far too easily replaced by the cheap sentimentality of a Broadway tunesmith; and the unabashed enthusiast of open feelings openly arrived at, is too often unable to distinguish between the two."

Into this atmosphere came the recognized luminary of mid-nineteenth century American popular songwriters—Stephen Collins Foster, who floated on the wave of sentimentality and at his best was a master at nostalgic expression.

Foster was born in a white cottage overlooking the Allegheny River and the village of Lawrenceville, near Pittsburgh, on July 4, 1826, the same day that Thomas Jefferson and John Adams died. His family belonged to the pioneer aristocracy of western Pennsylvania, prominent in the political, commercial, and social life of the Pittsburgh area. William Barclay Foster, Stephen's father, was of the rugged Scotch-Irish breed so significant in the conquest of the Appalachian frontier. A man of practical affairs, William became a successful merchant, prosperous enough to loan the government money during the War of 1812, and later served both as a member of the Pennsylvania state legislature and as mayor of Allegheny City, a Pittsburgh suburb. Stephen's mother, Eliza Clayland Tomlinson Foster, was descended from English stock that had settled on the east coast of Maryland prior to the American Revolution.

The Fosters were a close family, and after the death of a younger brother in infancy, Stephen grew up the baby. Petted and pampered not only by his parents but by his brothers and sisters as well, "little Stephy," as he was repeatedly called, spent his youth amid comfortable, happy, protected surroundings. Except for Stephen, the Foster children developed into stalwart types, well equipped to take their place in a society only a generation or so removed from the wilderness. The eldest son, William Barclay Foster,

Jr., about twenty years older than Stephen, became a civil engineer, built canals in Kentucky, Ohio, and Pennsylvania, and was in charge of constructing the section of the Pennsylvania Railroad that crossed the Allegheny Mountains. The other three sons—Henry, Dunning, and Morrison—all became successful businessmen. One of the daughters, Ann Eliza, was active in church work and married an Episcopal minister, Edward Young Buchanan—the brother of James Buchanan, later president of the United States.

But while the rest of the Foster children prepared themselves for a useful adulthood, their beloved Stephen was indulged and sheltered and encouraged to remain the immature boy. Of delicate constitution, the youth cared little for outdoor sports or strenuous activity, enjoyed only a few intimate friends, preferred seclusion, and nurtured a disposition that became more sharply sensitive and pensive. Kind, unassuming, impractical, Stephen struggled from childhood to adolescence, where he remained emotionally arrested for life.

Even as a small boy the gentle Foster evidenced a deep interest in music, although the cultural climate of western Pennsylvania was still relatively barren. Stephen's formal musical training was never very great, but as a child he somehow learned to play the flute and later the piano. A family legend has the lad at age seven accompanying his mother on a shopping trip to Pittsburgh, where he picked up a flageolet from the counter at Smith and Mellor's music store and within a few minutes amazed clerks and other shoppers by playing "Hail, Columbia." He also appears to have been strongly attracted to the stage as a youth, for his brother Morrison relates how Stephen and a group of his playmates fitted up a theater in a carriage house, where the nine year-old Foster as "star performer" sang the popular minstrel tunes of the day for the amusement of family and friends. Still another Foster tradition holds that a mulatto girl in the family's service made a practice of taking "little Stephy" with her to a black church, where the unrestrained singing of the congregation made a lasting impression on the boy.

In his schooling Stephen was never a very disciplined student, habitually erratic in his interests. While he showed a capacity for grasping material with little effort, he much preferred rambling through the woods by himself or reading at home alone to the routine of the classroom. He attended Allegheny Academy and had private tutors, in each case with marginal success. At thirteen he was sent to Bradford County, Pennsylvania, where his brother William was engaged in work on the North Branch Canal along the Susquehanna River. Stephen adored his older brother, looked upon him as a second father, and lived with William for a year and a half, while he attended two Bradford County schools—the Athens Academy and the Towanda Academy. His academic achievements at neither institution were particularly remarkable, but it was during his stay at Athens that the boy wrote his first musical composition, "The Tioga Waltz." The graceful, lilting melody was arranged for flutes and performed on a school program by Foster and some fellow students in April, 1841.

A few months later Stephen returned home to Allegheny, enjoyed a brief vacation with his parents, and then entered Jefferson College in Canonsburg. This exposure to higher education lasted a bare week, for homesickness and personal instability overcame him. He spent the next five years, 1841-1846, with his family in Pittsburgh, studying with private teachers, learning French and German, occasionally working in an office or warehouse, but devoting leisure hours to music. He was now fifteen years old and seems to have grown increasingly restless. He had no desire to return to school, was bored with drifting aimlessly, yet was unable to find either himself or his niche in the business society around him. His family became seriously worried. The youth showed no interest in selecting a career and held only temporary jobs. His "strange talent" for music, as his father referred to it, was seen as no real talent at all—not for determining a suitable profession and mapping out a future.

Yet music appears to have been the only interest Stephen was able to sustain. His first published song, "Open Thy Lattice, Love," was written in 1843 and issued by George Willig of Philadelphia the next year. Set to a verse Foster discovered in a New York weekly, the tune announced many of the characteristics of the composer's later sentimental parlor ballads. Its light, tripping melody is comfortably within the tradition of the English air, with a touch of Irish and Scottish song, while the text is well-mannered, remote, and restrained. The title page of the piece indicates that it was "composed for and dedicated to Miss Susan E. Pentland," a young girl who was living at this time with her father in the other half of the Foster's large two-family house in Allegheny City. There are suggestions that a romance existed between Susan Pentland and Stephen, but if such was the case, the affair could hardly have been taken seriously. At the time "Open Thy Lattice, Love" was written Susan was only eleven, Stephen sixteen. But ethereal romance is typical of the Foster love songs, and the object of their adoration is repeatedly physically unattainable.

While "Open Thy Lattice, Love" revealed a distinct advance in musical talent over "The Tioga Waltz," the work did not bring its composer notable financial returns. Very probably Foster sold the tune outright for a trifle. For two more years Stephen remained the "idle dreamer," living with his family and absorbing himself whenever possible with music. Under pressure to decide upon a career, he flirted with the idea of becoming a professional army officer, but early in 1846 learned that his application to West Point had been rejected. At this juncture his family determined action, arranging for Stephen to move to Cincinnati, where he would enter his brother Dunning's steamboat agency as a bookkeeper. Late in 1846 or early in 1847, the youth sailed down the Ohio from Pittsburgh, on his way—the family hoped—to learn an honest trade in the world of commerce. He would stay in Cincinnati slightly more than three years, living in the same boarding house as brother Dunning.

By this time Stephen had grown into a handsome young man—slender, not over five feet seven inches in height, but with a body well-proportioned. His feet and hands were small, his features soft and delicate. His nose inclined toward the aquiline with nostrils that were full and dilated. His lips were regular, his hair nearly black. His eyes were large and dark, lit by a marked suggestion of intelligence. He was modest, well informed on current topics, both an interesting conversationalist and an excellent listener.

The books Stephen kept for the Cincinnati firm of Irwin & Foster were models of accuracy and neatness, but the routine office chores demanded of him were at odds with the very substance of the youth's personality. From his brother's place of business, however, he could observe the black dock workers as they loaded and unloaded the Mississippi river boats. He listened to their singing as they sweated over the toils of the levee, songs of genuine human pathos. Across the river was Kentucky, from which wafted the mystic lore of the Old South. And to Cincinnati's theaters came the leading minstrel troupes of the day, as they plied their way down the waterways of America's heartland. Some of these performers Stephen had encountered in Pittsburgh, most of them he now came to know intimately, as he balanced the drudgery of bookkeeping with the excitement of talking with singers, theater managers, and music publishers.

Shortly after Stephen's departure for Cincinnati, Nelson Kneass, leader of one of the major minstrel companies of the 1840s, held a song contest in Pittsburgh. Young Foster was persuaded by his brother Morrison to enter a manuscript in the competition, sending Kneass his song "Way Down South, Where de Cane Grows." Foster's selection did not win the prize, but the contest did turn the youth's attention more seriously to song writing. In 1848 the Louisville music publisher W. C. Peters, whom the Foster family had known in Pittsburgh, brought out four of Stephen's tunes as *Songs of the Sable Harmonists*. The collection, which the novice composer virtually gave to Peters, included "Old Uncle Ned," "Oh! Susanna," "Away Down South," and "Lou'siana Belle." These numbers had all been written while Stephen was still in Pittsburgh for a singing group that met periodically in his parent's home. "Old Uncle Ned" contains one of Foster's best melodies and was enormously popular at once. In the piece the black is lifted above a clownish minstrel show caricature to become a sympathetic human being; yet the references to "old nigga" and "darky" made the song a scurrilous anachronism to a later age. The black appears more the buffoon in "Oh! Susanna," although the exaggerations and contradictions of frontier humor perhaps emerge even clearer. "Oh! Susanna," introduced publicly in a Cincinnati ice cream parlor, is a delightful bit of nonsense, quite outside the spectrum of Foster's genteel salon ballads, and discloses a boisterous rollicking wit that grew less evident in the composer's later, more introspective years. The infectious melody not only became an immediate sensation on the minstrel stage, but practically served as the leitmotif of the "Forty-Niners" on their way to the California gold fields. So familiar did the tune become that Bayard Taylor reported in 1853 that he had heard it sung by a Hindu musician in the streets of New Delhi!

Although Peters is said to have earned ten thousand dollars from *Songs of the Sable Harmonists*, Foster received very little. "Oh! Susanna" supposedly brought him about one hundred dollars, but appeared in many pirated editions from which the composer received nothing. The publication of these four songs, however, won Stephen a considerable reputation with itinerant minstrel performers and the general public alike. Impressed partly by the substantial amounts of money others were making off his music, Foster left Cincinnati in 1849 and returned to Pittsburgh determined to pursue song writing as a full-time career. He moved back into his parent's home, converted an upstairs room into a study, and—in the words of his brother Morrison—"devoted himself to the study of music as a science." In the evenings he often sat at the piano, improvising tunes and harmonies by the hour and occasionally singing one of his own songs or a traditional favorite. "At times," Morrison Foster recalls, "tears could be seen on his cheeks as he sang this song, so sensitive was his nature to the influence of true poetry combined with music."

The next two years were among the composer's most productive, probably his peak in terms of consistent quality. He published fourteen songs, five for the parlor and nine for the minstrel stage, and a piano piece. Of the minstrel tunes "Camptown Races" achieved the greatest popularity. A nonsense song celebrating the happy-go-lucky, "Jim Crow" type black, the number is dominated by a strong rhythmic pulse and the recurring chant, "Doo-dah-doo-dah day." While the sheet music sale numbered some 5000 copies for the seven years following the song's publication, Foster realized only $101.25 in royalties. "Nelly Bly," another of the big successes from this period, contains a simple melody and a lyric declaration of contentment and plenty.

Despite the popularity of his minstrel tunes, Foster felt that he should be writing music of a more genteel nature, works more suitable to the parlor. His piano quick-step "Santa Anna's Retreat from Buena Vista" was full of the elegant keyboard effects so much admired at the time, but the selection was never considered among the composer's more notable efforts. His salon pieces were far closer to Foster's ideal, since his patrician sense of decorum convinced him that his stature as a composer rested on refined airs like "The Spirit of My Song," rather than the more vernacular minstrel numbers, about which he always felt apologetic. Consistent with the fashion of the day, Foster's parlor songs drip with melancholy sentiment and are much concerned with fair, departed maidens, voices from the past, and blossoms that faded all too soon. "Lily Ray" was one of the first of the composer's laments to a lovely girl taken prematurely by death.

> *Grief, to thy memory,*
>   *Tuneth a lay,*
> *Lovely, departed one,*
>   *Sweet Lily Ray.*

"I Would Not Die in Summer Time" appeared in 1851, while "Wilt Thou Be Gone, Love," one of Foster's more elaborate compositions, in the form of a duet, is a musical paraphrase from Shakespeare's *Romeo and Juliet*.

By now the young songwriter had signed a favorable contract with the New York publishing firm of Firth, Pond & Company, paying him a royalty of three cents on each copy of his printed music. The terms were fair, reasonably profitable, and Foster's business relationship with the company proved generally satisfactory. Firth, Pond & Company would remain the composer's major publisher through 1860, although he occasionally entered short-term agreements with other firms, like F. D. Benteen of Baltimore.

In 1851 E. P. Christy, of Christy's Minstrels, the most popular blackface troupe of them all, asked Foster to write songs that his company could sing before they were published. Christy was willing to pay a nominal fee for the privilege, and almost any number performed by the Christy Minstrels was guaranteed an enlarged sheet music sale. Foster accepted Christy's offer, writing for him his masterpiece, "Old Folks at Home." So sensitive was the composer about his image of respectability, however, and so reluctant was he to have his name publicly associated with what he disdained as "Ethiopian songs" that he permitted E. P. Christy's name to appear on the title page as author and composer when the song was published by Firth, Pond & Company later that fall.

"Old Folks at Home" quickly achieved a popularity beyond anything Foster had known before, selling 40,000 copies within the first eleven months. The imperious John Sullivan Dwight, perplexed and disturbed by the song's universal appeal, wrote in his *Journal*, October 2, 1852:

> *Old Folks at Home* . . . is on everybody's tongue, and consequently
> in everybody's mouth. Pianos and guitars groan with it, night and
> day; sentimental young ladies sing it; sentimental young gentlemen
> warble it in midnight serenades; volatile young "bucks" hum it in
> the midst of their business and pleasures; boatmen roar it out . . . all
> the bands play it.

Before long even great operatic singers like Nilsson and Patti were including the piece in their repertoire.

Although Foster wrote the song in a crude, inconsistent black dialect, he was dealing with a theme close to his own heart, the love of home.

> *All up and down de whole creation,*
> *Sadly I roam,*
> *Still longing for de old plantation,*
> *And for de old folks at home.*

The composer merely transferred to the plantation black those same sentiments more genteelly expressed in the parlor ballad, sentiments that Foster, in his reluctance to leave the parental nest, had experienced intimately. Yet while the spirit of "Old Folks at Home" was genuine, the immediate setting was distant and artificial. Morrison Foster relates how his brother came to his office one day and asked him to suggest a two-syllable name of a southern river to use in a song. Morrison mentioned the "Yazoo," but this was rejected as no better than the "Pedee," which Stephen had penciled into the initial draft. The older brother then took an atlas down from the top of his desk and turned to a map of the United States. After a brief search, his eye fell upon the name "Swanee," designating a small river in Florida that emptied into the Gulf of Mexico. "That's it, that's it exactly," Stephen exclaimed, abruptly leaving the office without further conversation. When the song was finished, it began, "Way down upon the Swanee Ribber," referring to an inconspicuous stream Foster had never heard of before and would never see, yet became the very symbol of home.

Musically, the strength of "Old Folks at Home" lies in its honest simplicity, which reinforces the theme of lost innocence. The tune is restricted to five notes, while the harmony is almost consistently tonic, dominant, and subdominant. In Wilfrid Mellers' estimation, the song "owes its obsessive quality to its very rudimentariness: the fourfold repeated phrases make their effect because they are *worth* repeating, for the leaping octave followed by a pentatonic minor third contains an age-old yearning, while the declining cadential phrase brings us safe to the security of Home."

In his private life Stephen Foster was soon to have reason to yearn for the old folks and home. On July 22, 1850, he married Jane Denny McDowell, daughter of a leading Pittsburgh physician. The two families had known each other for some time, and Jane had been a member of the vocal quartet that met regularly in the Foster home. She was the contralto of the group; the soprano was Susan Pentland, the young lady to whom Stephen had dedicated "Open Thy Lattice, Love" years before. After a wedding trip to Baltimore and New York, the couple moved in with Stephen's parents, living there for the first year and a half of the marriage. Their daughter and only child, Marion, was born in Pittsburgh on April 18, 1851. Ten months later brother Dunning arrived from Cincinnati with his steamboat, the *James Milligan*, to pick up cargo for New Orleans. Stephen and his wife, made temporarily affluent by the success of "Old Folks at Home," boarded the ship for a month's pleasure trip down the Mississippi—the composer's only venture into the deep South and one of his few moments of marital contentment.

Encouraged by the popularity of his minstrel tunes and regretful that he had not claimed credit for writing "Old Folks at Home" himself, he wrote E. P. Christy, May 25, 1852:

As I once intimated to you, I had the intention of omitting my name on my Ethiopian songs, owing to the prejudice against them by

some, which might injure my reputation as a writer of another style
of music, but I find that by my efforts I have done a great deal to
build up a taste for the Ethiopian songs among refined people by
making the words suitable to their taste, instead of the trashy and
really offensive words which belong to songs of that order.
Therefore I have concluded to reinstate my name on my songs and to
pursue the Ethiopian business without fear or shame and lend all
my energies to making the business live, at the same time that I will
wish to establish my name as the best Ethiopian song-writer.

Perhaps inspired by his visit to New Orelans, Foster published "Massa's
in de Cold, Cold Ground" in the summer of 1852. The poignant, sorrowful
song contains one of the composer's loveliest melodies. "My Old Kentucky
Home," probably written late in the same year, stands as a Foster classic. Most
likely influenced by Harriet Beecher Stowe's novel *Uncle Tom's Cabin*,
published in 1851, "My Old Kentucky Home" reflects a number of the book's
sentiments and phrases, although Foster was certainly no abolitionist. The
piece, in fact, was originally entitled "Poor Uncle Tom, Good Night," and its
verses show a marked similarity to Mrs. Stowe's plot. The first stanza begins
happily, "the darkies are gay." Then "hard times comes a-knocking at the
door" and "the time has come when the darkies have to part." Evidently they
are sold to plantations down South, "where the head must bow and the back
will have to bend. . . in the field where the sugar canes grow." As in the piece's
companion, "Old Folks at Home," the black slave is treated with
understanding and affection rather than humor and ridicule. Interestingly
enough, Foster has forsaken the attempt at Negro dialect present in his earlier
blackface songs, bringing the selection closer to the genteel tradition of the
whites. Again the composer idealized a specific into a universal, as the house
in Kentucky became a symbol of the eternal home, filled with joys and
sorrows that are timeless. "Earthquakes may swallow Kentucky," Robert
MacGowan contends, "but the vision of that home will endure forever."
Structurally the work is quite simple, its melody employing only six notes.
    "Massa's in de Cold, Cold Ground" and "My Old Kentucky Home" were
both introduced by E. P. Christy, and each sold over 50,000 copies of sheet
music within a brief period. Foster would continue writing minstrel tunes,
although his output in that field became appreciably less, particularly after
Christy's retirement in 1854.
    Meanwhile Stephen's short-lived nuptial bliss was coming to an end.
The estrangement reached its initial climax early in 1853, when Foster left
Jane and his baby to live alone in New York, in part to be nearer his publisher.
The family attitude is glimpsed from a letter written by Stephen's sister
Henrietta, expressing concern for "poor Stephy," who has "had trouble
enough already." It is doubtful that Jane understood the impractical dreamer
she had married, and it is certain that Stephen's moody, instable,
temperament and gross indifference to financial matters did not fit him well

into the harness of a demanding marriage. His love for his parents was so consuming that his wife was bound to feel a neglect that was unintentional.

While the couple was separated, Foster wrote one of his best love songs, "Jeanie with the Light Brown Hair." "Jeanie" was probably the auburn-haired Jane, and into this lovely haunting melody the composer poured all of his feeling for his young wife. But typical of Foster, the love object is distant, adored in memory. Jeanie is contemplated with nostalgic yearning, but she is gone. As if "unable to face true passion or grief," H. Wiley Hitchcock suggests, "the dreamer finds the mournful dream delicious."

By the summer of 1854, Stephen and Jane were reunited and for a few months lived in a rented house in Hoboken, New Jersey. Then the longing for home and family became too great, and Foster suddenly proposed to his wife that they return to Pittsburgh. They sold their household belongings to a used furniture dealer and within twenty-four hours were on the road for Allegheny. According to Morrison Foster, Stephen arrived late at night, totally unexpected. His mother was awakened and immediately recognized his footsteps on the porch. As she hurried through the hall to let him in, she called out, "Is that my dear son come back again?" The sound of her voice so touched Stephen that when his mother opened the door she found him sitting on a porch bench weeping like a child.

The composer never left home again as long as his mother and father were alive. From 1853 to 1860 he and his wife remained together in Allegheny. Foster produced some of his most mawkish songs during this period, including "Willie, We Have Missed You," "Gentle Annie," and "Come Where My Love Lies Dreaming." Although still in his late twenties, Stephen was becoming increasingly obsessed with melancholy reveries of the old days, old friends, and an innocent happiness that could never return. Memories of the family dog, a beautiful setter given to Stephen by a friend, inspired the popular ballad "Old Dog Tray." Here Foster mourned a "once happy day," apparently that time in his childhood when he used to watch his dog playing with children on the Allegheny Common, days when the dog was his constant companion.

Then in January, 1855, his mother suddenly died. His father, who had been an invalid for four years, survived her only six months. The combined loss was a terrific blow to Stephen. His musical output trickled almost to a halt. In 1856 and 1857 he wrote only two songs, one each year, and both were among his more banal efforts. At the same time expenses began to mount, so that by early 1857 the musician's financial resources had become alarmingly depleted. In March he temporarily alleviated this distress by the short-sighted move of selling Firth, Pond & Company for approximately $2000 in cash all his future financial rights to the songs they had published to date, 1849 through 1856.

In 1858, forced by economic necessity, Foster began composing again, but the old inspiration was gone. He plodded industriously on in Allegheny until 1860, writing in an unimaginative, wooden fashion. The songs he produced were mediocre and lifeless, their motif increasingly contrived, yet repeatedly filled with a longing for the past. "Under the Willow She's Sleeping," "Sadly to My Heart Appealing," "Linda Has Departed," "Kiss Me, Dear Mother," "Poor Drooping Maiden," and "None Shall Weep a Tear for Me" are but examples of these sentimental effusions. Their sales were understandably light. Foster had drawn ahead on future royalties and was deeply in debt to his publishers. In desperation he sold Firth, Pond & Company in August, 1860, his complete rights to songs they had published since 1858. The $1600 he received from the transaction was almost immediately paid out to creditors, while the hopeless straits grew worse.

During the summer of 1860, at the urging of his publishers who agreed to pay him a small annual salary for a minimum of twelve songs a year, the composer moved to New York. His wife and daughter may have lived there with him for a while, but only for a brief time if at all. Life in the city for Foster was filled with excruciating loneliness, dark despair, and personal degradation. For several years he had been drinking heavily, and separated now from family and friendly surroundings, he drifted toward chronic alcoholism. He roomed on the Bowery, not far from later-day Chinatown, turning out the potboilers that earned him his pitiful income. Gradually the last vestiges of structure to his life began to break, as he turned more and more to the bottle for solace, accepting whatever he could get for his songs from any firm that would take them.

He pulled himself together twice, long enough to write the two masterpieces of his later years—"Old Black Joe" and "Beautiful Dreamer." Probably composed just before Foster came to New York, "Old Black Joe" was the last of his great plantation songs, published by Firth, Pond & Company in November, 1860. For a fleeting moment the creative spark returned, and out of the turmoil of his emotions Foster was able to gather a genuine expression of human grief—the grief he felt over the loss of his family and departed youth, intensified by his growing sense of insecurity and failure. "It is not a blackface minstrel who steps forward on the stage to sing *Old Black Joe*," Fletcher Hodges contends. "It is Stephen Foster himself, and he sings to us from his very soul!"

> *Gone are the days when my heart was young and gay,*
> *Gone are my friends from the cotton fields away;*
> *Gone from the earth to a better land I know,*
> *I hear their gentle voices calling "Old Black Joe."*

There is no hint of a black dialect now, for Foster is voicing his own feelings, only faintly disguised in the southern setting.

"Beautiful Dreamer," copyrighted in 1864, represents the last spurt from Foster's dying genius. Evidently he is seeking an escape from the grim realities of the world about him, a dream to eclipse the failure of his life in New York. He longs for the contentment of an earlier moment.

Sounds of the rude world, heard in the day,
Lulled by the moonlight, have all passed away.

Trite though some of the lines may be, the piece is musically among his best love songs. But again the love object is unattainable, since she is asleep, and emerges from the piece as fatuous as vapor.

In January, 1864, Foster was living at the American Hotel on the Bowery. He was taken seriously ill with a fever and confined to his bed. After two or three days he struggled up to wash himself and fainted, falling across the washbasin. The vessel broke, cutting a gash in the composer's neck and face. A chambermaid, bringing towels he had asked for, found him lying on the floor of his room, unconscious and bleeding. She called for aid and helped him back to bed. When he recovered his senses, Foster asked for a doctor. He was admitted to Bellevue Hospital on January 10, 1864, registered as a "laborer" and placed in a charity ward for the city's derelicts. Severely weakened by loss of blood and fever, he was unable to rally.

On January 13, it was snowing in New York City; Stephen Foster at thirty-seven lay alone, dying. The end came peacefully and quietly. His body was taken by William A. Pond to an undertaker's and placed in an iron coffin. His wife and brothers Morrison and Henry arrived from Pittsburgh to escort the remains home. As if to add to the anticlimax, the train met with an accident en route when a bridge gave way, dropping two passenger coaches into a stream; the baggage car containing Foster's body was unharmed by the wreck. Funeral services were held on January 20 at Trinity Church in Pittsburgh. On the way to the grave the cortege was joined by a volunteer band that played "Come Where My Love Lies Dreaming" and "Old Folks at Home." Stephen was buried in Allegheny Cemetery beside his mother and father, not far from the cottage where he was born.

Having grown up with a strong "angel view" of childhood, Foster was ill-equipped to accept his own frailties and unable to cope with the dissipation of his later life. As the pristine ideal of himself grew tarnished, his self-esteem shattered, and his will to live rapidly slipped away. In his helplessness in New York he called out in desperation for the mother who had imbued him with the impression of home as an oasis in a hostile desert, composing in quick succession "Oh! Tell Me of My Mother," "Farewell, Mother Dear," and "Farewell, Sweet Mother." Having rejected the wife who might have helped him mature, he clung to the end to a fantasy of innocence, security, and self-importance rooted in his infant past, hating himself for having blemished its image. To exist he turned to the only form of harlotry he knew, writing songs that were assured a momentary market. Taking advantage of the demand for Civil War songs, Foster—himself a staunch Democrat—wrote "We Are Coming Father Abraham, 300,000 More" in 1862, aware that its topical nature would cause it to sell. The next year he published a collection of Sunday school hymns, most of them feeble and undistinguished and long ago forgotten.

Viewed in a larger perspective, however, Foster's nostalgia was consistent with a greater national longing for the past. Americans, particularly in the more settled East, already were beginning to look back on a "once happy day" of unspoiled forests and virgin lands. Ruin and change followed in the wake of the pioneer, and as industry made its inroads into the Jeffersonian garden, the sense of uneasiness and dislocation grew. In literature Washington Irving, who incidentally adored the songs of Stephen Foster, early expressed resistence to the transition in progress through his legend of Rip Van Winkle. As Lewis Mumford explains in *The Golden Day*: "The old landmarks have gone; the old faces have disappeared; all the outward aspects of life have changed. At the bottom, however, Rip himself has not changed; for he has been drunk and lost in a dream, and ... he remains, mentally, a boy."

Still too steeped in optimism for gloom, Americans—like Foster— regarded the passing of their innocence with gentle melancholy rather than bitterness, glorifying the old in preference to depreciating the new. Yet in the face of a heightening sectional conflict, the waning of frontier abandon, and industry's exaggerated emphasis on materialism, aggressiveness, and a competitive spirit, there was cause for disquietude. Foster amazingly offered an urbanizing people a harmless escape from crass commercialism and the confusion of a changing world without denying any of the fundamental principles of the day.

Paradoxically, while Americans of the nineteenth century welcomed an opportunity to respond publicly to cheap sentimentality, they cherished from their Puritan heritage a cultural ideal of exercising restraint in the display of genuine emotions. Rather than violate this convention, or appear womanly, Foster employed the mask of the plantation slave, so much in vogue at the time. His more contrived sentiments he openly exposed in his parlor ballads, but his sincere feelings, those from the heart, he felt obliged to veil behind blackface. Unquestionably his minstrel songs, as a group, represent his most honest writing, once the popular Never-Never Land image of the South is scraped away. Initially, he used the black dialect to disguise the emotional flow more carefully, but the practice dwindled to a trace, then stopped altogether. As his personality and self-will disintegrated, the composer seems either to have forgotten or to have no longer possessed the strength to lift the mask before the last plaintive cries seeped from his tormented soul.

Far from a trained musician, Foster's musical strength lay in its simplicity. Introduced to music most likely by his mother and sisters, the composer's knowledge of sound technique never exceeded the rudimentary. Most of what he learned he picked up through his own efforts, and there is slight indication that his exposure to the European classics was more than perfunctory. On trips to New York, even during his happier days, there is little evidence that he sought out professional musicians or attended serious musical performances. By the time he decided to make a career of song writing, it was too late for intensive formal study.

Yet in some regards Foster's appeal stemmed from his very limitations. In a period when foreign musicians dominated the cities on the east coast, Foster's cultural isolation in Pittsburgh and Cincinnati allowed him the latitude to compose with a personality essentially his own. Growing up on the headwaters of the Ohio River, where the North and South often met, Foster caught a glimpse of the plantation life he would romanticize in song. Clearly he enjoyed his share of minstrel shows and mastered the blackface idiom through repeated exposure. From trips to Ohio as a boy he gleaned some knowledge of a vanishing frontier, while in Pittsburgh he observed intimately the emergence of an industrial society. He was able to write for a polyglot population in terms they understood, maintaining an air of dignity and at the same time directing himself to a simple people of a simple age.

A natural gift for melody is Foster's most striking musical gift, and he is often compared with Schubert by his champions. Vigorous and lilting, his melodies abound in wide intervals, sometimes leaping an entire octave, yet shine with an unembellished charm. His harmony is appropriately elementary, consisting of only a few standard chords. The beat is regular and firm. At his best when writing both music and lyrics, Foster's simple tunes are an affecting complement to his deliberately childlike verses. Much of his vocabulary consists of monosyllables. When polysyllables occur, the composer is prone to separate them musically by an adroitly spaced sequence of notes. Composing as he did—largely by instinct—it is understandable that technical ineptitude and amateurishness are evident on virtually every page. But Foster's calculated simplicity results in a flow of melody as easily sung and remembered as Lowell Mason's hymns and a haunting tenderness distinctly his own.

Altogether the composer wrote over two hundred selections, including one-hundred fifty parlor ballads, thirty minstrel tunes, and about two dozen religious songs. Over the course of twenty years, however, his style matured very little. "Beautiful Dreamer" shows no appreciable advance in technique over "Open Thy Lattice, Love," although the minstrel numbers do embrace a superior element. Melancholy though many of his pieces are, not one of them is in the minor mode. A true child of America, Foster set even his most morbid texts to tunes in the major mode, which is normally associated with vigor and optimism.

While Foster may have attended black church services as a boy and listened to black stevedores singing on the wharves of Cincinnati, his own music is squarely rooted in the Celtic-English-American folk tradition. Even his minstrel songs reflect little or no direct Afro-American influence, although some of them suggest characteristics related to the early white spirituals that appeared later in slaves' variants. Basically Foster refined the folk tradition in which he was grounded to the level of a vernacular art.

For later generations Stephen Foster's music has often seemed wistfully bound to the past, a dulcet souvenir from the age of crinoline and the daguerreotype. Yet in his singular way, the composer not only mirrored the spirit of his time, but phrased his personal nostalgia in terms sufficiently universal to achieve a permanent place in the nation's musical literature and more than casual recognition from abroad. While he received his share of attack from contemporary exponents of "scientific" music, Foster's reputation in the homely musical culture of his day was secure; at his peak he even earned a reasonably comfortable income from his songs. At the time of his marriage the composer was receiving royalties of approximately fourteen hundred dollars a year, and Firth, Pond & Company paid him over fifteen thousand dollars between 1849 and 1860. Most of this amount, however, came from the sale of a handful of his best works; once he cut himself off from rights to these, his income fell to a pittance.

Foster's recognition as America's first great songwriter must be viewed against the background of his age, for certainly his songs transcend the banal efforts characteristic of the popular music of the early nineteenth century. At his best Foster clearly rises above the bathos of "The Old Arm Chair" or the contrived tearfulness of "The Blind Orphan Girl," and even at his worst there is little of the oafish overstatement of the topical songs of the period or the hysterical unreality of trainwrecks, mountain blizzards, maniacs' clawing asylum walls, and eagles' snatching babies from mothers' arms. In his masterworks the sentimental predilections of his time are sublimated, allowing honest feeling to issue forth. Like his contemporaries, Foster offers escape, but in mitigated form, within the pale of credibility. His escape essentially comes from distance—distance in time (childhood, old age, the "good old days"), distance in place (the South), distance from reality (dreams), and distance from life (death—although usually softened in metaphor to sleep).

From the shipwreck of his life Foster was able to draw an expression of nostalgia in sympathy with the fears and longings of the urban frontier in which he lived. Far more reflective than philosophical, the composer was able to generalize his own experience into an attitude harmonious with young America's consciousness of vanishing innocence. When more adult personalities attempted to appeal in popular song to the puerile feelings of the burgeoning nation, their efforts as a rule were synthetic and theatrical, since the sentiments they voiced sprang from a designing intellect rather than from the heart. But in his inspired moments Stephen Foster conveyed genuine emotion through pure simplicity, an adolescent spirit serenading an adolescent land.

CHAPTER

XI

The Minstrel Stage

The growth of the city and the emergence of a clearly defined working class during the first half of the nineteenth century was accompanied by a gradual expansion of American entertainment. The softening of religious opposition, combined with a need to replace rural pastimes no longer available, encouraged the urban quarter of the nation to refashion its popular amusements. The new recreations, intended for the sweep of a democratic society, were generally something to be watched rather than enjoyed through active participation. Horse racing was revived, and other spectator sports began their evolution. Amusement parks were established, as were beer gardens and public dance halls. Despite lingering prejudice and restrictions from puritanical factions, an industrializing America was feeling its way toward a richer, more satisfying leisure for its urban masses.

Natural museums and itinerant circuses began to flourish, as direct contact with nature lessened. Theater continued to broaden its appeal, and by the time Jacksonian democracy reached its height three indigenous figures had become fixed in American drama—the Yankee peddler, the backwoodsman, and the blackface minstrel. Each was portrayed on stage as a larger than life stereotype; each possessed a comic dimension, yet reflected an element of reality and a fundamental aspect of the American character. All three preserved an Arcadian concept of rural America and mirrored the nostalgia of a society in transition.

Emerging in the 1840s, the rage for blackface minstrelsy soon swept the land, eclipsing every other form of theater on the American scene with the possible exception of the circus. Although it was very much considered a vernacular entertainment, the minstrel shows appealed to all classes of people and, with the disappearance of the ballad opera, became the major means of exposure for popular songs during the years preceding the Civil War. At a time when humorous songs were welcomed with caution into the family parlor and more elevated forms of music and theater catered almost exclusively to the genteel tastes of the upper classes, the minstrel stage thrived on unabandoned wit and nonsense and embraced songs both sentimental and whimsical.

While considered distinctly American, black minstrelsy bears striking similarities to the Italian *commedia dell'arte*, and the penchant for blackface had definite antecedents on the British stage as early as the seventeenth century. In this country Lewis Hallam, Jr. is known to have imitated a drunken black in 1769 during a New York performance of Isaac Bickerstaff's comic opera *The Padlock*. On the evening of December 30, 1799, Gottlieb Graupner—later organizer of the first American orchestra and one of the founders of the Handel and Haydn Society—rendered in blackface the comic "Song of the Negro Boy" at the Federal Theater in Boston, following the second act of the tragedy *Oroonoko, or the Royal Slave*. He won such applause that the song had to be repeated, and the German musician may in fact have been the first to sing on stage in blackface. In the years after 1800 comic songs delivered in blackface became increasingly popular in both the theater and the circus. When rendered on a dramatic program, these songs were either inserted between acts of a play or given between separate parts of the bill.

By the second decade of the century virtually every circus in the country boasted a blackface performer, and the number of British and American singers specializing in "Negro songs" had grown tremendously. George Washington Dixon, one of the most successful pioneers in black impersonation, appeared in Albany as early as 1827, while playing with a circus, singing "My Long-Tailed Blue." The song, which the entertainer supposedly wrote, depicted a black dandy out strutting on Sunday, dressed in his flashy blue swallowtail coat; later it proved to be a classic in minstrel music. In 1829 Washington introduced one of his favorite numbers at the Bowery Theater in New York, John Clements' "Coal Black Rose," and enjoyed great popularity in the city throughout that summer. In 1834 he sang "Zip Coon" in Philadelphia, another song he may have written. Although the words are no longer remembered, the tune became more commonly known later in instrumental form as "Turkey in the Straw."

George Nichols, a clown in Purdy Brown's Theater and Circus of the South and West, composed countless verses for comic songs, frequently impromptu, and is often credited with having sung "Jim Crow" years before Thomas D. Rice made it famous as a dance. Nichols presumably sang the song first in whiteface, then in blackface. Actors also became fascinated with portraying blacks. The English comedian Charles Mathews came to the United States in 1822 and during his year and a half stay grew enchanted with the Afro-Americans, particularly their dialect and humor. Observing the blacks in a variety of situations, he collected "scraps of songs and malaprops" from them and tried to transcribe on paper the peculiar speech of a black revivalist he heard in Philadelphia. When Mathews began incorporating this material into his skits, his characterization of the black was somewhat more realistic than earlier ones, although still basically stereotyped. The actor reproduced several songs indigenous to blacks on stage, such as "Possum Up a Gum Tree," imitating the dialect he had heard.

But the most significant personality in laying the foundation for American minstrelsy was undoubtedly Thomas Dartmouth ("Daddy") Rice, whose impersonation of "Jim Crow" supplied the early burnt cork tradition with its very heart. Rice was born in New York City in 1808, of poor parents, and as a boy he became a supernumerary at the Park Theater; later he journeyed up and down the Ohio River as an itinerant player. Although his specialty was comedy, he was employed for a time in Ludlow and Smith's Southern Theater in Louisville as a property man, lamplighter, and stage carpenter. One day while walking through the streets of some Ohio Valley town— Louisville in all probability—Rice discovered a slave crooning a curious melody and doing a strange shuffling step each time he reached the chorus of his song. Some accounts claim the slave was old and decrepit; others say he was a crippled black boy. The slave supposedly was rubbing down the horses in a stable-yard near the theater where Rice was playing. The man struck Rice as an engaging combination of pathos and humor. His right shoulder was deformed, drawn up high, while his left leg was stiff and crooked, causing him to walk with a limp—obviously painful, but nevertheless laughable to Rice. The tune the black sang as he went about his chores was mournful, yet at the end of each stanza he gave an odd little jump that caused bystanders to smile.

From this experience Rice drew the idea for his famous "Jump Jim Crow" routine. The comedian copied the walk and dress of his black model, but supplemented the stanzas of the slave's song with verses of his own. The performer also wrote new music for the number, later published by W. C. Peters, and while subsequent interpreters added numberless verses, the refrain stayed the same:

> First on de heel tap, den on de toe,
> Ebery time I wheel about I jump Jim Crow.
> Wheel about and turn about and do jis so,
> And ebery time I wheel about I jump Jim Crow.

It was probably during an engagement with Samuel Drake's company at the Louisville Theater that "Daddy" Rice first jumped "Jim Crow," most likely interpolated between acts of a local play by Solon Robinson entitled The Rifle, in which Rice was cast as a cornfield slave. The song's verses were largely nonsense, although this provided much of the appeal. Aside from what is suggested in the refrain, the exact nature of the dance is unknown. The few illustrations indicate a curious pose of bent knees, one heel up, the other down, one arm raised, the other on the hip, and the head cocked to one side.

According to Robert Nevin, who maintains that the routine originated in Cincinnati and was performed first in Pittsburgh, Rice initially had no clothes appropriate for the "Jim Crow" character. Noticing a porter in tattered attire similar to those of the stable slave, the entertainer appropriated the porter's garments for his dance. The porter, supposedly named Jim Cuff, stood in trepidation while Rice removed his ragged clothing, waiting in the stage wings practically nude as the comedian sang and danced "Jim Crow" for the first time. So well was the number received that Rice felt obliged to repeat the routine again and again. With each repetition the porter became more impatient, since he was expected back at his post by his superiors. In desperation the black finally ran out on the stage and proceeded to retrieve his clothing in full view of the audience. Nevin insists that the applause became so uproarious that the exit doors of the theater had to be thrown open, signaling the end of the performance.

On later occasions Rice presented his "Jim Crow" gyrations dressed in a dilapidated coat, straw hat, and worn out shoes, emphasizing the shiftless nature of his subject's character. The performer's tall, slender appearance enhanced his success considerably, although he was extremely clever in imitating a shambling gait and rustic black dialect. The routine was shortly expanded into an afterpiece, and in 1832 Rice jumped "Jim Crow" in New York for the first time during the interval between two serious dramas, *The Hunchback* and *Catherine of Cleves*. Three days later he danced and sang at the Bowery Theater following a performance of *Othello*.

Rice was before the public with his black impersonations for the next two decades, coining new verses for his songs to fit the particular locality in which he was playing. He played in New Orleans in 1835, where he likely observed authentic black entertainers like Corn Meal, whose popularity was soaring at the time. Rice returned to the Louisiana city in 1836 and again in 1838, on his second trip actually preparing a skit entitled "Corn Meal." In all probability Rice borrowed nuances from the black performer, as did a number of his blackface contemporaries.

Besides songs and dances, Rice wrote and acted in a number of burnt cork farces, often referred to as "Ethiopian Operas" and clearly precursors of the later minstrel sketches. As early as January, 1833, Rice introduced audiences at the Bowery Theater to *Long Island Juba* and *Where's My Head?* Within the next few years two of his most popular works of this sort appeared, *Bone Squash* and *Oh Hush!* or *The Virginny Cupids*, both of which drew ideas from the fading English ballad opera. Some of Rice's compositions were fairly vulgar in line and action, but they seem to have met with general success. Certainly the entertainer himself enjoyed a popularity in the 1830s and 1840s unmatched by any other American comedian of his time. He was well received in London and in Dublin and was paid six hundred dollars for a single performance. Late in his career, Rice participated in a few minstrel shows, but the solo act remained his specialty.

"Daddy" Rice's influence on other theatrical figures was considerable. During an engagement in Washington in 1833 he introduced to the profession four year-old Joseph Jefferson, later the great exponent of Rip Van Winkle. Rice reportedly carried the boy on stage in a sack and sang:

Ladies and gentlemen,
I'd have for you to know,
I'se got a little darkey here
That jumps Jim Crow.

At this moment he dumped the blackfaced boy onto the boards, and little Joe Jefferson proceeded to render a child's version of the "Jim Crow" dance. Rice was also instrumental in encouraging Stephen Foster to write songs for the minstrel stage and assisted the composer in his early days. Two of Foster's lesser songs, "Long Ago Day" and "This Rose Will Remind You" were written especially for Rice.

The original "Jim Crow" was imitated time and again in the decade before the first actual minstrel show. Barney Williams became famous for his blackface dances, although Jack Diamond's "Ethiopian breakdowns" were probably even better known. Bill Keller, Barney Burns, and Bob Farrell all made a stir, singing songs like "Coal Black Rose," "My Long-Tailed Blue," and "Zip Coon" in circus rings and theaters ranging from Niblo's Saloon to Barnum's Museum to frontier opera houses. While most of these blackfaced imitators worked independently at first, from 1840 on they began banding together, most often a banjoist teaming with a dancer.

But not until Dan Emmett and the Virginia Minstrels appeared at the Bowery Amphitheatre in New York sometime in February, 1843, was blackface minstrelsy actually born. Emmett, the group's leader, would become a legend later as the composer of the adopted Confederate anthem "Dixie," originally written as a minstrel tune. Of Irish descent, Daniel Decatur Emmett was born in Mt. Vernon, Ohio, in 1815, worked as a printer in Cincinnati as a young man, and later traveled as a circus musician. Impressed by Thomas Rice's "Jim Crow" act, he decided to write a similar routine for himself. Around 1839 he began composing Negro songs and performing in blackface, singing and accompanying himself on the banjo.

When the prolonged slump in the national economy continued into the early 1840s, actors and musicians across the country were temporarily thrown out of work, and Emmett's act like many others ran into trouble. One day in 1843 Dan Emmett and his friend Billy Whitlock were practicing the violin and banjo at Mrs. Brooke's boarding house on Catherine Street, where Emmett happened to be staying. Quite by chance they were joined by fellow musicians Frank Brower and Dick Pelham. In the ensuing conversation the four came up with the notion of joining forces in a blackface act. Perhaps the four together, in a different stage format, could prove sufficiently novel to win engagements the performers were unable to secure separately. A spontaneous rehearsal was held in Emmett's room. Whitlock played the banjo, Brower the bone castanets, Pelham the tambourine, Emmett the violin, and all sang— both solo and as a group. A trial performance was held either in Bartlett's billiard parlor on the Bowery or at the Branch Hotel, a favorite haunt for New York showmen.

Under the collective name of the Virginia Minstrels, the blackface ensemble was introduced publicly at the Bowery Amphitheatre, probably on February 6, 1843; a few nights later the ensemble repeated its act at the Chatham Square Theater. The four entertainers appeared in blue swallowtail coats, striped calico shirts, and white trousers. They sang, danced, played their respective instruments, engaged in banter in black dialect, and concluded the full evening's amusement with a general dance and "breakdown." Although the Virginia Minstrels sat on stage in a semicircle, Emmett later said the four members of the group were initially all end men and all interlocutors. According to the New York *Herald*, the performance was "entirely exempt from the vulgarities" and "other objectionable features" that had heretofore "characterized Negro extravaganzas."

The response from the public was amazing. Emmett's minstrel band became famous overnight, while any song advertised by its publisher as "sung by the Virginia Minstrels" was assured a notable success. Dozens of imitators formed within a matter of weeks, as the craze for minstrelsy spread like a fire to all reaches of the country. Meanwhile the Virginia Minstrels appeared at the Park Theater and Welch's Olympic Circus, then ventured into the provinces for a brief road tour; in March they paused in Boston for a series of performances before sailing for England. They arrived in Liverpool on May 21, 1843, and were well received by British audiences; however, the team broke up during their trip abroad. Emmett and Brower returned to New York on October 7, 1844, finding the minstrel show well developed, thriving more vigorously than before, and hailed as a unique American institution. The two entertainers quickly engaged an additional pair of musicians and, purposely avoiding the big cities, proceeded to Salem, Massachusetts, where they renewed their career in the United States. Despite ruthless competition the Virginia Minstrels shortly regained their reputation, and from then until the late 1850s Dan Emmett was in almost constant demand, performing in urban theaters during the winter and with traveling circuses during the summer months.

Even before the success of the Virginia Minstrels the basic stereotypes of the Afro-American had crystallized in the burnt cork tradition. One was the "Zip Coon" type, growing out of George Washington Dixon's characterization and the song "My Long-Tailed Blue." "Zip Coon" or "Dandy Jim," as he was also called, was the city "swell," modishly dressed in tight-fitting pantaloons, a lacy shirt, the inevitable blue coat with long swishing tails, a silk hat, and baubles dangling from his waistband. He frequently held up a *lorgnon,* which he peered through with an effeminate gesture, and occasionally carried a walking cane. His hair was delicately groomed, and he strutted before the footlights with precious dignity and an affected smile. Completely taken with himself, he sang with pompous deliberation and talked mainly of his suave appearance and tonic-like effect on women. He sometimes posed as the "larned skolar," although when he touched on topics of the day, his language usually became less arrogant.

"Jim Crow," the other blackface archetype, clearly evolved from the creation of Thomas D. Rice. Known also as "Gumbo Chaff," "Jim Crow" was the plantation hand, an uncouth tatterdemalion of low station but jolly spirits. His ragged costume was traditionally ill-fitting and thoroughly wrinkled, with large patches on his breeches and gaping holes in his shoes. A wide-brimmed hat sat perched on his woolly head, while his face beamed with a broad grin from an accentuated mouth. "Jim Crow" not only sang and danced, but later talked humorously of current affairs and from time to time evidenced flashes of rustic wisdom. Unlike the saucy "Zip Coon," the rural counterpart was illiterate but shrewd, in his own right a minor philosopher.

As with the other two early American comic heroes—the crafty, taciturn Yankee peddler and the lusty, boasting backwoodsman—the blackface stereotypes were sentimentalized caricatures of real life. Yet "Zip Coon" and "Jim Crow," although grossly exaggerated, contained an element of truth regarding the white as well as black, in that, stripped of their cartoonlike mannerisms, these American caricatures revealed a complex, growing minority becoming increasingly intolerant of Anglo-America's oversimplification of their lives. While the early burnt cork performers may have been influenced by black entertainers like Corn Meal or the famous dancer Master Juba, and perhaps had even picked up innuendoes from slaves and black workers observed along the Mississippi River system, the blackface archetypes fundamentally issued from the imagination of northern whites. Practically all of the first burnt cork troupers were either immigrants or showmen from the East and Middle West, whose firsthand knowledge of the South and plantation slavery was limited. What they brought to their blackface portrayals was barely a germ of reality indirectly received, but affably coated with the romantic attitudes and general misconceptions about the American black. Although incidentals of the caricature may have been drawn from direct experience, the essence was based on hearsay and popular lore and projected in overstated, exotic terms.

Plantation masters as far back as colonial days were prone to amuse guests by calling in slaves who could sing and dance, and when a southern gentleman gave a party, it was often his blacks who played the dance music. A precedent was therefore set early in America of the black serving as the entertainer of the whites. "The blacks," a traveler observed in 1795, "are the great humorists of the nation....Climate, music, kind treatment act upon them like electricity." How much the blackface performers later consciously attempted to imitate the antics of the plantation slaves is not known, but in the opinion of Charles Sherlock, "You would look in vain in real life for the counterpart of the traditional darkey of the stage as depicted so delightfully by a long line of Negro minstrels." Actress Fanny Kemble noted that the "Jim Crow" dances of the minstrel stage were tame compared with the dancing of the slaves on her husband's Georgia plantation. A survey of the first music associated with the burnt cork tradition indicates that a number of other factors were tamed down as well. The blackface songs contain few of the strong passions found in the actual lyrics of the southern slaves, and there are practically no references to harsh treatment, punishment, or the black's longing for freedom.

The minstrel performers were essentially concerned with devising a gainful form of theatrical entertainment, irrespective of historical authenticity. But a nation haunted by the question of slavery welcomed a benign characterization of the black as a happy, childlike figure, fundamentally content with his lot. Attacks by vehement abolitionists were in part balanced by the minstrel stage's view of plantation life for the black: a pleasant compound of singing, loafing, attending kindly "massas," making love, hunting coon and 'possum, fishing, and enjoying a subservient, happy-go-lucky existence. The burnt cork sketches, without question, viewed the black with gentle condescension, even while admitting his strengths and perception. Likewise the blackface songs, as so many of the sentimental novels of the antebellum South, quietly served to perpetuate the popular mythology regarding slavery and indirectly worked to maintain the status quo in a tension-ridden nation.

But the topical nature of Negro minstrelsy explains only part of its immediate success with American audiences. The shows also offered a nervous generation a release through nonsense, although much that was nonsense outwardly was less so on second glance. The two basic stereotypes of the early minstrel stage were each flexible enough for hurling a variety of lampoons at contemporary society. "Zip Coon" provided an excellent vehicle for deriding surface sophistication, foppery, pedantry, urbanity, and high society. "Jim Crow" was a no less capital device for exalting folk wisdom, traditional values, and rural customs. In their extreme the two original burnt cork archetypes suggested well the latent clash between city and country. And on the minstrel stage, as in most of the popular culture of nineteenth-century America, real knowledge came from the hinterland, while superficiality and pretense were attributes of the metropolis.

Even before the Virginia Minstrels left for England, their program pattern had begun to change, heralding the start of the minstrel show's evolution. The four performers continued to sit in a semicircle, turned partly to the audience, partly to each other. Emmett and Whitlock sat in the center, flanked by Pelham on the left, pounding the tambourine, and Brower on the right, rattling the bones. Unlike earlier blackface entertainers, composure was not part of the Virginia Minstrels' nature, and Pelham and Brower were the rowdiest of the lot, setting the precedent for the end men to come. Yet all four jumped up and down, stretched their legs out toward the audience, twisted their feet and toes, mouthed uncouth sayings, and roared with hoarse laughter. In their effort to be laughable and symbolic of the black epitome, the performers' makeup emphasized wide open mouths, bulging lips, and large, shining eyes. The evening's entertainment was divided into two parts, and an instrumental introduction acted as an overture, much like in the variety theaters of the day. The program presented by the Virginia Minstrels on March 7 and 8, 1843, at the Masonic Temple in Boston indicates the format employed on the eve of the group's departure for Europe:

PART I

AIR   JOHNY BOWKER   by the Band

SONG   OLD DAN TUCKER, a Virginian Refrain
           in which is described the ups and downs   Full Chorus by the
           of Negro life   Minstrels

SONG   GOIN OBER DE MOUNTAIN, or the
           difficulties between Old Jake and his
           Sweet Heart   FULL CHORUS

SONG   OLD TAR RIVER — or the Incidents
           attending a Coon Hunt   FULL CHORUS

A NEGRO LECTURE ON LOCOMOTIVES   by BILLY WHITLOCK
           in which he describes his visit to the Wild
           Animals, his scrape with his Sweetheart,
           and show[s] the white folks how the Niggers
           raise Steam

PART II

SONG   Uncle Gabriel—or a chapter on Tails   FULL CHORUS

SONG   BOATMAN DANCE—a much admired
           Song, in imitation of the Ohio Boatman   FULL CHORUS

SONG   LUCY LONG—a very fashionable song
           which has never failed to be received with
           unbounded applause   FULL CHORUS

SONG   FINE OLD COLORED GEMMAN—a
Parody, written by Old Dan Emmet, who
will, on this occasion, accompany himself on the BANJO, in a manner that will
make all guitar players turn pale with
delight

With the formation of the Christy Minstrels in Buffalo in 1846, the pattern of the minstrel show soon became standardized into the more common formula. Born in Philadelphia in 1815, E. P. Christy organized the most popular group in early American minstrelsy and often claimed that he—rather than the Virginia Minstrels—originated the whole concept. His troupe performed through the West and South and in 1846 appeared in New York at Palmo's Opera House. The next year Christy leased Mechanics' Hall on Broadway, where his company played for almost ten seasons. Sometimes referring to his shows as "Ethiopian Opera" to imply respectability, but charging an admission fee of only twenty-five cents, Christy appealed to the city's fashionable elite, as well as the humbler classes.

The program developed by Christy's Minstrels consisted of three major parts. The first, featuring song and comic repartee, was dominated by the interlocutor, essentially a master of ceremonies, and the end men, "Mistah Tambo" and "Mistah Bones." The entertainment began with the company's marching on stage and arranging themselves in the familiar semicircle. The interlocutor—usually a big man, attired in elegant fashion, without the conventional kinky wig of the other players—began the performance with the dictum: "Gentlemen, be seated! We will commence with the overture." Following an instrumental selection, a humorous interchange took place between the end men and the interlocutor in which the pompous interlocutor was made to suffer at the expense of either Tambo or Bones. As the merriment grew, the exchange was punctuated by the sounds of Tambo's tambourine and Bone's bone castanets, originally an actual pair of bones, but later ebony sticks. At the end of the first sally the interlocutor, in his most grandiloquent manner, introduced the opening song, usually a comic number from one of the end men.

After the song the amusing chatter resumed, the interlocutor continuing to serve as straight man and foil. The persistent victory of Tambo and Bones over this gentlemanly middleman bore a resemblance to the baiting of the circus ringmaster by the clowns and may in fact have been an outgrowth of the close association between early blackface and the sawdust ring. Certainly the triumph of end men was reflective of the nineteenth-century American's peculiarity for disdaining the elevated and the formally learned and was consistent with the democracy's delight in seeing the "high brow" vanquished by the nimble-witted buffoon. Much of the humor of the minstrel stage centered on current events and contemporary personalities, although puns, absurd answers, big words incorrectly used, and mispronunciations provided their share of the chuckles. It was largely the role of the interlocutor to keep the first part of the show moving, and he introduced the various entertainers, asked the proper questions, and announced the songs—all in flawless English. The purpose of the jokes and patter was in large measure to build toward the musical numbers. By no means were all of the songs humorous, and as a general rule the worst jests preceded the best and most serious ballads, creating an effect through contrast. Sentimental selections were ordinarily sung by "silver-throated" tenors, while the whole company often joined in the chorus of songs. Although his was mainly a speaking part, the interlocutor occasionally sang, normally possessing a resonant basso voice.

The climax of this first part, at least by the 1850s, was the walk-around, in which the entire company participated. Most of the troupe stood in a semicircle at the back of the stage, singing a lively tune, clapping their hands and stamping their feet to the music, while others played instruments. One by one the members of the group paraded around the inside of the circle three or four times and finished by doing a special dance in the center of the stage, each performer attempting to outdo the others. The walk-around may have been loosely patterned after the slave dances executed in the compounds of the great plantations, and possibly there were echoes of the field shouts and wailing cries of the plantation blacks in this aspect of early minstrelsy. Unlike the improvised, ecstatic dances of the slaves, however, the dances of the minstrel stage were consciously worked out and carefully calculated for theatrical effect. The minstrel dancers were showmen, and as such were expected to excel in speed, precision, endurance, and acrobatic flexibility. Planned variety was essential on the stage, and many of the minstrel dances emphasized clownishness to assure the audience's pleasure. As the instrumental postlude of the walk-around began, the whole group joined in a clamorous dance characterized by rowdy and exaggerated gestures. The "Lucy Long Walk-Around" was one of the most popular tunes for this first part finale, and Dan Emmett's "Dixie" was originally written as a walk-around number.

The second part of the format worked out by the Christy Minstrels was far less structured than the first. Known as the olio or free fantasia, the second part of a conventional minstrel show consisted of specialties, each performer displaying his particular talents. "Jim Crow" dances, imitations of Jack Diamond's "break-downs," slapstick comedy, banjo "jigs," dialect songs, sentimental ballads, satirical stump speeches, and "wench" numbers were all staples of the olio. Since the traditional minstrel shows offered no women, the "wench" roles were acted by female impersonators who generally became established features of most companies. Dan Gardner was probably the first to perform a "wench" number in blackface, as an independent act in 1835, and he likely was the first to do the "Lucy Long" routine, a female impersonation in song. Other olio specialties ranged from a performer's removing innumerable coats and vests to another's playing Paganini's "Variations on the Carnival of Venice" on a toy whistle. A public untutored in theater demanded variety of the stage, and the success of early American minstrelsy was in no small measure dependent upon the popularity of these individual numbers.

The third part of the show, sometimes considered an afterpiece of the olio, consisted of a burlesque or farce. Usually offered as a playlet employing the whole company, this part frequently parodied a current stage success or theatrical personality. "Daddy" Rice once wrote a travesty called "Sarah Hartburn," which received the attention of the great Bernhardt herself. Later blackface afterpieces burlesqued such perennials as *Macbeth* (in a skit entitled *Bad Breath, the Crane of Chowder*) and *Uncle Tom's Cabin*, the latter normally interspersed with "plantation" songs. The minstrels lashed out regularly at the pretentious, the arty, and the foreign—endearing themselves to an American public in an especially nativistic period. Jabs were made at Italian opera and foreign virtuosos. The reputations of Ole Bull and the fabled Paganini were both deprecated by burnt cork performers:

> *Loud de banjo talked away,*
> *An' beat Ole Bull from de Norway;*
> *We'll take de shine from Paganini,*
> *We're de boys from ole Virginny.*

And the *New York Clipper* took obvious delight in announcing in January, 1854, that Christy's Minstrels were lampooning in their current show the symphonic concerts then being offered in New York "for the masses" by the colorful Jullien. Although the scripts of these farces were generally written out in fairly detailed form, actors were nevertheless expected to insert whatever remarks of their own they thought appropriate, so that the air of spontaneity was maintained. One observer insisted that, "A minstrel having a speech of a dozen lines will make it twenty-five times and never make it twice alike."

The three-part structure formulated by E. P. Christy remained the accepted pattern of the minstrel show for more than half a century. The ragged, plantation type of black quickly came to be relegated to the second part of the program, while the northern dandy type appeared prominently in the first, highlighted in the end men. Gradually the semblance of a realistic black atmosphere, present in the early "Jim Crow" and "Zip Coon" impersonations, paled in the first two portions of the show as sentimental ballads and flashy virtuoso acts became increasingly characteristic. More subtle musical changes also began to occur. "The trend away from simplicity and primitive realism in minstrelsy which set in right after the appearance of the Virginia Minstrels," Hans Nathan contends, "reveals itself not only in the use of the accordion but in the adoption of four-part harmony by various troupes." By the 1850s the most genuine atmosphere of plantation blacks was contained in the show's burlesque section.

Meanwhile minstrelsy was being devoured from coast to coast, at times driving practically every other form of entertainment off the scene. The Christy Minstrels continued as the leading company until Ed Christy retired with a fortune in 1854. Falling victim to severe melancholia, the former banjo and tambourine performer died in 1862 after jumping from a second-story window of his New York home. Probably Christy's strongest rivals were the Campbell Minstrels, who had become so popular by the late 1850s that the country was swarming with troupes bearing their name. Sometimes two groups of Campbell Minstrels would even be playing a town at the same time, much to the confusion of the public. Like Christy's company, the Campbells introduced a host of enduring song hits, among them "Buffalo Gals."

Bryant's Minstrels, organized in 1857, was another particularly successful troupe, which from 1858 to 1866 was distinguished by the services of Dan Emmett. Emmett was engaged primarily to compose music for the company, but he also appeared as a blackface comedian, singer, and banjo player. Consisting of about a dozen entertainers, Bryant's Minstrels maintained excellent standards of performance, a more authentic quality of black life than most of their competitors, and gained a special reputation for their timely parodies. They drew enormous crowds for several years at Mechanics' Hall in New York City, weathered the national financial crisis of 1857-58 there, and a decade later moved into their own house, the well known Bryant's Minstrel Hall, where they played for another seven years.

Competition in minstrelsy became increasingly heated as the number of first-rate companies continued to mount in the years preceding the Civil War. James Buckley and his three sons entered the minstrel business in 1843, eventually taking the name Buckley's New Orleans Serenaders. Theirs was the first group to burlesque grand opera, making Donizetti's *Lucia di Lammermoor* the target in an afterpiece called *Lucy Did Lam a Moor*. As the rivalry for box office receipts grew more intense, advertising broadened to include all sorts of novel methods of reaching the public. "The Buckley Serenaders have invented a miniature handbill," pianist Louis Moreau Gottschalk noted in his journal. "They are miniature programs that you find stuck on your back, your hat, your gloves, by mysterious, indefatigable, and unseen hands."

There were the Alabama Minstrels, Kitchen Minstrels, Columbia Minstrels, Congo Minstrels, Georgia Champions, Kentucky Rattlers, Sable Harmonists, Nightingale Serenaders, Southern Minstrels, Virginia Serenaders, P. T. Barnum's Ethiopian Serenaders, and scores of others. Most of the major companies toured England sometime in their career, usually with great success, their shows attended by all segments of the British population. Back home, minstrel bands were traveling by railroad, steamboat, and stagecoach to all parts of the United States and its western territories. At one time there

were some ten companies playing simultaneously in New York City alone
Names of individual performers gradually came to stand out—star attractions
like "Billy" Birch, George Christy, Charley White, Billy Emerson, and Lew
Dockstader. Salaries for featured entertainers were often quite attractive;
George Christy—whose real name was Harrington—was reported to have
earned an astonishing $19,168.00 for a two and a half year period with
Christy's Minstrels. So enticing were the salaries in minstrelsy that a number
of legitimate actors and trained musicians resorted to the burnt cork stage at
least for a while. Edwin Booth did a turn in blackface before he became
known as a great tragedian, and Patrick S. Gilmore, the famous bandmaster
began his career as a minstrel.

For many of the smaller towns of mid-nineteenth century America the
minstrel shows were among the few means of public amusement, and the
arrival of a troupe marked a red-letter day indeed. Around 1850 the Ordway
Minstrels initiated the street parade as a way of promoting their productions,
an innovation undoubtedly borrowed from the circus. As the practice
developed, the entire troupe upon arriving in a town would parade through
the streets to their hotel by the longest possible route, headed by either a
"silver" or "gold cornet band." Marching in "twos" or "fours," depending
on its size, the band was strikingly attired in colorful coats and trousers, brass
buttons, and high silk hats. The company followed behind dressed in their
swallowtail coats, colored lapels, fancy vests, and gaudy trousers. Before each
performance the band usually gave a short concert in front of the theater, and
sometimes fireworks were shot off to the delight of the crowd and the town's
street urchins. During the heyday of minstrelsy a good company could
command the use of the best theater in practically any city, although in the
villages and frontier communities this might mean playing in town halls or
even makeshift canvas structures. Like P. T. Barnum, the blackface minstrels
represent an attempt to capture a mass audience by providing family
entertainment acceptable to the American middle class. Their universal
success remains a real phenomenon in theatrical history.

But minstrelsy in antebellum America demonstrated a rare harmony
between vernacular art, contemporary social conditions, and entrenched folk
attitudes. At the same time that the burnt cork performers bowed to
puritanical restrictions to win their popular following, they offered
audiences an escape from puritanism by depicting a happy dreamland in
which care and responsibility were of little consequence. Through the
symbol of the black the minstrel stage provided Anglo-Americans a vicarious
freedom from the very Protestant Ethic that had become the nation's
taskmaster. Borrowing from the sentimental lore of the Old South, the early
minstrels from the North created a carefree plantation paradise, where lusty,
rambunctious, joyous living prevailed and its blackface denizens were
seemingly unaware of the work ethic's mandates. As the setting gradually
shifted farther north, a black disguise remained to camouflage the sublimated
flight from a duty-bound world.

Until belligerents shattered the image, the industrializing North— uncertain of where its economic changes were leading—looked to the myth of the romantic southland as a symbol of rural tranquility. The nostalgia for a passing frontier and the uneasiness generated by the complications of urban living found sympathetic echoes in the blackface singer's intermittent homesickness and sense of oppression. Much of the merriment of the minstrel show, on the other hand, was a direct throwback to uninhibited frontier humor and was aimed largely at the pastoral mind. The backwoodsman's love for the tall tale was much present in the bragging of the burnt cork performers, while the black was often portrayed as a swaggering superman not unlike the frontier hero and river boatman:

> *My mama was a wolf*
> *My daddy was a tiger,*
> *I am what you call*
> *De Ole Virginny Nigger:*
> *Half fire, half smoke,*
> *A little touch of thunder,*
> *I am what you call*
> *De eighth wonder.*

Touches of the exaggeration characteristic of western humor frequently appear in the minstrel songs. A verse from one of "Daddy" Rice's most popular songs, "Sich a Gittin' Upstairs," tells of a "bone squash" captain who was cut in two in a fight, joined himself back together with glue, and vanquished his enemy. After the brawl he lay down to sleep, but as the day was hot, he awoke to find that the glue had melted and a thief had run away with his thighs. Dan Emmett's "Old Dan Tucker" pictures a vagabond, laughed at and scorned by his people, who got involved in all sorts of adventurous exploits. Having consorted with the fox and the jaybird, Dan Tucker was endowed with comical magic, enabling him to grow large as he combed his hair with a wagon wheel, shrink small and become ridiculous as he washed his face in a frying pan. But like the frontiersman, Dan Tucker remained the outcast of society, preferring to wander an uncharted course. With the passing years the black man of Dan Emmett's original song was transformed by later variations into a white, as the pressures of a complex society and the explosive nature of the racial issue became increasingly evident.

All three of the early American comic heroes were rebels in their own fashion. The stage Yankee headed the revolt against British civilization, while the backwoodsman revolted against all civilizations. The blackface minstrel's revolt was more cryptic and submerged, but nonetheless represented a cogent retreat from traditional American values. Along with his air of severance, each possessed an irreverent wisdom and a hearty resilience. "Comic triumph appeared in them all," Constance Rourke concludes in her classic study of American humor; "the sense of triumph seemed a necessary mood in the new country. Laughter produced the illusion of leveling obstacles in a world which was full of unaccustomed obstacles. Laughter created ease, and even more, a sense of unity, among a people who were not yet a nation and who were seldom joined in stable communities." At the same time that minstrelsy concealed a quiet revolt against the Protestant Ethic, it offered much that buttressed the great American belief in success. "It is, however, interesting," Wilfrid Mellers observes, "that the show's positive evocation of the American Hero—who still appears as the Backwoodsman— should now be subservient to the American Innocent, as represented by the Comic Negro. Both the Hero and the Anti-Hero are treated facetiously, and the main dramatic items are burlesques of European classics." Clearly, behind a mask of blackface, mid-nineteenth century Americans could admit in fun their ambivalence on key issues of national concern, disclosing that they were indeed a people in transition.

The triumph of the blackface minstrel was in the audacity of his humor rather than over the conditions of slavery—a humor frequently approaching the preposterous. In all the wild exaggerations of western myth-making, the excesses of the backwoodsman never spilled over into pure nonsense. But minstrel humor, distinctly unlike any other American form of its day, went off on a bold tangent into unmitigated absurdity. "To the primitive comic sense," Constance Rourke maintains, "to be black is to be funny, and many minstrels made the most of the simple circumstance." While the roots of this attitude toward the blacks lie deep in the past, the southern plantation experience certainly strengthened the notion in the United States. As historian Kenneth Stampp contends in his authoritative analysis of slavery in this country: "It was typical of an indulgent master not to take his slaves seriously but to look upon them as slightly comic figures. He made them the butt of his humor and game for a good-natured practical joke. He tolerated their faults, sighed at their irresponsibility, and laughed at their pompous pretensions and ridiculous attempts to imitate the whites." And so the concept was passed to the North, and so it was incorporated into the minstrel stereotype.

But if the blackface camouflage allowed Anglo-Americans to be more honest about their uncertainties, it also freed them to express pent-up feelings. Having internalized well the Puritan heritage of exercising restraint in the display of emotion, nineteenth-century Americans were inclined to suppress honest feelings under a ubiquitous mantle of utilitarianism, although regularly employing sentimentality as a decoy for real emotions. Behind burnt cork, however, white performers were at liberty to exhibit whatever feelings they liked, so long as they were not morally offensive. An entertainer could frolic, play the fool, and kick up his heels with utter disregard for the genteel tradition, since he was, after all, imitating the presumed eccentricities of a lower social class. In blackface a player might indulge in earthiness, while in his songs particularly he could voice passion and genuine pathos. The gentler emotions that a New England heritage worked to conceal, that materialism and the determination to win tended to crowd out, could surface on the minstrel stage without seeming effeminate. Spontaneous and unrestrained movement, unless lewd, came to be expected, as were lively rhythms and abandoned dancing.

Yet the point is less that blacks themselves were more emotional by nature than the whites, but more that Anglo-Americans were particularly reserved and underdeveloped in their emotions. Uncomfortable in exposing true feelings, the majority culture chose to transfer these sentiments to the blacks through minstrelsy. Even the "natural rhythm" the black was allegedly "born with" was more an outgrowth of the Anglo-American's own fetish for restraint than a special characteristic of the black. Because of his servile position in American life, blacks were simply less preoccupied with the image of respectability than their white contemporaries and far less engrossed with maintaining a premeditated composure. For the whites the black became the symbol of uninhibited expression. "He is our catharsis," Isaac Goldberg has written. "He is the disguise behind which we may, for a releasing moment, rejoin that part of ourselves which we have sacrificed to civilization. He helps us to a double deliverance. What we dare not say, often we freely sing. Music, too, is an absolution. And what we would not dare to sing in our own plain speech we freely sing in the Negro dialect, or in terms of the black." In this the minstrel stage launched a long tradition.

While there was clearly an undertone of defeat in minstrelsy's representation of the black, it was the festive side of the slave's life that was emphasized. For a time during the early 1850s the popularity of blackface waned slightly, in part perhaps a response to the tragic view of the southern black emerging from the pages of *Uncle Tom's Cabin* and its almost immediate dramatization. While Mrs. Stowe's picture of slavery continued to make its impact and won great support from abolitionist sympathizers, by the mid-1850s, when tensions over the Kansas-Nebraska question had brought the country to the edge of hysteria, the comic attitude toward the black was again welcome. With the issue of sectionalism raging more fiercely than ever, many Americans longed for the return of a day when the nation was happy and unified and its people knew their place. The burnt cork stereotypes were so outrageously incompetent and innocent that even the most anxiety-ridden members of the democracy could forget their troubles and roar with laughter. "So long as the Negro remained on the stage," Alan W. C. Green suggests, "he could be kept black, happy and harmless—a source of hilarity rather than shame, guilt, and anxiety." Not only was the black innocuous as drawn on the minstrel stage, but white audiences could look upon him and feel superior. "One could not help but feel an affection," Green continues, "for such an ego-building, permanently visible and permanently-inferior clown who posed no threat and desired nothing more than laughter and applause at his imbecile antics." Leaders of the antislavery movement might object—and did—to further delineation of the myth of contented darkies, kind old "massas," and pillared plantation mansions, but for much of the nation on the eve of the Civil War the pleasant fiction of minstrelsy was a comforting counteragent to more incendiary expressions. Possibly as a token concession to the protests from abolitionists, the minstrels by mid-century did emphasize the southern field hand less, the northern city black more. But when the blackface performers yearned for "de ol' plantation," many Americans yearned with them—partly for their rural past, more immediately for the restoration of a secure, harmonious Republic.

That the minstrel stage indicates in a guarded fashion many of the pressures, conflicts, and limitations of antebellum society there is little question. In their own day the black faces appearing behind flickering gas flames or candlelight on stages across the country provided not merely entertainment, but a means by which the young Union could air certain crises in its culture and to an extent come to grips psychologically with an inevitable national turning point. While the humor was pleasant in its time—aided as it was by gesture, intonation, and outlandish costume—much of it became dated quickly or grew cliche on repeated exposure. The songs, however, were often a different matter, for by far the most lasting contribution of black minstrelsy came with its music.

As early as 1849 Bayard Taylor wrote, "The Ethiopian melodies well deserve to be called, as they are in fact, the national airs of America." Although having roots in British, Scottish, and Irish folk songs, the minstrel tunes represent the first group of commercial songs in the United States to be more than mere echoes of the Old World. The airs of the English ballad opera, which customarily burlesqued the fancies of the nobility in the vernacular of the London rabble, had never really been suited to the new country, since it possessed neither nobles nor a fixed city rabble. But the songs of the minstrel stage concentrated on matters Americans understood and spoke to audiences on their own terms. While the lyrics usually focused on the black, Anglo-Americans sufficiently identified with the sentiments of these airs to realize a picture of themselves as well.

The songs which won minstrelsy its immortality were of all kinds—comic and serious, ribald and sentimental, naive and sophisticated. Some of the music was a simple borrowing of the popular parlor ballads of the day or even adaptations of airs from British and Italian opera. Yet from the early 1840s through the Civil War, the publication of independent minstrel tunes proceeded at an ever increasing rate, as the melange of troupes came to want their own special songs. The new idiom as a whole was less mawkish and trite than the middle class ballads of the period and distinctly more vigorous. This fact suggests to Hans Nathan that the minstrel songs "originated, for the most part, outside the city, and, above all, in a rough, realistically-minded social stratum."

Constance Rourke argues that the presence of satirical animal metaphors and bits of Afro-American fable in early blackface songs indicates a genuine black source. "Zip Coon," for instance, borrowed his name from the animal whose meat was considered most delicious by southern blacks. The crow was often used as a comic symbol for the black, while the white master or overseer became a bulldog or bullfrog. Sometimes, in disguise, blacks were shown cleverly outmaneuvering their social superiors:

A bullfrog dressed in soger's close
Went in de field to shoot some crows,
De crows smell powder an' fly away,
De bullfrog mighty mad dat day.

Still, most of the evidence supports the contention that the authentic black element in minstrel songs was incidental. Nathan admits that the constant musical intercourse between the slaves and white society resulted in "a blend of European and primitive melodic styles," but feels that the actual black influence on minstrel tunes was slight. "Excessive repetition of single tones and of phrases of narrow compass derives from the Negro," the musicologist maintains; "on the other hand, the symmetry of phrase structure is a white concept. The rhythm, too, is far removed from the Negroid complexities of banjo-fiddle music. As a matter of fact, the frequent use of equal note values, as well as tone repetitions in the opening phrase, seems to reveal the influence of white hymns."

Almost without exception, the songs for the early minstrel stage were written by whites. The first ones usually appeared under the label of "Negro Melody" or "Plantation Refrain," with no mention of the composer on the cover sheet until the 1840s. Even then there were often conflicting claims, as in the famous case of Stephen Foster and E. P. Christy. Foster may have been more genteel than most of the composers for minstrelsy, agreeing to unite with Christy "to encourage a taste for this style of music so cried down by opera mongers" only after much hesitation. His lack of direct acquaintance with the southern black, however, was less extraordinary.

Aside from Foster, Dan Emmett was probably the most significant composer for blackface. Unlike Foster, Emmett was a performer himself who had an intimate working knowledge of the theater. His familiarity with plantation slavery, while never great, was more extensive than that of his Pittsburgh contemporary. The house of Emmett's father, in Ohio, had served for a time as a station for the underground railroad, and the musician as a youth had been sent to Kentucky as a fifer and later to barracks on the Mississippi below St. Louis. Emmett claimed always to take into account in his music "the habits and crude ideas of the slaves of the South," although he insisted that his songs were of his own composition. His melodies are actually closer to white spirituals than to anything in genuine black music, and his verbal phrasing is decidedly unlike that of the black. A highly versatile composer, Emmett's most enduring songs are "Old Dan Tucker," written before the musician was sixteen; "De Blue Tail Fly," better known as "Jim

Crack Corn"; and "Dixie," originally called "Dixie's Land" and written in 1859 expressly for Bryant's Minstrels.

The gradual shift in Emmett's attitude toward the free black, as expressed in four of his songs first performed during the 1858-59 season, is particularly interesting in view of the controversy over slavery then storming the nation. Strongly opposed to southern secession and abolition from the beginning, Emmett in November, 1858, sympathetically pictured an escaping slave's longing for his southern home in "The Land of Freedom, or I Ain't Got Time to Tarry," his first song for Bryant's Minstrels. Home for the black was not only his girl Dinah, but the southern plantation so revered in minstrel music. Three months later, in "Wide Awake, or Dar's a Darkey in de Tent," the black was depicted as a worthless, troublesome commodity that the white man was free to dispose of at his leisure. Although cloaked in humor, the white was obviously annoyed with the black. By the middle of March, 1859, in "Jonny Roach," the black freely admitted that as contraband in the North he could not fare very well. Less than a month later, the black stated more firmly than ever in "Dixie's Land" that the South was the only place he belonged, the only place he felt happy. He essentially declared himself contented with his bondage, a declaration gladly received by most white audiences as a plea for the turmoil over slavery to end.

As with most of Emmett's songs, the original words of "Dixie's Land" were by the composer himself, the entire piece being written in about two days. Like virtually all minstrel musicians, Emmett relied on a stock of common phrases and word pictures. As was the custom in walk-around numbers, "Dixie" was initially sung in a manner reminiscent of the call-and-response system of the southern blacks, much slower than the beat later preferred by military bands. Consisting of the standard thirty-two measures, the first part of the song was sung alternately by a soloist and a small chorus in unison, which interjected at the end of every other line, "Look away! Look away! Dixie Land!" Like other walk-arounds, "Dixie's Land," as performed on the minstrel stage, contained an instrumental section, during which the members of the company rendered their dances. The song's longevity has been chiefly due to its modest, unpretentious qualities and, of course, its acceptance as a battle hymn by Confederate armies.

Firth, Pond & Company published "Dixie's Land" on February 11, 1861, after paying Emmett $300 for relinquishing further rights to the song. Although known as a "Southern Air," the piece retained its popularity in the North even after the outbreak of the Civil War. Lincoln was particularly fond of the tune, and when the future president first heard it, during a performance in 1860, he supposedly shouted from his box: "Let's have it again! Let's have it again!" The song was introduced to the South in New Orleans right before the war started, sung in a burlesque entitled *Pocahontas*. An immediate hit, the words were printed on a broadside and hawked in the streets. On February 18, 1861, "Dixie's Land" was played at the inauguration of Jefferson Davis in

Montgomery, Alabama, and bands shortly began playing the melody as a military quickstep. Gradually Confederate soldiers came to sing the tune to considerably modified words. The original chorus, meant so harmlessly by Emmett, a strong Union Democrat, now became a battle cry: "In Dixie Land I'll take my stand, To lib and die in Dixie."

The similarity between Emmett's music and antebellum religious spirituals is clearly evident in such songs as "Jordan Is a Hard Road to Travel." He wrote a number of banjo tunes, like the "Pea-Patch Jig," containing a beat that foreshadows ragtime, while some of his numbers— "Root, Hog or Die," for instance—even became popular in England. His strength as a composer lay chiefly in his naive freshness, his sinewy vigor, and his homespun humor. Looking at "Dixie," Hans Nathan observes, "there emerges a special kind of humor that mixes grotesqueness with lustiness and down-to-earth contentment—comparable, to overstate the case, to a blend of Brueghel and Mickey Mouse." Emmett was essentially a folk artist, who composed for the popular stage of his day with little thought of originality. "But since he was firmly rooted in a living tradition and in the local scene," Nathan concludes, "he was more genuine and more genuinely American than the professional composers of his time and his country."

Emmett retired from the stage in 1888, living quietly for a number of years in a small country home near his Ohio birthplace. In 1895 A. G. Field persuaded him to return to public life, and for one season he toured with Field's Minstrels. Returning to his rural home, he lived the rest of his life on a pension from the Actors' Fund of New York. His last appearance in minstrelsy was in an amateur performance for the Elks in Mt. Vernon, Ohio, in 1902. He died two years later, at the age of eighty-eight.

Almost every major minstrel troupe published its own song collection, while the favored Christy Minstrels eventually issued a half dozen. "Farewell Ladies" was introduced by the group, supposedly written by the leader himself, and "Stop Dat Knockin' at My Door" was a Christy specialty, providing all sorts of chances for action and clowning. The entire company would stand lined-up behind the soloist, with the tambourines, bones, and banjos all going full blast, as the end men shouted the spoken refrain back and forth: "Stop dat knockin'—let me in—stop dat knockin'—let me in."

Other dialect numbers to meet with long success include "Sittin' on a Rail," "Hard Times Come Again No More," and "The Yellow Rose of Texas." While many of the serious songs of early minstrelsy contain undertones of deep emotion, others were as sentimental as any of the parlor favorites of the day. Fred Buckley, one of the pioneers in burnt cork, wrote a series of particularly maudlin selections for the stage, among them "We Are Growing Old Together," "I See Her Still in My Dreams," and "I'm Turning Gray, Dear Kate." The sentimental numbers sung in blackface covered the gamut of human experience, but two examples of lasting popularity were "When I Saw Sweet Nelly Home" and "Silver Threads among the Gold."

Comic ditties like "All That Glitters Is Not Gold," "It's Not the Miles We Travel, But the Pace," and "You Never Miss the Water Till the Well Runs Dry," also became common, although these were looked upon by the guardians of good taste with almost as much disfavor as the dialect numbers. Minstrel audiences, nevertheless, carried these songs from the theater in their memory, and they were soon sung around the family piano and arranged for singing societies. Before long several representative minstrel tunes appeared in most of the music collections so common in middle class American households of the nineteenth century, thereby finding their way permanently into the nation's musical heritage.

The minstrel songs are characteristically simple in melody, elementary in harmony and rhythm, hence easily sung. The best of them contain a genuine, straightforward quality reminiscent of true folk music, while their comic element is generally of the deadpan variety, much within the tradition of American humor. At the same time the lyrics often express an attitude of indifference and lively abandon that is foreign to the mainstream of American thought. The make-up of the minstrel tunes is a hodge-podge to be sure, and even the most legitimate blackface numbers leaned heavily on European models. Musicologists, for instance, have traced the origins of "Zip Coon" to two Irish hornpipe melodies; "My Long Tailed Blue" is similar to a Scottish folk song; "Sich a Gittin' Upstairs" is a modification of an English dance tune; while "Jim Crow" is related both to an Irish folk song and an eighteenth-century piece from the English stage. And yet the black motif, however contrived, and the strong frontier ingredients combined with a natural evolution to produce a distinctly American atmosphere in minstrelsy that was lacking in the sentimental parlor ballads. Equally absent from the "heart songs" of the era were the better minstrel tunes' intrinsic verve and basic honesty. But the unique attributes that were the minstrel numbers' fundamental strength were the very features that disturbed the leaders of the "better music" movement most. Reluctant to accept any music associated with the primitive frontier past, the proponents of correctness in art looked upon a theatrical form symbolic of a servile race with absolute contempt. When the minstrel songs eventually made their way into the standard collections of parlor music after the Civil War, it was a victory of popular taste over the cultivated and a battle not easily won.

Not all of the artistic and intellectual community, however, was as negative about the "Ethiopian business" as the leaders of the "better music" movement. English novelist William Makepiece Thackeray was deeply moved by the minstrel melodies, while Edwin Forrest, America's first great Shakespearean actor, insisted that "he knew no finer piece of tragic acting than the impersonation of Dan Bryant as the hungry Negro in *Old Time Rocks*." Mark Twain recalled how the first blackface troupe to play Hannibal, Missouri, burst on the scene "as a glad and stunning surprise....Church members did not attend these performances, but all the wordlings flocked to them and were enchanted." And in his own caustic way, the humorist went on to express the American public's general attitude toward minstrelsy: "It seems to me that to the elevated mind and the sensitive spirit, the hand organ and the nigger show are a standard and a summit to whose rarefied altitude the other forms of musical art may not hope to reach."

Certainly the minstrel show remained the most successful form of theater in the United States for at least a generation after slavery had ended. There was a slight slackening of public interest during the opening months of the Civil War, but enthusiasm returned shortly thereafter. During the years immediately following the northern victory, the American people, in part reacting against the strain of four years of armed conflict, exhibited an unprecedented interest in all types of recreation, and minstrelsy thrived with a vigor, probably reaching its height around 1870. With the completion of the first transcontinental railroad in 1869, minstrel troupes invaded many of the western towns along its route. On the Mississippi and Ohio waterways showboats brought blackface entertainment to villages and towns nestled on the river banks. In the early 1880s there were at least thirty-two minstrel companies on tour at one time.

But despite minstrelsy's continued popularity, there were signs of trouble. During the financial panic of 1873-74 an estimated half of the blackface companies went broke on the road. In the East particularly, where the economic situation improved most noticeably, the minstrel troupes shortly regained much of their lost ground, although competition among the various groups grew sharper. To attract the desired audiences managers began emphasizing "bigger and better" offerings. "Colonel" Haverly advertised a troupe of "Forty, Count 'em, Forty," while Haverly's Mastodons in 1880 was a company of a hundred members. Elaborate stage settings also were employed, as the minstrel show evolved into a costly stage spectacle. Suddenly burnt cork entertainment was no longer modestly priced amusement, but a big business attempting to compete with the theatrical circuits then coming into power. In the struggle that followed, the minstrels' chances for success were slight, especially as admission charges rose to meet expanding production costs. Gradually the popularity of minstrelsy began to decline in the face of a more diversified American theater. The burnt cork players retained their drawing power longest in the southern states, but enjoyed some lingering professional success throughout the country until the early twentieth century, mainly in the smaller towns.

The decline of minstrelsy, however, stemmed in part from a degeneration of the shows themselves. As early as the 1850s there were isolated protests against the blackface stereotype of blacks, which grew increasingly less realistic as the burnt cork tradition evolved. The black was consistently viewed with good-natured affection, yet in an essentially belittling way. More and more the black came to be pictured as the lazy, good-for-nothing, innocently happy, broadly grinning inferior. He persisted in using an exaggerated dialect and words so long he twisted the syllables. He frequently consumed more gin than he could handle and loved chicken so much that he could not pass a henhouse without being tempted to sneak at least one. He adored the grand manner in dress, was passionately fond of watermelons, which he ate in a peculiar way, and was an expert wielder of the razor, an item he kept in readiness for special occasions like crap games. While this mosaic of the black reflected many of the prevailing attitudes at the turn of the century, the more enlightened segment of the American public was aware that myth was perpetuating injustice. "Following emancipation and the nominal guarantee of constitutional rights," Albert F. McLean, Jr. writes, "the image of the servile, childlike Negro not only lost its poignancy, but for cosmopolitan audiences, became actually absurd."

Yet while the blackface caricature was becoming more detached from reality, the black himself ironically found a place on the minstrel stage. The first all-black company was formed in 1865 by Charles Hicks and called the Georgia Minstrels. Curiously enough, these Georgia Minstrels employed the same burnt cork make-up and curly-haired wigs that the white performers used, although later black minstrels did capitalize on their natural color. The most distinguished of the post-Civil War composers for minstrelsy was a black trouper named James A. Bland, whose biggest success was "Carry Me Back to Old Virginny," later adopted as the Virginia state song. Born in Flushing, Long Island, on October 22, 1854—nine years before the Emancipation Proclamation—Bland came from a long line of free blacks. He grew up in Philadelphia and decided as a boy to become a professional entertainer, supposedly after hearing an old black playing the banjo. Bland worked for a time with the Georgia Minstrels, later reorganized into the Callender's Minstrels, as a comic, composer, lyricist, skit writer, and banjoist. Aside from his classic, "Carry Me Back to Old Virginny," published in 1875, his most successful songs include "Oh Dem Golden Slippers," "In the Evening by the Moonlight," and "Hand Me Down My Walking Cane." Black characteristics in Bland's music are few; rather he had a personal way with a sentimental song that is suggestive of Stephen Foster.

By the 1870s the olio section of the minstrel show in particular had become sufficiently removed from its original plantation setting that all sorts of alien material came to be interjected to vary the program—Irish ballad singers, complete with brogue, and Jewish comedians in great abundance. And to relieve the monotony of a wholly masculine show, female minstrels eventually appeared on the scene—most notable of whom probably was the young Lotta Crabtree. To compensate for their own limitations, less talented performers began to emphasize the vulgar and the grotesque; their jokes became stupidly obvious, their songs stale, and their dances mere exercises in contortion. The number of end men was increased to as many as four on each side, but the gimmick simply magnified the shortcomings of the offering. By the end of the century the shows were kept alive largely through the efforts of a few gifted entertainers, while the totality had stagnated into a murky reflection of the past. "The audience increasingly was there to be lulled by the familiar," Alan W. C. Green contends, "rather than delighted and entertained by artistry."

Certainly by the final decades of the nineteenth century, minstrelsy had been robbed of its unique features. At its best the minstrel show represented lively, continuous, coordinated entertainment derived from American materials *by* Americans. While the original sketches contained their share of romance and essentially viewed the black as an exotic intruder into a white man's world, the blend of realism and parody found in the early blackface caricatures ultimately revealed more about the Anglo-American than about either the plantation or city black. Referring to the three comic heroes of the pre-Civil War stage, Constance Rourke insists, "The young American Narcisus had looked at himself in the narrow rocky pools of New England and by the waters of the Mississippi; he also gazed long at a darker image." Americans not only gazed at the darker image, they made him a mouthpiece through which to voice their own frustrations, problems, and private sentiments. If the blackface effusion became too honest for comfort, or the response to it too severe, the mask was always there for protection, a smiling reminder that the confession had been, after all, no more than a joke.

From the musical standpoint, the minstrel stage brought to life a vast body of America's popular songs and served as the vehicle for spreading them across the nation. The "appearance of a new melody," an observer recorded in the 1850s, "was an event whose importance can hardly be appreciated by the coming generation. It flew from mouth to mouth, and from hamlet to hamlet, with a rapidity which seemed miraculous." Sheet music of current minstrel tunes was placed before an eager public as quickly as publishing houses could copyright and print them.

For a public hungry for amusement of all kinds, the antebellum minstrel shows were a refreshing change from Shakespearean melodrama, lectures on mesmerism and phrenology, "scientific" demonstrations, and museums of natural wonders. The minstrel stage was an essentially native form of entertainment and remains the only distinctively American contribution to the theater. When it declined in the late nineteenth century, minstrelsy did not so much die as it evolved into mutations better adapted to a new environment. For while the minstrel show itself had become a relic by the turn of the century, its spirit lived on in the revue, burlesque, and vaudeville.

CHAPTER

XII

A Nation of Sections

Each group of immigrants to the New World brought with them the musical heritage of their native land. They dotted the American map with little Hollands, little Swedens, little Germanies, little Frances, little Spains, and—later—clustered in urban quarters designated as little Italies, little Polands, little Russias, and little Bohemias, conveying in each instance the folk music of the country they had left behind. "Indeed," Alan Lomax contends, "the pedant may search in vain for a 'pure' American folk song," for the traditional music of the United States is a "mixture of mixtures," a cosmopolitan "hybrid of hybrids."

The primary compound, however, is an Anglo-Scots-Irish synthesis yet in evidence. When traditional British ballads were discovered still being perpetuated in the Southern Appalachians during the years encompassing American participation in World War I, much attention was given that isolated area as a sanctuary where the oral transmission of British folk songs had persisted almost undisturbed. While these mountain folk had indeed preserved an early musical heritage virtually intact, variations of Anglo-Scots-Irish ballads continued as a living tradition well into the twentieth century in pockets of the United States from the hills of New England to the upland South, from the woods of the Old Northwest to the Blue Ridge and Smoky Mountains on to the Ozarks and hills of Arkansas and Oklahoma, and perhaps beyond. Although the ingredients of American folk song are ultimately as multiple as the nation's ethnic origins, the foundation of the country's traditional music is predominantly British, much like its language, folklore, literature, and general heritage.

Some of these folk songs were sung in England, Scotland, and Ireland before Columbus discovered the New World, while others appeared and gained popularity during the centuries of American colonization. Some were brought over by the first settlers; others came with later arrivals, adding variety. A comparatively homogeneous society preserved this musical heritage with only slight modification, far less than might be expected of an oral tradition in a primitive country. As the colonial population pushed out toward the mountains, selected ballads of England, Scotland, and Ireland went with them. The early nineteenth century found trans-Appalachian frontiersmen singing of castles and ancestral halls, cavaliers with lances, ladies-in-waiting, court intrigues, and chivalric romances—much as their forebears had in the British Isles hundreds of years before. Changes in phrasing and melody gradually crept in, and geographical variations became increasingly defined as the decades went by, but the sentiment of these ballads remained essentially the same.

Among the most perennial of the Anglo-Scots-Irish folk songs in the United States have been "The Elfin Knight," "Lady Isabel and the Elf-Knight," "Lord Randal," "Barbara Allen," "The Gypsy Laddie," "Lord Thomas and Fair Elinore," "Earl Brand," "The Cruel Mother," "Lord Lovel," "Our Goodman," "Fair Margaret and Sweet William," and "Fair Annie." Of these American survivals "Barbara Allen" clearly leads both in the number of variants and in the number of tunes. A version noted in Mississippi began:

> *While in the merry month of May*
> *   The green buds were a-swelling;*
> *A young man on his death bed lay*
> *   For loving Barbara Allen.*

But "cruel Barbara Allen" laughed when she heard the death bells toll and laughed again when she saw the young man pale in death. Too late she felt remorse. As a Maine variant told her end:

> *When he was buried in his grave,*
> *   Her heart did burst with sorrow:*
> *"O mother, mother, make my bed,*
> *   For I shall die tomorrow!"*

> *"Now, maidens all, a warning take,*
> *   And shun the ways I fell in,*
> *Or else your heart like mine may break;*
> *   Farewell!" said Barbara Allen.*

Samuel Pepys in 1666 lauded the "little Scotch song of 'Barbary Allen'," and a century later Oliver Goldsmith declared that "the music of the finest singer is dissonance to what I felt when our old dairy-maid sung me into tears with 'Johnny Armstrong's Last Goodnight' or 'The Cruelty of Barbara Allen'." In varying forms the story was repeated time and again in mountain coves and lonely farm houses across the eastern United States during the early years of the new nation; but gradually it became extinct or outmoded in the larger towns.

Folk music, like folk art in general, synthesizes the values and anxieties of the group, and in expressing the feelings of the community reaffirms that community's basic values and social solidarity. Traditional music, therefore, is stated in simple, immediately comprehensible terms, utilizes familiar expressions and a common vocabulary, and is above all conservative in outlook. The folk song essentially applauds its community for feeling the way it does and serves to unite its society to the past. Unlike the art musician, who perceives life individually, freshly, and with the desire to go beyond the conventional, the folk musician seeks to maintain the status quo. Like the city that supports him, the creative artist favors change, while the folk artist, linked to the hinterland, emphasizes accepted values and existent experience and resists departing from a known that is understandable.

In the nineteenth century American backwoodsmen, through selection, censored the British folk song legacy to conform more closely to their puritanical ideals. The popular mind in America has traditionally drawn a particularly sharp distinction between pleasure and righteousness, inflaming—Alan Lomax insists—"the old wound of guilt and sexual anxiety which has so often characterized our civilization." The great majority of Americans in the nineteenth century looked upon sex with definite reserve. Only bad women enjoyed the experience; a dutiful wife suffered it merely in deference to her husband. "Thus the women of the frontier whose lives were hard, lonely and comfortless at best," Lomax continues, "found solace in romantic or vengeful fantasies. Their favourite ballads and love songs were shrouded in gloom, drowned in melancholy, and poisoned by sado-masochism." Love in the folk ballads of England, Scotland, and Ireland meant sorrow, invited betrayal, led to long separation, and brought lovers to an early grave. But primitive notes of joy relieved the gloom in these songs. The English maiden might be betrayed, but she was very pleasantly seduced first. In Scots songs she is often raped, but if she had pluck, she might gain a fine, noble husband. "But our pioneer folk censor," says Lomax, "struck these pleasurable realities from the songs, and, as far as possible, from life," leaving Americans to sing a sad moral:

> *The grave will decay you and turn you to dust,*
> *There's not one boy in fifty that a poor girl can trust.*

Most of the ballads which won lasting popularity in America have to do with sexual conflict viewed through the eyes of women. Barbara Allen's pride kills the young man who loved her. The greed of Lord Thomas' mother brings about the death of Fair Elinor. Faithful Lady Nancy Belle pines away to the grave when Lord Lovel abandons her for a year and a day. Pretty Polly strikes back at her seducer, the Elfin Knight, by pushing him over a cliff. Lord Randal dies in his mother's arms, poisoned by his wicked sweetheart. The married woman, who leaves her children and carpenter husband, is drowned with her Daemon Lover. Another lady of greater abandon, rather than return to her husband's castle, prefers to remain in the cold fields with the Gypsy Laddie. Lord Barnard runs through Little Musgrove, his wife's lover, before beheading the guilty woman. The Cruel Mother is haunted by the pitiful ghosts of her babies, whom she has stabbed. "Such are the themes of ballads cherished by the women of the backwoods, for whom love and marriage meant gruelling labour, endless childbearing, and subservience," Alan Lomax writes. "In the ballads one can see the women turning to thoughts of revenge, to morbid death wishes, to guilt-ridden fantasies of escape. Always the sorrows of women bring violence and death to those around them."

Similar emotions found comic release in humorous narratives. The Farmer's Curst Wife, sent off to Hell, thrashes the Devil and returns to earth to give her husband another trouncing. The wandering husband in "Our Goodman" is told that the man in bed with his wife is a cabbage head or a baby. Almost gone from American balladry are the jovial Scots songs of rape and pregnancy and the seduction songs of southern England. In their stead stand a host of later pieces telling of faithful and virtuous maidens who get their man. Yet this romantic image of virtue rewarded has a darker counterpart in a set of ballads bearing a sadistic, punishing theme. The "Cruel Ship's Carpenters," for instance, tells the story of a pregnant girl murdered by her treacherous lover. And this vein, Lomax observes, "has given rise to more than half of the ballads composed by white folk singers in America!" Curiously, for a frontier society in which the rugged, able-bodied male was a cultural ideal, the British ballads in which men play a hero's part have been little sung in America.

A guilt-ridden, repressed society found sex—and in turn, love—fearful, a contest that brought little happiness and was frequently a source of destruction. Not only must women not enjoy the sexual act, but love, if it became more than wifely duty, meant sorrow, abandonment, and possibly death. The virtuous maiden might get her husband, but men were not to be trusted. They were unfaithful and prone to desert, more loyal to imperious mothers than to their wives. The woman could, as Lomax suggests, contemplate revenge, think death wishes, and escape into fantasy, but for her to abandon her children meant endless guilt, and adultery for her would surely lead to violence and further unhappiness. Love, the subconscious seemed to hold, led to pregnancy, which for the woman resulted in death— spiritually, if not physically. To survive in a society that cast her as subordinate, the woman was left with little recourse but to become as aggressive, conniving, and vehement as she feared her husband potentially to be. In self-defense she must conquer him before he abandoned her, undermine his strength in an effort to reduce her feeling of inferiority. In the struggle what might have developed into love suffocated, and the woman's love-impulse became directed toward her children, particularly her sons, whom she must also vanquish lest they too abandon her.

Despite fervent expressions of hope and zeal for their labors, Anglo-Americans of the frontier, Lomax maintains, were latently angry. Rural common people in Great Britain, after long privation, had been forced off rich commons into city slums in the eighteenth century. The many who came to the New World arrived expecting a wilderness paradise, where wealth and position were theirs for the taking. Rather than a life of abundance and joy, they found in America hard work and a restrictive moral pattern. "To the religious," Lomax concludes, "death became a friend who freed them from continual struggle, and to the rebellious, death was a final break with a painful morality. The morbid hymns and bloody ballads expressed their unconscious wishes." They also reveal an appetite for violence and excitement, while the underlying psychological conflicts, evidencing a submerged composite of hate, suspicion, and desire for vengeance, may in fact temper the sincerity of America's recurring overstatements of optimism.

Clearly, beneath a placid surface, violent feelings were surging, emotions that a repressive society found too disturbing to express openly. Instead the tormented turned unconsciously to fantasy, murmuring their buried wishes and secret conflicts in ballads that had been passively accepted by a haunted civilization over long generations. If indeed folk songs are a record of community feelings, as collectors have consistently argued, then the Anglo-American hinterland must have been settled by an emotionally beleaguered people. Yet their fears and insecurities were voiced in the most traditional means, linking frontiersmen to their British roots and what they looked upon as cultural stability. In part their distress was eased by the familiarity of the cry. While the Anglo-American folk selected the songs they perpetuated from a far greater store that was popular in their ancestral land at the time their forefathers left, an appreciably larger number of the old-style ballads continued in North America as a living tradition than survived in Great Britain itself.

Alan Lomax masterfully sums up the experience of the British ballad in America:

> So, slowly, our folk songs grew, part dream and part reality, part past and part present. Each phrase rose from the depths of the heart or was carved out of the rock of experience. Each line was sung smooth by many singers, who tested it against the American reality until the language became apt and truthful and as tough as cured hickory. Here lies the secret of their beauty. They evoke the feeling of the place and of belonging to a particular branch of the human family. They honestly describe or protest against the deepest ills that afflict us—the colour bar, our repressed sexuality, our love of

violence, and our loneliness. Finally, they have been cared for and reshaped by so many hands that they have acquired the patina of art, and reflect the tenderest and most creative impulses of the human heart, casting upon our often harsh and melancholy tradition a lustre of true beauty.

The popular songs of early nineteenth-century America hinted at some of the same social ills, but in sublimated form and with much less honesty. Behind a veil of sentimentality were imperfectly hidden the sexual repressions in particular of a puritanical society, in which even love and joy were contemplated with suspicion. In commercial music, lovers were no longer murdered, but died instead, leaving behind a trail of grief. Seduction was reduced to the tender kiss, followed by a proposal of marriage. Wives did not so obviously vanquish their men, but rather created a quiet domestic nirvana that bordered on stagnation. Mothers no more were boldly domineering, but the gentle, gray-haired old ladies eulogized by popular songwriters commanded their children's unqualified devotion nonetheless. The fears and conflicts expressed in the traditional ballads were present in commercial music, but the statement was less granulated, the defenses more refined.

Since folk songs are rooted in fundamental social and psychological patterns, they change very slowly. New versions arise, and gradual modification takes place continuously as the songs are transmitted by word of mouth. But definite variations emerge little by little over considerable time. In remote areas, especially the Southern Appalachians, the whole way of life remained essentially conservative, and the Anglo-Scots-Irish ballad tradition blended into a hybrid that persisted with little contamination. In regions where the social pattern was more dynamic, these folk songs either died out or were altered more substantially. Proper names varied most often; in Virginia, for example, "Lord Randal" was sung as "Johnnie Randolph."

The method of singing traditional music was also resistant to change. The Anglo-American folk ballad was most widely sung without accompaniement. In the early nineteenth century a banjo, fiddle, or dulcimer might supply occasional accompaniment, but the guitar is a fairly recent innovation. The pioneers customarily sang long ballads, slowly and solo, employing highly embellished melodies. The voice was often high-pitched, with an almost "womanish" nasal tone. A tense throat permitted little shading in vocal color, but great delicacy in ornamentation. The effect was a plaintive wailing sound, consistent with the internal melancholy and conflict of the songs. The ballad singer became an impersonal, although highly effective story-teller. When the fiddle was used as accompaniment, it too became a high-pitched, wailing voice closely matching the singer's.

In the sequestered mountain valleys of the Southern Appalachians, Cecil Sharp, when he visited the region between 1916-1918, found the ancient ballads of Great Britain sung by young and old alike. This was in marked contrast to what he had discovered earlier in England, where he rarely found anyone under seventy who remembered the folk song tradition. Sharp also found the speech of the primitive Southern highlanders more English than American, and they were still using expressions that had long been obsolete in Britain. Most of them were illiterate, and they reminded Sharp very much of the English peasant. Not only was the singing of the old ballads widespread in the Southern Appalachians, but the art was closely associated with routine activities of everyday life. When Sharp asked one informant for a particular song, the singer faltered and sighed, "Oh, if only I were driving the cows home I could sing it at once!"

In content, however, few of the traditional folk songs have any direct connection with economic or political events. And while the fatalistic atmosphere of the Anglo-Scots-Irish ballads may have reflected hidden social conflicts and areas of psychological stress among the American folk, their tragic mood was far from consistent with either the national exuberance in politics or the urban excitement in commerce. Consequently by the mid-nineteenth century the old folk ballads had practically dropped out of existence in the more cosmopolitan Northeast, kept alive only among lumberjacks and in isolated communities of the Maritime Provinces. Taking their place with the common people was a myriad of native American songs, closely tied to the people, but not folk songs in the traditional sense. Many of these borrowed stylistically from the British originals. But the universal narratives of the traditional ballads were replaced by themes more immediately associated with specific aspects of a regional environment, often becoming quite topical.

Many of these early American songs emerging from segments of the folk community did center on political and economic matters. Since the beginnings of the eighteenth century vendors are known to have hawked their wares in the streets of the seaboard cities, voicing highly personalized street cries as they strolled. Some of these poignant tunes, like "Come Buy My Woodenware," eventually passed into the popular song repertoire. With the appearance of industry shortly after the Revolution, labor songs were soon to be heard, particularly from the textile mills, where the American factory system really originated. "The Lowell Factory Girl" was one of the earliest songs to express discontent among workers in the opening decades of the nineteenth century. Like true folk song, "The Lowell Factory Girl" was transmitted orally, spread over a wide geographical area, was sung for several generations, and its composer is unknown. As the industrial system expanded, songs protesting working conditions, long hours, and low pay became increasingly evident. In the years preceding the Civil War any number of songs were written manifesting agitation over the plight of the Irish workers, and certainly at no time were the folk at the bottom of the social and economic pyramid as optimistic about the state of American democracy as the classes nearer the top. But in the songs of the occupations, action is highly valued, and there is a sense of fulfillment present. While death is a common result of the workers' efforts toward improvement, it is a hero's death.

The songs of protest may qualify, but do not negate the vigor and enthusiasm present in the United States during the early years of industrialization. There was a freshness and an exuberance permeating the country that cannot be denied, and it was to be sure a period of vast expansion and national awakening. A lusty, dynamic people frequently enjoyed lusty music, and by the age of Jackson, comic songs—often uncouth, although seldom vulgar, smacking strongly of frontier humor—had become prevalent among the urban folk. Amid the working classes art music came to be sneered at as Federalist, aristocratic, and snobbish, while songs of a folk idiom, capturing the essence of rural salt, were held as the music of the common man and a true democracy. Although they were rarely welcomed into the parlor, the jaunty songs of the Jacksonian era were satiated with rustic exaggeration and incongruity, were often drawn from native lore, and were as egalitarian in spirit as the frontier tavern.

The building tension between rural and urban attitudes was repeatedly indicated in the vernacular songs of young America, as the nascent industrial system flexed its newborn strength. Fashionable classes might enjoy singing gaily about "Broadway Sights," but the great mass of Americans preferred lyrics reminiscent of the farm, songs like "Brother Jonathan" and "Jonathan's Visit to a Wedding." While such tunes generally had identified composers and were folk songs only in the loosest sense, they did voice common thoughts of a broad folk community anxious about the economic shifts taking place around them.

As industry and commerce expanded in the Northeast during the half century before the Civil War, maritime activity on the Atlantic seaboard quickened to keep pace. Enlarged markets called for enlarged shipping, and it was during these years that the sailing ship was brought to the peak of its efficiency. The long, thin clipper ship emerged, elevating sailing to a level of speed and grace undreamed of in preceding centuries. Especially aboard the clippers, where a rigorous time-schedule was kept, sailors developed the custom of singing while they went about their back-breaking toil. Chanteys, or work songs, were sung by the crew as they hoisted the canvases to the winds, weighed anchor, or labored at other heavy, manual tasks. Although English in origin, the chantey early became American in content—its wording simple, direct, and salty, like the seamen themselves. The rhythm of the song was supplied by the work being done, and the words had to fit whether they made good sense or not. The tune was often spirited, designed to lighten the labor at hand. Most of the chanteys consisted of short solo passages, each followed by a chorus, with many verses and much repetition. There was little attempt at harmony, although in the days when square-riggers carried large crews there was sometimes accompaniment from a fiddle or an accordion.

Most of the chanteys originated before 1850. While the airs were generally traditional, often having their roots in the ancient ballads, the words were of the sailors' own making. The chorus lines became standardized both in words and melody, whereas solo passages were subject to much improvisation and parody. Among the more famous sea chanteys are "Blow the Man Down," "Shenandoah," and "Whisky Johnny." Some of these songs were haunting, others humorous, many bawdy, even gross—in the "Christopher Colombo" genre. But this obscenity is jovial, forthright, and with little or no suggestiveness or *double-entendre*.

The solo lines of the chantey were normally sung by a leader or chantey-man, who was prized as one of the most valuable members of the crew. Since blacks or Irishmen often filled this role, characteristics of Irish balladry and the black spirituals crept prominently into the music of the sea. As the packets increased their speed, their crews were driven harder and harder, and the chantey became the rule. " A song is as necessary to sailors as the drum and fife to a soldier," Richard Henry Dana wrote in *Two Years before the Mast*. "They must pull together as soldiers must step in time, and they can't pull in time, or pull with a will, without it."

But the chantey did not die out with the sailing vessel, for when the old merchant seamen were transferred to steamships, they took along much of their old gear and many of their songs. These they passed on to the newer seamen, even after the work songs were no longer of much practical value. Traditionally there had been a strong taboo among mariners against singing their chanteys ashore; to do so would be courting disaster. When they caroused in port, or even sang on watch at sea, sailors would likely choose a ballad or popular love song. Later on, the work songs of the clippers not only had new themes fitted to them, but came to be heard with regularity on land, particularly in the woods of northern New England and eastern Canada.

There was in fact a close connection between lumbering in the Northeast and coastal seafaring. The same men who felled the trees in winter and directed the logs down the rivers in the spring would often take to the sea in summer for a voyage to South America or the West Indies. Lumbering and seafaring, therefore, were dovetailed occupations, sometimes employing the same men at different seasons. The bunkhouses of loggers were called "shanties," while the term "shanty-song" was frequently used in reference to the folk songs sung by the lumberjacks after they had concluded their work. The lyrics of the sailors' chanteys, which woodsmen had learned during intervals at sea, were slowly adjusted to fit more comfortably into a lumber camp environment, for improvisation remained characteristic. As with the seamen, the songs developed by lumberjacks were mainly associated with work, although the songs were sung for relaxation when the day's toil was over, rather than to set a cadence for pulling or hauling. The woodsmen's shanty-songs were filled with loneliness, nostalgia for home, and dreams—stated in a rough, masculine spirit. Emotions were expressed self-consciously and with restraint, while poignancy came largely from understatement.

Occasionally, a rigorous, rough-and-tumble humor was injected into the shanties, revealing the lusty, robust nature of the men who sang them.

When the Old Northwest was opened to Anglo-American settlement, the songs of the eastern woodlands were carried by lumbermen into the forests enclosing the Great Lakes, much as the British ballads and early folk spirituals were transported on a larger scale through the Cumberland Gap by the pioneers who were to settle the trans-Appalachian West. And like the merchant sailors and lumberjacks, the frontiersmen who moved into the Blue Grass of Kentucky and the fertile fields of Ohio devised variations of old songs and made changes that reflected their particular environment. But the pioneers also fashioned fresh tunes and lyrics by merging elements of the several oral traditions that found their way across the mountains. On the untamed frontier, where men and music were scarce, a song was treasured for its suitability to life more than for its source or inherited value. Settlers of different ethnic origins and from different sectors of America itself borrowed from one another as they came into contact in the interior, blending folk characteristics into a music that was new.

In the early days of westward expansion, when men alone probed the retreating wilderness, campfire balladry was plainspoken and coarse. The words were factual, repeatedly suggested the aggressive temper of everyday life, and frequently spoke of sudden death. Their very rawness supplied them the force of truth, for they sang the bald language of the vanguards of settlement. Later, as pioneer families continued their trek over wagon trails, down interior waterways, and on to the pathless prairies, frontiersmen experienced an increasing sense of rootlessness, a lonely, troubled feeling of somehow not belonging to the vast, awesome solitude enveloping them. Dispersed in the hinterland, the pioneers often sang "lonesome tunes," referring to themselves as sad, wayfaring strangers. While native American balladry discloses an air of rebellion and social protest, there are counter-balancing notes of wistfulness in the songs of the common people of the West.

But there is also that streak of laughter, capsuled in the tall tale, present in the music of the frontier—a wit in which the dangers and dimensions of the wilderness became too ridiculous to terrify any longer. Fun was made of the old class system, social airs, awkward lovers, and fumbling courtships. To the frontier humorist nothing was sacred; laughter became the great leveler. But the fiddlers and banjo players who crossed the mountains were no less determined to get some fun out of life, although this later meant facing the disapproval of more religious folk. "The one batch of white songs which catch sounds of untrammeled, earthy pleasure are the lyrics for the hoedown fiddle and the banjo," Alan Lomax observes. "I suspect that many of these rowdy and joyous songs were created in settlements far out on the frontier, beyond the reach of the preacher and his board of joy-killing deacons. They were kept alive by the reckless crew who roistered and drank, even though they were dancing beyond the pale of respectability."

Fiddlers played tunes from all over the British Isles, as well as American

originals. But the melodies, whether borrowed from Irish reels or the
contemporary minstrel stage, underwent substantial changes in mood,
structure, and style at the hands of frontiersmen. The imagination of the
rustic musician was permitted to wander freely about a given tune. Abrupt
intervals differentiated the lyric line, while rhythms became more energetic,
the beat clearly defined. Traditional melodies gained new figurations, as
frontiersmen expressed themselves in song, generally becoming wilder and
more aggressive. Individual playing mannerisms abounded; fiddlers often
ignored chin-rests, holding the instrument in any number of informal
positions. The hoedown fiddler played with less polish than his Scotch-Irish
equivalents, but his crisp, rhythmic attack and quick, heavy bowing infused
the tunes with an amazing vitality.

The folk dances for which these musicians played comprised a mosaic of
steps derived primarily from England, Scotland, and Ireland, essentially like
the songs themselves. Again improvisation produced local differences.
Dancing on the frontier tended to be less inhibited than in the more settled
areas, yet was cryptic and allusive nevertheless, depending on wild, foolish
images to impart hidden erotic desires.

But it was the element of unrestraint among early pioneers that the
religious folk who followed condemned as sacrilege, providing an immediate
impetus for the outbreak of the Great Revival in Kentucky in 1800. In the path
of the spiritual awakening that swept the frontier in the ensuing decades, a
renewed sense of guilt and shame was set ablaze among rural Americans,
causing them to spurn joy and equate the good life with work, duty, and
religious devotion. But in the camp meeting spirituals, as in other realms of
native folk song, the common man did issue forth as an individual. Unlike
the older types of hymns, folk spirituals like "Amazing Grace" and "How
Firm a Foundation" sang mainly of personal salvation, much as in American
balladry the first person singular tended to replace the impersonal narrator.
Yet the individual that emerged from the spirituals was no American giant;
he was a depraved sinner, groveling in fear.

> Amazing grace! how sweet the sound,
> That saved a wretch like me!
> I once was lost, but now am found,
> Was blind, but now I see.

While frontiersmen enjoyed singing these simple gospel hymns, the pleasure
was overcast by the hovering burden of obligation and the shame of being
human. The beloved fiddle had become damned as an instrument of the devil;
liquor, among lesser things, speedily ruined the best of voices; and pride was
the first of the Seven Deadly Sins. Still, the frontiersman labored with the
knowledge that he desired amusement, sometimes thirsted for drink, and
longed for enough self-assurance to end his tormenting guilt.

As the spirit of revivalism spread, a demand for camp meeting songbooks developed, most of them containing only the texts of hymns without musical notation. By 1829 the market had become so great that Orange Scott's pocketsized songster sold out its initial edition of 5000 copies within eighteen months, and a second edition was quickly bought. In 1835 "Singin' Billy" Walker of Spartanburg, South Carolina, published *The Southern Harmony*, which remained in use for years in the South. Through both music and sermons the camp meeting evangelists denounced the city as the special haven of wickedness and worldliness, placating rural Americans with the suggestion that while agrarian life might be hard and drab and limited, farmers in any case were more pious than their urban brethren and still remained the moral and spiritual backbone of the nation, even if their economic lead might be on the decline.

In some corners fanaticism appeared, as the religious zeal of the early nineteenth century continued to mount. Spiritualism, inspirationalism, and a whole rash of mysterious cults burst forth, while young America stammered its way toward some sort of self-identity. The Shakers—a celibate, communistic sect originating in England and planted in upstate New York in the late eighteenth century by Mother Ann Lee—believed in a mystical union of the believer with God's Holy Spirit. For the Shakers God was a duality, both male and female, and should be served by man with his total faculties. God gave man a tongue and feet and hands and a body. All of these should be employed in worshipping the Creator; otherwise the union with God would be less than complete.

Simplicity was one of the Shakers' most pervasive virtues, and their first music consisted of wordless tunes. Lyrics were added as Mother Ann's followers became instilled with the spirit of early American revivalism. A group of Shakers came out of the Great Revival in Kentucky, and others settled later in Ohio and Indiana. The hymns of these zealots were stirring diatribes against the flesh and man's carnal nature. Yet the songs of the Shakers offered a welcome emotional release from routine communal labors, while their whole form of worship—in sharp contrast with the camp meetings—demonstrated the joy experienced on the journey toward heaven.

Shaker hymns were of a distinctly folk character, fresh and imaginative in language, exhibiting a lively spontaneity and a sprightly tune. The Shakers were devoted to a free expression of primitive emotion and believed that the dance and bodily movement constituted the highest form of praise to God. Many of their songs were subordinant to the dance, the words essentially becoming a statement of the exhilaration of motion. While the Shakers engaged in group dances involving a precise, well-studied technique (slow "sacred" marches and quick dances entailing a lively, loping or trotting movement), the believers became notorious for their extemporaneous dances of ecstasy, in which participants broke from the ranks to shake, whirl, and sing in utter abandonment. This violent bodily movement expressed not only the joy of their religious faith, but a ridding of oneself of carnal appetites which made the union with God possible. For the Shakers religious gatherings became exalted pleasure, recreation transfigured.

But in the path of righteous excitement came prejudice and intolerance. For introducing dance into their worship, the Shakers suffered great criticism and persecution from their more puritanical neighbors. They were charged with engaging in wild orgies, drunkenness, playing cards, telling fortunes, and, most frequently, dancing naked. In the face of repeated hostility the Shakers clung to their beliefs, insisting that, after all, the children of Israel had danced on joyful occasions and had praised God's name in dance.

Severe as the persecution of the Shakers was, it was dwarfed by the suffering endured by the Church of the Latter-Day Saints, or Mormons. An extraordinarily musical people, the Mormons originated in western New York during the intense religious revivals of the 1820s, under the leadership of Joseph Smith. Loathed by more orthodox zealots around them—in part because of their exclusiveness, in part because of their economic success—the Mormons after much harassment splintered into groups, migrating into Ohio, Missouri, and Illinois, where Smith received a revelation in favor of polygamy. Increased hostility resulted in the killing of Joseph Smith and further mistreatment of the whole group. In the hope of leaving the United States altogether, a party of some 150 were led in 1847 into the valley of the Great Salt Lake by Brigham Young, where they soon formed the state of Deseret.

Once more under the jurisdiction of the United States, as a result of the Mexican Cession of 1848, the Mormons became the first of the western pioneers to use band and stringed instruments in their music or worship. They had no reservations about instruments associated with dance, for they strongly sanctioned "dancing before the Lord." The Mormons appear to have gotten more fun out of their religion than any other frontier faith, and church music was one source of this pleasure. Their bands included strings, percussion, and wind instruments, all of which were considered appropriate for making a joyful noise. Much of their music came directly from the Protestant hymn tradition of Great Britain. Some of it was reminiscent of the hymns of Martin Luther, while other songs were of folk and individual genesis. Several of these hymns declare and defend the doctrines of the Latter-Day Saints, while others depict the struggles between the Mormons and the "Gentiles" in Missouri and Illinois. Probably the best known of the Mormon hymns is William Clayton's "Come, Come Ye Saints," set to a tune that had apparently originated earlier in Georgia. Clayton was a member of the initial group of pioneers to make the trek to Utah with Brigham Young.

Unlike many religious denominations in America the Mormon Church encouraged its members in an appreciation and love for good music. The church taught that the life of a "Saint" should be filled with a wholehearted exuberance, which might well find expression in all types of music. Although bands and choirs were granted a prominent place in most Mormon meetings, music was particularly important in the general conferences of the entire church that came to be held in Salt Lake City each year. Here the choir sang a varied repertoire, ranging—according to one observer—"from original Mormon songs in the tune of 'Old Dan Tucker' to Bach's chants and Handel's oratorios." During the early years the Mormon Tabernacle Choir probably performed with more enthusiasm than artistic polish, but it would eventually grow into an organization of national importance.

Among the French in Louisiana and the German settlers in Texas, music fared considerably better, and on a more exalted plane, than with most Anglo-American frontiersmen. And certainly no population in the West were more given to singing and dancing than the Spanish. The music of Spain, both secular and religious, attained a high level of development during the time that colonization of Mexico and the American Southwest was beginning. The Spanish nobility had fallen under the spell of the troubador spirit, and there was a wealth of popular music as well. Life in the early Southwest was simple, as most of the Spanish-American settlements were remote from civilization. This provincial environment, however, was favorable for the development of folk music, both the perpetuation of sixteenth-century Spanish balladry and the creation of new songs by colonials.

By the time Anglo-American frontiersmen began to filter in, the Spanish borderlands from California to Texas reverberated with song. William Heath Davis reported that the people of southern California "seemed to have a talent and a taste for music. Many of the women played the guitar skillfully, and the young men the violin. In almost every family there was one or more musicians, and everywhere music was a famous sound." Each special event or *fiesta* had its musical accompaniment and was followed with a formal *baile* or informal *fandango*. *Fiestas* sometimes lasted for several days, and Davis was present at one wedding party where a hundred guests danced all night, slept three hours, enjoyed a picnic in the forenoon, and began dancing again—a cycle that continued for three days!

Music for *bailes* and *fandangos* was customarily furnished by violin, harp, and flute. Dances included traditional Spanish folk steps, as well as the newer quadrilles and waltzes—despite the Church's threat to excommunicate anyone discovered dancing the daring waltz. No *fandango* was complete without a *tecolero*, or master of ceremonies, who singled out each *señorita* for her turn. Singing and dancing were closely linked in the Spanish Southwest, and ballads improvised for the occasion were regular features of parties. During the festivities *cascarones*, or eggshells filled with small bits of colored paper, were broken over the heads of merrymakers, as the singing—good, bad, and middling—continued. Uneducated Spanish and Mexican singers tended to evidence a fondness for nasal tones and for ornamenting the melody with an abundance of turns, slides, and grace notes, in the fashion of southern Spain. This was part of the Spaniard's Moorish heritage, for the Moors often carried embellishment to the point that the original melody almost became unrecognizable.

Far and away the most beloved instrument throughout Spanish America was the guitar, or its predecessor the *bihuela*, a guitarlike instrument originating with the Moors. When accompanying songs the guitarist would ordinarily make his music simple, playing either chords or arpeggios, although on occasions he could perform extraordinary feats in virtuoso fashion. Pianos were first imported into the Southwest about 1840, but their presence, as throughout frontier America, was a sign of considerable wealth.

There were songs of the soil, the first introduced from Spain, later ones coming up from Mexico, and an abundance of church music. Mission choirs sang an extensive repertoire ranging from plain chants to complex masses. In California Padre Narcisco Duran compiled an extensive choir book in manuscript form in 1813, which was used for many years in the instruction of Indian neophytes at Missions San Jose and Santa Barbara. In his preface Father Duran included a summary of the curious methods he employed in training his choirs and mission orchestras from music with six-lined staves. The orchestras were comprised mainly of Indians, performing on homemade instruments. Since these same musicians often played for *bailes* and *fandangos*, they sometimes confused the selections appropriate for church and dance with naive disregard.

But the tranquility of Spanish-speaking California was interrupted by the "Bear Flag Revolt" in 1846 and, more decidedly, with the discovery of gold at Sutter's mill in the Sacramento Valley two years later. Within weeks word of the discovery had spread along the Pacific coast, and within months all America was brimming with the news that fortunes lay hidden in the mountainsides and streams of the Sierra Nevadas. By the end of 1849 thousands of Americans and Europeans had descended on California by the quickest route within their means—around Cape Horn by ship, across the Isthumus of Panama, overland through the Great Plains and Rocky Mountains. In the Sacramento Valley mining camps sprang up overnight, with their ramshackle saloons, ribald amusements, and shameless emporiums of vice. If the camp proved lasting, professional entertainers were attracted to its saloons and variety halls by the freshly panned, freely spent wealth from the hills.

The songs associated with the miners were not folk songs in the genuine sense. Their words were penned by professional broadside composers, were literary and ephemeral, and few of them passed into the oral tradition. Their tunes were either composed with the lyrics or pirated from current popular ballads and minstrel songs. While these songs often found their way into the pocketsized songsters published in California during the gold rush, most of them were introduced by professional entertainers, who sang in the saloons or on the stage with piano accompaniment. Their delivery was probably much like that accorded Stephen Foster's tunes and definitely not in the manner of rural folk music.

The miners' songs, nevertheless, reflect much of the atmosphere of the great gold rush—the long journey to California, the drudgery of mining, the hopes and disillusionments, the hardships and humor of life in the gold fields. The largest number and most popular of the gold rush songs were written by John A. Stone—"Old Put," as he preferred to be known. His "Sweet Betsy from Pike," a favorite with the miners and a tune that definitely did enter the oral tradition, described in spirited fashion the trek across the continent:

> *Did you ever hear tell of Sweet Betsy from Pike,*
> *Who crossed the wide prairies with her lover Ike,*
> *With two yoke of cattle and one spotted hog,*
> *A tall Shanghai rooster and an old yellow dog.*

> *Hoodle Dang fol-de di-do, hoodle dang fol-de day.*

The first gold rush song actually written in California was probably "Seeing the Elephant" by David G. Robinson, proprietor of one of San Francisco's earliest theatrical houses. Set to the tune of Dan Emmett's "De Boatman Dance," Robinson's lyrics told of conditions at the mines. The music of the forty-niners, like their way of life, reflected much adaptation. Parody was the most frequent result, although the borrowed tunes generally evoked a contemptuous humor in the transition. Some of the songs set to familiar melodies were clearly unhappy. "The Gambler," for instance, sung to the tune of "De Camptown Races," is a sorrowful song that reviewed the story of a miner who lost at games of monte, faro, and twenty-one. Other gold rush songs seemed cheerful enough on the surface, but contained an element of bite:

> *Hey what was your name in the States?*
> *Was it Thompson, or Johnson, or Bates?*
> *Did you murder your wife*
> *And fly for your life?*
> *Say, what was your name in the States?*

While the great preponderance of these songs were virile and rowdy, often cynical or complaining, there was a subordinate strain voicing the conventional and sentimental, praise to motherhood, children, and home—for example, "I Often Think of Writing Home."

The optimism and regard for rugged individualism considered so characteristic of the American West may indeed have been fostered by the mining experience, but the music identified with the various gold rushes does not support this. The lyrics that appeared in the popular press of the mining towns and in the miners' songsters tended to dwell on the loneliness and misery of men alone, despite frequently comic exteriors. Conversely, the most hopeful songs of the West were those of men who organized—the Mormons, the Wobblies, and at times, the Grangers. These groups either lived in reasonably settled frontier communities or, in the case of the Grangers, formed as frontier conditions were vanishing.

But songs and parodies were not the only music to be heard from the folk on the far western frontier. As settlement continued, a dimension of culture was added to the rustic population. When Sarah and Josiah Royce operated a store for a time in a mining camp near Sacramento, Mrs. Royce gathered together a few books, some knickknacks, a table, and a small organ, setting aside one room of their canvas shack as a parlor. The organ was Mrs. Royce's pride and joy, and she later recalled, "There was little time for music during the day, except on Sundays; but at night when the children were all in bed, and the store...kept my husband away, I used often to indulge myself in the melodies and harmonies that brought to me the most precious memories of earth, and opened up visions of heaven. And then those bare rafters and cloth walls became for the time a banquet-hall, a cathedral."

The trail blazers, however, were seldom so civilized and could be downright barbarous. As the vanguards pushed deeper into the prairies, deserts, and mountains of the great American West, they encountered, learned from, fought, concentrated, and murdered the aborigines in their path. Anglo-American pioneers readily borrowed much of immediate practical value from the Indians, those skills and implements that would help them adjust to a strange environment, but the white man's appreciation of primitive art and culture rarely became more than curiosity until after the frontier had been secured and tamed. Despite the more than casual interest in Indian music evidenced at times by American composers in the late nineteenth century, the red man's contribution to the development of music in the United States has remained relatively slight, far more significant in subject matter than in construction. Frances Densmore, the early authority in the field, specifically urged in fact "that Indian music be studied as an expression apart and different from our own music, and that its structure be compared with that of our music as little as possible."

Unlike European music, which for the most part was artistic or recreational, American Indian music was primarily functional—that is, an integral part of everyday life. Much of it originally was religious. Songs were indispensable in ritual, both public and private, and since ceremonial songs were believed to have come from a supernatural source, singing them was associated with the exercise of supernatural power. Songs were interspersed in legends and accounts of tribal or family history, although seldom were these truly narrative. Since food, health, and safety were of immediate concern to the Indians, much of their singing was an effort to assure these essentials. There were songs to insure a good hunt, songs to bring success in battle, songs to treat the sick, songs for games, special gambling songs, and lullabies. There were few work songs, and—despite fiction to the contrary—practically no love songs among the historical Indians, except those songs employed to work "love charms." The early Indians, although often highly sensitive, tended to favor silence in matters involving deep emotion and preferred to leave much concerning love unsaid.

Music, like other aspects of North American Indian life, varied a great deal over the spectrum of native cultures, yet with few exceptions it consistently had a purpose. To the Indian, music well performed was "good" rather than beautiful, meaning that it had accomplished the desired result. The three major classifications of songs were: those received in dreams, those purchased or inherited from their owners, and those praising a man's success or generosity. The first two types were felt to possess magic powers and were thus jealously guarded by the individuals or groups acquiring them. The third type was reserved for conveying special honors, and their singing usually was rewarded with gifts. All three categories were sung mainly by men, although lullabies were the particular province of women. These lullabies were neither composed nor received in dreams, but developed gradually from the gentle crooning sounds with which mothers quieted their children.

Indian singing was normally accompanied by percussion instruments and to the ear of Anglo-American frontiersmen possessed a harshness in tone. Songs tended to begin high, end low, and contain more rhythm than melody. Indians sang with their teeth slightly separated and their lips almost motionless, the tone apparently forced out by an action of the throat muscles. Their songs generally lasted from about twenty seconds to three minutes, including repetitions. If larger musical forms existed, they were composed by stringing a series of brief songs together. From the European viewpoint the most difficult aspect of the Indian's music was its rhythmic structure, for the rhythm of Indian songs was characterized by accents not equally spaced. Time units from two to five beats might occur within a single selection, and there were often conflicting rhythms between the voice and the beat of the percussion. Melodies were based on irregular intonation and at times on altered scales. Almost all songs were monophonic—containing only one melody, a single pitch sounded at a given moment. Harmony was absent; if women sang with men, they did so in a higher octave.

Two types of instruments were found among the North American Indians—wind and percussion. The first consisted of flutes and whistles, the latter of drums and various kinds of rattles. Dances were accompanied both by percussion instruments and singing. The importance of dance in the lives of the Indians is suggested by the fact that almost all of their more elaborate ceremonies became identified by the whites as dances.

The Indians' songs made only a slender impression on either the popular or serious music of the nation that rose from the Indians' primitive fields and hunting grounds. When American composers turned to Indian themes toward the close of the nineteenth century, they were, Frances Densmore wrote in 1926, "showing an appreciation of the fact that the old Indian, taking his music with him, is passing quietly into the Great Silence."

In marked contrast with the Indian, who remained essentially isolated from the mainstream of early Anglo-American civilization, the other major non-European element in the society—the black—exercised repeated influence on the development of a national music. In spite of his subordinate position, the Negro became far more amalgamated into the social structure of the United States than the Indian and thus possessed the avenue for making their contributions to the culture felt. For over two centuries the contrasting musical traditions of the blacks and Anglo-Americans lived together side by side, in a continual state of competition and stimulating exchange. Song material flowed back and forth between the races with such regularity that it became almost impossible at times to determine what had originated with what race. "Indeed," Alan Lomax speculates, "it seems very likely that one day all American music will be *cafe-au-lait* in colour."

Although frequently censured, African elements in the music of the southern slaves were too deeply rooted and vital to die out completely. Furthermore, the constant importation of more blacks worked to keep the West African heritage alive. Even after the slave trade was legally banned by the United States in 1808, contraband slaves were smuggled into the country directly from Africa until the eve of the Civil War. All of African origin, the work songs, field hollers, falsetto singing, and call-and-response system evident in colonial days continued. English actress Fanny Kemble, who lived in the South between 1838 and 1839 after marrying a Georgia rice planter, kept a perceptive journal of her experiences there. Some of the songs she heard among the slaves seemed "extraordinarily wild and unaccountable. The way in which the chorus strikes in with the burden between each phrase of the melody chanted by a single voice is very curious and effective." What she was probably hearing was a work song in which the leader set the rhythm of the labor by singing, while fellow slaves responded in unison. Some eighteen years later, landscape architect Frederick Law Olmsted, on one of his trips through the South by rail, was awakened by the singing of a black loading crew outside his car:

> Suddenly, one raised such a shout as I had never heard before; a long, loud, musical shout, rising and falling, and breaking into falsetto, his voice ringing through the woods in the clear, frosty night air, like a bugle call. As he finished, the melody was caught up by another, and then, by several in chorus.

The substance of these gang songs ranged from the ribald to the devout, for not all of the later work songs dealt with labor. Some were melancholy, many were trivial, others were extemporaneous. Most of them were quite free-spoken, although stoically accepting things as they were, often with a suggestion of humor. Sometimes the songs were more biting, leaning toward social criticism or ridicule. More frequently the gangs sang of women, lives gone wrong, the hard lot of the black, heroic events, places they had been or heard of, gossip, or salvation. The statement might be direct or metaphoric, but by the nineteenth century there was little overt connection between the words sung by southern blacks and native African dialects. Only part of the work songs came from plantations; many emanated from the woods and warehouses and levees of the Old South. And through them all seemed to run a fierce undercurrent of pain, as if the black were crying out in the only way he knew how.

Unlike the white backwoodsman, who sang with a tense body and throat, blacks sang with a relaxed voice and greater freedom. The sound characteristic of southern highlanders was high-pitched and nasal, their technique lending itself to ornamentation. The relaxed throat of the black, on the other hand, was capable of far greater shading, producing a wide range of color. Blacks were able to shape their voices to their changing moods, and their singing faithfully indicated—in sound more than words—whether an individual was happy, melancholy, or angry. As slaves, blacks found it expedient to temper their language, but the nuances of the black voice expressed feelings without restraint or shame. "When a Negro sings," Lomax observes, "the bridle is off."

The importance of music over words is illustrated repeatedly in the songs of the slaves. In part the blacks were handicapped by an inadequate vocabulary; in part they became too absorbed in the music to give words more than nominal attention. They were perhaps most verbal—and happiest— when singing about animals, which the blacks found eternally interesting. Animal songs had abounded in Africa and provided the American slaves with a means of expression that whites discounted as nonsense. In these songs the blacks made the creatures around them both objects of amusement and vehicles for philosophic comment. The slaves delighted in rhyming the characteristics of species, endowing them with their own range of thought and emotions.

But at the same time the blacks absorbed much of the music of their masters. Fanny Kemble heard in the blacks' singing "some resemblance to tunes with which they must have become acquainted through the instrumentality of white men." The old British folk ballads were sung by the families and guests of the early plantation owners, and with repetition these were picked up by house servants and passed on to their brethren in the fields. Gradually the ballads were modified by the blacks and incorporated into their own oral tradition. Sometimes the words became altogether different from those sung by whites, as the ancient songs were handed down from generation to generation around cabin firesides. Later blacks fashioned ballads of their own, which the whites in turn borrowed. The classic "Frankie and Albert" probably originated between 1850 and 1860, was sung in many versions, and later became more commonly known as "Frankie and Johnnie."

The blacks also sang parodies and lullabies. As was generally the case with slave songs, brevity, simplicity, repetition, and improvisation were characteristic. Since music was a more natural part of life for blacks than for whites, they tended toward greater flexibility in their songs, altering them to correspond with the moment. White singers, on the other hand, were far more controlled, adhering to the convention that ballads should be sung with little personal involvement and passed on essentially as they were heard.

With the passage of time the slaves' African heritage was discouraged, while instrumental music of a lively nature was seen as a way of insuring plantation morale. "I have heard," Fanny Kemble wrote, "that many of the masters and overseers on these plantations prohibit melancholy tunes or words, and encourage nothing but cheerful music and senseless words," fearing the effect that sadder strains might have upon the slaves, "whose peculiar musical sensibility might be expected to make them especially excitable by any song of a plaintive character, and having any reference to their particular hardships." Banjo and fiddle music was considered quite appropriate, and the blacks probably played many of the same tunes that were heard on the frontier and early river boats. "Sugar in a Gourd," in the style of an Irish reel, is known to have been played in the 1830s by blacks in Virginia and elsewhere. When playing the banjo, the plantation black frequently tapped his feet to the rhythm, and musicologist Hans Nathan has speculated that there was a preference for off-beats and irregular accentuation. The slaves often made their banjos out of long-necked gourds, the bowl of which they covered with coonskin. Tambourines were common among plantation musicians, and "bones" were made from rib bones of cattle, similar to the way they had been made in Africa. The blacks were intrigued with anything percussive and even fashioned a triangle from the U-shaped iron clevis used in hitching horses to a plow.

Music in West Africa was largely a group activity, and so it remained among the southern slaves. All sorts of instrumental ensembles formed on the plantations—banjo and drum; fiddle, tambourine, and sticks; banjo, jawbone, and tambourine. The musicians customarily were joined by onlookers who swayed, clapped their hands, danced, and sang, gradually evolving into a festive throng. The full burden of Puritanism did not weigh upon the blacks, for as second-class citizens the early slaves were not expected to adhere to the rigid principles that governed the whites. Their music could be joyous, sensuous, erotic, providing an outlet for tensions and feelings their masters suppressed. Blacks therefore escaped many of the anxieties and conflicts that plagued Anglo-America. Their dancing was initially encouraged by white overseers, who considered this spontaneous recreation a convenient means for keeping the blacks contented. Later, as the slaves came under the strong influence of evangelical Protestantism, they began to look upon such revelries as a sin, for religious leaders denounced dancing as heathen and obscene. The defiant youth might continue to dance, but their devout elders shuddered. When the youth "got religion," they were expected to cleanse their minds of "devil songs," and by the early twentieth century the acceptance of a more ascetic morality and increased social dislocation led blacks time after time to cry the "careless love" blues.

In urban areas, particularly those under Latin influence, there were less restrictions. The *laissez faire* attitude toward African singing and dancing that was common in the West Indies had its counterpart in the tolerance of New Orleans for the dancing in Place Congo. Here on Sunday afternoons, although part of secret ritual, primitive West African steps could surface. The *calinda*, the *congo*, the *bamboula*, and the *vodun* dances were all observed—those same dances Louis Moreau Gottschalk heard from his home as a boy. For the *bamboula* the black males attached metal strips to ribbons about their ankles, pranced, stamped, leaped into the air, and shouted, "Dansez Bamboula! Badoum! Badoum!" Meanwhile the women swayed from side to side and chanted. Drums, gourd rattles, and scrapers provided accompaniment. The *calinda* was associated with zombiism in Haiti, and there were other similarities between the dances in Place Congo and those of Haiti, Martinique, and the Virgin Islands. But it was in New Orleans that native African music, particularly rhythm, was most clearly preserved in the United States, performed in the open, where it could influence later developments. Gradually the dancers in Place Congo borrowed from the cultures around them, as more and more European elements came to be added to the African.

By the early 1820s, however, the dancing in Place Congo was meeting objections from those concerned with respectability and was eventually forbidden. The concept of the black folk musician as "a child of the devil" may derive from the Louisiana voodoo cult, in which as part of the initiation the black novice must learn to play a musical instrument. The novice was to go to the crossroads at midnight, protected only by a bone from a black cat. Here the black sat playing in the dark, until the devil approached, cut the black's nails to the quick, and swapped instruments with the neophyte. The voodooists therefore sold their souls to the devil in return for a mastery of the devil's instrument. Anglo-American yarns often told of fiddlers taking lessons from the devil in a graveyard at midnight, while old Gaelic tales insisted that the gift of music came from fairies. In any case unabandoned music was linked with Satan, and blacks—as they came into the camp of fundamentalist religion—were instructed in no uncertain terms to purge themselves of the old "devil songs."

In place of the forbidden songs came gospel hymns and spirituals. By 1800 the practice of giving slaves religious instruction was common, rising with the tide of revivalism. Blacks customarily took an active part in the camp meetings of the rural South, and by 1829 regular organized missions for the blacks were initiated in South Carolina under Methodist auspices. Christianity provided the slaves a degree of inner comfort, although religion for them remained more of an emotional experience than a dogmatic, philosophical or ethical system. A contemporary observed during the Great Awakening in Virginia that blacks were commonly noisier during preaching than whites, were more prone toward bodily movement, and could grow extravagant if permitted. In some instances church leaders attempted to compromise with the blacks' desire to dance by encouraging "shouts" or "holy dances" during religious services. Frontier populations were normally more tolerant of the emotional expressions of blacks than were residents in more settled areas. Sometimes blacks were not allowed to enter the church building at all, but invited to sit outside, since they disturbed quiet worship with their inclination to beat out the rhythm of hymns with their feet and hands.

Blacks sang the same gospel songs in these services as the whites, and by the mid-nineteenth century the standard Methodist and Baptist hymns were in wide use among the black population of the South. Yet the singing of the blacks was characterized by vocal effects peculiarly their own, punctuated by spontaneous outbursts of intense religious fervor. Syncopation was far more prevalent in the singing of blacks than among whites. The slaves initially employed no harmony, but each member of the group sang his or her own version of the melody, in much the same manner as rural southerners. The blacks, however, added a distinctive quality by injecting the call-and-response system into their gospel songs. Here, a melodic fragment was sung repeatedly by the chorus in answer to challenging lines from the leader; the leader then changed the call to illicit a new response. Although it bore a resemblance to the old "lining-out" method, this technique was rooted in Africa. In some songs the response eventually developed into a true chorus, becoming the most important part of the hymn and often assuming the position of the leading line.

The slaves' singing of gospel hymns, therefore, contained a half familiar, half exotic flavor—part jubilant, part plaintive. Often there was much hand clapping and feet stamping, and occasionally dancing. The songs conducive to bodily movement were sometimes called "runnin' sperichels," in contrast to the more sedate "settin' sperichels." But through most of this music ran the blacks' special emphasis on percussion, even when instruments were not actually employed. Unlike the whites, religious songs for the blacks were not confined to the church or meeting ground and might well serve as accompaniment for secular dances as well as sung in the fields or while performing tasks around the big house and cabin.

Blacks eventually created their own spirituals, probably fashioned after the earlier ones of the whites. By 1840 the long chants initially sung by blacks in a simple call-and-response manner were largely superseded by spirituals in stanzaic form. Blacks likely borrowed the notion of division into verse and chorus from the white hymns, but they maintained some of the original pulse. Both white and black spirituals contain groups of songs concerning slavery, bondage, the terrors of Judgment Day, and the joys of Heaven. It has repeatedly been suggested that blacks made many of their spirituals to bewail their position as slaves and acclaim the day when they could walk the golden streets of heaven in freedom and as equals. Two factors modify this contention appreciably. First, the blacks seem seldom to have contemplated their low estate until after the abolitionist attack had reached its heat. Second, the concept of spiritual slavery, the bondage of the children of Israel in Egypt, the shackles of sin, the joys of heaven after suffering, the glittering robe "that shall outshine the very sun," the wings and crown, are all to be found in minute detail in many of the hymns of whites, often in words identical to those used by blacks. The number of instances in which blacks definitely referred to physical slavery in their spirituals is small indeed.

The blacks probably did indeed apply a double meaning to many of the spirituals, often thinking of physical as well as spiritual slavery when they sang. But few of the spirituals were *created* to lament the black's enslaved condition. As the abolitionist attack continued and with internal dissent fermenting among blacks, bursting forth in Nat Turner's rebellion, the *double-entendre* of the black spirituals likely sharpened.

Go down, Moses,
Way down in Egypt land,
Tell ole Pharoh
Let my people go.

The blacks may also have communicated with one another between the lines of their folk hymns, even using them to convene secret meetings. "Steal Away" is thought to have been written by Nat Turner about the time of his call to be a prophet.

Steal away, steal away,
Steal away to Jesus,
Steal away, steal away home,
I hain't got long to stay here.

And runaways doubtlessly sang of their flight north.

Foller the drinkin' gou'd,
Foller the drinkin' gou'd;
For the ole man say,
"Foller the drinkin' gou'd."

The "drinkin' gou'd," of course was the Big Dipper, and the admonition was to go north until the "grea' big un" (the Ohio River) was reached. Historians have estimated that some 2000 slaves escaped annually after 1831, and while the fear of slave revolts persisted, insurrection was far less real than the fugitive problem.

I am bound for the promised land;
I am bound for the promised land:
O who will come and go with me?
I am bound for the promised land.

These spirituals were not originally solo or quartet material, but congregational outbursts sung with great religious conviction. The stories of the Bible gave black poets great play for graphic description, and their statement was characteristically dramatic and vividly colored. The style of the spirituals was concise and to the point, in contrast to the African tendency toward circumlocution. But the black spirituals represent a fusion of musical traditions, based largely upon white gospel hymns, but modified in execution by lingering techniques introduced from West Africa. When the songwriters of the minstrel stage fashioned their tunes upon what they thought to be native black music, they were in actuality employing as their model a black reflection of Anglo-American folk music.

Settled by diverse groups from colonial days on, later envisioning itself as a national melting pot, the United States on the eve of the Civil War remained a nation of sections. While its art music might have fallen into a reasonably well-ordered pattern, within the bounds of the genteel tradition, the country's folk music was as varied as its landscape and population. Many of the songs enjoyed in the hinterlands were ephemeral and crude, but they frequently possessed an honesty and a freshness that the more polished segments of American music lacked. The map of antebellum America sang from shore to shore, at times voicing anxieties and conflicts of the general cultural heritage, at times the flavor of life at hand. Sometimes the regions borrowed from one another, and basic melodies and a common storehouse of words and phrases were often evident in the songs of the people who carved out young America. And there were frequent borrowings between folk music and more commercial forms so that the demarcations between them became blurred.

But as the sections of the nation began to stabilize, conflicts developed, as the political and economic imbalance became obvious. While the North came to view itself as the bulwark of nationalism, it also saw itself as the embodiment of the American character, looked upon its own society and culture as the zenith of the national spirit. More and more, American music came to be what northern musicians, critics, and publishers thought it should be, less and less a genuine expression of the composite nation. After the Civil War, as the northern self-image came to be mistaken even more for the national image, the values of a middle class, industrial society came to shape the nation's values—in music as in American life generally.

CHAPTER

XIII

Reform and Crisis

Another type of musical entertainment to establish itself in antebellum America was the singing family. These groups mainly sang ballads that blended the popular and folk traditions, but while they came to be hailed as a distinctly American institution, the idea originated in Europe. Since the 1820s small ensembles of folk singers from the Swiss, Bavarian, and Austrian Alps had roamed the Continent, performing in beer gardens, theaters, and concert halls. Among the most popular of these Alpine troupes was the Rainer Family, two men and two women, who sang the mountain songs of their native Tyrol. The Rainers arrived in the United States in 1838, appearing for a time as the "Tyrolese Minstrels," and met with such success that a host of American imitators followed in the wake of their tour. There were the Bakers, the Cheneys, the Gibsons, the Burdetts, the Peaks, and the Browns—many of them coming out of the mountain regions of New England. But the most famous of the American singing families were the Hutchinsons from rural New Hampshire, who serenaded the country for more than twenty years.

The singing Hutchinsons numbered four, occasionally five—usually three brothers and a sister, the youngest children of Jesse and Mary Leavitt Hutchinson of Milford, New Hampshire. Three of the Hutchinson's sixteen children died in infancy; nine settled down either to business or farming; but the three youngest boys—Judson, John, and Asa—were smitten with a passion for music, which they in turn passed on to their smaller sister, Abby. All of the members of the "tribe of Jesse" sang in the meeting house and for their own pleasure, but their father, a staunch upholder of the work ethic and Baptist morality, categorized performing in public among the vanities of the world. The younger Hutchinson brothers, nevertheless, learned to read music in the village singing schools and church choir and acquired some skill on assorted musical instruments. Later they traveled to Boston to seek the advice of Lowell Mason on how to further improve their voices. They found the distinguished music educator cool and abrupt, for he obviously considered them country bumpkins with little musical background and even less money. "We departed with no material satisfaction," John remembered.

Sometime in 1842 the Hutchinson boys, over their father's protests, began singing in concert, calling themselves the "Aeolian Vocalists," in imitation of the Tyrolese Rainers, whom John had heard in Lynn. Shortly Abby, just turned thirteen, was invited to join the group, to lend a feminine touch. The singers often used "The Alpine Hunter's Song," a favorite of the Rainers, to advertise their early concerts, and Abby occasionally wore a Swiss bodice to give her "rather a foreign air." Frequently known at the beginning of their career as the "New Hampshire Rainers," the Hutchinsons were keenly aware of their foreign competition, even printing on their first programs:

> *When foreigners approach your shores,*
> *You welcome them with open doors.*
> *Now we have come to seek our lot,*
> *Shall native talent be forgot?*

The name "Aeolian Vocalists" was soon dropped as too theatrical, in favor of simply "The Hutchinson Family," which appealed more to church groups and reform organizations. The troupe also began to accompany its singing less on stringed instruments and more on a melodeon. Despite their rural upbringing and traditional orientation, the Hutchinsons sought the approval of genteel audiences and dressed in a discreet, fashionable manner. Abby was a pretty girl with large dark eyes and a round face, which enabled her to project an attractive image without appearing flashy in the customary stage sense. The group sang in rich harmony and prided themselves on their clear enunciation. Most of their songs were narratives, dealing primarily with sentiment and reform.

The Hutchinsons, like other singing families of the time, tried to convey through their songs an atmosphere of the American outdoors. "The Old Granite State," which they set to "You Will See Your Lord A-Coming," a hymn-tune popular around 1840, became their theme song:

> *We have come from the mountains,*
> *Of the "Old Granite State."*
> *We're a band of brothers*
> *And we live among the hills.*

They often sang the comic and dramatic ballads currently in vogue, and John made a specialty of Henry Russell's "The Maniac." Many of their songs they wrote themselves, their exuberant lyrics revealing the family's boundless optimism for America as the land of opportunity. "Uncle Sam's Farm," for instance, expressed a confidence both in the land and the inevitability of progress, while Judson's "The Vulture of the Alps," taken from a poem in an old school reader, looked back to Europe and, more specifically, was the type of song the Rainers were singing.

The songs of the New Hampshire singers were not intended for the concert platform alone, and many of them were welcomed into the hallowed parlor, especially dolorous ditties like "My Hopes Have Departed Forever," "There's Nothing True But Heaven," and "Where Can the Soul Find Rest?" The family's programs consisted of solos and ensembles, both vocal and instrumental. Later the quartet came more and more to sing without accompaniment. They performed in whatever buildings were available— churches, concert halls, even barns. Their singing style was informal, sometimes improvised, while their voices blended in close, simple harmony. To an unsophisticated American public, the Hutchinsons represented entertainment without the taint of the theater, gentility without affectation, communal fun without the sacrifice of rural principles.

Certainly the moral code of the Hutchinsons was above reproach, for they had been raised in a strict, puritanical environment that clearly delineated the world into right and wrong. In later life Judson and Abby drew close to spiritualism, and eventually John came to embrace the cult as well. Gradually the singers took to their hearts the humanitarian causes that stirred the nation during the decades preceding the Civil War: temperance, woman suffrage, dress reform, and most particularly, abolition. It was an age when national pride ran high, when there seemed no limit to American achievement, when the democracy seemed headed toward some resplendent millennium—a secular embodiment of the Puritan's "city on the hill." On the way any social or political reform appeared possible, and idealistic remedies covering the spectrum from blatant injustice to sentimental twaddle enjoyed more than fleeting champions. Many of these reforms the Hutchinson family sang, phrased in popular parlance and a quasifolk idiom that linked change with tradition.

"There's a Good Time Coming" sang the Hutchinsons, followed by temperance songs like "Clear Cold Water." But it was with antislavery songs that the family achieved both its greatest success and its most ardent criticism. Young Jesse, one of the Hutchinson brothers, who occasionally performed with the group, wrote a number of reform songs, among them "The Bereaved Slave Mother." The second stanza captures its mood:

The harsh auctioneer to sympathy cold,
Tears the babe from its mother and sells it for gold;
While the infant and mother, loud shriek for each other,
    In sorrow and woe.

Jesse's most controversial song, however, was "Get Off the Track," set to an old slave melody and using the railroad to symbolize the force moving toward freedom. Audiences were split wide open when the Hutchinsons performed the number, abolitionist sympathizers shouting their approval, the opposition hissing and yelling in anger.

Ho! the car Emancipation
Rides majestic thro' our nation,
Bearing on its Train, the story,
Liberty! a nation's glory
     Roll it along, Roll it along
     Roll it along thro' the nation
     Freedom's Car Emancipation.

The family singers could likely have drawn larger audiences and made more money if they had abandoned their causes and sung only popular ballads. But the Hutchinsons felt the reform zeal deeply and possessed enough Yankee stubbornness to hold their position in the face of growing resistance. Milford, their home town, had early taken a decidedly antislavery stand, and slavery had never been legalized, merely tolerated, in New Hampshire. During 1846 the crusading Hutchinsons added songs opposing the Mexican War, again thrusting themselves into the throes of controversy. As their reputation grew, the reception became more divided. Among their admirers the Hutchinsons counted Henry Wadsworth Longfellow, William Lloyd Garrison, John Greenleaf Whittier, Frederick Douglass, and many others, but with tension mounting from prolonged sectional turmoil, eastern audiences came to view the Hutchinsons as agitators, and their popularity dwindled.

While the family continued to sing abolitionist songs at political rallies and antislavery meetings, they began to rely on numbers like "The Snow Storm," "My Mother's Bible," and "The Ship on Fire" for their concert programs. Since temperance remained a more popular cause than abolition, songs denouncing liquor continued to play a part in the Hutchinsons' professional lives. Yet even when the family was quiet on slavery, their extreme views were known. New York City, once enthusiastic about the Hutchinsons, turned a cold shoulder on the group, in part tiring of the same old songs, in part considering the singers radical cranks. Little by little the family was driven into the interior for audiences, as they toured the cities up and down the Ohio River.

But extremist attitudes were only part of the explanation for the Hutchinson family's loss of favor on the east coast. They also became targets for the better music advocates. It was one thing for an Ohio editor to write of the Hutchinsons: "We like their music, because it is so simple and unadorned. It may not please those whose nice and critical taste love to hear music executed so that there is no music in it, but the people, the millions,

appreciate their notes for Liberty and the Right." The appraisal of eastern
sophisticates was another matter entirely. "Asa," John Hutchinson once said
to his brother, referring to the New York critics, "they're afraid of real
American music. All they want is operatic tra-la-la!" The singing family,
therefore, took in its stride such comments as those of a sour St. Cloud resident
who wrote the Boston *Post*: "The Hutchinsons have been around here, but
then you see they are yankees, and did not make much of an impression.
Besides that, they have a town laid out in a neighboring county, and that is *so
common*. The fact is we can only be delighted with genuine Italian *prima
dona* [sic]."

By the 1850s innumerable groups similar to the Hutchinsons were on the
road: The Alleghenians, the Spencers, the Continentals, Father Kemp's Old
Folks Choir, the Bliss Family, the Mountain Vocalists, and several more. The
Hutchinsons themselves splintered into three different troupes, much to the
bafflement of audiences and editors. The family singers competed with the
minstrel shows as well as one another, and eventually, as the musical life of
urban America grew richer, the upper classes paid them little attention. The
superior ability and showmanship of the Hutchinsons won them followers
for many years, but their refusal to mince words on a wide variety of reform
issues caused an increasing segment of the public to regard the singers as
downright weird. With the passage of time, they came to champion a half
dozen new *isms* and even interlarded their concerts with phrenological
speeches to attract the desired audiences.

The Hutchinsons exemplified an idealistic period in American history,
when optimism, aggressive nationalism, individualism, humanitarianism,
reform, militant nativism, and faith in progress ran rampant. Like the causes
they championed the personalities of the Hutchinsons were extreme. They
were like the nation they extolled in that they led paradoxical lives,
attempting to balance common sense and sound business judgment with
lofty, absolute idealism. And like the democracy on the eve of the Civil War,
the Hutchinsons teetered constantly between success and failure.

When the war came, Simon Cameron, Lincoln's initial Secretary of War,
issued a pass to members of the Hutchinson family, allowing them to cross
over into Virginia to entertain among the main lines of the Army of the
Potomac. Once again the Hutchinsons' reputation as radical abolitionists
preceded them, and they encountered violent antipathy. While most of the
northern soldiers opposed slavery, few were willing to accept in 1861 that they
were fighting a "nigger war." Many attended the Hutchinsons' concerts with
the prime purpose of disrupting them, and the *Washington Star* protested
loudly against turning military posts into "areas for political pow-wowing."
Seeing the havoc the singers were creating, the commander of the Union army
refused to let the Hutchinsons go on, and their permit to sing in the camps
was revoked. Later, as the war news grew worse, the family tried to bring
comfort and cheer to the home front by rendering current war songs. Abby,
who had married and retired, left her home in Orange to sing in behalf of the

Union and to shame Copperheads with songs of hope and patriotism. For a time Walter Kittredge, another New Hampshire ballad singer, performed with a group of Hutchinsons, and the family introduced Kittredge's famous war song, "Tenting on the Old Camp Ground."

It was during the Civil War that the music publishing business in America really came of age. The onset of catastrophe seems to have released in the country a lyric impulse that made the war as significant a catalyst in the nation's musical life as in its economic, political, and social development. "All history proves," the New York *Herald* maintained, January 11, 1862, "that music is as indispensable to warfare as money; and money has been called the sinews of war. Music is the soul of Mars." Certainly the enormous physical and emotional energy unleashed during the Civil War spilled over into song, among soldiers and behind both lines. "Perhaps the favorite recreation of the Confederate Army was music," historian Bell Irvin Wiley suggests, while his survey of the pastimes of Billy Yank prompted him to add, "Ranking close to reading among camp diversions was music."

Most of the songs popular during the early months of the war were the same ones that had been favorites before—sentimental melodies like "Lorena," "Annie Laurie," "Lilly Dale," "Sweet Evelina," the tunes of Stephen Foster, and such old reliables as "Home, Sweet Home" and "The Girl I Left Behind Me." But shortly the demand for timely numbers encouraged lyricists especially to turn out pieces dealing with every facet of the conflict at hand. The first war songs were largely jubilant, even audacious: "The Flag of Our Union Forever," "The War Drums Are Beating," "Brave Boys Are They, Gone at Their Country's Call," and "We Will Rally Round the Flag, Boys." Gradually, as the realities of war became painfully evident, the lyrics turned to haunting narratives of lonely bivouacs, the grief of mothers and sweethearts, and death: "The Faded Coat of Blue," "Just before the Battle, Mother," "When This Cruel War Is Over," and "The Vacant Chair."

In large measure the North and South shared the same songs, and far more new lyrics than melodies appeared during the course of the war. Many of these songs were inferior both musically and poetically, but their topical nature frequently gained them popularity. For the most part soldiers and civilians expressed themselves in song almost exactly as they had before the outbreak of hostilities, drawing from the popular tradition both sides shared. The songs created by soldiers were generally old tunes altered to give military life a passing context. The war songs penned by professional musicians were successful largely because they were phrased in the same musical idiom as the other popular tunes of the period—sounding much like the minstrel tunes, gospel hymns, or sentimental ballads of the antebellum years. A familiar musical style simply found a martial spirit added to the pre-war emotional pattern.

"In periods of conflict," Willard and Porter Heaps observe in *The Singing Sixties*, "the basic sentiments of people are the same as in times of peace—the love of home, family and friends and the security of the family group and the nation. During a war, however, these emotions are intensified and this magnification is evidenced in the subject content of songs which the people sing." In times of crisis the public leans more toward widespread ideas and universal emotions; thus popular culture becomes more immediate and group oriented, but remains strongly traditional. "Music during wartime," James Stone argues, "gives an air of normality to what is essentially an abnormal social condition." The old tune favorites and Civil War songs couched in banal, sentimental terms brought a feeling of continuity and comfort to an age of upheaval.

Interestingly enough patriotic tunes made up only a fraction of the wartime music and was generally restricted to ceremonial occasions—rallies of civilians or, at the front, in connection with some special event like parades, marching into a captured city, or signing an armistice. Patriotic songs, like flags, were essentially symbolic, sung at gatherings where unity needed reinforcement. Music best served as propaganda behind the lines. Hundreds of patriotic lyrics appeared in the wartime press urging solidarity and courage or commemorating a victory or some notable happening, but these were often never sung. The enlisted men seem to have been little interested in nationalistic music, preferring instead hymns, ballads, and minstrel songs. Since their commitment to the war effort was already indicated, stirring the emotions of volunteers seemed meaningless. Music was almost never heard on the battlefield. As one northern musician recalled, "The only time I remember music in battle was when General Devan's brigade was crossing the pontoon bridge at Fredericksburg . . . and this was long before the troops came under fire. . . . No drummer in my regiment ever played on the battle-field or could see any sense in doing it."

But patriotic melodies served to mobilize the civilian population behind the war effort, much as military orders marshaled the armies. Patriotic songs were among the few dictates that noncombatants would accept almost without question. "Acceptance is guaranteed," Stone concludes in his psychological study of war songs, "when the musical command is a go-ahead signal to sentiment that has already been prepared, and to action that is expected." Music during the Civil War became a mechanism for turning a heterogeneous crowd into a united people, casting an emotional spell over the indecisive that led them towards involvement. Mass singing stimulated a sense of participation and communicated to nonconformists the social pressure of the majority.

Obviously the standard patriotic hymns like "The Star-Spangled Banner," "America," and "Hail, Columbia" fell to the Union, shortly joined by the North's special Civil War anthem, Julia Ward Howe's "The Battle Hymn of the Republic." In November, 1861, a party which included Mrs. Howe, her husband (Samuel Ward, the editor of a Boston antislavery paper), and the Reverend James F. Clarke visited an outpost of the Army of the Potomac in Virginia, where they were scheduled to witness a review of troops.

A sudden Confederate assault, however, cancelled the review, and Mrs. Howe's party found themselves watching an unexpected skirmish instead. Later they heard the returning soldiers singing "John Brown's Body," to the tune of a southern camp meeting song. The rousing melody was still ringing in the Reverend Clarke's ears as he accompanied Mrs. Howe and her husband back to Washington, and he casually suggested to the lady that she write more dignified words to fit the sturdy martial air they had just heard. Inspired in the early hours of the morning, Mrs. Howe wrote down her lines, beginning "Mine eyes have seen the Glory of the coming of the Lord," by candlelight in a room at the Willard Hotel. They were published in the February, 1862, issue of the *Atlantic Monthly* and shortly considered among the finest lyrics produced by the war.

At first the Confederacy had little symbolic paraphernalia, including songs, to set it apart from the Union. In the early months of the war the South, particularly young idealists, even appropriated the French "La Marseillaise" as a rallying call. Later "Dixie" became the national air of the Confederacy, followed closely in popularity by "The Bonnie Blue Flag." Set to the well known Irish tune "The Irish Jaunting Car" by the Arkansas comedian Harry Macarthy, "The Bonnie Blue Flag" recites the chain of secession:

> *First gallant South Carolina nobly took the stand,*
> *Then came Alabama, who took her by the hand;*

broken with the refrain:

> *Hurrah! Hurrah! for Southern rights, hurrah.*
> *Hurrah for the bonnie blue flag that bears a single star.*

When Northern troops occupied New Orleans in 1862, commander Benjamin Butler threatened to levy a fine of twenty-five dollars on any person who sang, played, or whistled the tune. A. E. Blackmar, the song's publisher, was fined five hundred dollars, and all copies of the sheet music were ordered destroyed.

The Civil War, despite its brutality, had spiritual overtones, and hymn singing was important both at home and in the camps. The deep idealism that swept young men off to enlistment offices, the emotional pitch that soldiers commonly experienced before battles, and the patriotic fervor that repeatedly came over meetings of civilians were not unlike religious sentiments. The old hymns found a firm place among the activities of war, tending to alleviate fears and uncertainties. During the last two years of the conflict particularly the encamped forces on both sides stampeded to religious services, where they found in the lively gospel songs a bond with home and a flicker of hope to bolster their sinking morale.

A number of war tunes, like "Tramp! Tramp! Tramp!" or "When Johnny Comes Marching Home," bore qualities borrowed from the revival hymns, most notably their evangelistic flavor, vigor, repetition, and infectious simplicity. The minstrel tune style, on the other hand, adapted itself in songs depicting the less serious moments of the war. Songs of both types, not altogether dissimilar musically, were virile and cheerful, suitable for marching and improvisation.

Soldiers rarely sang about fighting, concentrating instead on camp routine and thoughts of family, home, and friends. Humor frequently crept into their lyrics, as in Frank Wilder's "The Invalid Corps," which told of a lucky man rejected on his draft physical:

I wanted much to be examined,
The surgeon looked me o'er and o'er;
My back and chest he hammered.
Said he, "You're not the man for me;
Your lungs are much affected and likewise
Both your eyes are cocked and defective otherwise."

Now and then lyrics that bordered on the stuffy contained elements of humor or a simile that irreparably damaged a serious mood.

Our bugle had roused up the camp,
The heavens looked dismal and dirty,
And the earth looked unpleasant and damp,
As a beau on the wrong side of thirty.

Topical songs were abundant, especially behind the lines. James Ryder Randall, a native of Maryland teaching in New Orleans, penned "Maryland, My Maryland" during the night of April 23, 1861, hoping to swing his home state to the Southern cause. Maryland, while supporting slavery, remained loyal to the Union, but Randall's lyrics, sung to the tune of the old German Christmas carol "O Tannenbaum," became a favorite throughout the Confederacy and proved one of the more lasting Civil War hymns.

On both sides there were hundreds of songs celebrating battles and campaigns, most of them enjoying only momentary popularity, perhaps sung for a brief while by one of the minstrel troupes. The retreat of Northern soldiers during the first battle of Bull Run brought forth "The Union Volunteers":

Ye loyal Union Volunteers,
Your country claims your aid,
Says Uncle Abe, a foe appears,
Are we to be afraid?
Are we to be afraid, my boys?
No, at them we will go;
On Potomac's banks we'll close our ranks,
And march to meet the foe.

But McClellan's appointment as commander of the Army of the Potomac renewed the confidence of the North, and before long Bryant's Minstrels were singing:

> For we'll have no more Bull Run affairs
>   Where the chivalry says we did knock under;
> For we've got a brave McClellan now
>   Who'll give them Northern thunder.

Lincoln's call for the drafting of 300,000 additional troops in 1862 produced the poem "We Are Coming, Father Abra'am, Three Hundred Thousand More," by the abolitionist writer James Sloan Gibbons and set to several different tunes.

Entertainment in New York during 1863 and 1864 was livelier than ever, including balls, circuses, minstrel shows, Italian opera, theater, concerts, lectures, itinerant menageries, spiritualist seances, and panoramas. An air of self-confidence and vigor had come to permeate the northern cities, in strange contrast with the grim war raging further south. The money situation, however, was not altogether happy. The government by then had issued millions of dollars in paper currency, and inflation was on. In March, 1863, the Bryants sang Dan Emmett's "How Are You, Greenbacks," a parody beginning:

> We're coming, Father Abra'am, one hundred thousand more,
> Five hundred presses printing us from morn till night is o'er;
> Like magic, you will see us start and scatter thro' the land
> To pay the soldiers or release the border contraband.

Meanwhile the South sang its current events in numbers like "Our Triumph at Manassas," "The Shiloh Victory Polka," "Fort Morgan Gallopade," and the humorous "Richmond Is a Hard Road to Travel," dedicated to the Union's General Burnside. The Confederacy's diplomatic battle to win the support of England found its way into verses of both North and South. Southern singers facetiously wooed Great Britain to the tune of "John Anderson, My Jo John":

> O, Johnny Bull, my Jo John! let's take the field together,
> And hunt the Yankee Doodles home, in spite of wind and weather,
> And ere a twelve-month roll around, to Boston we will go,
> And eat our Christmas dinner there, O, Johnny Bull, my Jo!

Far and away the most glaring characteristic of the Civil War songs, however, was a sentimentality perhaps exceeding that of the antebellum years. Emotions changed somewhat during the war, but emotional expression did not, except maybe to heighten a familiar sentiment. The feelings of peace—love of family and home, desire for comfort, irritation with the routine, the need for freedom from fear, and so forth—continued, but in intensified form, as the external threat produced a nostalgia for the normal. Underneath the saccharine surface of the sentimental war songs ran two major themes: love and death. Young boys going off to war were not legally accepted without their parents' consent, and the struggle between maternal and patriotic love was melodramatically drawn in "The Young Volunteer," in which a lad begs of his mother:

> Can you see my country call in vain
>   And restrain my arm from the needful blow?
> Not so, though your heart should break with pain,
>   You'll kiss me, bless me, and let me go.

The death of a drummer boy was fraught with special pathos, since the hero symbolized a soldier performing the duties of a man, yet retaining the innocence of a child. When "The Drummer Boy of Shiloh" died, "each brave man knelt and cried," while "The Dying Drummer Boy" called for his mother throughout the night but found peace with the dawn. In "The Standard Bearer" a young Confederate soldier died clasping the South's flag to his breast, and a Union boy's dying words were "Wrap the Flag Around Me, Boys." An expiring Confederate asked his comrades in "I've Fallen in the Battle" to send a lock of his sweetheart's hair home to his mother. In "Tidings Sad Must Be Conveyed" a soldier told his companions to notify his mother should he fall in combat, whereas another implored, "Break It Gently to My Mother." Still another announced, "Dear Mother, I've Come Home to Die," while "The Empty Sleeve" served to glorify the amputee, naming that sleeve "a badge of bravery and honor."

Soldiers constantly wanted to know "Do They Miss Me at Home, Do They Miss Me?" The joys of the family circle were expressed in "Home on Furlough," while a mother bade her parting son, "Keep This Bible Near Your Heart." Later the boy clutched the Bible as he lay dying. Another lad, hearing the surgeon tell those about him that he could not live, placed his hand over his forehead and with burning tears streaming down his feverish cheeks, asked in a trembling voice, "Who Will Care for Mother Now?" Mothers, usually aged, far outnumbered sweethearts and wives in Civil War songs, in part because of the extreme youth of many of the soldiers, in part because of the Platonic idealism of the age. Wives occasionally appeared, yet their love was more that of a sister than a mate. In "Take Your Gun and Go, John," a wife sent her husband off to war with a pair of blankets she had made as a girl—pretty blankets with roses in each corner and her name embroidered on them.

There was a morbid fascination with death in these songs and a horror that loved ones might die alone, without the comfort of family or friends. This fear was captured in John Hill Hewitt's "All Quiet Along the Potomac

Tonight,'' one of the most successful songs of the war:

> All quiet along the Potomac, they say,
> Except here and there a stray picket
> Is shot on his beat as he walks to and fro
> By a rifleman hid in a thicket.
> 'Tis nothing, a private or two now and then
> Will not count in the news of the battle;
> Not an officer lost, only one of the men
> Moaning out all alone the death rattle.
> "All quiet along the Potomac tonight."

"Somebody's Darling," among the most beloved Confederate poems, was set to music by both southern and northern composers and told of a young soldier who met death in strange, but tender, hands:

> Into the ward of the clean white-washed halls
> Where the dead slept and the dying lay;
> Wounded by bayonets, sabres and balls,
> Somebody's darling was borne one day.
> Somebody's darling so young and so brave,
> Wearing still on his sweet, yet pale face,
> Soon to be hid in the dust of the grave,
> The lingering light of his boyhood's grace.
> Somebody's darling, Somebody's pride,
> Who'll tell his mother where her boy died?

It was a bloody war with appalling casualties, although fraternization between the combatants was fairly common. In "Bill and I" two Union pickets shot a rebel youth, but broke into tears upon discovering that he had been a friend during an earlier assignment.

Henry Tucker's "Weeping, Sad and Lonely" or "When This Cruel War Is Over," with words by Charles Carroll Sawyer, was one of the most pathetic of the Civil War songs, a favorite of both sides. The piece was so mournful that the generals of the Army of the Potomac forbade their troops to sing it, fearing a lowering of morale and an increase in desertion. The ballad sold over a million copies, exceptional in those days, and dealt with the separation of sweethearts.

> Weeping sad and lonely
>   Sighs and tears how vain,
> When this cruel war is over,
>   Pray that we meet again.

Despite the fears of Union officers, touching tunes of this type, reminding soldiers of home-ties, may actually have produced an incentive for fighting, since they gave the conflict an undercurrent of meaning. The urge to fight for mother, home, and wife may have been more powerful than the impulse to fight for one's country, as suggested by the patriotic songs, since the first was more immediate and personal. Rather than causing desertion, the mawkish songs of home may have provided the war-weary soldier with an escape mechanism that substituted for overt action.

Although sudden death, home, and grieving families were appropriate topics for lyricists to wail over, the broader atrocities of war, the chaos and mass slaughters of the battlefield, rarely found their way into popular song. Larzer Ziff in his study of Civil War music could not locate a single song about the battle of Gettysburg, either by a northerner or a southerner. "It was one thing to sing of a bold dash at night," Ziff maintains, "it was another to catalogue the grim facts." In an uncertain time of unexpected disasters, it was easier for the populace to comprehend and accept the tangible—broken homes, crippled bodies, orphaned children, and the like—sad though those realities were, than to deal with abstraction. And individual heartbreak was made more palatable by the manner in which it was presented to the popular imagination—in songs and words that were lofty, ennobling, but artificial, somehow making the real seem unreal.

Sectional boundaries disappeared from such effusions of human emotion, as these songs came to be sung almost interchangeably by the blue and the gray, sometimes with a few substitutions in wordings. Evidence does not support the expectation that the lyrics of the North became more elated as the spirits of the Union rose while those of the South became more nostalgic as the Confederate hopes failed. The mood of the belligerents' songs remained remarkably similar until the end. Both sides had their songs of invective, particularly in the early months of the conflict, in which they poured out their wrath on Abraham Lincoln and Jefferson Davis, their scorn of their opponent's way of life, and their mockery of Rebs and Yanks, often with considerable humor. The Confederates taunted Lincoln's physical appearance and the President's frustration in finding suitable generals; northerners, on the other hand, made much of Davis as a small man with grandiose ambitions and threatened him with the noose. Both sides had their hero songs, although the adept southern leadership did give the Confederacy an edge in this area, in music as in maneuvers. As the war progressed, the songs behind both lines became sadder, more filled with fear, wariness, and personal tragedy. The common plight of the combatants was reflected not only in their appropriation of each other's songs, but was occasionally stated in a specific piece. George F. Root's "Foes and Friends" (with words by Ellen H. Flagg) pictured a soldier from New Hampshire and one from Georgia lying close to each other on a battlefield, both wounded and dying. Each man had a wife and small daughter. They talked of their loved ones and pardoned one another before dying.

There were actual events which suggested as well this mutual understanding between men caught in a political and economic squabble they did not fully understand. During the Rappahannock campaign in 1863 northern and southern troops were camped near each other across a small stream. At one point the Yankee band came down to the water and played "Dixie." The Confederates on the other wide of the river cheered and responded with "Yankee Doodle." The northerners applauded and struck up "Home, Sweet Home," in which the voices of the two sides joined.

Such fraternization makes clear how tunes were exchanged. The four years of Civil War produced a startling number and variety of songs, more than any other war in American history. Irwin Silber estimates some 10,000 songs in all related to the conflict, indicating why the war between the states has been called the "great singing war of all time." But it was an idealistic war wrapped in sentiment, and made all the more emotional by brother fighting brother. Although the Civil War was the most total and industrialized war the United States had yet fought, it was still more man against man, rather than technology versus technology. Human hardship, personal tragedy, and early adolescent bravado dominated the press and much of the public mind, and this was the stuff of which the popular war songs were made.

But the music of the Civil War was more than a succession of melodies and lyrics, for amid the turmoil American popular music struggled to break from its European legacy and took strides toward becoming a big business. As late as the 1830s vast numbers of songs published in America had originated in England. For two decades before the war gifted tunesmiths had been leading commercial music toward a more natural American idiom, but the rash of songs produced by the war, focusing on the immediacy of the situation at hand, forced a more native expression. Art more times than not was second to utility, yet the stylistic means of popular music moved toward more harmonious American ends. And just as the Civil War served as a giant stimulant to the burgeoning industrial system that cast a sooty image against northern skies, so did those crucial years nurture the roots of commercial music publishing in the United States.

Southern music publishers, however, quickened their activities tremendously during the early months of the war, and the outpouring of song from the Confederacy bordered on the phenomenal. Publishing houses had existed in Charleston, New Orleans, Mobile, and Nashville for a good many years, but these firms had remained relatively meager and had never broken the hold of northern publishers on the distribution of music in the South. A few days after the seccession of South Carolina, the first piece of Confederate sheet music was published in Charleston, "The Palmetto State Song" by George O. Robinson. Gradually the prewar stocks of music diminished, local songs became more abundant, and music publishing developed into a lucrative business in the Confederacy. Firms publishing sheet music increased five-fold during the course of the war, mainly producing songs rather than books. Songs were comparatively cheap to publish, required little paper, which was scarce, and were more easily distributed than books. Sheet music early in the war was printed on heavy paper, but as the conflict persisted, the quality became steadily poorer, the ink dimmer, and the size of the sheet music increasingly smaller. Costs, on the other hand, continued to soar. Inflationary prices of $1.50, $2.00, and even $2.50 a copy were not uncommon.

Harry B. Macarthy, the composer of "The Bonnie Blue Flag," was the most prolific southern songwriter, and while the wartime South produced little distinguished poetry, dramatist George H. Miles' "God Save the South" stands among the better lyrics. Songs were "plugged" by performers like Macarthy and Sallie Partington, a Confederate prima donna, who popularized "The Southern Soldier Boy" by singing it at every performance of the *Virginia Cavalier* at the New Richmond Theater. Reverses on the battlefield eventually doomed the music publishing industry in the South, and while a few of the firms lasted into the poverty stricken Reconstruction Era, these were all but eliminated as publishing came more and more to be concentrated in the metropolitan centers of the Northeast.

The manufacture of upright pianos had developed in the first half of the nineteenth century to the point that by 1860 their cost had been substantially reduced. Pianos, topped with fringed silk scarves, came ever more to occupy a conspicuous place in the homes of middle class Americans. As music lessons became a more accepted part of the education of children, the demand for sheet music blossomed, particularly for vocal selections whose piano accompaniment required little beyond a succession of simple chords. Choral singing had reached the height of its popularity in the United States by the 1860s, and quartet arrangements were in great demand. Before the war northern publishers like Firth, Pond & Company in New York, Oliver Ditson in Boston, and the John Church Company, also in Boston, had grown into thriving concerns. Firth, Pond & Company, of course, was Stephen Foster's publisher; Ditson would issue both "The Battle Hymn of the Republic" and "Tenting on the Old Camp Ground"; while Church would publish "Aura Lee," one of the most successful of the nonmilitary Civil War ballads, and later the sentimental favorite "I'll Take You Home Again, Kathleen."

Although Firth, Pond & Company dissolved in 1863, most of the publishers of the North expanded their operations beyond all precedents. By the Civil War the cylinder power press, invented in 1850, had become commercially available, permitting large runs and inexpensive preparation. While costs rose during the combat, the quality of northern printing remained fairly high. Whereas Confederate firms issued piano selections like the "Secession Quickstep," "Stars and Bars Polka," "Contraband Schottische," "Southern Rights March," and "Stonewall Lancer's Quadrille," the Union was offered such pieces as "The Emancipation Quickstep," "Gunboat Quickstep," and "The Young Recruit Galop." A series for piano that was widely purchased in the North was entitled *Pictures of the War*, in which there were several compositions celebrating Union victories. Typical of the showy piano standards of the day, these pieces depicted the roar of cannons through bass chords in double *fortissimo*, the whistling of bullets through the air in arpeggios, the advances of troops through exciting march passages, and the calm after battle through quiet, plaintive strains.

Songsters were published and supplied to soldiers in the field, cheap publications containing the words of popular favorites, nonsense songs, and patriotic airs. *The Stonewall Song Book*, published in Richmond in 1864, ran into eleven editions at least and had a host of northern equivalents. Hymn books were issued by both sides, often distributed to the armies by church groups, and broadsides poured from the presses. But the music publishing industry of the North, like that in the South, made its best returns on single song sheet music sales. And it was in this area especially that a commercial sensitivity developed into the concept of mass marketing popular music.

Out of the North's competitive music trade emerged the two leading composers of Civil War songs: George Frederick Root and Henry Clay Work. Both flooded the market with tunes that caught the public's fancy, and they became recognized moguls of their profession, riding the crest of the wartime boom in popular music.

George F. Root was born in Sheffield, Massachusetts, on August 30, 1820. Six years later his family, including eight children, moved to Willow Farm in North Reading, near Boston, where George Frederick grew up. His dream was to become a musician, and he made the most of the few opportunities that came his way, picking out tunes on whatever instruments he could find. Eventually he went to Boston to study and later began to have students of his own. He taught a number of singing schools, met Lowell Mason, and was asked to assist in the music program of the Boston public schools. He also taught classes at the Boston Academy of Music. Around 1845 he moved to New York, where he became a music teacher at Abbot's Institute for girls and five years later went to Europe for additional study. In 1853 he was back in New York, helping to organize the New York Normal Institute.

Encouraged by the success of Stephen Foster and others, Root decided in 1852 to try his hand at writing popular songs. Fearing that any association with commercial music might affect his career as a teacher, he published his first song, "Hazel Dell," under the Germanized pseudonym G. Friedrich Wurzel. The tune was a resounding success and highly profitable financially. This success was shortly followed by more studied efforts, namely *The Academy Vocalist*, a book for schools, and the cantata *Daniel*. The musician continued writing popular tunes, however, like "There's Music in the Air" and "Rosalie," publishing them on a royalty basis. For "Rosalie" alone he was paid $3000 in royalties.

In 1859 Root moved to Chicago, where his brother, in partnership with C. M. Cady, had opened a music store. By then the composer had become established as one of the leading American musicians of his day. In 1860 George Root was welcomed as a third partner into the firm of Root and Cady.

With the bombardment of Fort Sumter, he turned to writing war songs, beginning with "The First Gun Is Fired!" The piece was published by Root and Cady three days after Sumter's fall, and it was sung by the Lumbard brothers that same day at a patriotic rally in Chicago's Metropolitan Hall, with broadsides handed out to the audience. Root and Cady quickly expanded its publishing operations, had a great success with the "Zouave Cadets Quickstep," and over the next four years demonstrated a remarkable grasp of the public's taste in popular music.

Within six weeks after the war began the company had published five recruiting songs, three of them by George F. Root. These sold reasonably well throughout the Northeast and Midwest, but the firm and the composer both hit their stride with "The Battle Cry of Freedom" in 1862, introduced in Chicago by the Lumbards and later popularized across the country by the Hutchinson family. It was Root's greatest success, a favorite with soldiers and civilians alike. The tune afforded excellent opportunity for the display of technique on fifes and drums, while the recurrent phrase "shouting the battle cry of freedom," alternating with various verses sung by soloists, was ideal for group participation.

But Root scored again with "The Vacant Chair" (1862), "Just Before the Battle, Mother" (1863), and "Tramp! Tramp! Tramp!" (1864). These were all good tunes, well set to their words, easy to sing, and simply arranged. Their lyrics were much in the sentimental vein, and "Just Before the Battle, Mother" remains a classic statement of the penchant in nineteenth century popular culture for symbolically returning to the womb in the face of death:

Just before the battle, mother,
  I am thinking most of you,
While upon the field we're watching,
  With the enemy in view.
Comrades brave are round me lying,
  Fill'd with thoughts of home and God;
For well they know that on the morrow
  Some will sleep beneath the sod.

By 1863 George Root was devoting his entire time to composing and the supervision of Root and Cady. It was largely through his persuasion that the company came to publish the songs of Henry Clay Work, most famous for "Marching through Georgia." Work had come to Illinois with his family as a child, although he was born in Middletown, Connecticut, in 1832. The boy's father later maintained one of the "underground railroad" stations which helped runaway slaves escape into Canada; eventually he served in prison for these activities. Young Henry, therefore, grew up a vehement abolitionist, although from an early age music had been his primary interest. While still a youth, he sold a song, "We're Coming, Sister Mary," to Christy's Minstrels. Then in 1855 he went to Chicago, where he worked as a printer and eventually met George Root. Work's first war song, "Brave Boys Are They," was successful enough that Root and Cady offered him a contract, and he began to take composing more seriously. His new publisher issued "Kingdom Coming" in 1862 and proved real adroitness in advertising the piece. For a week before its publication the mysterious words *Kingdom Coming* greeted Chicago citizens from newspapers and street posters, causing all sorts of wild speculation. The Work song was introduced by Christy's Minstrels on April 23, 1862, and was an immediate success. Three months after its publication "Kingdom Coming" had already sold 8000 copies, and within seven months the sale had passed the 20,000 mark.

Not all of the songs published by Root and Cady during the Civil War years were war songs. Henry Work's "The Days When We Were Young" was issued in 1863 and the composer's more famous "Come Home, Father" was published the next year. The latter told the tearful story of a little girl coaxing her drunken father out of the saloon, as her younger brother lies dying at home and the steeple clock tolls the small hours of morning. Work was as ardent a temperance advocate as he was an abolitionist. While the line "Father, dear father, come home with me now" eventually became something of a national joke, it supplied prohibitionists with much emotional fodder during the crusade ahead. Work's most productive years were between 1861 and 1866, although he would show occasional bursts of energy later, writing "Grandfather's Clock" in 1876, his last successful song. He died suddenly in 1884 of a heart disease.

As the member of the house of Root and Cady in charge of publications, George F. Root was in a position to promote not only the career of Henry Clay Work, but other songwriters as well—notably Philip Paul Bliss, a writer of gospel hymns, and B.R. Hanby, composer of "Darling Nelly Gray." Meanwhile Root continued writing his own tunes, ultimately numbering some two hundred, including several sacred songs. Throughout his life Root remained a layman's musician, composing to suit the taste of the public at large, yet at their best his melodies, particularly the marches, were rousing and infectious. His songs fit the moment and "Tramp! Tramp! Tramp!" alone earned a profit of over $10,000. As in heavy industry, the wartime urgency repeatedly stimulated a process that under normal conditions might have taken generations to develop. So it was with the music publishing business. Songs were in extraordinarily great demand, and many of them— certainly any number of Root's—were turned out quickly and sung before the ink was scarcely dry.

After the war Root and Cady expanded, moving their offices to more spacious quarters in Crosby's Opera House, Chicago's new cultural center. Sheet music sales fell off somewhat, but the company continued to do a volume business in music books and teaching material. The firm suffered losses of over $25,000 in the great Chicago fire of 1871, and the partnership was shortly dissolved. C. M. Cady later opened a publishing firm in New York

City. George F. Root was president of the Chicago Musical College from 1872 to 1875 and taught choral singing. He continued an active career until his death in 1895.

In many respects the North was better prepared to meet the musical emergency of the Civil War than the South, and certainly no composer of the stature of Root or Work appeared within the Confederacy. Both sides often sang cheerfully, sometimes humorously, taunting their enemy's flaws and pompously affirming their own strength. But the combatants were fundamentally afraid and confused and, according to Larzer Ziff, "wrapped themselves in the comforting blanket of sentiment, and hugged it about them to ward off the awful facts they knew to lurk behind the simpering words." The music of the Civil War essentially was the music of peace, clearly within the high-flown, stilted spectrum of nineteenth-century popular song.

With Lee's surrender at Appomattox Court House on April 12, 1865, the Union could joyously sing "They Have Broken Up Their Camp" and "The Boys Are Marching Home." The Confederacy, staggering under fatal losses, was left with no alternative but to return to the Union, hopefully as smoothly as possible. The weariness, sacrifice, and pride of the South were captured with poignancy by Father Abram J. Ryan's "The Conquered Banner," set to music by Theodore von La Hache:

Furl that banner, for 'tis weary,
Round its staff 'tis drooping dreary,
* Furl it, fold it, it is best;*
For there's not a man to wave it,
And there's not a sword to save it,
And there's not one left to lave it
In the blood which heroes gave it,
And its foes now scorn and brave it,
* Furl it, hide it, let it rest.*

And so ended the bloodiest, most spiritually exhausting conflict in the young nation's history. And so the sun set on the garden that was once young America.

BIBLIOGRAPHICAL NOTES

GENERAL WORKS

Among the early histories of music in America and full of the prejudices of their time are Frederick Louis Ritter, *Music in America* (New York, 1883), Louis C. Elson, *The History of American Music* (New York, 1915), and Daniel Gregory Mason (ed.), *The Art of Music*, Vol. IV (New York, 1915). The standard work on the subject, but highly encyclopedic, is John T. Howard, *Our American Music* (New York, 1965). Gilbert Chase, *America's Music* (New York, 1955) is a more interesting, interpretative account, although somewhat uneven in coverage. Wilfred Mellers, *Music in a New Found Land* (New York, 1964) is a stimulating volume by a British musicologist. The work is best perhaps in its treatment of jazz, but often fairly technical. Shorter accounts include Irving Sablosky, *American Music* (Chicago, 1969) and H. Wiley Hitchcock, *Music in the United States: A Historical Introduction* (Englewood Cliffs, N.J., 1969). For juvenile readers John Rublowsky, *Music in America* (New York, 1967) is brief, readable, and informative, while Helen Kaufmann, *From Jehovah to Jazz* (New York, 1937) is a journalistic treatment with occasionally interesting points. Valuable to the serious student is Gilbert Chase (ed.), *The American Composer Speaks* (Baton Rouge, La., 1966), an anthology of essays by American composers from Billings to recent times.

CHAPTER I. THE NEW ENGLAND PURITANS

A significant interpretation of colonial Puritanism is contained in Daniel J. Boorstin's monumental *The Americans: the Colonial Experience* (New York, 1958), provocative throughout, and freqently controversial. Fundamental to any study of the Puritans is the work of Perry Miller, notably *The New England Mind: the Seventeenth Century* (New York, 1939); *Orthodoxy in Massachusetts* (Cambridge, Mass., 1933); and *Errand into the Wilderness* (Cambridge, Mass., 1956). No less valuable are Samuel Eliot Morison, *The Puritan Pronaos: Studies in the Intellectual Life of New England in the Seventeenth Century* (New York, 1936) and Thomas J. Wertenbaker, *The Puritan Oligarchy* (New York, 1947). More limited in scope, but vastly stimulating in viewpoint is Kenneth B. Murdock, *Literature and Theology in Colonial New England* (Cambridge, Mass., 1949), while William W. Sweet, *The Story of Religion in America* (New York, 1950) and *Religion in Colonial America* (New York, 1942) contain much general information on Puritan religious beliefs. For a broad survey of life during the colonial period Louis B. Wright, *The Cultural Life of the American Colonies* (New York, 1957) is both readable and scholarly, while an excellent chapter on music by Cyclone Covey may be found in Max Savelle's study of colonial civilization, *Seeds of Liberty* (New York, 1948).

Perpetuators of the belief that the Puritans hated music include George Hood, *A History of Music in New England* (Boston, 1846); Nathaniel D. Gould, *History of Church Music in America* (Boston, 1853); and Louis C. Elson, *The National Music of America* (Boston, 1924). Although Henry Davey, *History of English Music* (London, 1895) suggested that the Puritan attitude on music might not have been as negative as traditionals thought, the revisionist position was more effectively stated by Percy A. Scholes, first in "The Truth about the New England Puritans and Music," *The Musical Quarterly*, XIX (January, 1933), 1-17, and more definitively in *The Puritans and Music in England and New England* (London, 1934). Among Scholes' disciples is Henry W. Foote, *Three Centuries of American Hymnody* (Cambridge, Mass., 1940); "An Account of the Bay Psalm Book," *Papers of the Hymn Society* (1940), 3-18; and "Musical Life in Boston in the Eighteenth Century," *Proceedings of the American Antiquarian Society*, XLIX, Part 2, (1940), 293-313. The principal counterattack on Scholes' position came from Cyclone Covey, "Puritanism and Music in Colonial America," *William and Mary Quarterly*, Third Series, VII (July, 1951), 378-388, and "Did Puritanism or the Frontier Cause the Decline of Colonial Music?" *Journal of Research in Music Education*, VI (Spring, 1958), 68-78. A more recent and moderate interpretation may be found in Irving Lowens, *Music and Musicians in Early America* (New York, 1964).

Among the more valuable recent works on Puritan music are Ralph T. Daniel, *The Anthem in New England before 1800* (Evanston, Ill., 1966) and Zeltan Haraszti, *The Enigma of the Bay Psalm Book* (Chicago, 1956), while Robert Stevenson, *Protestant Church Music in America* (New York, 1966) includes two informative chapters on the subject. Older, but no less significant, is John A. Kouwenhoven, "Some Unfamiliar Aspects of Singing in New England," *New England Quarterly*, VI (Sept., 1933), 567-588. Also useful are Walso S. Pratt, *The Music of the Pilgrims* (Boston, 1921); Frank J. Metcalf, *American Writers and Compilers of Sacred Music* (New York, 1925); William A. Fisher (ed.), *Ye Olde New England Psalm-Tunes* (Boston, 1930); Hamilton C. MacDougall, *Early New England Psalmody* (Brattleboro, Vt., 1940); Leonard Ellinwood, *The History of American Church Music* (New York, 1953), and William J. Reynolds, *A Survey of Christian Hymnody* (New York, 1963). Samuel Sewall's *Diary* (New York, 1927) is an indispensable primary source on Puritanism, with a number of revealing comments on music, while John Tufts, *An Introduction to the Singing of Psalm-Tunes* (Philadelphia, 1954) gives probably the best insight into the methods of the eighteenth century advocates of regular singing.

CHAPTER II. THE MIDDLE COLONIES

An excellent survey of these diverse colonies is Thomas J. Wertenbaker, *The Founding of American Civilization: The Middle Colonies* (New York, 1938). Indispensable for an understanding of early American city life are Carl Bridenbaugh's *Cities in the Wilderness: The First Century of Urban Life in America, 1625-1742* (New York, 1938) and *Cities in Revolt: Urban Life in America, 1743-1776* (New York, 1955). Special attention to Philadelphia is given in Carl and Jessica Bridenbaugh, *Rebels and Gentlemen: Philadelphia in the Age of Franklin* (New York, 1962). Any number of penetrating comments on early American culture are contained in Constance Rourke, *The Roots of American Culture* (New York, 1942), although the author's overall thesis emphasizes the importance of the folk tradition.

Thomas C. Hall, *The Religious Background of American Culture* Boston, 1930) is helpful in understanding the religious tangle of the Middle Colonies, while Theodore Maynard, *The Story of American Catholicism* (New York, 1941) is the recognized work on that subject. Particularly useful on the Quakers is Frederick B. Tolles, *Quakers and the Atlantic Culture* (New York, 1960).

Gillian Lindt Gollin, *Moravians in Two Worlds* (New York, 1967) is a comprehensive account of the Moravians, although Donald F. Durnbaugh (ed.), *The Brethren in Colonial America* (Elgin, Ill., 1967) is of more immediate value to the Americanist. Of the older works Jacob John Sessler, *Communal Pietism among Early American Moravians* (New York, 1933); Joseph Mortimer Levering, *A History of Bethlehem, Pennsylvania, 1741-1892* (Bethlehem, Pa., 1903); James Henry, *Sketches of Moravian Life and Character* (Philadelphia, 1859); and Theodore M. Finney, "The College Musicum at Lititz, Pennsylvania, during the Eighteenth Century," *Papers of the American Musicological Society* (1937), 45-55, all contain useful information. Among the studies of Moravian music, Donald M. McCorkle, "The Moravian Contribution to American Music," *Music Library Association Notes* (1956), 559-606; Irving Lowens, "Moravian Music—Neglected American Heritage," *Musical America*, Vol. LXXVIII (Feb., 1958), 30-31, 122-126; Rufus A. Grider, *Historical Notes on Music in Bethlehem, Pennsylvania* (Philadelphia, 1873); Hans T. David, *Musical Life in the*

Pennsylvania Settlements of the Unitas Fratrum (Winston-Salem, N.C., 1959); Albert G. Rau and Hans T. David (comp.), *A Catalogue of Music by American Moravians* (Bethlehem, Pa., 1938); and Raymond Walters, *The Bethlehem Bach Choir* (Boston, 1923) are particularly noteworthy. On the Moravian composers in America, Donald M. McCorkle, "John Antes, 'American Dilettante'," *Musical Quarterly* (Oct., 1956), 486-499, and Albert G. Rau, "John Frederick Peter," *Musical Quarterly*, Vol. XXIII (July, 1937), 306-313, deserve special attention.

The best contrast between Moravian music and that at Ephrata Cloister is drawn by Hans T. David in "Ephrata and Bethlehem in Pennsylvania: A Comparison," *Papers of the American Musicological Society* (1941), 97-104. Also good on Ephrata are Julius F. Sachse, *The Music of Ephrata Cloister* (Lancaster, Pa., 1903) and Walter C. Klein, *Johann Conrad Beissel, Mystic and Martinet* (Philadelphia, 1942). Material on other Pennsylvania Germans may be found in Julius F. Sachse, *The German Pietists of Provincial Pennsylvania* (Philadelphia, 1895); Marion Dexter Learned, *The Life of Francis Daniel Pastorius* (Philadelphia, 1908); and Julius F. Sachse (ed.), "The Diarium of Magister Johannes Kelpius," *Proceedings and Addresses of the Pennsylvania-German Society*, Vol. XXV (1917).

Oscar G. Sonneck, *Early Concert-Life in America* (Leipzig, 1907) is the pioneer study of art music in early America, but William T. Upton, *Art-Song in America* (Boston, 1930) is also useful. Worth consulting is Virginia Larkin Redway, "Handel in Colonial and Post-Colonial America," *Musical Quarterly*, Vol. XXI (April, 1935), 190-207. The standard treatment of the ballad opera is Edmond M. Gagey, *Ballad Opera* (New York, 1937), although it covers the American scene only incidentally. A limited amount of information on the ballad opera in America may be gleaned from Oscar G. Sonneck, *Early Opera in America* (New York, 1915) and Henry C. Lahee, *Grand Opera in America* (Boston, 1901). The best single volume on theater in early America is Hugh Rankin, *The Theater in Colonial America* (Chapel Hill, N.C., 1965), although George O. Seilhamer, *History of the American Theater*, Vol. I (Philadelphia, 1888) and George C. D. Odell, *Annals of the New York Stage*, Vol. I (New York, 1927) are invaluable older works.

The outstanding study of early Philadelphia theater is Thomas C. Pollock, *The Philadelphia Theater in the Eighteenth Century* (Philadelphia, 1933). A logical beginning point for an investigation of that city's music would be Robert A. Gerson, *Music in Philadelphia* (Philadelphia, 1940), although Gertrude M. Rohrer, *Music and Musicians of Pennsylvania* (Philadelphia, 1940) contains interesting introductory material. Of a more specialized nature, but still excellent, is Robert R. Drummond, *Early German Music in Philadelphia* (New York, 1910). Much on early Philadelphia's concert life may be found in Oscar G. Sonneck, *Francis Hopkinson and James Lyon* (New York, 1967), while Thomas Ridgway, "Ballad Opera in Philadelphia in the Eighteenth Century," *Church Music and Musical Life in Pennsylvania in the Eighteenth Century*, Vol. III, Part 2, is the most complete coverage of that topic. Robert R. Drummond, "Alexander Reinagle and His Connection with the Musical Life of Philadelphia," *German-American Annals*, Vol. IX (1907), 294-306, contains some relevant background material on the colonial period, although the major subject is of a later period. The classic study of Benjamin Franklin is still Carl Van Doren, *Benjamin Franklin* (New York, 1938), and information on Franklin's interest in music is included. Also helpful is William Lichtenwanger, "Benjamin Franklin on Music," *Church Music and Musical Life in Pennsylvania in the Eighteenth Century*, Vol. III, Pt. 2, 447-472, while J. Henry Smythe (ed.), *The Amazing Benjamin Franklin* (New York, 1929) and Paul L. Ford, *The Many-Sided Franklin* (New York, 1899) are perhaps more interesting than valuable, but music is a consideration in both.

CHAPTER III. THE TIDEWATER SOUTH

Of the general histories of the South Francis Butler Simkins, *A History of the South* (New York, 1956) and Clement Eaton, *A History of the Old South* (New York, 1949) are among the best, while Thomas J. Wertenbaker, *The Old South: the Founding of American Civilization* (New York, 1942) is a fine study limited to the colonial period. Relevant material on colonial Williamsburg and Charleston may be found in Wertenbaker's *The Golden Age of Colonial Culture* (Ithaca, N.Y., 1949), and Carl Bridenbaugh, *Myths and Realities: Societies of the Colonial South* (New York, 1965) and Charles M. Andrews, *Colonial Folkways* (New Haven, 1919) are both worth consulting for general information on southern customs.

More detailed discussions of music in the colonial South are included in Francis Butler Simkins (ed.), *Art and Music in the South* (Farmville, Va., 1961) and W. T. Couch (ed.), *Culture in the South* (Chapel Hill, 1934). An excellent study of the itinerant music master is Maurer Maurer, "The 'Professor of Musick' in Colonial America," *Musical Quarterly*, XXXVI (October, 1950), 511-524. Albert Stoutamire's *Music of the Old South: Colony to Confederacy* (Rutherford, N.J., 1972) is a pedantic account of music in colonial Williamsburg and Confederate Richmond.

Louis B. Wright, *First Gentlemen of Virginia* (Charlottesville, Va., 1964), Philip A. Bruce, *Social Life of Virginia in the Seventeenth Century* (New York, 1964), and Richard Beale Davis, *Intellectual Life in Jefferson's Virginia* (Chapel Hill, N.C., 1964) all contain useful sections on music in early Virginia. Worth noting is Helen Cripe, *Thomas Jefferson and Music* (Charlottesville, Va., 1974). Claude G. Bowers, *The Young Jefferson* (Boston, 1945) deals in passing with that Virginian's concern with music, although Jefferson's own writings especially his *Notes on the State of Virginia* (Chapel

Hill, 1955), are more valuable. The musical interests of William Byrd are also viewed best from his own works, among them *Another Secret Diary of William Byrd of Westover, 1739-1741* (Richmond, Va., 1942). Maurer Maurer, "A Musical Family in Colonial Virginia," *Musical Quarterly*, XXXIV (July, 1948), 358-364, is a revealing portrait of the Robert Carter family.

On cultural life in colonial Charleston Frederick P. Bowes, *The Culture of Early Charleston* (Chapel Hill, 1942) and Eola Willis, *The Charleston Stage in the Eighteenth Century* (Columbia, S.C., 1924) are superior, although Robert Molloy, *Charleston: A Gracious Heritage* (New York, 1947) includes much general information, often superficially treated.

Two of the best post-war studies of slavery are John Hope Franklin, *From Slavery to Freedom* (New York, 1956) and Kenneth M. Stampp, *The Peculiar Institution* (New York, 1956). The controversial subject of early black music has probably been handled most penetratingly and objectively by Harold Courlander, *Negro Folk Music, U.S.A.* (New York, 1963). Henry E. Krehbiel, *Afro-American Folksongs* (New York, 1962), originally published in 1914, took the position that Afro-American songs owed much to African music. Newman I. White, *American Negro Folk-Songs* (Cambridge, Mass., 1928) insisted, on the other hand, that the Afro-American songs, particularly the Negro spiritual, were heavily indebted to the revival and camp-meeting songs of the whites. In a chapter of his book *White Spirituals in the Southern Uplands* (Chapel Hill, 1933) George Pullen Jackson argued convincingly that the Negro spiritual originated with the religious songs of the whites. Robert W. Gordon, "The Negro Spiritual," in the *Carolina Low-Country* (New York, 1931) also discusses the religious music of the Afro-American.

The secular songs of the black American are analyzed in Miles Mark Fisher, *Negro Slave Songs in the United States* (New York, 1963). Particularly interesting on this topic is Ernest Borneman, "The Roots of Jazz" in Nat Hentoff and Albert J. McCarthy (eds.), *Jazz* (New York, 1959), as are two articles by Richard A. Waterman: "'Hot' Rhythm in Negro Music," *Journal of the American Musicological Society*, I (Spring, 1948), 24-37, and "African Influence on the Music of the Americas" in Sol Tax (ed.), *Acculturation in the Americas* (Chicago, 1952). Noteworthy too are Romeo B. Garrett, "African Survivals in American Culture," *The Journal of Negro History*, LI (October, 1966), 239-245, and Howard W. Odum and Guy B. Johnson, *The Negro and His Songs* (Chapel Hill, 1925).

Dena J. Epstein, *Sinful Tunes and Spirituals: Black Folk Music to the Civil War* (Urbana, Ill., 1977) is vital.

CHAPTER IV. HOPKINSON AND BILLINGS

Oscar Sonneck's *Francis Hopkinson, the First American Poet-Composer* (Washington, 1905) is the pioneer biography of Hopkinson, although it is largely superseded by the more comprehensive study of George Everett Hastings, *The Life and Works of Francis Hopkinson* (Chicago, 1926). Most of the articles dealing with Hopkinson's music have been brief and fail to penetrate the subject as the scholar might like. Helpful, nevertheless, are Robert Cummings, "Francis Hopkinson: America's First Composer," *Music Journal*, XXV (March, 1967), 62-64; Allan J. Eastman, "The Beginnings of American Music," *Etude*, XL (March, 1922), 155-156; and Paul G. Chancellor, "Pennsylvania's Colonial Influences on American Musical History," *Etude*, LXVI (February, 1948), 75 and 122-123. The controversy created by Hopkinson's *The Temple of Minerva* is related by Lewis Leary, "Francis Hopkinson, Jonathan Odell, and the 'The Temple of Cloacina': 1782," *American Literature*, XV (May, 1943), 183-191, while passing references to Hopkinson are made in Carleton Sprague Smith, "The 1774 Psalm Book of the Reformed Protestant Dutch Church in New York City," *Musical Quarterly*, XXXIV (January, 1948), 84-96.

Containing information on both Hopkinson and Billings are Harold Vincent Milligan, "Pioneers in American Music," *American Scholar*, III (1934), 224-237; Garland Anderson, "Early American Music," *Showcase*, XLIII (February, 1964), 8-9; Neil Butterworth, "American Composers," *Music*, I (No. 2, 1967), 31-32; and especially Constance Rourke's stimulating *The Roots of American Culture* (New York, 1942).

The major biography of William Billings is David P. McKay and Richard Crawford, *William Billings of Boston* (Princeton, N.J., 1975), although J. Murray Barbour, *The Church Music of William Billings* (East Lansing, Mich., 1960) is certainly an excellent analysis of his work. Also of importance are Carl E. Lindstrom, "William Billings and His Times," *Musical Quarterly*, XXV (October, 1939), 479-497, Raymond Morin, "William Billings, Pioneer in American Music," *New England Quarterly*, XIV (1941), 25-33, H. Wiley Hitchcock, "William Billings and the Yankee Tunesmiths," *HiFi/Stereo Review*, XVI (February, 1966), 55-65, and Isaac Goldberg, "The First American Musician," *American Mercury*, XIV (May, 1928), 67-75. Edwin Hall Pierce, "The Rise and Fall of the 'Fugue-tune' in America," *Musical Quarterly*, XVI (April, 1930), 214-228 is a study of the "fuging tune" in general, but focuses on the influence of Billings.

A series of articles by Oliver Daniel contains interesting material on early American musicians, Billings in particular: "Journeyman Composers of New England," *Musical America*, LXX (February, 1950), 110-111, 222, and 248; "America's First Troubadour," *Music Clubs Magazine*, XXXII (January, 1953), 8 and 28; and "The Grass Roots," *HiFi Music at Home*, V (October, 1958), 33-37. All three are highly journalistic, however, and mostly repeat the facts found in the more scholarly treatments. Of the capsule surveys V. Gamet, "Billings Best," *Etude*, LVII (December, 1939), 777-778 and 816, is among the more noteworthy.

The primary source for Billings' views on music are his own introductions to his six tune books. Hans Nathan has edited a facsimile edition of

The Continental Harmony (Cambridge, 1961), which also provides examples of Billings' mature composition.

CHAPTER V. THE SEARCH FOR A NATIONAL IDENTITY

Stimulating background reading for any study of America's early national period is Daniel J. Boorstin's *The Americans: the National Experience* (New York, 1965). Russel Blaine Nye, *The Cultural Life of the New Nation* (New York, 1960) is a fine summary of the intellectual and artistic currents of the United States between 1776 and 1830, while Benjamin T. Spencer, *The Quest for Nationality* (Syracuse, N.Y., 1957), although primarily dealing with literature, provides keen insights into the whole problem of establishing an American identity.

Vera Brodsky Lawrence, *Music for Patriots, Politicians, and Presidents* (New York, 1975), is an excellent introduction to patriotic and campaign songs of the nation's first hundred years, while several of these songs are discussed briefly in both Sigmund Spaeth, *A History of Popular Music in America* (New York, 1948) and David Ewen, *Panorama of American Popular Music* (Englewood Cliffs, N.J., 1957). More comprehensive and detailed, although with no particular attempt at interpretation, is *The Story of Our National Ballads* (New York, 1960) by C. A. Browne and revised by Willard A. Heaps. The text to many of the revolutionary tunes may be found in Frank Moore's *Songs and Ballads of the American Revolution* (New York, 1855). An authoritative search into the origins of the most famous early patriotic songs is Oscar G. T. Sonneck's *Report on "The Star-Spangled Banner," "Hail, Columbia," "America," and "Yankee Doodle"* (Washington, D.C., 1909), while Frank Kidson, "Some Guesses about 'Yankee Doodle,'" *Musical Quarterly*, Vol. III (January, 1917), 98-103, contains interesting postulations concerning the nebulous source of that tune. Definitely worth consulting are John Atlee Kouwenhoven and Lawton M. Patten, "New Light on 'The Star-Spangled Banner,'" *Musical Quarterly*, Vol. XXIII (April, 1937), 198-200, and Leonora S. Ashton, "President's March: Hail Columbia," *Etude*, Vol. LXXI (July, 1953), 54-55.

A monumental account of Andrew Law's contribution to American music is Richard A. Crawford, *Andrew Law, American Psalmodist* (Evanston, Ill., 1968), one of the few thorough biographies of the early national composers. Virginia Larkin Redway, "The Carrs, American Music Publishers," *Musical Quarterly*, Vol. XVIII (Jan., 1932), 150-177, is splendid, although brief, as is John Tasker Howard's "The Hewitt Family in American Music," *Musical Quarterly*, Vol. XVII (Jan., 1931), 25-39. Invaluable is John W. Wagner, "James Hewitt, 1770-1827," *Musical Quarterly*, LVIII (April,

1972), 259-276. A highly scholarly analysis of early American ballad opera, particularly *The Archers,* is Julian Mates, *The American Musical Stage before 1800* (New Brunswick, N.J., 1962), indeed one of the landmarks in the historiography of American music. Chapters on phases of the work of Andrew Law, Benjamin Carr, and James Hewitt are included in Irving Lowens' outstanding collection *Music and Musicians in Early America* (New York, 1964), each of which represents an article previously published in journals.

Both primary and secondary material on folk music in early America have become fairly abundant in recent years, although George Pullen Jackson's pioneer study, *White Spirituals in the Southern Uplands* (Chapel Hill, N.C., 1933), is still among the best. Another classic is Cecil J. Sharp, *English Folk Songs from the Southern Appalachians* (London, 1932). The music of the frontier camp meetings is brilliantly discussed in Charles A. Johnson, "Camp Meeting Hymnody," *American Quarterly,* Vol. IV (Summer, 1952), 110-126.

CHAPTER VI. EARLY CONCERT LIFE

Any study of concert life in the United States before 1800 is indebted to Oscar G. Sonneck, *Early Concert-Life in America* (Leipzig, 1907), which remains the basic compendium of factual data on the subject. Broader in scope and far more lively is David Ewen, *Music Comes to America* (New York, 1947), while Julian Mates, *The American Musical Stage before 1800* (New Brunswick, N.J., 1962) stands as a modern classic.

The best single treatment of instrumental music in nineteenth century America is John H. Mueller, *The American Symphony Orchestra: A Social History of Musical Taste* (Bloomington, Indiana, 1951), although John Erskine, *First Hundred Years of the Philharmonic-Symphony Society of New York* (New York, 1943) and H. Earle Johnson, "The Germania Musical Society," *Musical Quarterly,* XXXIX (January, 1953), 75-93, are two specialized works worth consulting. A monumental encyclopedia of information is Charles C. Perkins and John S. Dwight, *History of the Handel and Haydn Society* (Boston, 1883), although interpretation is left to others. M. D. Herter Norton, "Haydn in America (before 1820)," *Musical Quarterly,* XVIII (April, 1932), 309-337, and Otto Kinkeldey, "Beginnings of Beethoven in America," *Musical Quarterly,* XIII (April, 1927), 217-248, give a broader insight into early concert music in America than might be assumed from their titles.

Cesar Saerchinger, "Musical Landmarks in New York," *Musical Quarterly,* VI (January, 1920), 69-90, and Ray Ellsworth, "Richard Grant

White and Music in Old New York," *HiFi/Stereo Review*, XIV (April, 1965), 47-53, offer interesting glimpses into the concert life of the city that by 1850 had become the nation's cultural center. Robert A. Gerson, *Music in Philadelphia* (Philadelphia, 1940) is the standard volume on the musical development of the Quaker city, but Louis C. Madeira, *Annals of Music in Philadelphia and History of the Musical Fund Society* (Philadelphia, 1896), contains a wealth of undigested facts. The key monograph on early Boston is H. Earle Johnson, *Musical Interludes in Boston, 1785-1830* (New York, 1943), although Thomas Ryan, *Recollections of an Old Musician* (New York, 1899) provides a chatty account of the city's musical highlights during the mid-nineteenth century, related by a member of Boston's Mendelssohn Quintette Club. Valuable for the researcher, but highly detailed for the general reader, is Louis Pichierri, *Music in New Hampshire, 1623-1800* (New York, 1960).

Arthur Loesser, *Men, Women and Pianos: A Social History* (New York, 1954) is a comprehensive, readable study of pianists and piano manufacturing, containing an interesting section on the United States. Walter Terry, *The Dance in America* (New York, 1956) presents a sound, enjoyable narrative, while Lillian Moore, "Ballet Music in Washington's Time," *Etude*, LXXIV (September, 1956), 17, 47, and 51, is almost too superficial to be of much interest or value to the serious student.

For a general biography of the first great American music educator consult Arthur Lowndes Rich, *Lowell Mason* (Chapel Hill, 1946), although a more intimate account may be found in Henry Lowell Mason, "Lowell Mason: An Appreciation of His Life and Work," *The Papers of the Hymn Society of America*, VIII (1941). A serviceable survey of music education in this country is Edward Bailey Birge, *History of Public School Music in the United States* (Philadelphia, 1937).

Excellent on the intellectual climate of the period are James H. Stone, "Mid-Nineteenth-Century American Beliefs in the Social Values of Music," *American Quarterly*, XLIII (January, 1957), 38-49, and Irving Lowens, "Writings about Music in the Periodicals of American Transcendentalism (1835-50)," *Journal of the American Musicological Society*, X (Summer, 1957), 71-85. Edward N. Waters, "John Sullivan Dwight, First American Critic of Music," *Musical Quarterly*, XXI (January, 1935), 69-88, provides the most stimulating analysis of that pioneer, but Ray Ellsworth, "Mr. Dwight's Dauntless Journal," *HiFi/Stereo Review*, XII (March, 1964), 58-62, and George Willis Cooke, *John Sullivan Dwight: A Biography* (Boston, 1898) are both useful. More general studies are Edward G. Lueders, "Music Criticism in America," *American Quarterly*, III (Summer, 1951), 142-151; Robert Sabin, "Early American Composers and Critics," *Musical Quarterly*, XXIV (April, 1938), 210-218; H. Earle Johnson, "Early New England Periodicals Devoted to Music," *Musical Quarterly*, XXVI (April, 1940), 153-161; and Christopher Hatch, "Music for America: A Critical Controversy of the 1850s," *American Quarterly*, XIV (Winter, 1962), 578-586.

Henri Herz, *My Travels in America* (Madison, Wisconsin, 1963) is an engaging journal of one of the prominent concert personalities performing in nineteenth century America. Mortimer Smith, *The Life of Ole Bull* (Princeton, N.J, 1947) is the major biography in English of the Norwegian violinist, although Sara C. Bull, *Ole Bull: A Memoir* (Boston, 1882) is an interesting personalized report. Concise and well-written is Ray Ellsworth, "Jenny Lind and Ole Bull in America," *HiFi/Stereo Review*, XV (September, 1965), 58-62. An extensive section of H.W. Schwartz, *Bands of America* (Garden City, N.Y., 1957) is devoted to a chronicle of the American career of Antoine Jullien.

Essential for the researcher attempting to put together the pieces of Jenny Lind's tour of the United States is C. G. Rosenberg, *Jenny Lind in America* (New York, 1851). While Joan Bulman, *Jenny Lind* (London, 1956) and most of the major biographies of the singer include chapters on her months under Barnum's management, Gladys Denny Schultz, *Jenny Lind: the Swedish Nightingale* (Philadelphia, 1962) is by far the most complete. The bulk of Edward Wagenknecht, *Jenny Lind* (Boston, 1931) is given over to the soprano's American experience, and the author includes a shorter version in his *Seven Daughters of the Theater* (Norman, Oklahoma, 1964). A primary source of great interest is Phineas T. Barnum's *Struggles and Triumphs* (New York, 1872), the showman's seldom modest autobiography. A lively, but reliable biography of Barnum is Irving Wallace, *The Fabulous Showman: The Life and Times of P. T. Barnum* (New York, 1959), a lengthy chapter of which deals with the Jenny Lind tour. M.R. Werner, *Barnum* (New York, 1923) also includes a spritely account of Barnum's management of the Swedish soprano. Less revealing are Henry Scott Holland (ed.), *Memoir of Madame Jenny Lind-Goldschmidt* (London, 1891); W. Porter Ware and Thaddeus C. Lockard, Jr., *The Lost Letters of Jenny Lind* (London, 1966); Francis Rogers, "Jenny Lind," *Musical Quarterly*, XXXII (July, 1946), 437-448; and Davis A. Weiss, "The Swedish Nightingale in America," *Etude*, LXX (April, 1952), 18-19 and 49.

CHAPTER VII. EUROPEAN OPERA AND A CRYSTALLIZING
            SOCIAL ORDER

A number of the references suggested in the bibliographical notes for Chapter VI also include information on grand opera in early America. A definitive general work on opera in the United States, however, still remains to be written, and most of the volumes on individual cities hold more interest for the opera enthusiast than for the cultural historian. Oscar G. Sonneck,

Early Opera in America (New York, 1915) contains a mass of factual information on the period before 1800, while Henry C Lahee, *Grand Opera in America* (Boston, 1901) sketches developments in the nineteenth century. An interesting chapter by Philip L. Miller, "Opera, the Story of an Immigrant," may be found in Paul Henry Lang (ed.), *One Hundred Years of Music in America* (New York, 1961). Julia Cline, "Opera in America, 1735-1850," *Poet Lore*, XLI (Summer, 1930), 239-250, and Josephine K.R. Davis, "Young Opera in Young America," *Music Journal*, XXI (October, 1963), 30-32 and 69-71, are both brief, but worth consulting.

Henry A. Kmen, *Music in New Orleans: The Formative Years, 1791-1841* (Baton Rouge, La., 1966) is a superlative study, emphasizing the importance of opera in that city. A brief discussion of music in the river city, but a wealth of background material, is provided by Howard Mumford Jones, *America and French Culture, 1750-1848* (Chapel Hill, N.C., 1927). Ronald L. Davis, *A History of Opera in the American West* (Englewood Cliffs, N.J., 1965) offers two short chapters on opera in New Orleans, while Andre Lafargue, "Opera in New Orleans in Days of Yore," *Louisiana Historical Quarterly*, XXIX (July, 1946), 660-678, and Harry Brunswick Loeb, "The Opera in New Orleans," *Publications of the Louisiana Historical Society*, IX (1916), 29-41, are pioneer efforts.

George C.D. Odell, *Annals of the New York Stage* (New York, 1927) is indispensable for the researcher, and Lorenzo Da Ponte, *Memoirs of Lorenzo Da Ponte* (New York, 1967) is valuable on the arrival of Italian opera in New York City. William G.B. Carson, *St. Louis Goes to the Opera* (St. Louis, 1946) is informative, but contains only a sketch of the years before the Civil War. Ronald L. Davis, *Opera in Chicago: A Social and Cultural History, 1850-1965* (New York, 1966) is the most recent volume on that subject; Karleton Hackett, *The Beginnings of Grand Opera in Chicago* (Chicago, 1913) and George P. Upton, *Musical Memories* (Chicago, 1908) are significant early accounts.

Material on the frontier opera house is included in Edmond M. Gagey, *The San Francisco Stage: A History* (New York, 1950), George R. MacMinn, *The Theater of the Golden Era in California* (Caldwell, Idaho, 1941), Works Progress Administration, *History of Opera in San Francisco* (San Francisco, 1939), Margaret G. Watson, *Silver Theatre: Amusements of Nevada's Mining Frontier* (Glendale, Calif., 1964), and Ronald L. Davis, "They Played for Gold: Theater on the Mining Frontier," *Southwest Review*, LI (Spring, 1966), 169-184. Greater interpretation may be found in Davis, "Culture on the Frontier," *Southwest Review*, LIII (Fall, 1968), 383-403; Louis B. Wright, *Culture on the Moving Frontier* (New York, 1961); and Davis, "Sopranos and Six-Guns," *The American West*, VII (Nov., 1970), 10-17, 63.

CHAPTER VIII. THE ROOTS OF SERIOUS COMPOSITION

Material on Alexander Reinagle is scant, as no complete biography exists. Ernst C. Krohn, "Alexander Reinagle as Sonatist," *The Musical Quarterly*, XVIII (January, 1932), 140-149, is an excellent study of the composer's major works, while R.R. Drummond, "Alexander Reinagle and His Connection with the Musical Life of Philadelphia," *German-American Annals*, IX (1907), 294-306, offers valuable information on the musician's later accomplishments.

William T. Upton's *Anthony Philip Heinrich* (New York, 1939) is the classic study of the Bohemian-American composer, and Upton's *William Henry Fry: American Journalist and Composer-Critic* (New York, 1954), although not of the same quality as the author's biography of Heinrich, is nevertheless the best study of Fry to date. Important chapters on both Heinrich and Fry may be found in Irving Lowens, *Music and Musicians in Early America* (New York, 1964), while Upton's *The Musical Works of William Henry Fry* (Philadelphia, 1946) includes an interesting sketch of the composer. A brief treatment of Fry and George F. Bristow, with special reference to their operatic writings, is contained in Edward Ellsworth Hipsher, *American Opera and Its Composers* (Philadelphia, 1927). Bristow presents great problems for the researcher, since no in depth discussion of his life and works has been published.

Scattered information on early composition may be gleaned from Robert Sabin, "Early American Composers and Critics," *The Musical Quarterly*, XXIV (April, 1938), 210-218; William T. Upton, *Art-Song in America* (New York, 1930); Neil Butterworth, "American Composers: The Awakening of Nationalism," *Music*, I (1967), 24-25; and Christopher Hatch, "Music for America: A Critical Controversy of the 1850s," *American Quarterly*, XIV (Winter, 1962), 578-586.

CHAPTER IX. LOUIS MOREAU GOTTSCHALK

Paul Arpin's *Life of Louis Moreau Gottschalk* (New York, 1852), a short brochure translated from the French by Henry C. Watson, is the earliest source of biographical information on the New Orleans pianist-composer, ending with the musician's return to the United States from Europe. H.D., probably Henry Didimus, wrote a brief sketch, *Louis Moreau Gottschalk, the American Pianist and Composer* (Philadelphia, 1853), likely drawing most of his information from Arpin and essentially covering the same material. The first important biography of the musician was written by Octavia Hensel, *Life and Letters of Louis Moreau Gottschalk* (Boston, 1870), although the author had studied with Gottschalk and tends to portray him as a paragon of virtue. Particularly interesting on the pianist's years in Latin America is Luis Ricardo Fors, *Gottschalk* (Havana, 1880), written in Spanish and including a fabricated account of the composer's death in Rio de Janeiro.

Gottschalk's own *Notes of a Pianist* (New York, 1964) was originally published in 1881, but the later edition, with an introduction by Jeanne Behrend, is superlative. The diary was kept chiefly for the pianist's private amusement during his long travels. The musician, although occasionally given to distortion, is generally frank, rarely self-conscious, and often introspective. The real Gottschalk comes through better in his own writing than in the hands of most of his biographers, and he emerges from his own pages as much less the wax puppet creation.

The most comprehensive recent life of Gottschalk is Vernon Loggins, *Where the Word Ends* (Baton Rouge, 1958), which despite having been published by a university press, is a highly romanticized account. A significant study of the composer's music is John Godfrey Doyle, *The Piano Music of Louis Moreau Gotschalk* (Ann Arbor, Michigan, 1962), an unpublished dissertation available through University Microfilms. Carl E. Lindstrom, "The American Quality in the Music of Louis Moreau Gottschalk," *The Musical Quarterly*, XXXI (July, 1945), 356-366, and John Tasker Howard, "Louis Moreau Gottschalk, as Portrayed by Himself," *The Musical Quarterly*, XVIII (January, 1932), 120-133, are both of primary importance.

Well worth consulting are Jeanne Behrend, "The Peripatetic Gottschalk," *Americas*, XI (October, 1949), 20-26; Manuel Marquez Sterling, "Gottschalk, Musical Humboldt," *Americas*, XXII (January, 1970), 10-18; Jeanne Behrend, "Louis Moreau Gottschalk, First American Concert-Pianist," *Etude*, LXXV (January, 1957), 14, 48, 58-59; and Ronald Eyer, "Louis Moreau Gottschalk, America's First Musical Celebrity," *Musical America*, LXXIX (February, 1959), 10-12. Irving Lowens, *Music and Musicians in Early America* (New York, 1964) contains a valuable chapter on Gottschalk, while interesting information is available in Arthur Loesser, *Men, Women and Pianos: A Social History* (New York, 1954) and Harold C. Schonberg, *The Great Pianists* (New York, 1963).

CHAPTER X. SENTIMENTAL SONGS IN THE AGE OF INNOCENCE

Interpretative studies of early American popular music are few indeed, and the field remains virtually untouched by serious scholars. Most of the chronicles become little more than lists of titles, dates, and composers, with brief descriptions of the immediate circumstances surrounding the appearance of the major songs. Superficial analysis is occasionally attempted, but rarely with sufficient grasp of the intellectual forces shaping the age to satisfy the cultural historian. Within these limitations, the best of the general works on the subject are probably Sigmund Spaeth, *A History of Popular Music in America* (New York, 1948), and David Ewen, *Panorama of American Popular Music* (Englewood Clifs, N.J., 1957). Less comprehensive, but containing passages of real insight, is Lester S. Levy, *Grace Notes in American History: Popular Sheet Music from 1820 to 1900* (Norman, Okla., 1967).

Scattered data may be gleaned from Philip D. Jordan and Lillian Kessler, *Songs of Yesterday* (Garden City, N.Y., 1941), and Frank Luther, *Americans and Their Songs* (New York, 1942), while short, factual discussions of the popular songs of the early nineteenth century and their composers, along with music and lyrics, are included in Helen Kendrick Johnson, *Our Familiar Songs and Those Who Made Them* (New York, 1887). Definitely worth consulting are Sigmund Spaeth, *Weep Some More, My Lady* (Garden City, N.Y., 1927), Isaac Goldberg, *Tin Pan Alley* (New York, 1961), and Arthur Loesser, *Humor in American Song* (New York, 1942).

A rich examination of the early music publishing business is James H. Stone, "The Merchant and the Muse: Commercial Influences on American Popular Music before the Civil War," *The Business History Review*, XXX (March, 1956), 1-17. Charles Seeger, "Music and Class Structure in the United States," *American Quarterly*, IX (Fall, 1957), 281-294, is valuable in setting the social context for the development of commercial music in a democratic state, while Carl Bode, *The Anatomy of American Popular Culture, 1840-1861* (Berkeley, 1960), and Meade Minnigerode, *The Fabulous Forties, 1840-1850* (New York, 1924), both provide partial chapters on the popular songs of the antebellum period; each pose a number of stimulating theoretical questions.

The emergence of "scientific" hymns is outlined in Henry Wilder Foote, *Three Centuries of American Hymnody* (Cambridge, Mass., 1940). Lowell Mason's compositions are treated best in Arthur Lowndes Rich, *Lowell Mason: "The Father of Singing among the Children"* (Chapel Hill, 1946), and Henry Lowell Mason, "Lowell Mason: An Appreciation of His Life and Work," *The Papers of the Hymn Society*, VII (New York, 1941). Mary Browning Scanlon, "Thomas Hastings," *The Musical Quarterly*, XXXII (April, 1946), 265-277, is outstanding, viewing Hastings' life and music as a manifestation of the religious zeal of the age and drawing an interesting contrast between Hastings' work and Mason's.

The career of John Howard Payne, in both music and the theater, is authoritatively presented in Grace Overmyer, *America's First Hamlet* (New York, 1957), while Henry Russell, *Cheer! Boys, Cheer!* (London, 1895) is a fascinating personal account by a popular English entertainer and song writer who enjoyed an extended success in the United States. No less enchanting are the memoirs of John Hill Hewitt, *Shadows on the Wall* (Baltimore, 1877), although a better evaluation of the composer's career is found in John

Tasker Howard, "The Hewitt Family in American Music," *The Musical Quarterly*, XVII (January, 1931), 25-39.

Of the several biographies of Stephen Foster, the classic is John Tasker Howard, *Stephen Foster, America's Troubadour* (New York, 1953). Two articles by Howard supplement this study: "Stephen Foster and His Publishers," *The Musical Quarterly*, XX (January, 1934), 77-95, and "Newly Discovered Fosteriana," *The Musical Quarterly*, XXI (January, 1935), 17-24. A primary source of major importance is Evelyn Foster Morneweck, *Chronicles of Stephen Foster's Family* (Pittsburgh, 1944), a two-volume collection of letters compiled by a niece of the composer, and Morrison Foster's often sentimentalized *My Brother Stephen* (Indianapolis, 1932) contains intimate material available nowhere else.

Despite its age, Harold Vincent Milligan, *Stephen Collins Foster: A Biography of America's Folk-Song Composer* (New York, 1920) is an account of enduring merit, while H. Wiley Hitchcock, "Stephen Foster," *HiFi/Stereo Review*, XVIII (January, 1967), 47-58, is among the best of the shorter studies. Fletcher Hodges, Jr., *The Swanee River and a Biographical Sketch of Stephen Collins Foster* (White Springs, Florida, 1958) is a useful summary by the longtime director of the Stephen Collins Foster Memorial of the University of Pittsburgh. Hodges has also written *A Pittsburgh Composer and His Memorial* (Pittsburgh, 1938) and *Stephen Foster, Democrat* (Pittsburgh, 1946). Raymond Walters, *Stephen Foster, Youth's Golden Gleam* (Princeton, 1936), is a narrative of the composer's life in Cincinnati, and Robert MacGowan, *The Significance of Stephen Collins Foster* (Indianapolis, 1932) is a brief analysis of some interest. Of the books for children, Claire Lee Purdy, *He Heard America Sing: the Story of Stephen Foster* (New York, 1940) stands among the more notable.

Most of the later writers have drawn heavily from Robert P. Nevin, "Stephen C. Foster and Negro Minstrelsy," *The Atlantic Monthly*, XX (November, 1867), 608-616, although the facts in the article have frequently been questioned. Excellent in shedding light on the influences shaping Foster's music are George Pullen Jackson, "Stephen Foster's Debt to American Folk-Song," *The Musical Quarterly*, XXII (April, 1936), 154-169, and Otto Gombosi, "Stephen Foster and 'Gregory Walker,'" *The Musical Quarterly*, XXX (April, 1944), 133-146.

CHAPTER XI. THE MINSTREL STAGE

The classic monograph on minstrelsy in the United States is Carl Wittke's *Tambo and Bones: A History of the American Minstrel Stage* (Durham, N.C., 1930), although the work decidedly reflects the racial attitudes of its age. In large part Wittke's work has been superseded by Robert C. Toll, *Blacking Up: The Minstrel Show in Nineteenth-Century America* (New York, 1974). A less scholarly vintage account worth consulting is Daily Paskam and Sigmund Spaeth, *"Gentlemen, Be Seated!"* (Garden City, N.Y., 1928). Without question one of the best studies of the subject in recent years is Hans Nathan, *Dan Emmett and the Rise of Early Negro Minstrelsy* (Norman, Okla., 1962). The book is supplemented by three important articles by Nathan: "Dixie," *The Musical Quarterly*, XXXV (January, 1949), 60-84; "The First Negro Minstrel Band and Its Origins," *Southern Folklore Quarterly*, XVI (June, 1952), 132-144; and "Early Banjo Tunes and American Syncopation," *The Musical Quarterly*, XLII (October, 1956), 455-472.

Constance Rourke's chapter on blackface in *American Humor: A Study of the National Character* (New York, 1931) is unsurpassed for depth of insight and provocative analysis. A number of the author's major points are repeated in *The Roots of American Culture* (New York, 1942). Another valuable chapter on the minstrel show may be found in Richard Moody, *America Takes the Stage* (Bloomington, Ind., 1955), certainly one of the best factual summaries available. Alan W. C. Green, "'Jim Crow,' 'Zip Coon': The Northern Origins of Negro Minstrelsy," *The Massachusetts Review*, XI (Spring, 1970), 385-397, contains excellent material and significant interpretation, while occasional points of interest may be gleaned from Orrin Clayton Suthern, II, "Minstrelsy and Popular Culture," *Journal of Popular Culture*, IV (Winter, 1971), 658-673. Also see Alexander Saxton, "Blackface Minstrelsy and Jacksonian Ideology," *American Quarterly*, XXVII (March, 1975), 3-28.

An early biography of merit is Charles Burleigh Galbreath, *Daniel Decatur Emmett: Author of "Dixie"* (Columbus, Ohio, 1904), and H.T. Burleigh's collection of famous minstrel tunes, edited under the title *Negro Minstrel Melodies* (New York, 1909), provides both music and lyrics in workable form. Two primary accounts offering glimpses into the American minstrel stage are Noah M. Ludlow, *Dramatic Life as I Found It* (Bronx, N.Y., 1966), and Sol Smith, *Theatrical Management in the West and South for Thirty Years* (New York, 1868).

Minstrelsy in California, focused around the career of young Lotta Crabtree, is discussed in Constance Rourke, *Troupers of the Gold Coast* (New York, 1928), and Philip Graham, *Showboats* (Austin, Tex., 1951), includes a sketch of blackface on the Mississippi-Ohio waterways. Brief mention of the minstrel show is made in F. Garvin Davenport, "Cultural Life in Nashville on the Eve of the Civil War," *The Journal of Southern History*, III (August, 1937), 326-347, while the work of James A. Bland, the leading composer for the minstrel stage in the late nineteenth century, is the subject of John Jay Daly, *A Song in His Heart* (Philadelphia, 1951).

An excellent summary of recreation in the United States, including a short section on the burnt cork tradition, is Foster Rhea Dulles, *America Learns to Play* (New York, 1952). Most of the general surveys of popular music in America offer passing references to the songs of the minstrel stage, but Isaac Goldberg, *Tin Pan Alley* (New York, 1961), and Marshall W. Stearns, *The Story of Jazz* (New York, 1956), provide more than fleeting insights. The thesis of Albert F. McLean, Jr., *American Vaudeville as Ritual* (Lexington, Ky., 1965), holds interesting possibilities for future studies of minstrelsy.

The contrast between the minstrel tunes and authentic songs of the American blacks is made evident by volumes like Newman I. White, *American Negro Folk-Songs* (Cambridge, Mass., 1928). Kenneth Stampp, *The Peculiar Institution* (New York, 1956), is a superlative modern study of slavery in the United States, which serves as an interesting comparison with the stereotype of the black depicted on the minstrel stage, while Stanley Elkins, *Slavery* (Chicago, 1968), contains a stimulating examination of Anglo-American attitudes toward the institution of slavery and suggests a number of psychological implications.

CHAPTER XII. A NATION OF SECTIONS

Compilations of folk songs of the United States are abundant, but penetrating analysis of their historical meaning in American life is rare indeed. Alan Lomax fortunately manages to say much in his seminal introduction to *The Folk Songs of North America in the English Language* (Garden City, N.Y., 1960), as provocative as it is beautifully written. Far less interpretative, although significant nonetheless, are John A. Lomax, *Adventures of a Ballad Hunter* (New York, 1947), and John A. and Alan Lomax, *American Ballads and Folk Songs* (New York, 1934), and *Folk Song U.S.A.* (New York, 1947). A great deal of factual information may also be found in Ray M. Lawless, *Folksingers and Folksongs in America* (New York, 1960). A good summary of the nature of folk music in this country is Roger D. Abrahams and George Foss, *Anglo-American Folksong Style* (Englewood Cliffs, N.J., 1968), while Bruno Nettl, *An Introduction to the Folk Music in the United States* (Detroit, Mich., 1962) should provide helpful background material for more specific work on early American folk song.

The classic study of the traditional British ballad in America is Cecil J. Sharp's two-volume *English Folk Songs from the Southern Appalachians* (London, 1932). Worth consulting are Tristram P. Coffin, *The British Traditional Ballad in North America* (Philadelphia, 1963), Richard Chase, *American Folk Tales and Songs* (New York, 1956), Josephine McGill, "'Following Music' in a Mountain Land," *The Musical Quarterly*, III (July, 1917), 364-384, and C. Alphonso Smith, "Ballads Surviving in the United States," *The Musical Quarterly*, II (Jan., 1916), 109-129. Outstanding among the more specific collections are Eloise Hubbard Linscott, *Folk Songs of Old New England* (New York, 1939), Phillips Barry, Fannie Hardy Eckstorm, and Mary Winslow Smyth, *British Ballads from Maine* (New Haven, Conn., 1929), Mary O. Eddy, *Ballads and Songs from Ohio* (New York, 1939), Emelyn Elizabeth Gardner and Geraldine Jencks Chickering, *Ballads and Songs of Southern Michigan* (Ann Arbor, 1939), Mellinger Edward Henry, *Folk-Songs from the Southern Highlands* (New York, 1938), John Harrington Cox, *Folk-Songs of the South* (Cambridge, Mass., 1925), Reed Smith, *South Carolina Ballads* (Cambridge, Mass., 1928), Arthur Palmer Hudson, *Folksongs of Mississippi and Their Background* (Chapel Hill, N.C., 1936), Arthur Kyle Davis, Jr., *Traditional Ballads of Virginia* (Cambridge, Mass., 1929), and Josiah H. Combs, *Folk-Songs of the Southern United States* (Austin, Tex., 1967).

Some insight into early work songs of the industrializing Northeast may be gleaned from John Greenway, *American Folksongs of Protest* (New York, 1960), while serviceable acounts of the sea chanties include Joanna C. Colcord, *Songs of American Sailormen* (New York, 1938), Frank Shay, *American Sea Songs and Chanteys* (New York, 1948), Stan Hugill, *Shanties from the Seven Seas* (New York, 1961), and Frederick Pease Harlow, *Chanteying Aboard American Ships* (Barre, Mass., 1962). Information on lumberjack songs is contained in William Main Doerflinger, *Shantymen and Shantyboys* (New York, 1951), as well as Edith Fowke, *Lumbering Songs from the Northern Woods* (Austin, Tex., 1970).

George Pullen Jackson's works remain fundamental in any study of white spirituals, particularly *White Spirituals in the Southern Uplands* (Chapel Hill, N.C., 1933), *Another Sheaf of White Spirituals* (Gainesville, Fla., 1952), *Spiritual Folk-Songs of Early America* (Locust Valley, N.Y., 1953), *White and Negro Spirituals* (New York, 1943), and "Buckwheat Notes," *The Musical Quarterly*, XIX (Oct., 1933), 393-400. William Walker's *The Southern Harmony Songbook* (New York, 1939), has been reprinted with shape notes, while L. L. McDowell, *Songs of the Old Camp Ground* (Ann Arbor, Mich., 1937), is a collection of religious folk songs from the Tennessee hill country. "The Early Camp-Meeting Song Writers," *Methodist Quarterly Review*, XLI (July, 1859), 401-413, may prove interesting, but Charles A. Johnson, *The Frontier Camp Meeting* (Dallas, Tex., 1955), is much more informative. An article by Samuel E. Asbury and Henry E. Meyer, "Old-Time White Camp-Meeting Spirituals" in J. Frank Dobie (ed.), *Tone the Bell Easy* (Dallas, Tex., 1965), is worth observing.

The best source on the music of the Shakers is Edward D. Andrews, "Shaker Songs," *The Musical Quarterly*, XXIII (Oct., 1937), 491-508, while Howard Swan, *Music in the Southwest, 1825-1950* (San Marino, Calif., 1952), includes sketches of the musical life of the Mormons and Spanish. More specialized material on the songs of the Spanish is available in Arthur L. Campa, *The Spanish Folksong in the Southwest* (Albuquerque, 1933), Charles F. Lummis, *Spanish Songs of Old California* (Los Angeles, 1923), and Eleanor Hague, *Spanish-American Folk-Songs*, published as part of the *Memories of the American Folk-Lore Society*, X (New York, 1917). Basic for understanding the forces shaping the cultural life of the American West is Louis B. Wright, *Culture on the Moving Frontier* (Bloomington, Ind., 1955). Richard E. Lingenfelter, Richard A. Dwyer, and David Cohen, *Songs of the American West* (Berkeley, Calif., 1968), is an outstanding compilation with an intelligent—if all too brief—introduction. Dwyer and Lingenfelter, *The Songs of the Gold Rush* (Berkeley, Calif., 1965), and Eleanora Black and Sidney Robertson, *The Gold Rush Song Book* (San Francisco, Calif., 1940), are both valuable, although a more narrative treatment of the miners' songs would be found in general accounts like David Ewen, *Panorama of American Popular Music* (Englewood Cliffs, N.J., 1957), or even better in this instance, Philip D. Jordan and Lillian Kessler, *Songs of Yesterday* (Garden City, N.Y., 1941). An Excellent collection of traditional songs is Ethel and Chauncey O. Moore, *Ballads and Folk Songs of the Southwest* (Norman, Okla., 1964).

Frances Densmore's pioneer work on the music of the North American Indians is still valuable, especially "The Study of Indian Music," *The Musical Quarterly*, I (April, 1915), 187-197, and *The American Indians and Their Music* (New York, 1926). More modern treatments may be found in Harold E. Driver, *Indians of North America* (Chicago, 1961), and Bruno Nettl, *Music in Primitive Culture* (Cambridge, Mass., 1956). An interesting article by an American composer who attempted to incorporate Indian themes into his music is Charles Wakefield Cadman, "The 'Idealization' of Indian Music," *The Musical Quarterly*, I (July, 1915), 387-396.

The complexity of black spirituals was treated in 1914 by critic Henry Edward Krehbiel, *Afro-American Folksongs* (rev. ed., New York, 1962) who essentially concluded that the spirituals reflected a style learned in Africa. Krehbiel was answered by Newman I. White, *American Negro Folk-Songs* (Cambridge, Mass., 1928), who insisted that the texts at least were in large measure borrowed from the gospel songs of whites. Guy B. Johnson, *Folk Culture on St. Helena Island, South Carolina* (Chapel Hill, N.C., 1930), argued that the melodies as well often came from white spirituals. George Pullen Jackson made this point even stronger; "The Genesis of the Negro Spiritual," *The American Mercury*, XXVI (June, 1932), 243-248, is a summary of his position. The African influence was stressed later by Richard A. Waterman, "'Hot' Rhythm in Negro Music," *Journal of the American Musicological Society*, I (1948). An early collection is William Francis Allen, Charles Pickard Ware, and Lucy McKim Garrison, *Slave Songs of the United States* (rev. ed., New York, 1929), while the introduction in Miles Mark Fisher (ed.), *Negro Slaves Songs in the United States* (Ithaca, N.Y., 1953) may prove useful.

Of considerable importance are Dorothy Scarborough, *On the Trail of Negro Folk-Songs* (Cambridge, Mass., 1925); Howard W. Odum and Guy B. Johnson, *The Negro and His Songs* (Chapel Hill, N.C., 1925), and *Negro*

Workaday Songs (Chapel Hill, N.C., 1926); John W. Work, *Folk Song of the American Negro* (Nashville, Tenn., 1915), and *American Negro Songs and Spirituals* (New York, 1940); and Robert W. Gordon, "The Negro Spiritual," in Augustine T. Smythe (and others), *The Carolina Low-Country* (New York, 1931), 191-222. Worth considering are Paul Fritz Laubenstein, "Race Values in Aframerican Music," *The Musical Quarterly*, XVI (July, 1930), 378-403; Percival R. Kirby, "A Study of Negro Harmony," *The Musical Quarterly*, XVI (July, 1930), 404-414; Edgar Rogie Clark, "Negro Folk Music in America," *Journal of American Folklore*, LXIV (July, 1951), 281-287; and Melville J. Herskovits, *The Myth of the Negro Past* (New York, 1941). More recent studies include Alan P. Merriam, "The African Idiom in Music," *Journal of American Folklore*, LXXV (1962), 120-130; Robert Stevenson, "The Afro-American Musical Legacy to 1800," *The Musical Quarterly*, LIV (Oct., 1968), 475-502; and, most notably, Harold Courlander, *Negro Folk Music, U.S.A.* (New York, 1963). Dena J. Epstein, "Slave Music in the United States before 1860," *Music Library Association Notes*, XX (Spring, 1963), 195-212, and XX (Summer, 1963), 377-390, is a fine survey of sources. George Washington Cable, "The Dance in Place Congo," *The Century Magazine*, XXXI (February, 1886), 517-532, and "Creole Slave Songs," *The Century Magazine*, XXXI (April, 1886), 517-532, are classic accounts by a distinguished man of American letters.

CHAPTER XIII. REFORM AND CRISIS

The story of the Hutchinson family has been engagingly told by Philip D. Jordan, *Singin' Yankees* (Minneapolis, 1946), and Carol Brink, *Harps in the Wind* (New York, 1947).

Of the several volumes on the music of the Civil War perhaps the most valuable is Willard A. and Porter W. Heaps, *The Singing Sixties* (Norman, Okla., 1960). Two highly significant articles, James Stone, "War Music and War Psychology in the Civil War," *The Journal of Abnormal and Social Psychology*, XXXVI (October, 1941), 543-560, and Larzer Ziff, "Songs of the Civil War," *Civil War History*, II (September, 1956), 7-28, provide excellent interpretations. An entire issue of *Civil War History*, IV (September, 1958), edited by Albert T. Luper, is devoted to music. Hans Nathan, "Two Inflation Songs of the Civil War," *The Musical Quarterly*, XXIX (April, 1943), 242-253, probes with skill one aspect of the subject, while Kenneth A. Bernard, *Lincoln and the Music of the Civil War* (Caldwell, Idaho, 1966), offers information on another. Useful is Richard B. Harwell, *Confederate Music* (Chapel Hill, N.C., 1950), supplemented by Harwell's *Songs of the*

Confederacy (New York, 1951), a collection of sheet music. Clearly worth consulting are Irwin Silber, *Songs of the Civil War* (New York, 1960), Silber's *Soldier Songs and Home-Front Ballads of the Civil War* (New York, 1964), and Paul Glass, *The Spirit of the Sixties* (St. Louis, 1964).

An informative study of the rise of the commercial music business in the United States is Dena J. Epstein, *Music Publishing in Chicago before 1871: the Firm of Root and Cady, 1858-1871* (Detroit, 1969). George F. Root has recorded his own career in *The Story of a Musical Life* (Cincinnati, 1891), although Lydia Avery Coonley, "George F. Root and His Songs," *New England Magazine*, XIII (January, 1896), 555-570, is of some interest. Also important is Richard S. Hill, "The Mysterious Chord of Henry Clay Work," *Music Library Association Notes*, X (March, 1953), 211-225, and X (June, 1953), 367-390.

Index

A NOTE ON THE AUTHOR

Ronald L. Davis was born in Cambridge, Ohio and raised in Dallas. He attended the University of Texas at Austin, where he received his B.A. in anthropology and his M.A. and Ph.D. in American history. He has taught cultural history at Kansas State College at Emporia, Michigan State University, and since 1972 has been Professor of History at Southern Methodist University in Dallas. He has written *A History of Opera in the American West* (1965), *Opera in Chicago* (1966) and edited *The Social and Cultural Life of the 1920s* (1972). He is the director of the DeGolyer Institute for American Studies and the SMU Oral History Program on the Performing Arts.